The Triumph of Textiles

The Triumph of Textiles

Industrial Dundee, c. 1700–1918

Christopher A. Whatley and Jim Tomlinson

EDINBURGH
University Press

Edinburgh University Press is one of the leading university presses in the UK. We publish academic books and journals in our selected subject areas across the humanities and social sciences, combining cutting-edge scholarship with high editorial and production values to produce academic works of lasting importance. For more information visit our website: edinburghuniversitypress.com

© Christopher A. Whatley and Jim Tomlinson, 2024

Edinburgh University Press Ltd
13 Infirmary Street
Edinburgh EH1 1LT

Typeset in 10.5/13pt Sabon by
Manila Typesetting Company
and printed and bound in Great Britain

A CIP record for this book is available from the British Library

ISBN 978 1 3995 3781 0 (hardback)
ISBN 978 1 3995 3783 4 (webready PDF)
ISBN 978 1 3995 3784 1 (epub)

The right of Christopher A. Whatley and Jim Tomlinson to be identified as author of this work has been asserted in accordance with the Copyright, Designs and Patents Act 1988 and the Copyright and Related Rights Regulations 2003 (SI No. 2498).

Contents

List of Figures	vi
List of Tables	vii
List of Abbreviations	viii
Acknowledgements	ix
Introduction: Rewriting the History of Industrial Dundee	1
1 Dundee: The First Town in Great Britain	24
2 The English East India Company and Dundee's Emergence as a Global City, 1830s–1870s	60
3 Entrepreneurial Endeavour, from Angus Flax Merchants to 'Lords o' Juteopolis'	92
4 Dundee's People and the Headlong Chaos of Industrial Transformation	132
5 The Darker Side	171
6 Calcutta Bites Back: The One-industry City under Duress	187
7 The City Divided, c. 1876–1918	214
8 The City and the First World War	245
Afterword	277
Index	283

Figures

I.1	Baxters' Dens Works, 1904	4
I.2	Ships crowding the harbour at Dundee, c. 1887	6
I.3	View of 'Cox's Stack'	8
I.4	Barnagore Mill, Calcutta, 1862	10
I.5	Dundee Chamber of Commerce exhibition stand, 1947	12
I.6	Albert Square, Dundee's post-1850s commercial hub	14
2.1	Collapsed jute warehouse, 1891	62
2.2	Gilroy Brothers' Tay Works	70
2.3	Castleroy, 'the greatest of the jute palaces'	85
3.1	Sir David Baxter, Baxter Brothers' leading partner and chairman during the golden age of Dundee's textile industry	96
3.2	Peter Carmichael, of Baxter Brothers	98
3.3	Sketch by Peter Carmichael of Baxter Brothers, 1865	113
3.4	Mr G. Brown (c. 1865), a mill manager in Baxters' Dens Works	124
4.1	View of the interior of an unknown Dundee spinning mill	140
4.2	Postcard depicting female spinners, late nineteenth century	140
4.3	Handloom weaver, mid-nineteenth century	150
5.1	Map of Dundee, late nineteenth century	176
5.2	Demolition of Whitehall Close	180
5.3	Scouringburn feus	182
6.1	Total raw jute production and Dundee imports, 1851–1911	195
7.1	Caldrum Works Dinner Hour, early twentieth century	221
7.2	Striking workers, 1912	231
8.1	Camperdown Works, Cox Brothers, Dundee	247

Tables

2.1	Jute imports, 1838–70	72
4.1	Population of Dundee, 1755–1891	134
7.1	Structure of jute spinning, 1908	217
7.2	Prices in Dundee, 1893 compared with 1847	223
8.1	Cox Brothers' pre-tax profits, 1912–19	247
8.2	Women's occupations in Dundee, 1911 and 1921	257
8.3	Gender composition of jute workers in Bowbridge Works, 1914–18	258
8.4	Employment at Cox's, 1914 and 1917	259

Abbreviations

AJSM	Association of Jute Spinners and Manufacturers
CHAR	Churchill Archive, Churchill College University of Cambridge
DCA	Dundee City Archives
DCC	Dundee Chamber of Commerce
DCL: LHC	Dundee City Library: Local History Collection
DDMFOU	Dundee and District Mill and Factory Operatives Union
DDUJFW	Dundee and District Union of Jute and Flax Workers
DSU	Dundee Social Union
DTC	Dundee Trades Council
DWCA	Dundee Women Citizens' Association
DYB	*Dundee Year Book*
ECA	Edinburgh City Archives
FCC	Food Control Committee
FVC	Food Vigilance Committee
GUA	Glasgow University Archives
IJMA	Indian Jute Manufacturers' Association
ILP	Independent Labour Party
JIMPA	Jute Importers Mutual Protection Association
LRC	Labour Representation Committee
NRS	National Records of Scotland
OSA	Old Statistical Account 1791–1799
PKCA	Perth and Kinross Council Archives
SLP	Scottish Labour Party
TNA	The National Archives
UDA	University of Dundee Archives
UDC	Union for Democratic Control
WE: WNC	War Emergency: Workers' National Committee

Acknowledgements

This book would not have been written without a seedcorn grant awarded by the Research Committee of the University of Dundee in 1997. This was used to initiate the History of Dundee research project. Funded at the start were a PhD and a researcher, Dr Louise Miskell. Over subsequent decades the project has expanded and, supported by the Fleming Trust and other funders, led to the publication of three edited volumes on the history of Dundee, as well as several articles in scholarly journals. It is this pioneering body of work carried out by some forty historians that has provided much of the source material for this book which, we hope, is now presented in an accessible format and style.

We are extremely grateful to the archivists whose knowledge and support we have drawn upon in the writing of this book and in finding appropriate images. Especial thanks to Caroline Brown, Jan Merchant and Kenneth Baxter at the University of Dundee Archives, location of an incredibly rich but still underutilised collection of records relating to the textile industry of Dundee and Tayside. The interest Caroline and Jan have shown in our project has been a comfort during the long hours we have spent poring over hard-to-read documents. Erin Farley and her colleagues at the Local History Centre in Dundee Central Library have been enormously helpful too. Sarah Aitken and Martin Allan at Dundee City Archives have played their part, as has Mel Ruth Oakley of Dundee Heritage Trust. David Powell, Archivist at D. C. Thomson & Co., Ltd, kindly found and supplied images from the company's important photographic collection on the Kingsway. Archives & Special Collections at the University of Glasgow have also been generous in allowing us access to the materials in their care. Thanks are due too to national repositories, mainly the National Library of Scotland, the National Records of Scotland and the National Archives at Kew. We are particularly grateful to Robin Urquhart, formerly of the National Records of Scotland, who assisted us in obtaining digital copies of some invaluable primary material. Others who have helped deepen our understanding of textiles and textile manufacture in the United Kingdom and overseas have been Sally Tuckett, University of Glasgow, and Fabrice Bensimon of Sorbonne Université, Paris. We should acknowledge too the work of previous generations of historians of Dundee and its textile industry, who have done much of the heavy lifting, so to speak, which has made our task so much easier. This includes the monumental legacy left by Alexander J. Warden, and his seminal *The Linen Trade, Ancient and Modern*, first published in 1864, as well as the pioneering work by Bruce Lenman, Enid Gauldie and the late Charlotte Lythe. Their *Dundee and its Textile Industry, 1850–1914*, published by the Abertay Historical Society in 1969, is a demonstration of what a local history can be at its best. Few if any of the several fine historians of aspects of the industry and its owners and workers in subsequent decades have omitted references to the foundations laid in these publications.

Last but not least, our thanks are due to Eddie Clark and the editorial team at Edinburgh University Press, as well as the indexers, Sue Tricklebank and Sheree Mosley, for their forbearance and professionalism during the production process.

Introduction: Rewriting the History of Industrial Dundee

Dundee has had a hard time at the hands of its critics. In 1929 the popular and prolific South Africa-born travel writer H. V. Morton crossed the Tay to explore the town. Its situation was 'bonnie', but that was it. The smoking chimneys that created a low-hanging pall over Dundee reminded him of the steel-manufacturing town of Sheffield, the 'deep rumble' of jute wagons on the cobbled streets, of Manchester. Dundee was the archetypical industrial city. But it was also 'a place of fearful inequality; riches and poverty are side by side; opulence and squalor hand in hand.'[1] Morton was not alone in his assessment. Perhaps the most acerbic comments ever made about Dundee were those of the nationalist poet Christopher Grieve, otherwise known as Hugh MacDiarmid. For MacDiarmid Dundee was 'a great industrial cul-de-sac', a 'grim monument to man's inhumanity to man'. Unlike Morton, who at least liked Dundee's location as well as the Howff, the city's vast central graveyard, he could find nothing to mask its 'utter degradation'.[2] This was in 1934, the year in which the city fathers decided to demolish the town house designed by the eminent Scottish architect William Adam two centuries earlier, an act of civic vandalism that further reduced Dundee in the eyes of contemporary observers.[3]

To an extent such comments were justified, but they refer to the period between the First and Second World Wars, when Dundee's staple industry, jute, was suffering from fearsome competition from India and elsewhere. Morton averred that Dundee had Calcutta (now Kolkata) 'in its pocket'. The obverse was truer; some years were better than others, but unmistakably jute was under pressure from the 1880s. The consequences were periods of high unemployment, acute poverty, widespread drunkenness and a millenarian longing for salvation, preferably temporal but otherwise divine. The search was led by James Scrymgeour, the father of Edwin Scrymgeour, the temperance advocate and religious evangelist who, representing the Scottish Prohibition Party, unseated Winston Churchill in the 1922 General Election.[4] Within, there was also some embarrassment about Dundee's aesthetic inadequacies at a time when the elites in manufacturing cities elsewhere were vying with each other to use some of their new-found wealth to improve and enhance the urban fabric. In 1863 the Rev. Dr Archibald Watson, who had recently taken up his charge in Dundee's East Church after leaving a post in Glasgow, remarked (rather boldly) that there was 'no town in the world' where so little effort had been devoted to 'acquiring public treasures of beauty and literature as Dundee'. Visitors, he went on, would be struck by the town's great mills and factories and foundries and their numerous chimneys, and quickly discern the overriding ethos, that is of a place devoted to manufacturing, making money and eating and drinking.[5] 'Where are your monuments?', it was proposed that others might ask, and compare what could be seen in London, Edinburgh and Glasgow with their absence in Dundee, where, despite the town's debt to them, 'we have not even erected a stone of remembrance to WATT or Arkwright'.[6]

In more recent times historians have compounded this dismal picture.[7] Some (including one of the present writers) have condemned Dundee as 'The closest Scottish equivalent to Charles Dickens' part-mythical Coketown', and delighted in repeating the colourful remarks made by the circuit court judge Lord Cockburn in 1842.[8] He lamented the fact that some citizens of Perth were envious of Dundee, with its 'steam engines, its precarious wealth, its starving, turbulent population, its vulgar blackguardism'. Even better known is his uncompromising depiction of Dundee a decade later, as 'a sink of iniquity, which no moral flushing seems capable of cleansing'.[9] At least one book which draws on Cockburn's scathing remark in its title has been published, which, its publisher claims, reveals 'the real nineteenth century Dundee'.[10] Even more solidly academic historians have been inclined to stress the negative aspects of the town, the most eloquent of whom, William Walker, was at one with Mary Macarthur, general secretary of the Women's Trade Union League, who concluded that in no town in the United Kingdom did men and women labour under worse conditions than in Dundee.[11]

Others have focused on the number and impact of Irish immigrants to Dundee, and the extent to which the textile industry dominated. Apart perhaps from Paisley none of Scotland's other large industrial towns were so dependent upon a single industry (and even in Paisley there was greater diversification, certainly for male workers).[12] Condemned too are the low wages paid to jute workers. These were lower than in other branches of the British textile industry. Shocking too for many contemporaries was the poverty of many of the recruits to the vast army of female workers, with their raucous street culture and characteristics that challenged Victorian males' assumptions about appropriate women's roles and behaviours. Drunkenness, as we have already noted, was rife, and disorderly behaviour even more so; contemporaries were especially concerned about the degree to which female spinners (but less so weavers) were culpable. Pointed out are aspects of Dundee's historical record where the town seems to have performed particularly poorly: thus, the water supply was 'more inadequate' than anywhere else, while in housing, only Paisley was more overcrowded. And while wages were low, prices including rents were high, higher even than in London, the most expensive English city. Partly in consequence, Dundonians – that is, working-class Dundonians employed in textile manufacture – were undernourished and more prone to disease and premature death.[13]

There is no denying the validity of many such findings, based as most of them are on incontestable empirical evidence. But not all, and there is at least some room for alternative readings. For example, we might ask why Lord Cockburn took such a visceral dislike to Dundee. Was it that the world with which he was familiar and the environments in which he felt most comfortable tended to be rural, steeped in history and dignified? His acceptance of manufacturing towns was grudging; if they were to exist, they should not be 'made out of the ruins of natural beauty', a process which was certainly taking place in Dundee.[14] Was his anti-Dundee ire based in part on the shock he felt when *female* prisoners at the bar swore at and cursed him – to the extent that after sentencing them, confinement 'never was more cordial'? And while Peter Carmichael was troubled to the core about conditions in Dundee, he recognised that in most similar towns there was 'too little room for the living' and 'too little for the dead'. But nowhere was as bad as Oldham, which he described after a visit in 1846 as being 'in a state of *barbarism* in the very centre of England and in the 19th century'.[15]

We should also be careful about periodisation. Almost universally, the most authoritative published work on the textile era in Dundee begins in or after 1850 and is often concerned with the decline of the jute industry and the social challenges associated with this.[16] Consequently, more than half a century of growth and achievement is excluded. While what were probably Dundee's most buoyant decades ever – the 1850s and 1860s – are usually but not always covered, the bulk of such histories are necessarily concerned with the competitive pressures which Dundee faced from around 1870 and their economic and social effects. Many of these were dire, as paternalistic industrial relations broke down and employer–worker conflict became more apparent. The town's institutional infrastructure could no longer deal with the immense social problems that resulted as living standards deteriorated during bouts of wage cutting and unemployment.

Accordingly, this book encompasses a longer time span and outlines and accounts for the remarkable rise of Dundee to become the UK's principal flax processor and manufacturer of linen cloth – which had happened by the 1840s. This was after overtaking Barnsley, England's leading weaving centre, and Leeds in spinning. It is certainly grossly misleading, mistaken even, to argue as some historians have, that jute became important for Dundee in the 1820s and had even become well established as a jute-manufacturing centre by 1841.[17] It was not until 1863 that the term 'Juteopolis' was applied to Dundee. What can be said is that Dundee's *association* with jute began sometime in the 1820s. But it was not until the 1850s that imports of jute overtook those of flax and hemp, and even then, linen continued to be made in Dundee, not least by the world's largest linen manufacturer, Baxter Brothers Ltd.

The fact is that until mid-century the dominant manufacture in Dundee was linen. Indeed, such was the importance of flax spinning and weaving linen cloth and canvas to Dundee that, long before the ascendancy of jute, the town had powered its way to become Britain's premier linen- manufacturing centre.[18] It was not jute but linen that made industrial Dundee. It is surely significant that the Dundee textile industry's first historian, A. J. Warden, called his monumental book, published in 1864, *The Linen Trade: Ancient and Modern*. As late as 1868 David

Figure I.1 Baxters' Dens Works, 1904. Established in 1818 on the side of the Dens burn, over the following decades the owners created a vast integrated industrial enterprise, employing some five thousand workers. Although utilitarian in purpose, status-building flourishes are also evident, in the bell tower on the original site, which once housed a statue or bust of James Watt, and the tall obelisk-like chimneys. © University of Dundee Archives.

Bremner, in a survey of Scottish industries, was still able with conviction to declare that Dundee was 'the metropolis of the linen trade', not least due to the late American Civil War, 'the most fortunate that ever occurred for the linen manufacturers of Dundee'.[19] 'Juteopolis' did not appear out of the blue; its roots were long and deep. Without an understanding of these, and the importance of linen, the story of jute is without a beginning or foundation, while its 'meteoric' rise becomes an illusion.[20]

Having said this, we have no intention of ignoring the half century and more after 1850. We will argue that from early on, Dundee's success in jute was bound up with Britain's imperial project, primarily India, literally and metaphorically the jewel in Queen Victoria's crown. In the twentieth century, it was the British government's desire to conciliate the forces of Indian nationalism that was partly to blame for the slow, tortuous demise of the jute industry in Dundee and which has merited serious academic investigation.[21]

But it was through the notorious East India Company that Dundonian merchants and manufacturers were first alerted to the potential of jute as a raw material. One date given for this is 1824. This was more than two decades prior to 1850. Even earlier, in the eighteenth century it was partly due to the support of the British state, and the interventions of the Board of Trustees for Fisheries, Manufacturers and Improvements established in 1727, that Dundee's linen trade became established. At this stage too, vital for the town's success was the ability of merchants and manufacturers to supply colonial markets in the Caribbean and elsewhere with the town's ubiquitous plain, coarse Osnaburg cloth – it was legal access to these that had been behind some Scots' thinking that closer union with England in 1707 would be to Scotland's benefit.[22] As so much Dundee (and district) cloth was used to clothe slaves, we acknowledge the city's largely indirect role as a beneficiary of what is now recognised as the despicable plantation system.[23]

However, the emphasis on jute is understandable. The term 'Juteopolis' signalled Dundee's spectacular success in spinning and weaving jute, a coarse raw material that was imported from the other side of the world, Bengal. It hints too at the extent to which jute dominated Dundee by the 1860s. It was far and away the town's biggest employer. Numerous ancillary trades depended upon it: engineering, machine making, manufacturers of hackles and other equipment used to process the jute fibre. The city's docks and dockers were involved too, unloading the thousands of bales of jute that arrived annually from Calcutta in ships that were often owned by the jute companies – indeed, it was the move into direct shipment of jute to Dundee that seems to have established the town's reputation as the world's centre for importing, manufacturing and exporting the commodity.[24]

Nowhere else, either in Britain or indeed the rest of the world, at this time had such a command of this product, turned out in millions of yards from imposing mills, factories and calenders, proudly embellished by their owners with all manner of architectural flourishes.

Even the height, construction and appearance of works chimneys were considered by the industry's leaders to be more than functional matters: they had to say something, a display for the outside world of Dundee's dominant textile industry. From the vantage point of 1866, Peter Carmichael, a leading partner and engineering guru at Baxters' Dens Works, surveyed what he could see of Dundee's 120 or so works chimneys and reflected that it was 'almost comical to note what one would call the individuality of these erections', built, it seemed, without 'much respect for the laws of symmetry'. Yet, he was pleased to conclude, those constructed more recently were 'lofty, handsome and well-proportioned for the most part'. Waxing as eloquently as he would when viewing a great artwork, Carmichael was sure that Dundee's chimneys formed 'one of the most picturesque features of our town, whether

Figure I.2 Ships crowding the harbour at Dundee, c. 1887. The river Tay was Dundee's global artery, through which Archangel and Baltic flax and Bengal jute were directly imported. Until the era of the railway, manufactured goods were exported in virtually equal measure. © Libraries, Leisure and Culture, Dundee.

seen in storm or in sunshine, in the early dawn or when moonlight sleeps upon our noble river'. Not surprisingly, Carmichael – who was respected far beyond Dundee for his expertise in chimney design and construction – took the greatest satisfaction from those at Dens, built in 1844, 1854 and 1864 respectively and distinguished by their 'taper-top[s] from which the smoke ascended very freely'.[25] But it is the great Italianate campanile at Lochee, which served Cox's vast jute works, that is best known, and still stands today, visible from miles around, a monument to the city's golden age. Unfashionable it may be to argue thus, but in material form it symbolises the belief of James Cox, one of the brother owners of Camperdown Works, the largest jute concern in Scotland, that business success was part of a moral mission. He obtained much satisfaction later in life from the thought that through their global involvement in jute, and by the shuttle (and plough) rather than with cannons, he and his brothers had done more for the cause of world peace by uniting peoples across the planet than any of 'the greatest warriors that ever lived'.[26]

The story of jute has frequently been told. Received wisdom is that its success owed much to the global demand there was for bagging and sacking materials. These were used to hold and convey the vast quantities of bulk commodities that were shipped in the nineteenth century, prior to refrigeration and large-sized containers. The importance of wartime requirements too has been emphasised, justifiably, given the coincidence of prosperity in Dundee with the main military conflicts that occurred in the nineteenth century and up to 1918. The war in Crimea was described later as a 'decided Godsend to Dundee . . . coming as it did after the crisis of the early forties', and similar sentiments applied to other nineteenth-century conflicts.[27] Along with this go assumptions that Dundee's spinners and weavers were concerned only with volume as opposed to quality. Yet, as will be revealed in later chapters, there were individuals and firms keen to raise the value of their products. Baxter Brothers, who manufactured canvas for the Royal Navy (and until the early twentieth century were its major suppliers), necessarily had to maintain the highest standards, as did others who wished to be distinguished from those firms who by 'hard driving' early on earned Dundee its reputation for poor-quality yarns and cloth. As competition with India intensified in the late nineteenth century, several firms not only diversified into new products such as cords, twine and ropes, but also spun lighter yarns in efforts to move upmarket from the hessians, bagging and sacking which were the staple Calcutta products.[28] However, even coarse cloth, which was the town's specialism, was not always low-grade cloth. In fact, there were almost countless variations according to type, quality, design,

Figure I.3 View of 'Cox's Stack', the remarkable 86-metre-tall Italianate chimney erected by the Cox Brothers in 1865 at their Camperdown Works, Lochee. Chimney design and appearance was the source of much rivalry between the leading textile firms. © D. C. Thomson & Co. Ltd.

weight and length. There were several varieties even of the ubiquitous Osnaburgs, which were to became Dundee's staple (linen product) from the middle of the eighteenth century. Much later, towards the end of the period covered by this book, one commentator found it 'impossible to enumerate' all the jute fabrics turned out in Dundee, from narrow goods to the widest linoleum cloths and, additionally, 'a great variety of plain and figured fabrics, in all colours . . . as well as millions of wrappers and bags of all kinds and sizes used in transporting and storing various kinds of merchandise', with which Dundee has traditionally been associated.[29]

But success was by no means a given. Competition in flax and linen – the foundations upon which Dundee's primacy in jute was built – locally, from elsewhere in Britain as well as on the continent of Europe, was intense. As will be seen, the textile industry in Dundee suffered a series of setbacks, with numerous sole traders and partnerships failing and cast adrift during the sharp downturns that were a feature of the linen and jute trades – as between 1825 and 1826, 1837, 1842, 1845, 1854 and periodically thereafter.[30] Even in the best of times, short working and shutdowns were never far away. Dundee, however, does appear to have been blessed with a rich pool of capitalist talent, determined to succeed, with some entrepreneurs clearly adopting and embodying many of the features of the Protestant work ethic. Their attributes included an acute awareness of the market and shifts and openings therein, and a preparedness to adapt accordingly. Often the individuals concerned had a keen understanding of and active interest in mill and factory machinery, and workplace design. They were prepared too to learn, by diligent observation of how machines worked and how they could be improved, from each other and by adapting best practice from elsewhere, mainly the linen and cotton districts in the north of England, but Glasgow too, where much was gleaned about power loom weaving which, in cotton, had commenced earlier than in Dundee. Star names in this regard stand out – James Ivory, William Brown, William and David Baxter, Peter Carmichael (who patented several of his inventions), the Cox brothers, James in particular, and many more besides.

But what has also become apparent is how important certain mill and factory managers and foremen were for the successful running of the works, or departments as the various works grew in size and complexity.[31] Usually drawn from the ranks of the tradesmen who serviced the first mills, the best of them were retained by their employers for many years if not decades, and treated well, not only in Dundee but also Calcutta, where they played vital roles in the establishment and smooth running of the mills that sprang up there after 1855. In 1862 one of the first of them, Barnagore, with 240 looms (both hand and power), was employing a manager and seventeen assistants from Dundee.[32]

Names of the town's supervisory staff – such as Donald M'Intosh, heckling manager at Dens for more than forty years in 1871, or Robert Chalmers, at the same works but in charge of spinning – and their contributions are as worthy of record as many of Dundee's linen and jute barons.

What our research for this book has uncovered too – much to our surprise – is the extent to which Dundee's rise was attributable to carpets, first of flax and hemp and afterwards made from jute. These, dyed in bright colours, were well-designed products, and sought after by domestic consumers who wanted a cheaper alternative to the fashionable

Figure I.4 Barnagore Mill, Calcutta, 1862. Barnagore was one of the first Calcutta jute mills (the earliest was founded in 1855) that would soon rival Dundee's pre-eminence in the global jute trade. Most of this group of young men came from Dundee and district – sought for their experience as overseers, managers and mechanics, in which capacities they played a key role in the emergence of the Calcutta industry. In India they were able to enjoy relatively affluent lifestyles and retain their national and cultural distinctiveness. © University of Dundee Archives.

woollen varieties known by the names of the places where they were made – Brussels, Axminster, Wilton and Kidderminster. This last was relatively cheap, but not as much as carpets made in Dundee. Strangely, Dundee's remarkable success in this market, which began to be apparent from the 1830s, has hardly been recognised by historians. No mention of Dundee producers is made in the standard study of Britain's carpet industry.[33] And this is despite the fact that some of Dundee's most important textile firms, not least Cox's of Lochee but also others such as the Grimond Brothers, manufactured vast amounts of carpeting. The Grimonds' 'Brussels' carpets made from jute were world-renowned, and able to compete with the traditional and expensive Brussels carpets made from wool.[34] Again, it was the quality of Dundee's carpets that struck observers. Jute-based 'Brussels' and 'Wilton' carpets were the 'most elaborate' made in the city, but equally, 'considerable ingenuity and taste' were displayed 'in connection with other types of carpets and rugs'.[35] In the later nineteenth century, expanding carpet production was an important element in the attempt to move Dundee's jute products further upmarket as Indian competition intensified. Rather than seeing the jute sack as epitomising Juteopolis, we should note that when, much later, in 1932, the newly elected MP, Florence Horsbrugh, gave her fellow MP, Dingle Foot, a wedding gift, she chose a highly patterned Dundee-made carpet.[36]

In turn, with jute carpeting and rugs very much at the heart of the home, we have looked more critically at the part played by whale oil in accounting for the global lead Dundee took in jute production. It has been accorded a key role as a softener of the brittle jute fibres as they were unpacked from their bales and prepared for spinning. The fact is that whale oil gave off an obnoxious smell. Accordingly, it was unsuitable for jute yarn that was woven into domestic carpets. Thus other means had to be found for softening the jute fibres; part of the answer was to use mineral oil. However, given this domestic use for jute, not as a product for carrying huge quantities of guano – the accumulated excrement of seabirds and bats, found in bulk especially in South America – but for carpeting millions of working-class households, it is ironic that for a long time Dundee's jute spinners and weavers were reluctant to admit their association with the fibre. When in 1835 good-quality flax was in short supply, some firms in Dundee began to take jute more seriously. Alarmed that its use would 'tend to lower the character of our manufactures very much', the *Dundee Advertiser* warned against its further employment. And despite the arrival in 1840 of the first direct shipment to Dundee from Calcutta, prejudices against it remained, not least as the machinery used to prepare and spin flax was unsuitable for the heavier jute fibres. Apocryphal perhaps, but one manufacturer was later quoted as having said (in Dundee dialect), 'Eh, laddie, yir maisters are doing an awfu' thing in pittin' a' their eggs in ae basket turning oot a' their gude machinery to spin sic a feckless thing as Jute.'[37] He was wrong. But it was some time before those working with jute, especially where it was mixed with flax, were prepared to admit this publicly. Thus, even though Cox's extensive premises at Lochee, which spread over twenty-eight acres, comprised the largest jute production unit in the world, for a long time its proprietors preferred to use the name Camperdown Linen Works. In short, the triumph of jute was strangely muted.

Returning to the issue of social conditions and the character of industrial Dundee, attention will be paid to the ways in which civically minded manufacturers and leading citizens including members of the town council rose to the challenges they faced. Indeed, they had not been entirely neglectful of the desirability of public monuments as a means of instilling

Figure I.5 Dundee Chamber of Commerce exhibition stand, 1947. Carpets were a major component of Dundee's success as a textile town, yet pictures of them are hard to find. The two rugs in the left of this picture are an exception. © University of Dundee Archives.

civic pride; in 1853 the Royal Arch, paid for by subscription, had been unveiled near the docks, to commemorate Queen Victoria's presence there in 1844.[38] The mid-century awareness of the town's unflattering image as a place dedicated largely to making things, work, wages and the bustle of business, inspired the construction of the grand Albert Institute, first and foremost a library and museum designed by the eminent architect Sir George Gilbert Scott. Paid for by subscriptions, this was one of Britain's finest memorials to Prince Albert, Queen Victoria's consort, who had died in December 1861. It is true that Glasgow's George Square was by this time well on the way to becoming that city's pantheon of heroic figures. However, as early as 1863 Dundee had its first public statue, of the leading manufacturer and benefactor Sir David Baxter, erected in the park he had gifted and which was named after him. Less than ten years later a second statue was unveiled, by the same sculptor, Scotland's most eminent practitioner, Sir John Steell, but this time in Albert Square, the new business heart of Dundee.[39] This addition, of the Radical MP George Kinloch, paved the way for a group of statues, including one of pioneering local engineer James Carmichael and another of the nation's poet, Robert Burns (also by Steell), an acquisition – and status symbol – sought by all of Scotland's main towns.[40] What is suggested by this and other material evidence – such as the laying out of parks, publishing ventures, the promotion of fine art and popular literature – is that Dundee was no cultural backwater.[41]

But it would be foolhardy to try to argue that Dundee did not have a dark side, and that many thousands of ordinary people – men, women and children – endured miserable existences in appalling conditions in both their workplaces and beyond. And there is no doubting that in several respects Dundee did differ from Scotland's other big cities; for example, there was the preponderance of women employed in textiles (jute especially – 70 per cent of those employed by the industry in 1907 were females) and the unusually high percentage of married women who were in employment. While boys were as common as girls in jute factories until they reached an age when they would have to be paid adult wages, many were then dismissed and had to seek alternative work, often as unskilled labourers, although we will show later that the extent of this has been exaggerated.[42] For these and other reasons Dundee has rightly been called a women's town.[43] Even so, albeit hugely significant, such features do not tell Dundee's nineteenth-century story in full. They can conceal much which is well worth putting on record and even celebrating.

It is not intended in this book to deny that the rapid industrialisation of Dundee presented a range of unprecedented challenges for the authorities, whether as employers or town councillors. It is, however, to suggest that the experience of urban life for the thousands of migrants who arrived and settled in Dundee was not wholly negative – certainly in the century or so from the 1780s – and that there were periods of optimism during which the prevailing mood was of relative contentment and social harmony. To be fair, some historians have acknowledged this.[44] We would suggest, however, that greater emphasis should be placed on such evidence. There is much of this. Louise Miskell has made a powerful case that certainly up until 1850 Dundee may have been more socially integrated than some other industrial cities; the town's leading employers and the better-off middle classes tended not to flee for the suburbs.[45] The class divisions that became apparent later in the century were less so earlier, when there are signs of some collective pride in Dundee's unplanned and sometimes chaotic transition from a port town to a modern manufacturing hub. In 1822, for instance, a large crowd watched and cheered when the 'riggin stane' was placed upon the chimney stack at the new and extended Lower Dens Works with its 15 horsepower steam engine.[46] The firm's next big building, opened in 1836 at Upper Dens, attracted even more attention, with some considering its spacious weaving sheds

Figure I.6 Albert Square, Dundee's post-1850s commercial hub. On the right is the Albert Institute, designed by Sir George Gilbert Scott, opened in 1867; on the left, the Chamber of Commerce (1854) by David Bryce. The Square was also the location of Dundee's main public statues, of Kinloch, James Carmichael, Robert Burns and Queen Victoria. © D. C. Thomson & Co. Ltd.

to be one of the wonders of the world. For Dundonians, as the town's first power loom factory, it was, or seemed to be.

Although in the 1820s and up to the 1840s there were clashes between employers and some tightly organised groups of workers such as the hand hecklers over the introduction of new machinery, during the midde decades of the nineteenth century there are signs of close collaboration of employers and employed, notably where marginal but significant improvements to machines and their better operation were concerned. One commentator wrote of an atmosphere wherein workers recognised their part in the success of the linen and jute trades, and made such suggestions in recognition of 'the manifest benefit' to both their employers and them in 'keeping Dundee in the foremost rank of the textile trade, first gradually, then rapidly'.[47] This was not simply wishful thinking on the part of an outside observer. One of several examples of this kind of intervention comes from Dens Works in 1873, when a new labour-saving device for the lapping process, where the finished webs were folded and tied up, was introduced. The result was a loss of jobs, while wages were to be paid for piece work rather than at a daily rate. Despite his fears of opposition, however, Peter Carmichael noted that some of the men involved, 'offered suggestions and pointed out defects'.[48] Other relevant evidence of employer–employee harmony takes the form of processions, such as that which preceded the opening of Baxter Park in 1863, when more than 7,000 workers from most of the town's workplaces proudly displayed flags and banners that showed their attachment to their employers.[49] They also subscribed to a fund to erect a statue of their benefactor. In more prosperous years, textile workers participated in works outings and soirees, often held around Christmas time or new year. How typical or popular songs and poems written by workers such as the well-known 'Factory Girl' Ellen Johnston were, is not clear. But there were many of them. They extolled the virtues of foremen, for example, and hint at affectionate relations within the workplace. (Equally, however, there were instances where male supervisors exploited their position and humiliated, beat and even raped females under their command.) There was pride too in the product Dundee was most closely associated with. Thus in 1877, D. Taylor, a handloom weaver poet, was evidently struggling to deal with one of the jute industry's episodic downturns. Nevertheless he was still able to sing, in verse, the praises of jute, the cloth with which he worked, and its many and perhaps surprising uses:

> It's mixed amon' silk, an' ca'd by that name,
>> In cotton, tae, often it's tried;
> It looks gey weel on the back o' some dame,
>> When in braw, bricht colours it's dyed.
> It's int ae *oor* hets, it's into *your* shawls,
>> It's mixed in maist a'thing wi wear;
> An a' the gaudy and gay fal-de-rals
>> Three-fourths o' them's jute you may swear.[50]

But not everyone in Dundee was employed in textiles. Among those who were, either directly in works' engineering workshops and the like, or indirectly, they appear to have relished living in Dundee. Admittedly these were more often males, and more especially skilled males. But something around a quarter of the biggest linen and jute firms' employees were men and shouldn't be overlooked when we are characterising nineteenth-century Dundee. In addition, some 3,000 individuals worked in the dozen or so engineering companies that were in existence in the 1860s, which were vital for the textile industries' operations; few firms could afford to employ mechanics, joiners, engineers, masons and others to the extent that larger enterprises such as Baxters, Cox's or the Gilroy Brothers did. While such engineering works made marine engines and other equipment for the town's shipbuilding industry, most of their output – outlined above – was destined for the textile mills and factories. Nearly all of the machinery for opening bales and softening jute and for weaving and finishing was made in and around Dundee. Preparing and spinning machinery was more often made in Leeds and Belfast – but also locally, by James F. Low & Co. at Monifeith.[51] Many Dundee-made machines used in the flax and jute trades are on display in the city's Verdant Works, Dundee's industrial museum which opened in 1996.

Although the men who were engaged in such work were by no means sheltered from the sporadic downturns that brought a halt to new mill and factory construction and shut down those already in existence, on the whole they fared better than the production workers. They enjoyed higher and more regular wages, and a much less regimented workplace environment. Part of Victorian Britain's class of respectable artisans, they were more often than not literate, avid readers of improving literature, religious, inclined to temperance (although not to abstention) from all alcohol, and thirled to the notion of separate spheres – that is, their place was in the workplace while women's place was in the home.[52] What little evidence we have is that men of this cast as well as supervisory staff tended to steer clear of the female preparers and spinners, with their 'immodest' comportment, language, songs and wayward habits. They were prepared, however, to socialise with and even marry weavers, who were altogether, although not always, more respectable.[53] They may have had much in common with James Myles, author of *Chapters in the Life of a Dundee Factory* Boy (1850), who, despite his lingering fondness for the countryside of his youth, and conscious of the worst excesses of the factory system, relished urban life. This included the employment generated by steam engine-powered industry, as well as 'all the intellectual, religious and social apparatus of a huge town wherein nearly a hundred thousand mortals live'.[54] William McGonagall may have been a poor poet and an object of mirth, but he had his finger on his fellow townspeople's pulses as far as local – and national – issues were concerned. The 'Poet Laureate of Paton's Lane' recognised that broadsheet verse that talked up Dundee's virtues, from its civic buildings, hotels, shops, tramways and parks to its two rail bridges across the Tay, is what attracted readers – and sales.[55] There were events too that seemed to unite massive numbers of the town's inhabitants, such as the unveiling of the statue of Robert Burns in the recently laid out Albert Square in 1880. There were unifying causes too, as for instance the campaign, fought partly on patriotic grounds, for a second MP.[56]

That industrial Dundee was more than a lopsided, poverty-stricken, disease-ridden frontier town is a central premise of this book.

Notwithstanding the opinions of twentieth-century commentators when the city was struggling against foreign competition, and the views of historians who have been inclined to emphasise the negative aspects of Victorian and Edwardian Dundee, there was much from which contemporaries could take comfort. Indeed, much with which they could be pleased. Where they could, industry leaders and town councillors addressed and often effectively tackled many of the great challenges with which they were faced, from removing narrow, airless roads and allowing fresh air and light into the heart of the old medieval town to transforming the town's grossly inadequate water supply through a series of improvement acts in the 1860s and 1870s. Although their record overall is patchy, what can be said with certainty is that not a few of the most important textile magnates played active parts in these schemes, while many more contributed large sums of money to fund and support key institutions. Especially rewarding were favourable comments from visitors. We will see later in this book the desire there was from the USA to emulate Dundee's unparalleled success in jute, not only as an industry but as a means of wealth creation for those who owned and promoted it. Even more effusive about Dundee's merits was a commercial commentator from Australia. His observations were published in *The Australian Trading World* in August 1887, in what primarily was a feature article on the Cox brothers at Camperdown. It was what was said about the city, however, that is of note here. With jute, Dundee had risen to become the third most populous town in Scotland. The Tay bridge impressed. But its 'street architecture and public buildings . . . [keep] pace with its commercial progress'. The writer went on: 'The intellectual wants of the community are supplied by all the usual agencies, and its picture gallery, technical and medical schools, University College, noble infirmary . . . the public parks are second to none in the kingdom for beauty of situation and effective landscape gardening, while the esplanade or public promenade along the river side is an inestimable boon to the denizens of the central parts of the town.'[57] By the time the British Association made what was that prestigious body's second visit to Dundee in 1912 (the first had been in 1867, when those concerned had struggled to find suitable accommodation), Dundonians could vaunt an even longer catalogue of civic attainments.

In seeking to rebalance the historical record by emphasising the dynamism and growth of the city, especially in the first seven decades of the nineteenth century, we do not deny that there was a significant shift thereafter. This is not to say that the years after 1870 were a time of 'decline'. Output and employment in the textile industries and the city generally grew until the First World War. Innovation and technological advance continued, while new markets and new products were developed. Real wages rose significantly from the 1870s, largely because of cheaper food. But both the challenges faced by the city and the temper of responses to these challenges shifted.

Most obvious among those challenges was the rise of Indian competition in the staple products of sacking and bagging, alongside a loss of markets in Europe as countries there built up their own jute industries.[58] Expansion of higher-end products such as carpets and linoleum backing could partly compensate for losses elsewhere, and the total world market for jute goods continued to increase until 1914. But the rise of Calcutta was a harbinger of doom for Juteopolis. In the shorter run it cemented Dundee's position as a relatively low-wage city, and it was increasingly recognised that these low wages were largely responsible for the widespread poverty and appalling housing conditions. Dundee's position as the worst city in Scotland for infant mortality reveals starkly the limits of the prosperity of Juteopolis.

There was no overnight shift in the political and ideological temper of the city. The free trade liberalism of the mid-nineteenth century, with its accompanying class-collaborative politics and paternalistic social relations, remained strong. But from the 1880s it was under pressure. On the employers' side, Conservatism advanced, especially after the split in Liberalism over Irish Home Rule in the 1880s but underpinned by growing doubts about the seeming loss of economic superiority. Protectionist views, once almost unheard in the city, resurfaced as international competition in jute stiffened. Protectionism among employers tended to be allied with a more assertive stance against the claims of labour, with less willingness to see benign class collaboration as the best solution to all problems.

On the labour side, there was no great upsurge in trade unionism; the strongest unions in the city were in engineering and transport, with the much more numerous textile workers very poorly organised until the eve of the First World War. Liberalism remained strong among the working class, as they gained the vote and became politically more assertive. But the ideas of socialism, though fragmented and diverse in character, were making some headway. Labour as a distinct political force was on the rise, even if in many respects its ideas, most notably on free trade, overlapped strongly with Liberalism. The election of Alexander Wilkie as Dundee's first Labour MP in 1906 symbolised the ambiguity of the 'rise of labour'; he had previously stood as a Liberal candidate, and in parliament was a loyal supporter of the Liberal government.

There was no death of Liberalism in the Edwardian years, but the industrial unrest of the immediate pre-war years, alongside women's suffrage agitation and the renewed battle over Irish Home Rule, were precursors of a much sharper discontinuity in social relations and political allegiances brought about by the war. In Dundee, this shift was underpinned by a decisive loss of competitive power of the jute industry via-à-vis Calcutta. While large wartime profits were made in both places, for Dundee these were the product of highly artificial and temporary wartime conditions, not evidence of competitive capacity. After a brief post-war boom, the story of Dundee jute was to be one of unambiguous decline.

The city's links with flax and jute, however, have never been entirely severed. Some jute continued to be processed in Dundee until the end of the twentieth century. Firms which began as flax and jute spinners and manufacturers in the nineteenth century have diversified and are still in business today. Halley Stevensons at Baltic Works, founded in 1864, no longer manufacture jute products, but they are still in textiles, albeit waxed cotton and other weatherproof fabrics in which they are global leaders. Although since 2020 Low & Bonar has been in German hands, the firm was founded in Dundee (in 1903) as a vehicle for selling jute goods around the world. Don & Low, Forfar-based and now part of the Thrace Group, boasts a pedigree going back 231 years, and for many decades manufactured jute at Ward Mills in Dundee. The firm was one of the first in the Dundee region to transfer from jute to polypropylene; many of those who failed to make this step, or to diversify, closed down.

It was as early as 1889 that Verdant Works ceased to spin and weave jute. The mill was built in 1833 for David Lindsay, a merchant and flax spinner. Having been purchased by Dundee Heritage Trust in 1991, and opened as a museum five years later, it is now one of Scotland's best industrial museums and a fitting material record of Dundee's textile heritage. That it was a mid-sized steam engine-powered works, employing no more than 500 or so workers in its mid-Victorian prime, and situated in the Scouringburn district, where so many of the town's first mills were erected, gives it an added resonance and importance. Camperdown Works in Lochee and Dens Works in Dundee were world-ranking in scale and significance, but it was the smaller concerns – of which there were many more – like Verdant Works that were more typical.

The most spectacular instance of Dundee's present-day association with the golden age of flax and jute is the V&A Dundee, the first Victoria and Albert Museum in the United Kingdom outside London. The idea came from Georgina Follett, then Dean of Duncan of Jordanstone College of Art and Design. Now incorporated with the University of

20   THE TRIUMPH OF TEXTILES

Dundee, Duncan of Jordanstone was established as a school of industrial art, its benefactor James Duncan insisting that its 'chief purpose was the teaching of textile manufacture and design'.[59] With several of Dundee's jute manufacturers competing in the market for fancier goods and long having been involved in carpet weaving, by the end of the nineteenth century the need for formal training in textile design was becoming intense. It is appropriate therefore that Dundee's V&A is the first museum of design in Scotland. (The city was designated a UNESCO City of Design – the only one in the UK – in 2014.) Opened in 2018, a decade after it was first mooted, the V&A is also a key element in the regeneration of the waterfront, which no longer serves its main purpose as the transit point for the import of raw jute, the industrial city's lifeblood. In place of shipyard workers, sailors, dockers, porters, carters, warehousemen and engine drivers, the western end of the waterfront now teems with visitors from elsewhere in Scotland, the UK and abroad, around two million of whom have been attracted to the V&A over the past six years. Rather than jute, it is tourism in part based on Dundee's unique history and heritage but also its transition from post-industrial decline that is generating income for the city; £109 million by 2023 as well as several hundred jobs.

This number is nothing like that when textiles in Dundee were triumphant. Yet the deep roots laid centuries ago continue to produce new growth. This book should ensure that sight is not lost of the debt today's Dundonians and others interested in the city as it is now and may be in future owe to those who caused it to flourish as never before, nor since.

Notes

1. H. V. Morton, *In Search of Scotland* (London, 1929), pp. 105–6.
2. Quotation from Christopher A. Whatley, David B. Swinfen and Annette M. Smith, *The Life and Times of Dundee* (Edinburgh, 1993), p. 160.
3. George Blake, *The Heart of Scotland* (London, 1934), p. 50.
4. William W. Walker, *Juteopolis: Dundee and its Textile Workers 1885–1923* (Edinburgh, 1979), pp. 18–27; Jim Tomlinson, 'Churchill's defeat in Dundee, 1922, and the decline of liberal political economy', *Historical Journal*, 63 (2020), pp. 980–1006.
5. *Dundee Advertiser*, 27 November 1863, p. 3.
6. *Dundee Courier and Argus*, 7 January 1862, p. 2.
7. Christopher A. Whatley (ed.), *The Diary of John Sturrock, Millwright, Dundee 1864–65* (East Linton, 1996), pp. 2–3.
8. Christopher A. Whatley (ed.), *The Re-Making of Juteopolis, Dundee c.1891–1991* (Dundee, 1992), p. 12.

9. *Circuit Journeys by the Late Lord Cockburn* (Edinburgh, 1975), pp. 163, 383.
10. Malcolm Archibald, *A Sink of Atrocity* (Edinburgh, 2012).
11. Walker, *Juteopolis*, p. 32.
12. Catriona M. M. Macdonald, *The Radical Thread: Political Change in Scotland. Paisley Politics, 1885–1924* (East Linton, 2000), pp. 46–50.
13. Examples of such negative views on Dundee include Bruce Lenman, Charlotte Lythe and Enid Gauldie, *Dundee and its Textile Industry 1850–1914* (Dundee, 1969), pp. 77–102; Ian Adams, *The Making of Urban Scotland* (London, 1978), p. 83; Richard Rodger, 'Employment, wages and poverty in the Scottish cities 1841–1914', in George Gordon (ed.), *Perspectives of the Scottish City* (Aberdeen, 1985), pp. 40–1; T. M. Devine, 'Urbanisation', in T. M. Devine and R. Mitchison (eds), *People and Society in Scotland, Vol. 1, 1760–1830* (Edinburgh, 1988), pp. 40–1.
14. *Circuit Journeys*, p. 163.
15. UDA, MS 102/1/2, p. 30.
16. For instance, Lenman, Lythe and Gauldie, *Dundee and its Textile Industry*; Walker, *Juteopolis*; Eleanor Gordon, *Women and the Labour Movement in Scotland 1850–1914* (Oxford, 1991); as well as more recent studies such as Jim Tomlinson, *Dundee and the Empire, 'Juteopolis' 1850–1939* (Edinburgh, 2014) and Jim Tomlinson, Carlo Morelli and Valerie Wright, *The Decline of Jute* (London, 2011).
17. An early instance was Michael Flinn (ed.), *Scottish Population History from the 17th century to the 1930s* (Cambridge, 1977), p. 466; on the 1841 date, see Rodger, 'Employment, wages and poverty', p. 40.
18. Louise Miskell and Christopher A. Whatley, '"Juteopolis" in the making: Linen and the industrial transformation of Dundee', *Textile History*, 30: 2 (1999), pp. 176–98.
19. David Bremner, *The Industries of Scotland: Their Rise, Progress and Present Condition* (Newton Abbot, 1969), pp. 247, 251.
20. The term is used by T. M. Devine, 'Industrialisation', in T. M. Devine, C. H. Lee and G. C. Peden (eds), *The Transformation of Scotland: The Economy Since 1700* (Edinburgh, 2005), p. 58. The same author massively exaggerates the numbers employed at Camperdown works in Lochee. Yes, this was the world's largest jute-manufacturing complex but at its height 5,000 workers were employed, a third of the 14,000 quoted (p. 36).
21. Tomlinson, Morelli and Wright, *Decline of Jute*, pp. 119–33.
22. Christopher A. Whatley, *Bought and Sold for English Gold? Explaining the Union of 1707* (East Linton, 2000 edn), pp. 56–84.
23. For a recent, award-winning study of the slave trade and the plantation system, see David Alston, *Slaves and Highlanders: Silenced Histories of Scotland and the Caribbean* (Edinburgh, 2021); for Scotland's role more generally, see the contributions in T. M. Devine (ed.), *Recovering Scotland's Slavery Past: The Caribbean Connection* (Edinburgh, 2015).

24. Christopher A. Whatley, 'Contesting memory and public places: Albert Square and Dundee's pantheon of heroes', in Christopher A. Whatley, Bob Harris and Louise Miskell (eds), *Victorian Dundee: Image and Realities* (Dundee, 2011 edn), p. 175.
25. Carmichael, Life and Letters, 1, pp. 306–10.
26. UDA, MS56/2/5/2, Cox MSS, James Cox's Diary, pp. 105–6.
27. H. R. Carter, *Jute and its Manufacture* (London, 1921), p. 186.
28. Thomas Woodhouse, 'Spinning and weaving', in A. W. Paton and A. H. Miller (eds), *Handbook and Guide to Dundee and District* (Dundee, 1912), pp. 286–7.
29. Ibid., p. 288.
30. A. J. Warden, *The Linen Trade: Ancient and Modern* (London, 1868 edn), p. 612.
31. The classic text on this subject is Sydney Pollard, *The Genesis of Modern Management* (London, 1968 edn).
32. D. R. Wallace, *The Romance of Jute: A Short History of the Calcutta Jute Mill Industry, 1855–1909* (Calcutta, 1909), pp. 19–21.
33. J. Neville Bartlett, *Carpeting the Millions: The Growth of Britain's Carpet Industry* (Edinburgh, n.d.).
34. Ibid., p. 12.
35. Woodhouse, 'Spinning and weaving', p. 287.
36. Cutting in Florence Horsbrugh papers, Churchill Archives Centre, University of Cambridge, HSBR2/3.
37. D. Ritchie, 'Textiles', in Paton and Miller (eds), *Handbook and Guide*, p. 278.
38. Rob Duck and Charles McKean, 'Docks, railways or institutions: Competing images for mid-nineteenth-century Dundee', in Whatley, Harris and Miskell (eds), *Victorian Dundee*, pp. 165–6.
39. Whatley, 'Contesting memory', in Whatley, Harris and Miskell (eds), *Victorian Dundee*, pp. 173–6.
40. Christopher A. Whatley, *Immortal Memory: Burns and the Scottish People* (Edinburgh, 2016), pp. 115–21.
41. See, for example, Matthew Jarron, *Independent & Individualist: Art in Dundee, 1867–1924* (Dundee, 2015).
42. W. A. Graham Clark, *Linen, Jute, and Hemp Industries in the United Kingdom* (Washington, 1913), p. 127.
43. Gordon, *Women and the Labour Movement*, p. 142; Jim Tomlinson, 'The First World War in a "Women's Town"': Dundee 1914–1922, *Women's History Review*, 31 (2021), pp. 173–97.
44. Rodger, 'Employment', p. 41.
45. Louise Miskell, 'From conflict to co-operation: Urban improvement and the case of Dundee, 1790–1850', *Urban History*, 29: 3 (2002), p. 353.
46. UDA, MS102/1/1, Peter Carmichael, Reminiscences, I, p. 182.
47. Woodhouse, 'Spinning and weaving', p. 279.

48. UDA, MS102/1/3, Baxter MSS, Peter Carmichael, Vol. III, Life and Letters, 2, p. 44.
49. Christopher A. Whatley, 'Altering images of the industrial city: The case of James Myles, the "Factory Boy" and mid-Victorian Dundee', in Whatley, Harris and Miskell (eds), *Victorian Dundee*, pp. 79–81.
50. Kirstie Blair (ed.), *Poets of the People's Journal: Newspaper Poetry in Victorian Scotland* (Glasgow, 2016), pp. 130–2.
51. Clark, *Linen, Jute, and Hemp*, pp. 116–17.
52. Whatley, *Diary of John Sturrock*, pp. 5–26.
53. Gordon, *Women and the Labour Movement*, pp. 153–4.
54. Whatley, 'Altering images', pp. 77–8.
55. See Norman Watson, *Poet McGonagall: The Biography of William McGonagall* (Edinburgh, 2010), pp. 92–117.
56. Ibid., pp. 90–3.
57. Reprint from *The Australian Trading World*, 12 August 1887.
58. Jim Tomlinson, 'Orientalism at work? Dundee's response to competition from Calcutta, circa 1870–1914', *Journal of Imperial and Commonwealth History*, 43 (2015), pp. 807–30.
59. Matthew Jarron, *'"Independent and Individualist": Art in Dundee, 1867–1924* (Dundee, 2015), p. 156.

1

Dundee: The First Town in Great Britain

The manufacture of linen is now . . . our principal article of trade . . . and Dundee is considered, in regard to this kind of manufacture, the first town in Great Britain.

That Dundee would become the British, let alone the world centre of anything would have seemed beyond belief to a visitor to the burgh in the years either before or immediately after the Union of 1707. Along with many of the other Scottish towns, Dundee was in the doldrums, suffering from a 'great decay of trade', one visible sign of which was 'ye many ruinous tenements' and other signs of disrepair 'even in the most public places of the Town'.[1] Both a cause and consequence of the burgh's condition was that the harbour was becoming silted up, thereby losing several feet of water. The contrast with the position little more than a century beforehand was stark. Dundee had vied with Aberdeen and Perth to be the second most important – and wealthiest – town in Scotland, behind the undisputed capital, Edinburgh. What went wrong during the seventeenth century we'll return to below.

The relationship with England forged in 1707, that went beyond the union of the crowns in 1603, is seen by many historians as having provided an unprecedented opportunity for the Scots to advance their economic interests. Indeed, as we will see, it would provide the political and economic framework within which Dundee was able to propel itself onto the global stage, although some roots of this remarkable transformation, although tenuous, can be traced further back in time.

DUNDEE IN THE DOLDRUMS, AND A WAY OUT THROUGH UNION

In the decade or so prior to 1707, Scotland's economy was confronted with a series of interrelated challenges. True, prior to this, individuals had done well in overseas trade, in merchant shipping and as privateers. These were state-sanctioned pirates such as Dundee-born captain William Kidd, later of New York, who was hanged for piracy and murder in the gallows in Wapping in May 1701.[2] Others grew prosperous in domestic luxury trades like gun making (in which Dundee was pre-eminent) and silver smithing, and extractive industries such as lead and coal mining. There were greater strengths to the Scottish economy than is sometimes assumed.[3]

Visible signs were status-enhancing estate purchases, new or extended grand houses in the countryside and reconstruction work in some burghs. In their dimensions, quality and modern-ness Dundee's grander houses, according to Robert Edward in 1678, resembled 'palaces', even if some of this impressive building work dated back to the later sixteenth and early seventeenth centuries. This was when Dundee – led by its merchants and craftsmen – had enjoyed several decades of export-led prosperity. Growing imports of flax from the Baltic – the raw-material basis of the burgh's future – added to the town's economic buoyancy. By the end of the sixteenth century, 'hemp claith' and 'lyning' were substantial contributors to this.[4] After the Restoration of 1660, with Charles II as monarch, in the surrounding countryside the burgh's merchants were again acquiring estates and becoming substantial landowners in Errol, Longforgan and Lundie – all within an hour's horse ride of Dundee.[5]

This was just as well. Population losses had partly resulted from two outbreaks of plague in the 1640s. Twice during the civil wars of the early and mid-seventeenth century Dundee had been sacked, 'fearfullie defaced' according to the burgh's representative in parliament. The second of these, by which time Dundee was 'already in a pitiful state', was led by the Cromwellian general George Monck and his forces in 1651.[6] The siege and assault that followed resulted in a massive loss of shipping (sixty ships were said to have been seized) and personal wealth, with soldiers rampaging through the town and plundering at will.[7] Lives were lost too (how many is unknown, but over one thousand is plausible), as they would be again as the effects of the 1690s famine became apparent. For some five or even seven years of poor harvests had led to hunger, destitution and the deaths of perhaps 15 per cent of the population, a sign of Scotland's underdevelopment. In Dundee, as with many other Scottish towns, famine conditions led to an increase in the numbers of the poor – many of whom, starving, had flocked in from the surrounding countryside as crops failed. These were the survivors: in the hinterland, hundreds had died on the road. They were buried in simple coffins or a bier – a common coffin – paid for from funds of the parishes where the famine victims had perished, although in some places the kirk session might allow the body of the deceased to be buried using the communal mortcloth.[8] Large numbers of the labouring poor, fearing they would soon go hungry as ships carrying scarce grain for shipment elsewhere were loaded at the harbour, rioted. Dundee felt the mob's fury at such a prospect in the early spring of 1699, the first of several food riots that would periodically erupt over the next century and more. The town's population of just over 8,000 was only three-quarters of what it had been half a century earlier.[9]

Coinciding with the famine was another blow, the impact of which, this time, was felt most acutely by the country's political elite, landowners and burgh merchants. The well-known, ambitious but probably imprudent attempt by the Company of Scotland to establish an international trading centre at Darien, 'New Caledonia', on the Isthmus of Panama that narrowly separated the Atlantic Ocean from the Pacific had ended ignominiously in 1700.

Between them, these two disasters had cost the country dear. Getting on for perhaps half of Scotland's capital had been poured into the Company of Scotland's venture, investors of all ranks having been enticed by the heady promise of vast returns. Dundee burgh officials and merchants had joined the rush to subscribe. In the forefront was future provost John Scrymgeour, who pledged most, £300 sterling.[10]

By the turn of the eighteenth century, cash – needed for everyday transactions – was in desperately short supply, even though the note-issuing Bank of Scotland had been founded in 1695, a year after the Bank of England. The confidence of the nation's traders and manufacturers was further sapped as tariffs overseas began to impact on Scottish goods. There was a growing recognition that at a time when the success of Europe's more aggressive leading states depended on the acquisition of overseas colonies and powerful navies to protect their merchant ships on the high seas, Scotland would struggle to compete on its own in this age of muscular mercantilism. From the later 1690s onwards, ideas proliferated, and debate intensified, often in pamphlet form, about the steps required to revive and strengthen Scotland's ailing economy.[11] Closer union with England was one of the solutions proffered.

There were those who were convinced that such a step, provided it involved open trade, would bring benefits. Indeed, for more than a century a free trading arrangement with England had been high on the agenda of a number of Scottish thinkers, pamphleteers and politicians. In the Scottish Parliament, even opponents of the incorporating or parliamentary union that was debated from 1705 onwards could see the merits of tariff-free trade with England; access to England's overseas possessions across the Atlantic that by 1706 had also become part of England's offer – lure even – to the recalcitrant Scots. Accordingly, many members of the Country party opposition in the Scottish Parliament voted in favour of the fourth article of the treaty. This promised the Scots unimpeded access to English consumers as well as entry to England's expanding colonial markets overseas under the protection of the Royal Navy.

It is notable that Dundee's aforementioned John Scrymgeour – of Kirkton, a merchant and successively a burgess, bailie, dean of guild and the town's provost from 1700 until 1702 – was one of the country's burgh commissioners (MPs) in the Scottish Parliament who voted for the proposed union. In so doing, Scrymgeour had to ignore the pressure there was from Jacobites within Dundee as well as in nearby towns such as Forfar and Perth and surrounding counties to oppose incorporation. Yet as a 'Glorious' Revolution-supporting Presbyterian Whig and a beneficiary of an appointment as a collector of customs (potentially a lucrative office which may well have helped fund his purchase of the estate of Tealing around 1705), it was not surprising that Scrymgeour should have adopted the Court – or government – line.[12]

Yet it seems entirely reasonable to suppose that Dundee's material circumstances also played a large part in Scrymgeour's calculus. Prior to the furore over union, the burgh's merchant guild – a formal body representing the interests of the town's buyers and sellers – had given him a strong steer about how he should vote when trade matters were debated.

Although burgh finances across Scotland in the early 1700s were precarious, the size of Dundee's debt in 1704, £120,000 (Scots) and increasing yearly, stands out.[13] At the same time, it sits alongside a national balance of trade deficit which may have been in the region of £2 million Scots. The costs of what was a skeletal government machine far exceeded the nation's tax revenues.[14] In Dundee the former staple manufacture, coarse grey woollen cloth or plaiding, was, like most of the rest of the woollen industry in Scotland, struggling, despite the sporadic support of the state. While hopes for a revival were sufficiently buoyant that the union treaty included an agreement that funds would be devoted to stimulating it (in some places, but not Dundee, this happened), a more likely future lay in those commodities in which Scotland had a comparative advantage: black cattle – and linen.[15]

From the perspective of this book, what matters most is the state of and prospects for the linen trade. The skill base upon which the burgh would later flourish was laid down early; as will be seen, other continuities in terms of long associations with textile manufacturing stretching far back in time can be identified running through to the twentieth century. The master weavers had formed themselves into a formal trade body or 'craft' towards the end of the previous century, when they had petitioned the town council for permission to put in place an altar for their patron saint, Severus, in the town's kirk, St Mary's – one of Scotland's finest medieval churches, the tall tower of which still stands.[16] By the later seventeenth century, hand spinning and weaving had spread far out into the surrounding region, with thousands of rural dwellers in Tayside engaged in these activities on a part-time basis, as an adjunct to agricultural work. As agricultural surpluses were small, what rural dwellers could earn from yarn and cloth sales was many households' main source of cash earnings. The ubiquity of hand spinning among females of all ages is attested by the familiarity of the tune and song, 'The Rock and the Wee Pickle Tow', which not only dates back to seventeenth-century Forfarshire but also captures the process, rhythms and culture of this domestic occupation.[17]

Such growing dependence on by-employment in flax and linen corroborates what we know of linen sales, and exports. Apart from local purchasers, who included hundreds of individual hawkers who travelled over the border with an array of goods to sell in England, most of the output from such by-employment was purchased by merchants from Dundee, Montrose and Perth (the country's main market for linen cloth at the time). This was then sold either in the towns concerned, sent by sea to London or taken overland to the south-west of Scotland.[18] Despite sharp fluctuations, over the course of the seventeenth century exports of linen cloth to England, by far the most important external market, rose spectacularly, from 18,000 ells to 650,000 ells.[19] By around 1700, linen was Scotland's principal manufactured export. But, heavily reliant on English buyers, it was vulnerable to rising tariff levels which by 1698 had reached 15 per cent. One consequence of this growing pressure on price was that in order to reduce production costs, Scottish weavers compromised on quality – a constantly recurring issue for Dundee's reputation as a cloth-making centre. This was despite the periodic efforts made by the Weaver Trade in Dundee to ensure that journeymen within the burgh bounds maintained high standards. The Weaver Trade was one of Dundee's nine craft incorporations. Formally founded in 1512, the Trade played a prominent part in Dundee's religious, economic and social life, its main function being to control numbers working at the craft and to maintain high standards of cloth-making.[20] The need to monitor the quality and amount of cloth woven by the 'unfree' weavers who resided and worked outside the burgh – in a line of roadside dwellings and work-shops that went up the 'Hill' or Hilltown to the north of Dundee prior to its incorporation as part of the burgh of Dundee in 1697 – added to the challenge. On the other hand, as the numbers of such weavers grew, and their labour was cheaper than that of craft-approved freemen weavers inside the burgh boundaries, their cloth was readily bought by the burgh's merchants.[21]

A second and more immediate consequence of the rise in English tariffs was a reduction in work available in spinning and part-time weaving and a squeeze on incomes, thereby exacerbating the effects of the famine in Dundee and on Tayside. Low levels of baptisms in Dundee during and after the worst of the famine was over, suggest that recovery was relatively slow; in fact, according to the Rev. Robert Small, writing of the parish in 1793, it was 'several years after the rebellion in 1745' that Dundee recovered from the 'calamity' of the 'ill years' of the 1690s.[22] And with the threat of a total prohibition of exports into England as relations between Scotland and England deteriorated in 1704 and 1705 – over the Scots' unwillingness to discuss union – a 'national panic' ensued. And little wonder. Westminster's so-called Aliens Act of February 1705 threatened to impose a blockade on all livestock, coal – and linen – from Scotland, if by Christmas Day the Scots failed to accept the Hanoverian succession (that is, to succeed heir-less Queen Anne on her death) and engage in serious discussions about a British union. Having established a foothold in London for its linen, the danger for Dundee was acute.

Indeed, for Scotland more generally to have been cut off from by far and away the main market for what was becoming the Scottish staple would have been disastrous.[23] Yet as the articles of union were debated in the Scottish Parliament in Edinburgh in the last weeks of 1706, petitions arguing against the proposal flooded in – in part orchestrated by members of the nobility, the Country Party and others.[24]

Very different was the attitude of the provost and council of the burgh of Montrose, thirty miles to the north of Dundee. Heavily dependent on the income and employment generated by exporting linen cloth to London, they urged their commissioner (MP) James Scott to act with them in 'common cause', fearing that if agreement with England was not reached, the 'English Prohibitory Laws' would be reimposed with a vengeance. Consequently, Scotland 'would be deprived of . . . the only trade by which the ballance [sic] is on our side'. Without such access,

30 THE TRIUMPH OF TEXTILES

it was crystal clear 'what shall be the fate of this poor blinded nation in a few years'.[25] Similar thoughts would have been in the forefront of Dundee's John Scrymgeour's mind when he considered the most likely environment in which Dundee might flourish.

Even more active on behalf of the burgh's economic interests was Scrymgeour's close successor as lord provost, George Yeaman. A wealthy West India merchant who had spent time on India's Malabar coast, Yeaman was Dundee's provost between 1706 and 1708. He was returned as Westminster MP for Perth Burghs (which after 1707 included Dundee) in 1710.

UNION, THE BRITISH STATE AND SCOTTISH LINEN

The much-vaunted advantages of incorporation were slow to arrive. Indeed, the distinctly negative immediate economic effects of the Union in the east of Scotland induced unrest among ordinary people as well as the country's landed and commercial elite and their representatives at Westminster. As is well known, in 1713 Scottish MPs initiated a move that came close to repealing the Union that had been agreed only six years earlier. Ironically, given what had been hoped for, linen was the manufactured commodity most adversely affected, now labouring under the weight of new duties on exports and other measures that directly and indirectly led to a sharp reduction in cloth sales.[26] The medium and finer fabrics, associated with the west of Scotland, were in addition faced with intense and successful competition from Dutch, German and French linen.[27]

It quickly became apparent that the Union only provided an opportunity for Scots to improve their circumstances, not a guarantee. Those with an interest in trade and manufactures recognised that they would have to fight hard to make the Union work for them, not least against the vested interests of both English and Irish merchants and producers. Accordingly, within six months of the Union coming into effect (on 1 May 1707), Dundee's guildry had met to consider 'what they had to inform' the new British Parliament on trade issues. Among the topics they discussed were measures to regulate linen.[28] For some decades thereafter, the guildry kept a watchful eye on matters relating to the burgh's business, including linen, where necessary lobbying the town council, the Convention of Royal Burghs (which in its turn was active on behalf of Scottish interests) and Parliament.

In the vanguard for Dundee – as well as on behalf of the neighbouring Perth – was Yeaman, to whom it was claimed later the district was more indebted 'than to any representative ever sent from Scotland'.[29] Within months of his election in 1710, supported by his town council colleagues, he had begun to agitate for an area-specific reduction in the coal tax – which benefited in particular the two main burghs he represented. As significant was Yeaman's promotion of a bill to better regulate linen manufacturing in Scotland. His first attempt failed but in 1712 he succeeded in taking a second measure through Parliament.[30] In one respect the effect was immediate, with Dundee town council taking advantage of the legislation to appoint a stampmaster to inspect linen cloth sold in the burgh.

Earlier, in response to the burgh's parlous situation – above all, the need to stimulate trade and overcome labour shortages that had become a concern in the years following the recent famine – the provost and council had taken a series of radical countermeasures. In 1706 they had ordered that the daughters of guild brethren should be admitted as free burgesses just as their sons were. Not long afterwards, the dean of guild had been instructed to employ free of any entry money anyone who applied with a testimonial as a shore porter, numbers of which the council wished to double given how important they were for carrying essential items such as coal, salt and 'market goods' into the heart of the burgh.[31] Before long further freedoms from medieval restrictions were sought by the burgh's shipmasters and seamen fraternity for wrights such as anchor smiths and John Adamson, a shipbuilder from Scarborough, who they hoped would establish a ship-repairing dock at the shore and therefore bolster the recent increase in shipping.

But most important of all, then and, as it happened, for the burgh's future prosperity, in December 1707 the council slashed the petty customs (local taxes) applied on white linen brought to Dundee for sale from May into June, as did some smaller burghs. This was a direct challenge to Perth's ancient midsummer market, the country's largest, so much so that as early as 1713 the burgh's inhabitants, including the tacksmen of the ports or entries to Perth, were complaining that 'Country people who were used to resort to this burgh with their cloath' were 'going all to Dundie'.[32] In fact, the move was a masterstroke, and recognised as such by authorities on Scotland's economic circumstances such as Edinburgh's lord provost Patrick Lindsay.[33] On his tour through northern Scotland around 1725, Daniel Defoe observed the town's thriving linen trade with England and was impressed too by Dundee's 'stately houses, and large handsome streets'.[34] In 1735 Dundee was able to boast the grandest new townhouse in Scotland, designed by the country's leading architect, William Adam.

Progress, however, was far from straightforward. For one thing, Dundee had its long-standing local rivals to contend with: Perth obviously but also Coupar Angus, and Forfarshire burghs such as the county town itself and Arbroath, Brechin, Kirriemuir and Montrose.[35] Some merchants continued to purchase uninspected cloth, which could be bleached with 'lime, pidgeons dung or other harmful stuff', thereby damaging the burgh's reputation. There was unease too about English protectionism, with woollen and silk manufacturers in England demanding a prohibition on imports and the wearing of printed or dyed textiles – from home as well as abroad. Apprehension about the impact of this on employment and incomes among flax spinners and linen weavers north of the border may have contributed to the unprecedented bout of food rioting that took place along Scotland's east coast, including Dundee, in the winter of 1719–20, which the authorities in Edinburgh and London feared might have been Jacobite-tinged. The Secretary of State the duke of Roxburghe was convinced that if conditions worsened in the linen trade in Scotland the consequences would be 'very bad' and urged government intervention.[36] Once more Dundee but also Perth were in the forefront of the flood of protests sent to Westminster against the proposed legislation, arguing that linen was now Scotland's 'only Staple Commodity and the main work and business wherein the common people . . . are Imployed [sic] and Enabled to maintain themselves'.[37] Such was the ferocity of this campaign (which included Irish producers) that British-made linen was exempted from the terms of what was known as the Calico Act of 1721.

This concession heralded a distinct change in the British state's treatment of Scotland and the Scottish economy. The government, with the Whig Robert Walpole as prime minister (the country's first) from 1721 until 1742, had become increasingly concerned about the situation in Scotland. The strength of support for the Jacobites had led to the serious rising of 1715 and an attempted invasion in 1719, and showed little sign of waning despite the punitive actions taken in the wake of the '15 by the British state. Disorder too was widespread, with the collectors of the customs and excise officers who had been appointed shortly after the Union being subject to violent assaults by mobs and unable to carry out their duties. The Malt Tax disturbances further focused the minds of the authorities; Scotland was close to being ungovernable. If the 'flame of sedition' was to be doused, the British government should support Scottish interests within the Union on the same terms as those of England, otherwise Scotland would become a burden, 'fit for no other purpose, than to as an open Back-door for the enemies of our happy Constitution to enter by'.[38]

THE FIRST TOWN IN GREAT BRITAIN

Employment creation was one way of reducing unrest, while at the same time benefiting the nation at large. Funds provided by the Equivalent, agreed as part of the Union settlement, were devoted to what in effect was an economic development agency, the Board of Trustees for Fisheries and Manufactures, in 1727. Although the Board provided some assistance to the west coast fisheries, by far and away the biggest beneficiary was linen. A range of measures was implemented, including studying Irish bleaching methods (in this the Scots were 'lamentably deficient'), subsidising bleachfields, setting up spinning schools and raising skill levels among weavers, this last to be achieved partly by appointing a small but nationwide army of stampmasters to inspect and approve cloth brought to market for sale.[39] The Board's work was supplemented in 1746 with the establishment of the British Linen Company, which at first managed the manufacture at all stages as well as the marketing of vast quantities of linen cloth, before transitioning to finance and banking in the later 1760s.

For Dundee both of these bodies were of crucial importance. Above all was the introduction to Scotland, first by the Board of Trustees around 1741, and in 1745 by the British Linen Company, of Osnaburgs – for a time sold under the more patriotic name 'Edinburgs'.[40] Until this time none was made in Scotland. Osnaburg was an imitation of a fabric made in and around Osnabrück, the centre of a flax- and hemp-growing district in Germany. Previously, re-exports of these and other foreign linens from Britain to the plantations had actually been favoured with a drawback worth around 17 per cent of the total value of the cloth, much to the chagrin of Scottish and Irish merchants and manufacturers who could see the immense gains to be had if they had such favoured access to this market.[41]

Over time Osnaburgs would become Dundee's and its region's staple manufacture. A plain, coarse cloth, Osnaburg provided one of the pathways that led, almost a century later, to jute, just as in the 1770s and 1780s, capital and expertise in fine linen production helped facilitate the transition to cotton spinning and weaving in the west of Scotland.[42] Although at first the manufacture of Osnaburgs (in Scotland) was more successful in Edinburgh, by 1750 out-working, part-time spinners and handloom weavers in and near Dundee as well as in Angus and the Mearns had raised their game. But to produce them was relatively simple, to the extent that master weavers 'in and about town . . . think any person and any sort of utensils good enough' for making such cloth.[43] And inexpensively.

Not much more than ten years after it was first made in Scotland, 2.2 million yards of Osnaburgs were produced, a spectacular achievement not matched by any of the other varieties of linen made in the country.[44] Little wonder then that Dundee's town council spared no expense on lavishly celebrating the birthdays of kings George II and George III and other members of the royal family, or that they paid for flags to be hoisted on the old steeple and for the townhouse bells to be rung on the news of British military and naval successes during the Seven Years War with France.[45] With victory in 1763, Britain under the terms of the Treaty of Paris added to its colonial possessions in the Caribbean and North America, and *de facto* became the world's greatest maritime trading power. Dundee's inhabitants were among the winners.

In helping to forge links between Dundee and the metropolis at the heart of Britain's expanding global empire was another MP. This was the prosperous and influential John Drummond of Quarrell in Perthshire, who had established himself as a merchant in London in the immediate pre-Union decade. Drummond, who represented Perth Burghs from 1727 until 1742, recognised that additional political pressure was essential if Dundee's and other Angus towns' ordinary brown (that is, unbleached) linen was to find a larger market. There was no point in looking to the European continent, where flax was grown successfully, and all kinds of cloths made relatively cheaply and well. By far the most promising customers were the British slave plantations in the Caribbean, Virginia and the Carolinas. Indeed, in his capacity as a director of the Royal African Company – Britain's principal state-sponsored slave trading vehicle, formed in 1672 – Drummond had encouraged the use of Scottish linen.[46] England, following in the wake of Portugal and Spain, had begun in the late sixteenth century to amass its colonial empire in the Atlantic maritime world, which by the time of the outbreak of the American Wars of Independence in 1776 comprised thirteen colonies in North America and a string of islands in the Caribbean, including Jamaica, Barbados, Antigua, Nevis and St Kitts – places the Scots could now exploit too.[47]

Drummond's lobbying on behalf of the Scottish linen interest may have contributed to another key intervention on the part of the British government, now recognising that targeted policies were required to kick-start Scotland's flagging economy.[48] In 1742 one manifestation of this was the introduction of a bounty on exports of coarse linen. By such a mercantilist measure, another London-based supporter of the Scottish linen industry had anticipated some five years earlier, 'how soon we should outdo other Nations . . . in coarse linens . . . to the British plantations'.[49] Increased in 1745 so that even the cheapest cloths received the bounty (a half-penny a yard on export for linen valued at less than five-pence sterling), its effect was transformational, the means according to one of Dundee's ministers some decades afterwards by which 'the industry of the inhabitants was first set in motion'.[50]

Now able to compete on price with the thousands of makers of cheap linen cloth elsewhere in Europe, not least Osnabrück, which had been the main supplier to the plantations, sales of Scottish-made Osnaburgs soared. Sir John Clerk of Penicuik, who had been an advocate of and negotiator for union in 1707, pronounced gleefully that the 'vast incress of our Linnen Manufactories' was a direct result of the Scots being able to trade with England and the 'vast advantages which flow to Scotland from the plantation-Trade'.[51] Just how true this observation was became clear between 1754 and 1756 when the bounty payment was withdrawn: exports plummeted.[52] Significantly, however, even before this short-term setback, in January 1754 there were at least sixteen individuals or partnerships in or near Dundee weaving substantial quantities of 'Edinburgs', or Osnaburgs.[53] Dundee was one of the places that benefited most from the new financial incentive, the amount of stamped linen increasing from 817,416 yards in 1747 to 1,275,689 yards twelve years later.[54] This was when a petition signed by as many as forty-seven of the burgh's cloth merchants claimed that the linen trade was providing 'daily subsistence' to 'the greatest number of the Inhabitants'.[55] Over the course of the next half century, roughly nine-tenths of the linen exported from Scotland, most supported by the bounty system, was destined for use in the plantations.

For British planters in the Caribbean and the North American colonies, Osnaburg was the ideal cloth with which to clothe their African slaves, although it was used too by white indentured servants and other workers. Slave numbers expanded alongside the rise in the output of colonial products such as sugar, cotton, tobacco and coffee. By the 1760s British vessels were transporting across the Atlantic some 42,000 slaves each year, and by 1775 over 1.8 million Africans had been enslaved in what from 1707 were British colonies.

By 1830, after two centuries of British participation in the transatlantic slave trade, there were over two million Africans in the Caribbean sugar islands and the tobacco-growing plantations in the Chesapeake.[56] This created a massive market for provisions – and for clothing, one considerably bigger than that of Scotland alone, with its population of 1.2 million in 1755 and 1.6 million in 1801.[57] Once they became the property of the plantation owners, slaves who had survived below deck in the horrendously cramped hulls of ships which had carried them across the Atlantic were almost immediately dressed as Europeans, but in the lowest grades of 'negro' cloth. Such clothing was deliberately plain

36 THE TRIUMPH OF TEXTILES

– buff was the colour of the unbleached material, very different from the clean white linens that became an eighteenth-century fashion statement for the free.[58] Cloth designed for slave use was also uniform, befitting and making clear their lowly social status, although agencies such as the British Linen Company were aware that demand differed according to location; 'fine threaded & Bright Colours' were more suitable for the 'sugar Colonys [sic]' of the West Indies, while the 'stronger kind' of linen was better suited to the North American colonies.[59] Here, some 140,000 African men, women and children arrived between 1725 and 1775, literally a captive market for Scottish cloth manufacturers.[60] Critically too, coarse linen from Scotland was cheap, a major consideration given plantation policies designed to keep all labour costs at a minimum.[61] Owners in Virginia were required by law to clothe their slaves, but this applied elsewhere too. In addition, Osnaburgs and its variants had the virtue of being easily accessible, sturdy and durable (it was also used as bagging and for sacks), even if its coarseness meant it was harsh on the skin. The several yards of cloth allocated to each slave yearly was relatively easily made into loose-fitting shirts and trousers, dresses and, for children, shifts.[62] It was one of the distinguishing features of runaway slaves, as in July 1779 when owner Clayton Littlehales advertised in the *Royal Gazette of Jamaica* for the capture of a boy named 'Sharper', who had the letters IE marked on his right shoulder and was wearing 'blue Breeches' and an Osnaburg 'Frock'. Later, and even easier to identify, was 'Charles', who wore 'a check frock and trousers', while 'over the whole' was an 'Osnaburg frock with the letters BOB marked on the breast'.[63]

The importance of this market for Dundee and the surrounding region is easily demonstrated: of ten million yards of Osnaburgs made in Scotland 1819, over eight million came from Angus. At the heart of this was Dundee, with 4.2 million yards being sent off as early as the later 1780s, propelled to this position by a combination of its promoters in London, an ambitious town council, the Board of Trustees and the bounty. Another factor was the enterprise of Dundee's merchant-manufacturers, some of whom seem to have been prepared, by using low-cost, part-time spinners and weavers, to sell unevenly made or 'indifferent' cloth, and at the lowest prices. In 1760 they were accused by the British Linen Company of 'hurting . . . the trade of the Nation', by resisting the Company's attempt to introduce to the district what was called Pomerania linen (which was a degree finer than Osnaburg) by gathering in British Linen Company banknotes as a means of putting a stop to their business.[64] While further attempts were made to use finer yarns to

THE FIRST TOWN IN GREAT BRITAIN

make better cloth – and there were distinct gradations within the genus – Dundee's coarse linen was perfectly adequate for most colonial uses. Consequently, a few decades later, if a merchant or manufacturer wished to target more lucrative markets (as in New York) for better grades of linen such as diaper, they had to differentiate themselves from the Dundee norm. Thus in Forfar, Robert and William Don, that burgh's leading cloth manufacturers and dealers in the early nineteenth century, went to extraordinary lengths to discredit the Dundee product while boosting their own. But there were Dundee manufacturers too who boasted that their product was better, for example, than 'deficient' Osnaburgs from Kirriemuir, which was lighter (20 and 22 porter instead of 24) and of lower quality. The Don brothers, as well as some Dundee manufacturers, added to their range 'Strelitz' Osnaburgs, which were slightly wider and used higher-quality yarns, although a tow variant (using shorter flax fibres) was also made. Lint or tow, Strelitz commanded a higher price and was sought by London dealers who also served the transatlantic market.[65]

Most of the Osnaburgs as well as other varieties of cloth made in and near Dundee was shipped across the Atlantic via Glasgow and Liverpool – and London, the connection with which was underpinned by the presence in the capital of numerous Scottish agents and specifically Dundee and Angus émigrés and their kinsmen.[66] The Dundee merchant James Syme, for example, was a major purchaser of tow and lint Osnaburgs, sheeting and sailcloth, consigning it to ships bound for London or Liverpool. Typical was a shipment of over 5,000 yards of tow Osnaburgs from thirteen weavers in 1797 which he shipped to a merchant in Liverpool, Patrick Fairweather.[67] Fairweather, a Scot from Angus, had been a slaver and senior trader at Calabar on the west African coast in what is now Nigeria. He had made at least eighteen voyages trading slaves from Calabar to Jamaica, Grenada and Dominica, before retiring from slaving in 1793 and setting up as a merchant.[68] It seems beyond doubt, given his background, that the cloth he acquired from Dundee was intended for enslaved people in the West Indies. Others – William Baxter and Sons, for example – even based one of their family members (in this case, Robert Baxter) in the capital.

A smaller direct trade from Dundee was established early on, perhaps to avoid the London merchants (who expected to be supplied with higher-quality materials and sometimes accepted offers from American customers at lower prices than the Dundee merchants anticipated), the heavy charges of middlemen or the costs of shipping the bales coastwise to the Thames. Taking advantage of Dundee's enviable riverside location and the fact of its established if small harbour, from around 1751 a growing number of ships carrying linen, mainly Osnaburgs, left Dundee for Charlestown, Savannah and a handful of other American ports. A similar West Indian trade commenced in November 1753 when the *Dolphin* sailed for Jamaica carrying only linen. By 1815 direct exports reached some 300,000 yards in some years, along with other goods such as sailcloth, iron and tanned leather – another local speciality.[69] Return cargoes were mainly of plantation products such as rice, tar, turpentine and pitch. This was important as otherwise it could be many months before payment for direct consignments of linen was made, leaving sellers short of liquidity. Increasingly, however, it was through Glasgow that Dundee cloth went overseas, even if at times this was costly as commission agents chose to sell what they had on hand rather than waiting for the market to strengthen and prices to rise. Dundee merchants seized the opportunity presented by the opening of the Forth and Clyde Canal in 1790 of sending their cloth to their agents by this shorter route to Port Dundas in the centre of Glasgow, which could be reached almost as fast as a letter sent overland.[70]

Dundee's textile products were not wholly confined to the lower end of trade, with white (that is, bleached) linen being manufactured along with specialist products such as brown sheetings and others with names such as Baltic bagging. For a time too, the town diversified its range of textiles, with cotton spinning and coloured-thread making being carried on in the 1790s.[71] Merchants such as James Duncan and John Moir traded in these and other commodities at the turn of the nineteenth century, consigning goods to many of the places listed above.[72]

During the wars with Napoleonic France the attention of several of the burgh's merchants and manufacturers had focused on sailcoth. Indeed, Dundee-made canvas was reckoned 'superior in quality to any other in Britain'. Worth noting too at this stage is that for the next century (and beyond), wartime demand and Dundee's fortunes were to be inextricably linked.

The town's success with canvas, insiders were convinced, was due to three factors. The first was the application since the early 1790s of steam-powered spinning machinery, which allowed more tow or 'shorter materials' to be incorporated into the yarns, which improved the coarser canvases – although not immediately. Introduced by Messrs Fairweather & Marr and located in a badly lit former currying house or leather works in Chapelshade, the old sun and planet steam engine of 20 nominal horsepower, by Matthew Boulton and James Watt, frequently broke down.

THE FIRST TOWN IN GREAT BRITAIN

Reputedly, on occasion the engineers employed to repair it 'had to fly out at the doors to see how the pieces were thrown about'.[73] But even when they were going, the rocking motion made the early engines unsuitable for spinning.[74] Despite these misadventures, the use of steam-powered mill machinery in Dundee – where the flow of running water from the burgh's two main watercourses, the Dens burn and the Scouringburn, was inadequate to drive mill wheels – was a harbinger of the future, of 'Juteopolis'. Prior to the advent of steam, a couple of mills for scouring linen yarn were powered by the 'water of Dens' – 'no other than a torrent', which raged during spells of heavy rain but not at all during dry summers, and was generally sufficient for the burgh's earlier corn mills. It was the Dichty stream, which ran strongly beyond the burgh boundaries, that earlier had served the needs of the burgh's waulking mills for scouring, cleansing and finishing woollen cloth that had been made within Dundee itself.[75] Along its banks by the end of the eighteenth century it was flax spinners who were drawing on it for their kinetic energy needs.

Second, what were eventually more even yarns than could be spun by hand, were better boiled and bleached.[76] Third, and crucial at this stage, was the export bounty of two-pence per ell – without which, the Chamber of Commerce argued, Dundee would lose customers to Russia, where the bulk of the flax they used was grown.

We can add a fourth explanation: the success of John Baxter, of the family that would before long become Dundee's largest linen manufacturer, in winning contracts with the Royal Navy for sail canvas of an acceptable quality (it was reputed to have been used on Nelson's ships at Trafalgar) and at a competitive price.[77]

LINEN, OSNABURGS AND DUNDEE: IMPACTS TO c. 1830

The impact of colonial demand for cheap coarse linen from Dundee and the surrounding region was immense. This was in addition to a small group of returnees from the West Indies who had amassed small fortunes there as planters or officials and then purchased estates in Dundee's hinterland, as for example David Fyffe at Logie.[78]

These apart, while there were some well-off Dundonians, there is nothing to suggest that the burgh's cloth merchants were anything like as wealthy as Glasgow's 'tobacco lords'; Osnaburgs sold in bulk but usually with wafer-thin margins. This would become a major feature of the jute trade too. This is not to deny that substantial amounts of money could be made from coarse linens: on his death in August 1833 the merchant

40 THE TRIUMPH OF TEXTILES

and banker John Baxter of Idvies had stock worth just over £31,664 (well over £3.6 million at today's prices), the vast bulk of it (other than some coffee at Hamburg) in the hands of agents in the Caribbean islands. Jamaica was top of the list, but important too were slave states such as Brazil – with the world's largest slave population – and the southern states of North America.[79]

Many of those in textiles simply failed, with too little capital to survive business downturns, which were frequent and deep. Demand, from London and the plantations, could drop off without warning and remain depressed. On the supply side, shortages of flax from St Petersburg, Riga and elsewhere in the Baltic and of yarn slowed or even stopped production. Hefty price rises had the same effect. Slowing down output too was the propensity of weavers to abandon their looms in accordance with the agricultural cycle – to sow in the spring and then take a week or two off for the later summer harvest, and even refuse to weave certain kinds of cloth, greatly to the frustration of the merchants who employed them.[80]

For the labouring-class households whose womenfolk prepared and spun the flax into yarns, and the young and adult males who wove webs into linen cloth, the second half of the eighteenth century and even beyond was on the whole a period of relatively good fortune. As in other parts of Europe – Ireland, for example – where linen was made domestically, most handloom weavers were either small-scale farmers, or rural cottagers or the inhabitants of small settlements who had access to some land upon which to keep a cow and perhaps some other livestock and grow vegetables.[81]

This was the situation in the early nineteenth century in the parish of Liff and Benvie, immediately to the west of Dundee. There was a mix of household formations. These ranged from families such as that of John Tinder who with his son Jamie wove, while his daughters wound pirns for the looms and his wife 'attended to the corn'. At the other extreme were lone widows who scraped a living from pirn winding. Others – such as men like Robert Thom who had a wife but no children, or who lived alone – rented out looms to those whose accommodation was too cramped to house one. One contemporary observed that 'betwixt the produce of the ground and the income from the loom, with their pig or two [the inhabitants] could live like little kings, in a very plain way of course, but substantially'.[82]

This impressionistic comment is supported by harder evidence in the form of better earnings and rising real wages data during what was a brief (if much exaggerated) 'golden age' for Scotland's linen handloom weavers.[83] From the 1770s demand for the skills in textile manufacture of weavers in rural Angus, Lowland Perthshire and Fife increased. Household incomes rose as thousands of women (and children), attracted by cash payments, turned out more hand-spun yarn for the market from the spindles and distaffs and spinning wheels that were found in virtually every home.[84] Indeed, as pressure grew across the board for those concerned with textile work to devote more time to it, the compensating earnings made for a more varied diet that was less dependent on oatmeal and might include meat and tea; in fact, this seems to have been part of a virtuous circle wherein better-nourished workers were able to increase their productive hours.[85]

Even more conducive in persuading them to commit more hours to manufacturing employment was the unleashing of a desire among ordinary people for consumer goods, including hats, better-quality clothing, watches, clocks and kettles.[86] Furthermore, with demand for labour intense until after 1815, such households were able to live in accordance with patterns of work that varied in intensity, and allowed time for leisure pursuits which around Dundee in the weaving villages included gardening (flower growing was much favoured) and intense religious devotions. Female spinners often worked in groups across the age range, conversing and singing in what were called 'rock-ins'. So-called 'prime spinners' were especially favoured by employers – and suitors – unlike the colourfully named 'slubber spinners' whose yarns were uneven, prone to break on reeling and, owing to their haste, made more waste.[87] So important were the spinners in the textiles production process that at Glamis Mill, for example, the proprietors laid on new year balls for them, although similar rewards were commonplace among employers who wished to hold onto the best spinners and handloom weavers.[88] By exerting some control over the proceedings, not least the amount of liquor that was consumed, there was a greater chance that work would not be long interrupted.[89]

Although the temptation to paint an overly rosy picture of life prior to the mills and factories should be resisted, there is a sense in which the combination of industriousness in agriculture and even more so at the spinning wheel or loom offered a greater degree of personal autonomy – control over the allocation of time and the ranking of priorities – than would be the case within only a few years. Working hours in the first mills were long (at least thirteen and a half hours with two half-hour breaks) and regulated by the clock and the clanking, hissing steam engines that powered the spinning frames, relieved only when boilers broke down, coal or water supplies were interrupted, or machine parts gave way.

This, though, was in spinning. However, the pressures of change affecting the growing numbers of more or less full-time handloom weavers clustered in the burgh's Bucklemaker Wynd and the Chapelshade, Hilltown and Seagate districts often using looms handed down by fathers and grandfathers were not dissimilar, although unlike the spinning frame the power loom lay some way in the future. Beetling too – whereby cloth off the loom was hammered with wooden mallets to bind the threads flat – continued as a hand-craft, with the 'quiet tip-tap' of the beetlers working away in their cellars being 'one of the common sounds of the town'. Even so, there was greater concentration, in workshops of various dimensions. Therein more control could be exercised by employers, albeit that most operated on a small scale. By around 1830 there were some four hundred 'manufacturers' (also termed 'household weavers') in Dundee who between them had between four and five thousand looms, an average of between ten and twelve each. Most had far fewer.[90] A handful had more. Those employed worked under close supervision in weaving sheds like the handloom 'Factory' belonging to Thomas Webster & Co., in Hawkhill. The grim and soul-destroying nature of work in the weaving shed was articulated by the weaver-poet William Thom, who from 1814 spent seventeen years in such an environment in Aberdeen.[91] For cloth merchants like John Moir, however, there were distinct advantages in being able to assure buyers that the bales of cloth in question had been made by their own weavers and were therefore of good quality throughout.

Increasingly, Dundee was assuming the characteristics of a manufacturing town. This was evident not only in the number of handloom weavers but also as there were substantial numbers of working women (mainly spinners), recognisable by being 'wrapped in coarse plaids'. Silk cloaks and bonnets were a rarer sight.[92] Although some females wove the lighter fabrics, it was as spinners that they began to stand out. Prominent too were large numbers of young people; more than half of the 3,000 or so employees in the spinning mills in 1830 were aged between ten and eighteen.[93]

As in so many other Scottish municipalities, it was the weavers who were most commonly found in the ranks of the radical societies that were active during the early years of the French Revolution. The Dundee weaver George Mealmaker was a leading figure in the clandestine United Scotsmen movement later in the 1790s.

THE FIRST TOWN IN GREAT BRITAIN

On the other hand, led by the town's propertied classes, large numbers of weavers joined the loyal volunteers as fears of a French invasion grew while the earlier enthusiasm for the Revolution cooled. Despite Dundee's reputation at the time, as well as subsequently, as a hotbed of radicalism, recent research has concluded that militant support for the Friends of the People and the authority-alarming planting of Trees of Liberty during 1792 was confined to a 'committed minority' which had shrunk by the end of the 1790s.[94] In accounting for this apparent passivity, the part played by the town's staple trade seems to have been significant. Wartime demand for sailcloth and plain brown linen was high, and exports were still underpinned by the government bounty. With wages at high levels for much of the time, Dundonian weavers and their dependants experienced a relatively comfortable war. Certainly, their situation contrasted well with their continental and Irish rivals.[95] Marching armies and battles had devastated competitor regions such as Saxony, Silesia and Westphalia; recovery was slow or even non-existent, with linen 'doomed by the widespread use of cotton'.[96]

Yet there were difficult times in Dundee during the war years. Most distressing were the steep fluctuations in the availability and price of flax from St Petersburg resulting from Napoleon's decrees of 1806 and 1807 that were intended to block British trade. Mill closures and some bankruptcies followed.

Nevertheless, over the period of conflict, imports of flax and hemp to Dundee increased roughly seven-fold, while linen cloth exports tripled. The years immediately afterwards, however, were more difficult. Along with peace came the curtailment of government contracts for sailcloth, hammock and cheap shirtings, with many individuals and partnerships going under as a result.[97] This presaged a pattern of periodic and drastic thinning out of individual merchant-manufacturers or small partnerships that would recur on three more occasions before the middle of the century. The impact of the collapse in demand during 1815 and 1816 was catastrophic. Well over sixty enterprises went out of business.

Incomes too plummeted. While a handloom weaver prior to the battle of Waterloo in June 1815 could earn twenty shillings for a piece of cloth 150 yards long, by winter this had been slashed to five shillings. With peace too came the return of youths and younger men from military service in search of work and the dilution of the labour market. The following year the harvest failed and, with prices high, many households necessarily subsisted on a diet of potatoes, mashed or turned into soup, three times a day; oats and other grains were almost impossible to buy.

Food riots ensued, attracting nationwide attention and the condemnation of the judiciary. Meal sellers' stores and houses were sacked, while within the weaver community of Hawkhill, effigies of 'one Thomson', a weaver who had dealt in meal as a secondary occupation, were burnt, as he had allegedly been 'giving little weight' and raised the price of his meal to twenty pence when others were selling at two-pence less.[98] This though was simply the prelude to an 'explosion' as a crowd that swelled to some two thousand proceeded to break the windows of almost every one of the hundred-plus meal sellers' premises in Dundee, before pillaging the house of a more prominent merchant at Carolina Port.[99] If political radicalism was less potent than has been assumed, the attachment of the labouring classes in Dundee to what has been termed the 'moral economy' of the poor was both long-standing and flourishing and would be in evidence for some decades.

So too were what might be termed the weapons of the weak – the traditional means adopted by ordinary people when participating en masse in an event in which they had an interest, but no formal means of expressing it. One of these was the monarch's birthday. The disorder that had accompanied this annual event, when for a few hours large but disciplined crowds had turned their local worlds upside down by chasing magistrates and other authority figures off the streets, had petered out in most places by the early nineteenth century. In Dundee, however, the occasion continued to be marked as late as May 1853 – Queen Victoria's birthday, a Monday, which among the weaver population was still considered to be a day of rest and for copious alcoholic refreshment. The Town House in the High Street was sacked, while passers-by were ordered by the crowd – prominent among which were 'the lowest and most ignorant grade of working lads' – to remove their hats. Refusal led to their involuntary removal and the conversion of such prized accoutrements into footballs, stark if temporary reminders to the town's middle classes that any assumptions they had about the extent to which they controlled public spaces was conditional.[100]

Dundee's small business elite – merchants, shipmasters, small-scale manufacturers and shopkeepers – who survived the fifteen years of war with Napoleon's armies appear to have lived modestly. They are vividly depicted in Henry Harwood's well-known 1821 painting, *The Executive*. Most lived in the central districts of the burgh. Even the top of what is now the Constitution Road was viewed by some as a move too far, 'distant from all Markets and in the winter . . . an uncomfortable residence', the grocer and spirit merchant Thomas Handyside Baxter reflected as new 'Cottages' there were under construction.[101] There was

THE FIRST TOWN IN GREAT BRITAIN 45

though an identifiable drift to larger houses that were scattered in an unplanned manner at and beyond the outer fringes of the town – along the Nethergate, down Roseangle where they fronted onto the shore and along the riverbank at Magdalen Green. As the better-off moved away, their residences in the central districts, including what had been the burgh's grandest house, were subdivided and inhabited by tradespeople.

But what little evidence is available indicates that the resident merchant elites had much in common with the 'middling sort' elsewhere in Scotland in the later eighteenth and early nineteenth centuries. In their homes, reception rooms and separate dining rooms were introduced, along with mahogany furniture, more glass (including mirrors), and chinaware, silver spoons and prints. The numbers of tradesmen offering what might be termed luxury services grew, to include by 1825 cabinet makers, a clock maker, portrait painter and the like. There were shopkeepers selling books, notably the establishment of the Radical poet Robert Nicol, who later edited the *Leeds Times*. Other providers included dancing masters and a music teacher, and Helen Lindsay's cookery shop at the head of the Seagate.

Cultural life was enriched too, in spite of the unusually powerful opposition up until the 1760s of the Kirk and other stern religious sects that had emerged in Dundee. Relished by the burgh's most prominent citizens in subsequent decades were concerts, assemblies, balls and a couple of theatres (the fine Theatre Royal in Castle Street was opened in 1808), newspapers – the weekly *Advertiser* and the *Courier* – and literary magazines. For the more studious there was a subscription library and Enlightenment-influenced scientific and speculative societies.[102] Overall the impression gained is that there were less overt signs of luxury than in other similar-sized towns in Georgian Britain. The low number of servants, both male and female, points to a similar conclusion.

For the authorities, however, there was another side to Dundee's religiosity. The moral renewal sought by some dissenting ministers was to align them with the movement for parliamentary reform, which spilled over into Radical politics. Unusually, in Dundee such individuals found themselves propelled into leadership roles, as in the case of Thomas Fyshe Palmer, the Unitarian minister who was sentenced to be transported for his part in the Friends of Liberty society in the politically febrile years of 1792 and 1793.[103] But this was uncommon.

Some historians have written off Dundee at the turn of the nineteenth century, convinced that even at this stage the burgh and its pennypinching, unimaginative civic leadership was on the slippery downward path that would later earn it its reputation as a 'frontier town'; a grim, poverty-stricken, industrial quagmire from which its better-off inhabitants fled, to the eastern suburb of Broughty Ferry or even safely over the Tay to Newport. This view has been challenged by more benign accounts of the burgh's condition in the pre-jute decades.[104]

The flight of the wealthy, for example, was largely although not entirely a post-1850 phenomenon.[105] There seems to have been less desire than there was in towns like Edinburgh and Glasgow for social segregation. In those places, new towns, distinct from the old, were self-consciously laid out on rational lines as exemplars of modernity. By contrast, the late Charles McKean, an architectural historian, was struck by the extent to which the classes in Dundee intermingled, with the middling sorts opting to stay in the older, central parts of the burgh, defending their shops and business premises from what was perceived to have been a sharp rise in crime after the Napoleonic wars by instigating and paying for watching schemes. It was not until 1824 that Dundee acquired its first Police Act, some years after Scotland's other industrial towns.[106]

The modest retreat to the suburbs just noted was overshadowed by the move from the 1790s of the proprietors of small mills and tanneries to districts just beyond the pre-1831 burgh boundaries, such as the Hawkhill and the Scouringburn. It was to their misfortune that it was here that workers' housing – low, cramped and poorly built – was hastily put up, creating what before long would become overcrowded disease-ridden slums. And even though Dundee lacked a new town, within the burgh bounds there were notable instances of improvements in the form of new streets and buildings – Crichton Street (1783) and Castle Street (1795) and the Exchange Coffee Room on the newly raised Dock Street (1828) – part of an improvement programme taking place by the docks. Similarly, in the same year, 1828, Union Street made for an easier opening to the shore. If the town council was lackadaisical and uncoordinated in its attempts to improve the old and build from new, the burgh Trades and private individuals proved more than capable of stepping into the breach.[107]

However, despite the improvements to the urban fabric alluded to above, there were signs of problems that not many decades later would become overwhelming.

Dundee was not alone among Britain's manufacturing towns in these respects. But from the 1820s so strong was the surge of mills and factories along with the unprecedented rates of increase in the numbers of migrants to work in them, that the medieval infrastructure was soon overwhelmed. The kinds of law-breaking associated with the unchecked

THE FIRST TOWN IN GREAT BRITAIN   47

flow of migrants without fixed abodes, supporting networks and steady incomes rocketed: vagrancy, drunkenness, theft and riotous and disorderly conduct multiplied.[108] We will further explore conditions and social relations in industrial Dundee by the mid-century in chapter 4.

LINEN: GROWTH, CONSOLIDATION AND LEADERSHIP

The foundations just outlined were those upon which Dundee's future as a mill- and factory-dominated industrial town were laid. In part they are also consequences of that process. The growth trajectory of coarse linen production in Angus continued to be steeply upwards, with output almost doubling from 8.8 million yards in 1790 to 16.3 million in 1820. Concerns that would later become part of the economic bedrock of the town were established, as for example Baxter Bros, who set going the first of their mills at Dens in 1818 – a 'wonderful year' for the spinning trade, according to one witness.[109]

But it was in the decade that followed when Dundee's pre-eminence in linen – reflected in the assessment of Dundee's ministers quoted in the title of this chapter – was established. The pace of change was remarkable – as rapid as it would be in the 1860s when jute became Dundee's main manufacture.

The five or so spinning mills that succeeded Fairweather & Marr's initial venture were small and undercapitalised, struggled to produce profits and tended to go in and out of business. But the first country mill owners too had struggled with credit shortages as the banks were inclined at this stage to view flax spinning as a 'low disreputable trade' and too risky to support.[110] Total capacity at the turn of the nineteenth century was only two thousand spindles. Larger mills were built after 1800. James Brown, previously a pioneer in water-powered spinning in the Angus countryside outside Dundee, built West Ward or Bell Mill in the burgh's Guthrie Street, and his sons, who took over nearby East Ward Mill from George Wilkie (successor to Fairweather & Marr), stand out in this regard.[111] Yet even in 1816, according to James Carmichael, who became one of Dundee's leading and most highly regarded textile engineers, machine spinning 'was hardly an accomplished fact'; hand spinning was still widespread.

There were, however, men who were keen to spearhead change (who they were, their backgrounds and characteristics are the focus of Chapter 3). They made it their business to try to tackle the technical challenges not only of mill spinning but of processing the heavier yarns used in Osnaburgs and similar cloths. These were serious impediments that had been apparent almost from the time the flax-spinning frame invented by the Darlington partnership of Kendrew & Porthouse was first used in Scotland, at Inverbervie (1787) and at Kirkland in Fife, possibly in 1788.[112] Indeed, the problems associated with the raw material – especially tow, the rough, brittle part of the fibrous flax plant that was removed during the preparatory processes of heckling and carding – were apparent during the hand-spinning era and continued to focus the minds of the leading mill proprietors.[113] Overcoming this to allow for a 'long draw' of strong, even yarn was crucial if large-scale machine spinning at high speeds was to be a success. Although attempts to get to the bottom of the 'grand secret' (successful carding) bore some fruit and allowed mill spinning to get under way, the problem was not fully resolved until the 1860s, as will be seen later. Related were the prodigious quantities of waste produced by some spinners – 30 and even 40 per cent of the flax bales in some cases, a level which could not be sustained.

Of the many other hurdles that the early proprietors had had to overcome, not the least was the lack of mechanics to build and repair the new machinery. They had little knowledge, either, about how a mill should be laid out. Descriptions of the first of them are suggestive of unplanned ramshackle organisation and technical inefficiency made worse by lax management – although with few local models to guide mill managers and overseers as they attempted to impose the new workplace regime this is hardly surprising.[114] The wheelwrights who had attended to water-powered mills had to adapt and acquire new skills. Another challenge related to management deficiencies (although not unique to Dundee) was the recruitment of workers into the mills, training them in new skills and techniques, and above all inculcating the discipline and regular habits demanded by the clock and the steam engine in a working environment that for most was alien.[115] For this reason, recruitment practices familiar to agricultural workers were adopted, with masters of mills attending country hiring markets and paying arles – effectively signing-on fees – for six-month or annual engagements contracts. Another of the first proprietors turned to Edinburgh's charity workhouse and procured boys and girls – under certain conditions concerning their upkeep, training and education.[116]

This all tends to support the scanty evidence there is that, again as elsewhere in early industrialising Britain, there was resistance to mill work. Charles Mackie, for example, a mill manager in the early nineteenth century, recalled that the spinners had been 'all up in arms against the . . . Mills'. There were, it seems, cases of arson, with those women affected by the introduction of mill work regretting the loss of their way of life,

THE FIRST TOWN IN GREAT BRITAIN 49

fearing the injuries that might result from working with the water- and steam-driven frames, but above all anxious about the threat mills posed to their skill-derived status. And income. Over time, those who were left behind suffered a sharp fall in wage rates as more mills were opened. The flax dressers – hecklers, of whom there were between three hundred and four hundred – also stood firm in defence of their handicraft skills and pre-industrial workplace practice that included periodic 'pint' or drink breaks.[117] Through taking collective action in what were early instances of trade unions, and strikes in 1822 and 1827, they managed to resist the introduction of machinery long after its use had become commonplace in Leeds.[118] It is no surprise then that few if any mill owners made any money from their pioneering endeavours. The attrition rate was crushingly high.

Yet the problems faced by early entrants to the trade in Dundee were remarkably soon overcome by some of the more determined venturers. Indeed, while the first steam engines to be used in Dundee came from English firms such as Messrs Boulton and Watt, Fenton, Murray and Jackson of Leeds, and John and George Rennie of London, and Glasgow's Robert Napier & Co., within a few years and certainly from around 1820 most were made locally, with the Glasgow-born and trained brothers James and Charles Carmichael, who established their Ward Foundry in 1810, in the vanguard.[119] By 1818 Dundee was host to two dozen firms of 'wrights' and 'millwrights', vital contributors as the town established critical mass as the centre of Scotland's coarse linen trade. Preparing machinery too was imported, as were spinning frames, again from Leeds, at this point the country's linen capital, but adapted and improved by local spinners with a mechanical bent. By close observation and scrupulous attention to detail, Dundee's more successful textile enterprises were able to avoid the trouble, expense and disappointment associated with inventing from scratch, 'a great mistake', according to the industry's master mechanical and production engineer Peter Carmichael.[120] Notwithstanding the initial shortage of skilled mechanics, by the first years of the nineteenth century Dundee had its first machine makers – James Low and Robert Fairweather, and Meldrum & Co. – while in and around the town sufficient confidence and expertise had been amassed to tempt spinners from Dundee to establish mills in the north of Ireland.

The period of post-war dislocation over, by the end of the decade demand for linen goods had once again surged. The United States was by far the main market, as the population soared from 5.3 million in 1800 to 12.8 million in 1830 – over 30 per cent in each decade during

50   THE TRIUMPH OF TEXTILES

the first half of the nineteenth century. Flax was difficult to grow in North America, so shipments of linen from Dundee, including better grades such as diaper (used for household purposes), most of which went to New York, rocketed. In 1815 just over 164,000 yards left Dundee for this destination. By 1829 almost five and a half million yards were sent out. Cheaper grades did even better, including hemp bagging for America's cotton crop, and also twine. Incredibly, total linen sales from Dundee to the United States, including the plantations of the south-east, increased more than ninety-fold.[121]

Mills already in existence were brought back into production, while in less than two years, between 1820 and 1822, at least another eleven new flax-spinning mills – many small, 'little mills' – were erected and opened. The times were heady, the optimism of the period reflected in the very public whisky-drinking celebration in 1822 that followed the placing by the mason of the last stone (the 'riggin stane') of the chimney stack of the new Lower Dens Works that were built by William Baxter and his son Edward.[122]

Total horsepower was now 178, and the number of spindles had quadrupled, to eight thousand. Even this early, Dundee was well on the way to becoming Scotland's leading importer of flax and the main source of spun yarns. By 1826 Dundee had overtaken Hull as Britain's most important flax port, from which England's major linen manufacturers such as Marshalls of Leeds obtained their supplies. This rise to pre-eminence would have come as a surprise to many of those manufacturers who had feared the consequences of the withdrawal in 1822 of the bounty on linen exports that had been in place since the time of the battle of Culloden. Its removal, a result of British economic policy at the time moving in the direction of free trade, had been resisted by flax spinners and the linen interest in Dundee as well as other places where linen was a major source of income and employment, and from whence campaigns for its retention had been waged on the grounds of its 'vital importance'.[123]

The prop was no longer required. However, in what was largely a seller's market, it appears that many firms were initially tempted to prioritise quantity over quality. In the past this has often been seen as paving the way for jute, as manufacturers sought cheaper raw materials than flax and hemp and customers sought coarser goods.[124] Yet what has become clear as we carried out our investigations for this book is that this not only oversimplifies Dundee's move into jute but in some respects is simply wrong. It is true that in general Dundee's reputation was for coarser cloths, in contrast to Leeds where finer varieties were made. We have noted already that low margins per yard encouraged volume production,

THE FIRST TOWN IN GREAT BRITAIN 51

a consequence exacerbated by cut-throat competition between individuals and small firms anxious to secure and hold their position in the market. Yet there were merchant-manufacturers like the aforementioned John Moir who deliberately differentiated their cloth from other producers in Dundee by its quality – something buyers were concerned with too: 'put your Glass to one of his webs', he wrote to one of his Glasgow customers, Matthew Mackay & Co., for whom he had shipped Osnaburgs from a 'very good manufacturer in Dundee', and you will 'find only ten threads in the Warp'. Moir, keen to obtain a higher price for his own cloth in a market where a fraction of a penny could make the difference between break-even and profit, explained that his weavers used eleven threads to make a 'superior Article'. Nevertheless, he wrote, if Mackays were not prepared to pay, reluctantly, he would 'make it the same as other people do'.[125] In spinning, James Carmichael too bucked the trend, and made 'decent tow yarns to please the manufacturers'.[126]

In 1825, however, the London stock market collapsed, leading to the failure of several banks. Across the country, credit dried up. Business in Dundee ground to a halt, the second of the pre-c. 1850 shocks that rocked the town. The five banks with branches in the burgh withdrew what had been notoriously generous credit lines. Orders dried up, crippling individuals and firms who had 'little real property' (the humbleness of the origins of many of Dundee's employers is striking), 'but much genuine imprudence'.[127] According to one account, over two hundred businesses had to cease trading. This included the forerunners of what would become Dundee's biggest manufacturers: James Cock or Cox of Lochee and William Thomas Baxter of Baxter and Sons, who had just built the first of their mills at Lower Dens.[128] One contemporary, struck by the silence that descended as spinning mills, weaving sheds and foundries closed down, remarked that for months on end, well into 1826, every day was like the Sabbath. When it would end, another despairing witness asked in May, 'heaven knows'.[129] With the price of flax low, some spinning continued in hopes that once the worst was over, yarn prices would soar.[130] More works, however, were put up for sale but attracted risible offers. For their owners, emigration seemed like the only way out. Just how many departed is not clear, although there is no doubt that for several of those worst affected a fresh start elsewhere was their best option. Intriguingly, we now know that there was some interest from struggling Dundonians in Calcutta, where some of their townsmen were already located.[131] We will return to this connection in the next chapter.

By 1827 not only had most of the former mills begun spinning again. Proprietors who had survived the cull, such as William and John Brown, extended their works, while in 1828 and 1829 entirely new mills were erected, notably to the west of the Scouringburn. By 1830 there were around thirty of them, almost double the number prior to 1826. Steam engines – now made locally – were more powerful, some putting out 20 horsepower, so much so that water-driven country mills (of which there may have been as many as sixty pre-1830) found it difficult to compete, not least as they were burdened by the additional cost of transporting their cloth to Dundee. In Dundee itself, spinners increased their productive capacity by putting in additional frames as well as using larger spinning frames of forty spindles. They were powered by what would soon be fifty-three steam engines with a combined 930 horsepower.

By raising productivity levels by driving the frames faster and with a shorter draw, according to Charles Mackie, 'a new era in spinning' was heralded.[132] Also important for the future was that greater amounts of tow were being spun, a step made possible by improvements in carding and preparing this much less malleable fibre.

As the new decade dawned, Dundee was now the leader in Scotland in flax-spinning know-how and technology, with an international reputation for its flax- and hemp-based products. The importation of thousands of tons of the raw materials and the export of linen cloth valued at some £1.5 million (in 1833) had been facilitated by the merchant-led conversion in the two decades after 1815 of Dundee's 'wretched tide harbour' into a substantial port. This second transformation of the town's waterfront on the river Tay, an integral part of the artery through which the town's lifeblood flowed, was the object of immense civic pride. Grand processions were organised as its component facilities such as Thomas Telford's King William IV Dock (1825) were opened, with others following for similar reasons on many occasions for the rest of the century.[133]

Economic activity on this scale created new job openings. As a result, in-migration proceeded apace, with most of the arrivals coming from rural Angus and elsewhere on the east coast. But in addition, there was what was described as an 'extraordinary influx' of immigrants from rural Ireland into the industry – almost immediately making a mark that within a few years would become indelible. Over the decade the town's population had risen by 42 per cent, to over 45,000 people by 1831. But notwithstanding assumptions to the contrary, none of this owed anything to jute.[134]

In 1823 several bales of jute had arrived in Dundee, but very little of this or subsequent small shipments was processed during the rest of the decade. Most spinners preferred to stick with flax and hemp. What changed in this regard, why and how, is the subject of the following two chapters.

Notes

1. UDA, Council Minute Books, VIII, 1704–15, 1 April 1706; Edinburgh City Archives [ECA], Moses Collection, SL30/223, Reports and Visitations, Dundee, 1710.
2. Eric J. Graham, *Seawolves: Pirates & the Scots* (Edinburgh, 2005), pp. 137–42.
3. See, for example, Allan I. Macinnes, *Union and Empire: The Making of the United Kingdom in 1707* (Cambridge, 2007), pp. 137–240.
4. Elizabeth P. D. Torrie, *Medieval Dundee: A Town and its People* (Dundee, 1990), pp. 36, 70–1.
5. Karen J. Cullen, Christopher A. Whatley and Mary Young, 'Battered but unbowed – Dundee during the seventeenth century', in Charles McKean, Bob Harris and Christopher A. Whatley (eds), *Dundee: Renaissance to Enlightenment* (Dundee, 2009), pp. 67–9.
6. Alan M. Macdonald, 'Dundee and the crown, 1550–1650', in McKean, Harris and Whatley (eds), *Dundee*, pp. 51–2.
7. John D. Grainger, *Cromwell Against the Scots: The Last Anglo-Scottish War, 1650–1652* (East Linton, 1997), pp. 158–60.
8. See, for example, W. Mason Inglis, *Annals of an Angus Parish* (Dundee, 1888), pp. 143–4; Flora Davidson, *Glen Clova Through the Ages: A Short Guide to the History of an Angus Glen* (Dundee, 2013), p. 37; Karen J. Cullen, *Famine in Scotland: The 'Ill Years' of the 1690s* (Edinburgh, 2010), pp. 117–22.
9. I. D. Whyte, 'Scottish and Irish urbanisation in the seventeenth and eighteenth centuries: A comparative perspective', in S. J. Connolly, R. A. Houston and R. J. Morris (eds), *Conflict, Identity and Economic Development: Ireland and Scotland, 1600–1939* (Preston, 1995), p. 24.
10. Derek J. Patrick, 'Dundee in the nation, c. 1686–1746', in McKean, Harris and Whatley (eds), *Dundee*, p. 92.
11. Roger L. Emerson, *An Enlightened Duke: The Life of Archibald Campbell (1682–1761), Earl of Ilay, 3rd Duke of Argyll* (Kilkerran, 2013), pp. 227–32.
12. E. Cruickshanks, Stuart Handley and D. W. Hayton (eds), *The House of Commons 1690–1715, II, Constituencies* (Cambridge, 2002), p. 926.
13. Patrick, 'Dundee in the nation', p. 93.
14. Christopher A. Whatley, *Scottish Society 1707–1830: Beyond Jacobitism, towards Industrialisation* (Manchester, 2000), pp. 36–7.
15. Clifford Gulvin, *The Tweedmakers: A History of the Scottish Fancy Woollen Industry 1600–1914* (Newton Abbot, 1973), pp. 28–9.
16. Annette M. Smith, *The Nine Trades of Dundee* (Dundee, 1995), p. 158.
17. Christopher A. Whatley, 'Sound and song in the ritual of popular protest: Continuity and the "Nob Songs" of 1825', in Edward J. Cowan (ed.), *The Ballad in Scottish History* (East Linton, 2000), pp. 153–6.
18. Karen J. Cullen, Christopher A. Whatley and Mary Young, 'King William's Ill Years: New evidence on the impact of scarcity and harvest failure during

the crisis of the 1690s on Tayside', *Scottish Historical Review*, LXXXV, 2 (October 2006), pp. 262–3.

19. T. C. Smout, *Scottish Trade on the Eve of the Union, 1660–1707* (Edinburgh and London, 1963), p. 233.

20. Annette M. Smith, *The Nine Trades of Dundee* (Dundee, 1995), pp. 157–68.

21. Smith, *Nine Trades*, pp. 161–5.

22. <https://stataccscot.edina.ac.uk/static/statacc/dist/home≥ (hereafter *OSA*), Dundee, County of Forfar, Vol. VIII (1973), p. 213.

23. William Seton, *The Interest of Scotland in Three Essays* (London, 2nd edn, 1702), pp. 58–9.

24. Christopher A. Whatley, *The Scots and the Union* (Edinburgh, 2007 edn), pp. 281–2; see also Karin Bowie (ed.), *Addresses Against Incorporating Union 1706–7* (Woodbridge, 2018), pp. 15–24.

25. S. G. E. Lythe, 'Early modern trade, c. 1550 to 1707', in Gordon Jackson and S. G. E. Lythe (eds), *The Port of Montrose: A History of its Harbour, Trade and Shipping* (New York and Tayport, 1993), pp. 95–6.

26. Whatley, *Scots*, pp. 337–8.

27. Alastair J. Durie (ed.), *The British Linen Company 1745–1775* (Edinburgh, 1996), p. 2.

28. Annette M. Smith, *The Guildry of Dundee* (Dundee, 2005), pp. 62–3.

29. *OSA*, Dundee, p. 241.

30. Eveline Cruickshanks, Stuart Handley and D. W. Hayton (eds), *The House of Commons 1690–1715, V, Members O–Z* (Cambridge, 2002), p. 954.

31. UDA, Council Minute Books, VIII, 1 April 1706, 17 October 1707; General Petitions to Dundee Town Council, 'The Shipmasters and Fraternity of Seamen', 1721.

32. Perth and Kinross Council Archives [PKCA], B59/26/4/1, Petitions, 1689–1739, for example, 'Petition of Thomas Craigdallie, late tacksman of the Bridge of Tay port' (1711); Cullen, Whatley and Young, 'Battered but unbowed', pp. 75–7.

33. Patrick Lindsay, *The Interest of Scotland Considered* (London, 1736), p. xxvii.

34. Daniel Defoe, *A Tour Through the Whole Island of Great Britain* (London, 1986 edn), p. 651.

35. Torrie, *Medieval Dundee*, p. 33.

36. Whatley, *Scottish Society*, pp. 192–3.

37. PKCA, B59/24/86, 'Council Petition to Parlt Anent the Linen', 1721.

38. Anon., *Reasons for Improving the Fisheries and Linen Manufacture of Scotland* (London, 1727), p. 16.

39. Durie, *British Linen*, pp. 2–4.

40. Alastair Durie, 'Imitation in Scottish eighteenth-century textiles: The drive to establish the manufacture of linen', *Journal of Design History*, 6, 2 (1993), p. 72.

41. ECA, Moses Collection, SL 30/244, Alex Dundas, London, anent Duty on Foreign Linens exported, 1 December 1737.
42. Brenda Collins and Philip Ollerenshaw, 'The European linen industry since the Middle Ages', in Brenda Collins and Philip Ollerenshaw (eds), *The European Linen Industry in Historical Perspective* (Oxford, 2003), pp. 16–19.
43. Durie, *British Linen Company*, p. 85.
44. Alastair Durie, *The Scottish Linen Industry in the 18th Century* (Edinburgh: John Donald, 1979), p. 27.
45. See UDA, Burgh of Dundee, Treasurer's Accounts, 1733–53, 1753–1778.
46. Andrew Mackillop, 'Dundee, London and the Empire in Asia', in McKean, Harris and Whatley (eds), *Dundee*, pp. 162–3.
47. Kenneth Morgan, *Slavery and the British Empire* (Oxford, 2007), pp. 7–11.
48. Bob Harris, 'The Scots, the Westminster parliament, and the British state in the eighteenth century', in Julian Hoppit (ed.), *Parliaments, Nations and Identities in Britain and Ireland, 1660–1850* (Manchester, 2003), pp. 131–3.
49. Quoted in Whatley, *Scottish Society*, p. 106.
50. *OSA*, Dundee, p. 223.
51. Douglas Duncan (ed.), *History of the Union of Scotland and England by Sir John Clerk of Penicuik* (Edinburgh, 1993), p. 177.
52. Durie, *Scottish Linen Industry*, pp. 51–3.
53. Alastair J. Durie (ed.), *The British Linen Company 1745–1775* (Edinburgh: Scottish History Society, 1996), pp. 58–9.
54. Alastair J. Durie, 'The markets for Scottish linen, 1730–1775', *Scottish Historical Review*, 52, No. 153, Part 1 (1973), 30–49, p. 30.
55. ECA, Moses Collection, SL30/4/6, 'Petition of the Merchants of Dundee to the Convention of Royal Burghs', 1768.
56. Joseph E. Inikori, *Africans and the Industrial Revolution in England* (Cambridge, 2002), pp. 192–5; Simon P. Newman, 'Freedom seeking slaves in England and Scotland, 1700–1780', *English Historical Review*, 134: 570 (October 2019), p. 1141.
57. T. M. Devine, 'Did slavery make Scotia great?', in T. M. Devine (ed.), *Recovering Scotland's Slavery Past: The Caribbean Connection* (Edinburgh, 2015), p. 235.
58. Jan de Vries, *The Industrious Revolution: Consumer Behaviour and the Household Economy, 1650 to the Present* (Cambridge, 2008), p. 135.
59. Lloyds Banking Group Archive, British Linen Company, GB1830 BLB1/4/7/2, Foreign Letters 1750–1752, letter to Tubman and Hartley, Whitehaven, 17 October 1751; we are grateful to Dr Sally Tuckett for this reference.
60. See Simon P. Newman, 'Rethinking runaways in the British Atlantic World: Britain, the Caribbean, West Africa and North America', *Slavery and Abolition*, 38: 1 (2017), pp. 49–75.
61. See Stuart M. Nisbet, 'Early Scottish planters in the Leeward Islands, c. 1660–1740', in Devine (ed.), *Recovering Scotland's Slavery Past*, pp. 70–3.

THE TRIUMPH OF TEXTILES

62. Shane White and Graham White, 'Slave clothing and African-American culture in the eighteenth and nineteenth centuries', *Past & Present*, 148 (August 1995), pp. 149–55; Katherine E. Gruber, 'Slave clothing and adornment in Virginia', *Encyclopedia Virginia* <https://www.encyclopediavirginia.org/Slave_Clothing_and_Adornment_in_Virgina>, accessed 15 October 2020.

63. *Royal Gazette of Jamaica*, 31 July 1779, p. 10; 15 April 1793, p. 12.

64. Durie, *British Linen Company*, pp. 122–3.

65. Christopher A. Whatley, *Onwards From Osnaburgs* (Edinburgh, 1992), pp. 31–62; NRS, CS 96/4030, Letter Book of John Moir, 1823–27, 24 February, 14 March 1823.

66. Mackillop, 'Dundee, London and the Empire in Asia', p. 164.

67. NRS, CS96/2195, Court of Session, Stock account book of James Syme, merchant, Dundee, 1763–1797; see Sally Tuckett and Christopher A. Whatley, 'Textiles in transition: Linen, jute and the Dundee region's transnational networks, c. 1740–c. 1880', in Emma Bond and Michael Morris (eds), *Transnational Scotland: Legacies of Empire and Slavery* (Edinburgh, 2021), pp. 38–54.

68. Trans-Atlantic Slave Trade Database, Slave Voyages, <https://www.slavevoyages.org/voyage/database>, accessed by Dr Sally Tuckett, 24 July 2020; see also Stephen D. Behrendt, A. J. H. Latham and David Northrup, *The Diary of Antera Duke, an Eighteenth-Century Africa Slave Trader* (Oxford, 2010), p. 72.

69. Charles McKean, Claire Swan and Malcolm Archibald, 'Maritime Dundee and its harbour, c. 1755–1820', in McKean, Harris and Whatley (eds), *Dundee*, pp. 276–80.

70. See NRS CS 96/4030, Letter Book of John Moir.

71. *OSA*, Dundee, pp. 216–17.

72. Bob Harris, 'Merchants, the middling sort, and cultural life in Georgian Dundee', in Harris, McKean and Whatley (eds), *Dundee*, p. 245.

73. UDA, MS 102/1/1, Peter Carmichael, Reminiscences, 1, p. 81.

74. William Brown, *Reminiscences of Flax Spinning* (Dundee, 1962), p. 14.

75. NRS, I Inglis D/2/19, Waulker Trade of Dundee v. David Brown and others (1764).

76. DARC, Forfarshire Chamber of Commerce and Manufactures, Vol. 3, 'Copies of Memorials and Petitions', c. 1818.

77. Enid Gauldie, *The Dundee Textile Industry, 1790–1885* (Edinburgh, 1969), pp. xvii–xix.

78. Harris, 'Merchants', p. 246.

79. UDA, MS 11/5/43, Inventory of the personal estate and effects of the late John Baxter Esq of Idvies, Merchant in Dundee who died upon the 25th day of August 1833.

80. Whatley, *Onwards From Osnaburgs*, pp. 43, 50–1.

THE FIRST TOWN IN GREAT BRITAIN

57

81. Collins and Ollerenshaw, 'European linen industry', pp. 18–19.
82. UDA, MS56/2/5/2, Diary, James Cox (c. 1885), pp. 33–42.
83. Durie, *Scottish Linen Industry*, p. 100.
84. A. J. S. Gibson and T. C. Smout, *Prices, Food and Wages in Scotland 1550–1780* (Cambridge, 1995), pp. 349–56.
85. For a discussion of what has been called the industrious household, see de Vries, *Industrious Revolution*, chapter 3.
86. Gibson and Smout, *Prices*, pp. 236–8, 339–40.
87. UDA, MS11/5/4, Charles Mackie, 'Reminiscences of Flax Spinning from 1806 to 1866', pp. 17–18.
88. UDA, MS 11/1/3, Glamis Mill Account Book, 1806–15, p. 63.
89. Diary, James Cox, p. 62.
90. Carmichael, Reminiscences, I, pp. 90, 92, 180.
91. William Thom, *Rhymes and Recollections of a Hand-Loom Weaver* (London, 1845), pp. 7–20.
92. Charles McKean, Bob Harris and Christopher A. Whatley, 'An introduction to Georgian Dundee', in McKean, Harris and Whatley (eds), *Dundee*, pp. 138–44.
93. 'Parish of Dundee', in *New Statistical Account, XI, County of Forfar*, pp. 4–5.
94. Bob Harris, 'How Radical a town? Dundee and the French Revolution', in McKean, Harris and Whatley (eds), *Dundee*, p. 206.
95. Louise Miskell and Christopher A. Whatley, '"Juteopolis" in the making: Linen and the industrial transformation of Dundee, c. 1820–1850', *Textile History*, 30: 2 (1999), pp. 177–8.
96. Miskell and Whatley, '"Juteopolis" in the making', p. 176.
97. Gordon Jackson with Kate Kinnear, *The Trade and Shipping of Dundee, 1780–1850* (Dundee, 1991), pp. 6–7.
98. NRS, AD 14/16/58, Papers relating to food riots in Dundee, Declaration of Thomas Stewart.
99. *Caledonian Mercury*, 9 December 1816.
100. Whatley, 'Altering images', pp. 81–2.
101. UDA, MS15/114/2, Diary of Thomas Handyside Baxter, 1829–30, 2 April 1830.
102. Harris, 'Merchants', pp. 249–59.
103. John Stevenson, 'Scotland and the French Revolution: An overview', in Bob Harris (ed.), *Scotland in the Age of the French Revolution* (Edinburgh, 2005), pp. 250–1.
104. Louise Miskell, 'From conflict to co-operation: Urban improvement and the case of Dundee, 1790–1850', *Urban History*, 29: 3 (2002), pp. 350–71.
105. Christopher A. Whatley, Bob Harris and Louise Miskell, 'Introduction: Altered images', in Christopher A. Whatley, Bob Harris and Louise

58 THE TRIUMPH OF TEXTILES

Miskell (eds), *Victorian Dundee: Image and Realities* (Dundee, 2011 edn), p. xxxi.

106. David G. Barrie, *Police in the Age of Improvement: Police Development and the Civic Tradition in Scotland, 1775–1865* (Cullompton and Portland, 2008), pp. 93–103.

107. See Charles McKean, '"Not even the trivial grace of a straight line; Or Why Dundee never built a New Town', in Whatley, Harris and Miskell (eds), *Victorian Dundee*, chapter 1.

108. DCA, Dundee Police Board Minutes, 1824–32, 12 July 1830, Comparative view of the numbers and descriptions of cases for this and the previous year.

109. Mackie, 'Reminiscences', p. 46.

110. Ibid., p. 32.

111. John R. Hume (ed.), *Early Days in a Dundee Mill, 1819–23* (Dundee, 1980), pp. 1–2.

112. For dates of mill openings and extensions, see Mark Watson, *Jute and Flax Mills in Dundee* (Tayport, 1990), pp. 11–24.

113. Hume, *Early Days*, pp. 83–7.

114. Ibid., pp. 9–37.

115. Ibid., pp. 14–15.

116. Brown, *Reminiscences*, pp. 33–4.

117. Ibid., p. 25.

118. Dennis Chapman, 'The combination of hecklers in the east of Scotland 1822 and 1827', *Scottish Historical Review*, 27: 104 (October 1948), pp. 156–62.

119. Watson, *Jute and Flax Mills*, p. 124.

120. Quoted in Miskell and Whatley, '"Juteopolis"', p. 183.

121. Calculated from Jackson and Kinnear, *Trade and Shipping*, p. 16.

122. Carmichael, Reminiscences, I, p. 182.

123. DCA, GD/CC/1/1, Forfarshire Chamber of Commerce, Minute Book, 3 March 1819–4 April 1822, 3 March 1819, resolution from Mr Edward Baxter.

124. Diary, James Cox, p. 58.

125. Letter Book of John Moir, 24 June 1823, p. 35.

126. Mackie, 'Reminiscences', p. 54.

127. *Perthshire Advertiser*, 20 April 1826; see also, Miskell and Whatley, '"Juteopolis"', pp. 186–7.

128. Diary, James Cox, p. 65; NRS, CS96/4624, Minute Book in Sequestration of William Baxter and Sons, Dundee, 13 July 1826.

129. *Glasgow Herald*, 12 May 1826.

130. *Caledonian Mercury*, 5 June 1826.

131. Letter Book of John Moir, 20 May 1825, p. 140.

132. Mackie, 'Reminiscences', p. 54.

THE FIRST TOWN IN GREAT BRITAIN

133. William Kenefick, 'The growth and development of the port of Dundee in the nineteenth and early twentieth centuries', in Whatley, Harris and Miskell (eds), *Victorian Dundee*, pp. 34–8.
134. Michael Flinn et al., *Scottish Population History from the Seventeenth Century to the 1930s* (Cambridge, 1977), pp. 466–7.

2

The English East India Company and Dundee's Emergence as a Global City, 1830s–1870s

A success that has enriched Scotland and promoted the commerce of the world.

In truth, as we have seen, Dundee had already become a presence in global trade before 1830, importing flax from Russia and the Baltic and exporting, mainly across the Atlantic, linen cloth of various kinds and grades. Indeed, perhaps less well appreciated than it should be, is that even as Dundee and jute were becoming synonymous, according to the Scottish industrial commentator David Bremner, in an article in *The Scotsman* newspaper, as late as 1868 the town continued to be recognised as 'the metropolis of the linen trade'.[1] And this with good reason.

LINEN: CHALLENGES AND OPPORTUNITIES, c. 1830–c. 1850

The recovery from the calamitous years of the previous decade carried on apace as the 'new era' dawned. This was in spite of what was perceived to be a threat to the town's trade with the Caribbean and both North and South America. Campaigning for the abolition of slavery was becoming more intense, while there were slave revolts in St Dominique, Barbados, Demerara and, in 1831, Jamaica.

With their heavy dependence on selling into the slave plantations, Dundee manufacturers - along with similarly placed London hatters, Manchester cotton masters, Yorkshire wool producers, Welsh iron masters and west of Scotland coal masters and herring fishermen – feared the effects of emancipation on their businesses.[2] Opinion among the town's cloth merchants, flax spinners and linen manufacturers was divided about how to deal with 'the question of the abolition of Negro Slavery in the West Indies'. At a Chamber of Commerce meeting held to consider the matter in December 1830, George Boase, a banker, argued that the subject was 'a moral and not a commercial' matter. There was agreement too by those present that abolition was demanded 'by every consideration of justice and humanity'. They also agreed, however, that it was not 'expedient' to petition Parliament, given that the Chamber's express role was to protect the commercial interests of the town and county.[3] Money and morality were uneasy bedfellows.

In Dundee, however, such fears were quickly dispelled – even if the home (UK) market for sheetings and similar cloths had more or less collapsed in 1831, the 'finest houses in London', it was reported, having never seen the trade so depressed.[4] After a short hiatus, overseas shipments of Osnaburgs surpassed those preceding the Abolition Act of 1833 as the attention of manufacturers and their agents was directed from Britain's slave islands in the Caribbean to places where the practice of using bound labour continued to be carried on, as in Cuba and Brazil.[5] As was observed by British government ministers at the time as they attempted to placate traders anxious about the commercial impact of abolition, 'the negroes must still have clothing . . . and the demand will only be changed from one set of customers to another'.[6] An example relevant to Dundee was Santo Domingo in Haiti. Despite slavery having been abolished in 1793, it was in the early 1830s the destination for an estimated £70,000 worth of Dundee cloth – roughly £4.7 million nowadays.[7]

There were other continuities. The decades-old bounty on exports had been extended during the 1820s but at reduced rates and was due to be removed altogether in January 1832. Dundee's merchants and manufacturers worried, as they had a decade earlier, about the consequences for their businesses and sent off petitions to the Treasury and elsewhere. Catastrophe was forecast, but they had lost the argument. So instead, they urged further delay, although only for months, partly on the grounds of the suffering that would result among the working classes if the bounty was taken off during the winter when the cost of living was highest and opportunities for employment – at the harvest, for instance – were minimal. The manufacturers and merchants on the other hand did well, sending off 11.3 million yards of cloth in the last quarter of 1832. The annual average between 1824 and 1827 had been 2.8 million yards.[8]

Demand for bagging from the United States grew strongly, at least until 1835. Such was the level of confidence in the trade that existing mills were extended, with J. and W. Brown leading the way. Baxters at Dens were not far behind. New mills were erected too. The early 1830s witnessed the appearance of at least another eleven mills, most of which,

Figure 2.1 Collapsed jute warehouse, 1891. Warehouse collapses were fairly common occurrences, partly owing to poor building quality and the overloading of top floors, but also as in damp conditions jute bales could swell and put pressure on warehouse walls, causing them to bulge and fall. Fire too was a constant hazard. © Libraries, Leisure and Culture, Dundee.

with iron frames, were fireproof.[9] These though came too late to prevent as many as sixteen fires in 1835, the worst of them at James Watt of East Mill's warehouse on Dock Street in which were stored 300 tons of jute hemp and 200 barrels of tar. The tightly packed bales of jute swelled in the heat, causing a wall to collapse, which crushed and killed five men.[10]

A few of the new plants were very large, a tranche that included Upper Pleasance, Hillbank and Wallace Craigie, this last completed in 1836 to spin flax by a partnership of Robert Brough, James Gilroy and William Halley. By 1837 the works was operating as William Halley & Co.[11]

In 1833 Thomas Bell had begun to manufacture wide canvas when he established Belmont Works.[12] In hindsight this was perhaps too many, with some owners having been persuaded to add productive capacity owing to fears that the anticipated Factory Act (1833) would curtail output from their existing plant owing to the fewer hours their workers could be employed for.[13] This was the time too when Harry Walker, who would also become a prominent player in Dundee's textile industry, established Dura Works.[14]

Such was William Halley's faith in the future of the linen trade that in 1834 he purchased the *Thomas*, the first of three brigs which his firm would employ to ship flax direct to Dundee from the Baltic ports.[15] This was also an attempt to reduce the company's costs by cutting out the dealers who imported the raw materials. A few former employers also re-entered the fray. Following the collapse of their father's business in 1826, the Cock/Cox brothers had gone their separate ways. James had even considered joining the trickle of broken employers who had left Dundee and emigrated. At the end of 1834, however, Robert Cox was tiring of his status as a weekly paid employee as a mechanic in a Belfast mill, and the 'pigsty' where he was lodging. Having watched somewhat enviously as his employer's fortunes in canvas making had improved, he wrote to William in Dundee suggesting that the two of them and their other brother James take on a mill of their own.[16]

As earlier, other than for periods of peak demand, the key element affecting the profitability of a spinning mill was the price at which the raw material could be purchased. It follows that it was also in the spinners' interest to reduce the quantity of waste, a recurring priority for the industry's leading engineers like James Carmichael.[17] With other cost pressures – coal, oil, storage, depreciation, and wages in what was a highly competitive market – there were many failures, which the success of Dundee's better-known textile concerns has somewhat hidden from the historical record.[18] For as ever, progress was lumpy, with short bursts of heady optimism and heavy investment being followed by sharp downturns that instigated bankruptcies for owners and reductions in wages and working hours and, worse, unemployment for their workers.

It was not long before another blow struck. Within a couple of years of the promising early to mid-1830s, a warehouse fire in New York that consumed vast quantities of bagging had encouraged the manufacturers in Dundee to overproduce to replenish the lost stocks. The result was another local crisis.

Yet there was no sign of this at the start of 1836. Then, Dundee was being lauded by, among others, Robert S. Rintoul, editor of the

Spectator, for the speed and extent of its rise from 'an obscure provincial town' twenty years earlier to a port and manufacturing centre of 'national importance'. Dundee was the fastest-growing manufacturing town in the British empire, according to the *Fife Herald*. This was despite its lack of coal and the shortage of running water to drive mill wheels. Deep wells had to be sunk for sufficient water for other industrial uses such as steeping flax, bleaching and dyeing, and to fill the cooling ponds required by the growing number of steam engines – the crucial source of power without which the town's textile industry could never have grown as it did. All this is reflected in the value of the town's forty mills, which had increased over fifteen years or so from less than £2,000 to £475,000. Such had been the expansion in shipping capacity (tonnage had risen from 16,698 in 1815 to 39,400 in 1835) that the port – 'one of the finest in Britain' – seemed set to become the 'Liverpool of Scotland'. The mills then in process of erection, it was forecast, would result in five thousand new jobs – and put greater pressure on housing accommodation, which was already in short supply, a problem that would intensify in coming years.[19]

In November 1836, however, within weeks of the last of these glowing assessments of the town's progress and prospects, news of the stoppage of some mills began to be broadcast, mainly due to problems in the American market. Very soon, some six works were said to be closing down every week.[20] In December the talk locally was of commercial 'disaster'.[21] Soon, a total of sixty-one firms in and near Dundee had 'given in', yet another brutal 'weeding out' process that lasted well into 1838.[22] Unsurprisingly, such 'unfavourable circumstances', according to one somewhat understated comment, had 'rendered the past season [1836] rather unpropitious to the labouring population'.[23]

However, despite such periodic and devastating shocks that shook the trade to its foundations, there were still those who either held on in hopes of better times or who were prepared to try and establish themselves in Dundee. Given what is an astonishing rate of attrition, replenishment of the entrepreneurial talent pool was critical: looking at a list of the town's thirty-four spinners in business in the mid-1830s from the vantage point of 1885, James Cox was 'astonished' that only one 'has been able to stand his ground and keep his works going until now'.[24]

Collectively, the endeavour of those firms that kept going is reflected in the steady rise in imports to Dundee of flax, codilla and hemp, which becomes apparent when sharp year-to-year fluctuations are discounted. Imports of the three main fibres averaged 20,227 tons each year between 1830 and 1832 inclusive, 24,696 tons for 1840 to 1842 and 32,925 in the equivalent three years a decade later.[25] The peak year was 1853, when 47,112 tons were unloaded, much of it at the new Earl Grey Dock, opened in 1834, further to the east of the existing harbour. Yet by and large there was sufficient mill and factory capacity to process this.

There was little new construction during the 1840s, in part a consequence of nervousness among some owners about pushing too hard with new steam-driven machinery at a time when memories of earlier violent opposition in Dundee but also other parts of the country were still vivid. Adding to their anxieties were the Chartists, some of whom in Dundee in 1842 were of a militant inclination.[26] Total horsepower from the industry's steam engines rose only slowly, from 1,436 in 1836 to 1,947 in 1851.[27]

'LINENOPOLIS': DUNDEE IN THE 1850s AND 1860s

As in the pre-1830 years, underlying such figures were the decisions and actions taken by individuals and firms. Some continued to turn out yarn and cloth by volume with little regard to quality. However, in the aftermath of the crisis of the mid-1830s a few began to experiment further with jute, the price of which had risen but not as much as hemp (the relative prices per ton were £19 and £41). The development caused concern: it would 'tend to lower the character of our manufacturers very much', declared the *Dundee Advertiser* early in 1835. The hope was that the move 'will not continue long enough to ruin it altogether'. Not everyone took heed, however, and, with the benefit of hindsight, J. R. L. Halley of Wallace Craigie Works reflected many years later, 'Such was the birth of the jute industry.'[28]

The period of gestation though was prolonged. Rather than turning to jute, a number of spinners sought new markets for their flax-based products. It was as the situation deteriorated in 1836 that Baxters at Dens began to spin yarns that were sold in France for the linen manufacturers there.[29] Nor were Baxters alone in this regard; before long the French market was credited with 'giving employment to thousands of industrious working people'. France was an outlet that for a few years kept Baxters as well as other firms reasonably buoyant and helped Dundee survive the next depression, of 1842 and 1843, although only with difficulty; literally hundreds of works were stopped or failed. Owners who had borrowed to extend their premises were bankrupted, their creditors crippled: James Gilroy of Douglas Mill was reputed to have offered his creditors one penny in the pound.[30] By this time the French government under Louis Philippe had begun to impose prohibitive tariffs on imported flax yarns –

at least on those coming from the United Kingdom, in retaliation for British bars on French goods.[31] Overseas markets for flax and linen were becoming increasingly difficult for Dundee firms to compete in.

Even so, and notwithstanding Dundee's reputation – or at least that of some manufacturers – for turning out low-grade cloth, there were others who were determined to maintain the highest standards and to operate in the upper reaches of the coarse linen trade. Reference is often made to the attempts made by some Dundee firms to manufacture jute carpeting as a substitute for the better-known, more fashionable and also more expensive woollen carpets. Indeed, the introduction of jute to Dundee has sometimes been attributed to this very market and the prospect of competing with Abingdon, near London, where jute yarns were being used to make carpets from early in the century.

This, however, is slightly misleading. Striking is the fact that in spite of their place later as Dundee's premier jute company, the Cox brothers in Lochee fought hard to make and sell carpeting made from tow and hemp. Only in sacking did they employ jute, and this tentatively and when the price of hemp was unduly high. During 1840 – for part of which year a richly detailed letter book survives – James Cox was in frequent dialogue with buyers in London, Liverpool and elsewhere in England about making imitation carpeting from flax and hemp with a range of patterns and colours. In June he proudly advised a principal customer, London's Fleet Street-based Edward & Banister, that he had just dispatched bales of narrow carpeting as well as broad with 'the most splendid patterns' so far. Over the summer he and his brother William (who had just taken charge of the weaving department) were endeavouring to make 'new' carpeting with patterns, colours and widths specified by London and other purchasers, using not only local yarns but also brighter and lighter coloured worsted yarns possibly bought from John Crossley & Sons in Halifax but certainly from spinners in Glasgow. By September they had added 'hearth ruggs with fringes' to their repertoire. Throughout, the brothers' aim was to match the quality of other manufacturers of similar goods anywhere in Britain, but at a lower cost, at the same time being ready to reduce their quality threshold – and prices – if that is what their customers preferred.[32]

It was somewhat later than this that jute supplanted flax in the manufacture of carpets in Dundee, although as we will see, there were some pioneers in the 1830s. But it was not until the mid-1850s that what was described as a 'comparatively new branch of industry' began to take off, led by pioneering firms like the Grimond brothers at Maxwelltown Works (erected in 1847, initially for handloom weaving, and dyeing)

DUNDEE'S EMERGENCE AS A GLOBAL CITY 67

and Thomsons of Seafield Works. Joseph and Alexander Grimond may have been the first in the world to manufacture jute carpets in imitation of the high-end Brussels variety, although other firms too made a product the colours of which were said by local promoters to glow 'brighter than those of the brightest productions of the looms of Kidderminster'.[33] Certain is the high quality of the Grimonds' product, which was acknowledged by their being the only jute-weaving carpet firm to win a medal at the 1878 Paris International Exhibition. Thomsons had formerly been makers of sacking cloth but, like the Cox's before them, they strove to emulate the most fashionable varieties of carpeting from flax, hemp and tow. However, they were not long in recognising the potential of harder-wearing jute carpeting that imitated Kidderminster, Paris Twill, Dutch and Venetian varieties. Selling at between five-pence and 1s 3d a yard, a visitor to Seafield observed that the 'poorest housewife' could now 'decorate her canny parlour' with 'these luxuries for the multitude'.[34] Few 'who have any respect for appearances want [for] their carpeted floor and papered walls', wrote a contributor to the *Dundee People's Journal*.[35] By 1857 some half of Dundee's jute carpeting was being distributed around the United Kingdom, but the other half went overseas.[36]

The other non-jute product made in Dundee was sail canvas, although there were other varieties, uses and demands for this type of cloth which other Dundee firms exploited, most notably A. & D. Edward & Co., although by the 1850s the firm was using jute. But sailcloth manufacturing was not as straightforward as it might appear. For their warships the Admiralty laid down criteria which became increasingly strict, with stringent testing taking place at Deptford, where the royal dockyards had been established in 1513. The requirements for canvas for merchant shipping were less demanding, so that tow or shorter fibres could be incorporated, as could hemp (incidentally, a source of cannabis, from which the name canvas derives). For royal naval purposes, however, only certain qualities of long flax could be used (the preference was for Irish-grown, although named alternatives from the Low Countries and Russia were acceptable). Before being woven, warp yarns were to be boiled in chlorine-free water infused with 'best American pot and pearl ashes' for six minutes (fifteen for weft) and then washed in 'clear running water'.

The damage chlorine bleaching could do by weakening the canvas had been recognised towards the end of the Napoleonic wars. This presented a challenge as the Admiralty's preference was for white sailcloth, rather than the darker hue of the flax-based material that Baxter's made.

THE TRIUMPH OF TEXTILES

All traces of vegetable matter had to be removed; the mildewing that resulted otherwise made the cloth less durable.[37] Widths and weights too were precisely specified.[38] Failure to meet requirements resulted in rejection, as happened to Baxter Brothers in 1847 and 1852 (and probably at other times too). The 1847 disappointment may not have come as a surprise, however, them having been warned in March by their near neighbours Turnbull & Co. of Claverhouse bleachfield that the yarn Baxter's had sent them had so many 'broken ends hanging loose' they would be unable to return it in 'good order'.[39] The brothers stood firm against compromises, recognising that while long jute fibres mixed with flax and hemp were hard to spot, such adulteration 'could not deceive any one accustomed to handle canvas' and cloth so made would only be used by shipowners anxious to purchase sailcoth cheaply – a false economy as such a combination made for an unstable product as well as one that had less than half the strength of flax-made canvas.[40]

Provided they maintained the highest standards, Baxter's at Dens – the market leaders in Dundee – were able to exploit what continued to be a substantial demand for sailcloth from what was the world's largest navy, the seaborne defender of Britain's imperial assets. By mid-century the navy's largest battle ships of 110 guns were each carrying over 20,000 yards (almost 12 tons) of sail, while even cutters required over 4,700 yards, including spare sets in both cases.[41] Add to this the requirements for sailcloth of the world's expanding merchant fleet and it is little wonder that long after the Napoleonic wars had ended, canvas continued to be the 'staple manufacture of Dundee'; in the mid-1830s it was still the town's single most important cloth export, having recently overtaken Osnaburgs and sheetings.[42] However, while canvas continued to be made in Dundee (partly in response to government purchases for military uses post-1850), it was never again as important as the other main varieties of linen and jute cloth. The end of the dominance of sailing ships in the mid-Victorian decades saw to that.

Concurrently, and apart from periodic and punishing dips, demand for Dundee's staples, including Osnaburgs and bagging, continued to rise, albeit slowly. Contrary to expectations (of a downturn in trade and widespread unemployment), the Crimean War offered something more, for a short time at least, when imports of flax, tow and hemp reached their all-time peak (of over 47,000 tons), until flax shipments from Russia were interrupted and eventually curtailed.

The American Civil War, however, from 1861 to 1865, was much more important: 'the most fortunate event that ever occurred' for Dundee's linen manufacturers, according to David Bremner, with orders for cloth

DUNDEE'S EMERGENCE AS A GLOBAL CITY

coming from the armies of both sides in the conflict. For the workforce there was full employment and for the owners unprecedented profits and capital accumulation.[43] It was during the 1850s and early 1860s that many of the town's great mills and mill and factory complexes were built, either from scratch or, more often, by extending existing works.

Leading the field were the Baxter brothers at Dens, where William Baxter and his son Edward had erected a small, 15 horsepower spinning mill in 1822. Upper Dens was begun in 1833, after which for the next three decades further buildings and steam engines were added. By the early 1860s there were sixteen engines with a combined nominal 615 horsepower, 20,000 spindles and 1,200 power looms. Although the firm bought much yarn from other spinners, there were several spinning mills within the 10 acres (4 hectares) over which the works were spread, and most of the machinery was made and engineered on site. With over four thousand employees, Dens had become the world's largest linen-manufacturing plant.

A. & D. Edward & Co.'s Logie Works, at the west of the Scouringburn district, followed a similar trajectory, extending in a series of steps in accordance with the proprietors' reading of market opportunities. The first mill was constructed in 1828, powered by a 30 horsepower engine. By 1846 the mill was over 90 metres in length, and four storeys high, the largest building in Dundee at the time. This was soon supplemented by an equally large power-loom factory which also contained preparing, winding and warping flats. Not far short of twenty years later its 17,000 spindles, and 600 power looms driven by five steam engines amounting to 250 horsepower were employing some 2,500 workers.

Vying for the honour of being the grandest of the great mill and factory complexes was the Cox's Camperdown Works in Lochee, a weaving village on the north-western fringe of Dundee. Although the Cox family had been active in the textile trade in the district since the early eighteenth century, it was only in 1850 that the foundation stone was laid for a power-loom factory; at the time, most of Cox's carpets were being woven by hand weavers in their own homes. Over the next few years other operations that had previously been carried out elsewhere were concentrated at Camperdown, 'so as to have everything under immediate supervision'. According to Warden, Cox's was the only local firm 'who take in the raw material and send out the cloth in bales from their own [fully integrated] premises'.[44] By 1855 a yarn warehouse, dyeing, bleaching, washing and drying facilities, warp-winding machinery and a calender had been added to what was a 13.5 acre (5.5 hectare) site. After a lull, in 1858 work began on a new, larger spinning mill, as well as a chimney and tower, which incorporated a large clock – and bells, for the 'villagers' but mainly for the company's employees. Powering all of this were several steam engines, including a 100 horsepower beam engine – then the largest in Scotland used for manufacturing purposes – from James Carmichael & Co.'s Ward Foundry.

Within but at the western edge of the burgh, 'the largest and most imposing' building was the Gilroy Brothers & Co.'s Tay Works, most of which was constructed after 1851. Its frontage, extending for just under 200 metres along Lochee Road, was to become the longest of any textile works in Dundee. It may even be the longest in Britain.[45] As with Camperdown, all processes were integrated at the site, where by 1863 over 1,700 workers were employed.

The primary reason for this immense investment in mills, factories, calenders, warehouses and machinery was to exploit local (UK) and global markets for linen cloth. And several of Dundee's less well-known firms continued to focus on the manufacture of linens. Ogilvy Gourlay Miller, for example, who had succeeded to the three mills of J. & W. Brown, not only spun more flax yarn than most Scottish spinners but also achieved

Figure 2.2 Gilroy Brothers' Tay Works, possibly the longest textile mill frontage in Britain. The site of the works had long been used by flax spinners, and was developed by the Gilroys solely for jute spinning and weaving in 1848. The elaborate pediment is dated 1865, a proud statement of the firm's success during the American Civil War. © D. C. Thomson & Co. Ltd.

the highest international standards.[46] St Roque's Mill, with its four thousand spindles, was similar in concentrating on flax. However, other than at Baxter's Dens Works, which publicly at least disavowed jute (certainly it wasn't spun there), some part of the expansion of Dundee's industrial stock was due to the introduction of jute, both as a fibre, yarn and cloth in its own right, and in combination with the material that for a century had put Dundee on the edge of the global stage.

THE SLOW, SURREPTITIOUS BUT IRRESISTIBLE RISE OF JUTE

Indeed, it was the premises built specifically to spin and weave jute that were beginning to draw the eye of contemporaries. In October 1859 the *People's Journal* waxed lyrical about Messrs J. & A. D. Grimonds' Bow Bridge Works, at Clepington, then under construction. Even though not complete, this 'noble'-looking building was 'the most splendid of the kind yet built'. And little wonder: unlike many of the other works which had been established early on and grown like topsy with a series of extensions, the Grimonds' complex was altogether new, and fit for purpose.[47]

We've already seen that some small quantities of the raw material that was to give Dundee its appellation 'Juteopolis' had been landed at the port in 1823. Yet while imports increased in the 1830s, volumes were hardly impressive, even if some jute was listed in the harbour accounts under the heading 'hemp'.[48]

Even by the start of the 1860s the quantity of raw jute imported to Dundee was still well below the hundreds of thousands of tons that were landed at the docks during the industry's heyday. In 1902, the peak year, some 414,550 tons were imported.[49] Furthermore, up until 1857, when 38,300 tons of flax, codilla and hemp were imported, against 24,342 tons of jute, in every previous year it was the former fibres that dominated the rapidly expanding dockside area and filled the numberless cobblestone-rattled carts in which the bales were transported to the mills.

Indeed, it was just at this point that commentators were proclaiming that over the past three years Dundee, 'the principal emporium of the linen manufacture in the United Kingdom', had been 'active beyond all precedent'.[50] So buoyant was the town's staple trade, with new works under construction, that concerns were expressed that even if over two thousand of the necessary additional workers could be recruited, they would struggle to find accommodation, the town being 'already more than full'.[51] It seems there had been a 'total cessation' of immigration

Table 2.1 Jute imports, 1838–70

Jute imports (tons)	
1838	1,136
1845	8,313
1850	14,080
1855	26,891
1860	36,965
1865	71,000
1870	73,878

from Ireland, with deleterious effects on the heckling and preparatory processes in particular.[52]

It was the following year, 1858, that marked the point at which jute imports overtook those of the former staples – and never again fell behind.[53] Rising imports reflect what was happening on the ground, at individual works, with the Cox's first spinning jute in 1855, and others following suit at around the same time. It is no coincidence that building work for the Grimonds' Bow Bridge Works began in 1857.

The transition had been loosely signalled in 1856. In December the *Dundee Advertiser* carried a lengthy article headed 'Extension of Local Manufactures', which provided details of a rapid expansion in flax-spinning capacity extensions to existing mills. But also noted was the greater use of heavier yarns and, above all, increases in the numbers of power looms – and handlooms.[54] It is striking that even those works that were heralded for their modernity and efficiency continued to employ handloom weavers. Development was uneven and not simply a transfer from one system to another. A new raw material; age-old technology. It was the latter upon which most jute carpeting was woven, thereby offering a lifeline to handloom weavers of weightier fabrics who, otherwise, would have joined the nationwide exodus of broken men and women from the weaving trade whose skills were now redundant; half a century earlier this was one of the most prestigious and well-remunerated occupations in the country.

Until recently, historians have been inclined to explain the transition to jute by reference mainly to local (that is, Dundee-based) factors. Put simply, the oft-listed sequence of events usually begins with the assertion that the market in which Dundee linen producers mainly operated became increasingly difficult owing to interruptions in the supply of their raw materials, flax and hemp, and rises in their price.[55]

DUNDEE'S EMERGENCE AS A GLOBAL CITY

Jute, which had been sent from London to Dundee sporadically on a trial basis, was a possible substitute. Then, after the fortuitous discovery that whale oil (from Dundee's pre-existing whaling industry) could be used to soften the fibres which were otherwise difficult to machine-spin, jute began to supplant hemp and flax. Being cheaper in its raw state relative to flax, jute was well suited to the growing global requirements for gargantuan quantities of sacks and bagging. It also served the battlefield requirements of the Crimean War (1853–6) and the American Civil War (1861–5), which included wagon and gun carriage covers, and sandbags. As a result, 'Juteopolis' was born, with Dundee the hub of a nexus of outlier producer towns such as Arbroath, Brechin and Forfar.

This is an entirely credible version of events. But the explanation for Dundee's move into jute is slightly more complicated – and, arguably, more interesting than the traditional account allows.

Most explanations for Dundee's turn to jute have acknowledged – in passing, at least – the role of empire in its ascendancy.[56] They usually include a reference to the fact that in or around 1791 and periodically thereafter (1793 and 1796 are other dates given) the English East India Company (EIC) sent small parcels or 'specimens' of jute from the alluvial plain of Bengal, where the raw material was grown, to Britain. Indirectly, as most was landed at and sold in London, some of this found its way to Dundee.

There is a case, however, for situating Dundee (and other places in the United Kingdom where jute spinning and manufacture was carried on) more firmly within the British imperial project, as with cotton and as has recently happened in the case of the silk industry.[57] What follows is a more explicit presentation of this proposition, with greater emphasis being placed on the EIC's motivations and actions, and Dundee's pre-existing Asian links including the symbiotic relationship that developed between Dundee and imperial India.

Jute, as it had been for centuries, was cultivated by small peasant farmer-proprietors – *ryots* – in the marshlands of the Ganges delta, along with rice, oilseeds, pulses and spices.[58] After the laborious process of harvesting the crop with sickles, the stalks from the twelve feet or so high plants were then 'retted', allowing the fibres to be stripped and dried, before being hand spun and woven into coarse cloth (*tat*). This was done either in the same peasant households for the makers' own clothing and bedding or distributed to a vast army of full- and part-time hand weavers (of whom there were an estimated 638,000 in the middle of the century), spread across much of the province of lower Bengal where gunny bags,

74   THE TRIUMPH OF TEXTILES

mats, rugs and screens were produced, and colourfully hand-dyed where appropriate.[59] Most of this was exported.[60]

In comparison to the other textiles the EIC promoted and exported, jute was of minor significance. Nevertheless, the incentives that lay behind the EIC's determination to buy through intermediaries the better-known fibres, yarns and cloth and export them, also applied to jute.[61]

Robert Clive's victory at the battle of Plassey in 1757 meant the EIC seized administrative control of the territories the company wanted to exploit, including the Bengal province and Calcutta, as well as the *diwani* – that is, the 'right' to collect revenues from land taxes.[62] As few manu-factures from Asia were welcomed in Britain, the Company's directors were persuaded to concentrate on importing groceries such as tea and spices – but also new raw materials.[63] It is in this context that the trial bales of jute found their way to London.[64] Yet clearly this was specula-tive, and had little to do with textiles. In 1801 the *Caledonian Mercury* reported that 'jute, a species of yarn' was to be brought home with a cargo of rice 'by way of dunnage' (that is, as packaging for the rice) so that it could be tried for use in paper making, 'of which great expecta-tions have been formed' and for which purpose it had long been used in India and elsewhere.[65] This impetus was carried on by the free merchants and agencies who succeeded the EIC.[66]

The question arises then about who and what determined that Dundee should be considered as a possible user of this hitherto largely unknown plant for which until 1791 there was no English name. The answer partly lies in the complex networks that overlapped local, national and inter-national (imperial) boundaries. The last is most clearly seen in Scotland's connections with the EIC. Scots had had a long-standing involvement dating back to the immediate post-1707 period. This intensified after around 1760.[67] Conspicuous is the extent of the involvement of promi-nent individuals from Dundee and its hinterland in the EIC. MPs repre-senting the burgh reached the highest levels inside the Company.[68] While there is no evidence linking these men with the introduction of *jute* to Dundee (they were active in the eighteenth century rather than later), John Drummond and other of the region's merchants were ardent pro-moters of and (mainly) successful players in the Dundee–London linen trade and the subsequent export of coarse linen to the West Indies – and, dyed, to India.[69] The Dundee–London relationship was further fostered by Dundonian merchant firms with representation in the capital, acting as the umbilical cord between Scotland's east coast and the world's great-est trading emporium.[70]

DUNDEE'S EMERGENCE AS A GLOBAL CITY

At lower levels, however – into the nineteenth century – it is noticeable how many of the scions of Dundee's merchant families found employment in India, thereby creating a direct channel of communication between Dundee and the Far East. And even though such individuals mainly served as surgeons, mariners (and even as commanders of the EIC's ships) and officers in the EIC's armies, it is entirely reasonable to suppose that in their letters home they would relay commercial intelligence. That there was an established Dundee presence in Calcutta is evident from correspondence of the linen merchant John Moir. In 1825 Moir wrote to Hugh Cathro, possibly a merchant ship's captain, and John Tandy, both from Dundee and resident in Calcutta, commending another recently arrived Dundonian to them and asking that they should 'acquaint him with the customs of your Country'.[71]

Significant too is that one of the sources of East Indian information was William Roxburgh, a Scot who had been a surgeon employed by the EIC prior to becoming, in 1793, head of the Royal Botanical Garden in Calcutta, a project 'intended solely for the promotion of public utility and science'.[72] Among Roxburgh's interests were hemp and jute, his research on the subject gaining him three gold medals from the Society of Arts, which was keen for manufacturers to exploit other potentially useful fibres identified by the EIC.[73] Familiar with the EIC's ropeworks near Cuttack, it may have been Roxburgh who had arranged for bales of jute to be sent to London, some of which found its way to Abingdon, where it was used to make wool substitute carpets similar to those made in India.[74] Around the same time, in 1804, the possibility that Dundee spinners might find a use for Indian sunn hemp (with which jute was sometimes conflated) resulted in modest quantities being sent north, where it was used in the manufacture of sailcloth and cordage.[75] Using established lines of communication, some London dealers also sent small quantities of jute to Dundee, either on their own initiative or upon invitation from curious Dundee merchants and flax spinners.

Not to be overlooked is the direct shipping connection between Dundee and London, more important for some Dundonians than Edinburgh. The sea route was further secured in 1834 with the launch of the Dundee, Perth and London Shipping Co.'s 'magnificent and powerful' steam vessels, the *Dundee* and the *Perth* – at the time reputed to be 'the swiftest in the world'.[76] The journey from Dundee to Hoare's Wharf, one of the 'Scotch Wharfs' on the Thames, could be completed in less than forty hours, quicker than by the mail coach. The return voyage, leaving from Downe's Wharf, was only slightly slower. The costs of the

76 THE TRIUMPH OF TEXTILES

raw material were further reduced and the importation process simplified when for the first time, in April 1840, jute was shipped direct to Dundee from Calcutta.[77] The cargo, 1,226 bales of jute, along with other colonial produce including '40 buffalo horns', was carried in the Dundee-built barque the *Selma*, which after a 156-day voyage was towed into the Earl Grey Dock, watched by a sizeable crowd. Those present would have had little inkling of how momentous an event in Dundee's history this docking was.[78]

Just who in Dundee began to spin jute and manufacture it, and when this began, is steeped in mystery. Indeed, the transition process was so subtly incremental that just three decades after jute first began to be used, the memory of what had happened, and exactly when, had been lost. Even the industry's first historian, Alexander Warden, who had first-hand experience of the textile trades in Dundee as the manager of a calender works (where cloth was pressed and finished), credited more than one of his fellow citizens with the distinction of being the front runner. Indeed, the debate over which flax merchant, spinner or manufacturer (the roles were often combined) could claim to be 'the father and founder of the jute trade in Dundee' was still a matter of dispute in 1891 – and is yet to be settled.[79] There were several claimants to the title, including George Leighton, William Anderson, Thomas Neish, James Watt, James Taws, William Boyack, Alexander Rowan, Messrs Bell, Balfour & Meldrum, John Halley, John Hadden, James Grimond, John Sharp, Henry and James Cox, and Robert Gilroy. Part of the problem of identifying a clear winner in this respect is that in the early years there was great market resistance to jute, which was seen as an inferior fibre that was difficult to spin, unsuitable for the warp threads, and made for an inferior cloth. Accordingly, spinners who dared to incorporate it into flax yarns usually did so on a small scale, and then surreptitiously. Memory of its use was deliberately forgotten.[80]

George Leighton may have been the first man in Dundee to have received one of the bales of jute sent north in 1823 (a bale then weighed around 300 lb or 136 kg). William Anderson's London-based brother also shipped some jute to the Tay. With experience of working up EIC hemp, Anderson, whose mother was apparently an accomplished hand spinner, was in pole position to experiment with the new fibre.[81] On a small scale he even had some success, using hand-spun jute yarn in the heavy fabrics he manufactured.[82] Thomas Neish too appears to have shown an early interest in the fibre, and also persisted in trying to spin it into a viable yarn which, apparently, he had done by 1832. Neish, however, may have been beaten to the starting line by the Gilroy brothers, who had a small mill at Lilybank from 1827. William Boyack too may have tried to spin jute around this time although, as with the others, this was a composite yarn, comprising flax and tow or hemp along with jute.[83] The other names listed above were also actively experimenting at the time, with variable degrees of success. However, it was apparently not until the mid-1830s that a pure jute yarn was spun – by James Taws, who, Warden suggests, 'may have been the first to do so'.[84]

Samples of Abingdon hand-spun jute yarn had been brought to Dundee – in 1833 – by Alexander Rowan, a well-travelled, savvy merchant who had a 'strong faith in jute'.[85] It was Rowan who encouraged James Neish to attempt to spin jute twist and manufacture jute carpets, an alternative to those made from wool (although, as has been seen, Dundee's first carpets were made from flax).[86]

Balfour and Meldrum were reputed to have made jute carpets at around the same date, 1833.[87] This was also the way into jute for the firm of Cox Brothers, proprietors of what would become the world's largest jute works.[88] But Cox's adoption of jute was by no means straightforward, as we have seen. And it wasn't until 1855 that the brothers began to spin jute at Camperdown. Arguably even more significant was that in 1838 Rowan had persuaded the Dutch government to use jute yarn instead of flax tow in the manufacture of bags for coffee grown in Indonesia, formed from the territories held by the hegemonic Dutch East India Company. It was this initiative – and the resulting proof of the suitability of jute bagging for bulk transportation – that gave Dundee its 'proper start' as a jute-making centre.

It seems that few firms gave up flax altogether. While there were some which concentrated exclusively on either flax or jute, all the others, observed David Bremner in 1868, 'work both fibres, sometimes mixing them in certain proportions . . . at others keeping them distinct'. The nervousness with which individuals and firms left linen behind to embark on the journey into jute is seen most vividly in company names: it was not until the 1870s that the ubiquitous terms flax spinner and linen manufacturer were dropped and jute spinner and manufacturer became a label which they could publicly proclaim.[89]

Yet even if it is difficult to identify a single individual, what is certain is that by the mid-1830s a number of firms were not only incorporating jute into their flax and tow yarns but also in a few cases focusing almost entirely on jute.[90] But even at the lower-value end of the trade – in sacking, for example – there was still some customer resistance.[91] 'Juteopolis' was born not of a revolution in the raw material used, but of a drawn-out evolutionary process.

DUNDEE'S CONVERSION TO JUTE, CONTINUED

It is certainly the case that the quality of flax and hemp from Russia had begun to deteriorate during the Crimean War, with less attention being paid to cleaning, which included the removal of seed remnants that made preparation and spinning more difficult and expensive. Slower land transport times within Russia and longer exposure to the elements led to alternate wetting and drying of the fibres, which in turn became brittle. At this time too, the vulnerability of the supply chain also became apparent, with direct shipments coming to a halt at times. Post-war dislocation meant that there was no improvement in the situation: indeed, contemporaries felt that whatever its source – Archangel, Riga, St Petersburg – things got worse as far as the quality of imported flax was concerned.[92] Whereas in 1853 just over 47,000 tons of flax, tow and hemp were landed, this fell to 25,842 tons in 1858. Raw jute imports to Dundee more than doubled.[93]

Just as the impetus to eighteenth-century linen production in Scotland came from post-Union support from the British state and burgeoning market demand, external factors were central in stimulating Scottish jute manufacture and drawing it further into transnational networks. The interruption in the supply of flax from Russia just noted, allied to strong wartime requirement for canvas and sacking, persuaded many linen manufacturers around 1855 to switch to jute. Reports from India of the extent to which EIC initiatives in irrigating vast tracts of land and connecting the ports by rail were opening up the 'undeveloped resources of that rich and fertile country' to be 'dispersed over the whole world' were avidly read. *The Indian Review* newspaper was available in Dundee from May 1842.[94] Of particular interest were the opinions of 'persons who have passed a number of years in India', who were convinced that the supply of jute was secure and inexhaustible. The argument that 'the only limit is as to its being wanted', underpinned the optimism that swept through the town in the later 1850s.[95] At the same time, demand for bagging and sacking of various kinds, both from within the UK as well as overseas, was growing.

During the Crimean War jute was used as a flax substitute in some products. Indeed, the quantity of jute brought to Dundee more or less doubled during the period of the conflict, thereby underlining the significance for the town of the mid-1850s, discussed earlier. Necessarily this ushered in a new phase of mill and factory building from 1850 onwards, although there was a hiatus at the end of the decade before yet another surge of new construction in the 1860s. Firms that had already taken the

DUNDEE'S EMERGENCE AS A GLOBAL CITY

plunge and worked with jute invested in more spindles, power looms and labour.[96] Even those which had been reluctant to use jute began to adopt it. We have already seen that Cox's of Lochee added jute spinning to their other operations in 1855.

Dundee's textile business community was close-knit, which made it more likely that a decision taken by any individual entrepreneur would very soon be common knowledge. Inter-marriage between members of families connected with the flax and related engineering trades was commonplace.[97] Detailed information on trade, technical issues, markets, productions, prices and prospects was shared or overheard when the burgh's merchants and manufacturers met informally, congregating as they did in the Cowgate area of the burgh close to the docks. In 1835 forty-eight men, mainly merchants, spinners and manufacturers (plus a few others) had leased two shops from the Union Bank and established the Baltic Coffee Room between the Cowgate and the Wellgate. Information sharing was its prime purpose. Open six days a week, one of the first steps the directors took was to order daily newspapers from London, Liverpool, Glasgow and elsewhere, for reading *in situ* or to buy.[98] It is in such an environment that conversations about the rewards and risks of transitioning to jute are likely to have taken place. Business leaders gathered formally too in associations like the Chamber of Commerce, formed in 1819 and which from 1854 had its own premises in Albert Square.[99] Many of the same men – and it was mainly men – collaborated in many of the civic and philanthropic projects that played such an important part in fostering relatively warm social relations in the town, up until the 1870s at least.

One topic that would have interested the spinners was whale oil. Whale oil, as well that of seals, it is argued, was critically important during the early, batching stage of jute production, softening the otherwise brittle and unworkable fibres. These were sprinkled with oil and water in a series of layers. It has been argued that the ready availability of whale oil was a factor that differentiated Dundee from its rivals and gave the town a headstart in the production of jute.

Whaling from Dundee had begun in the 1750s and expanded slowly thereafter. Although in the very early days of what would become the jute era Dundee was far from being the most important whaling port either in the UK or Scotland, by the mid-nineteenth century it had assumed pole position, with average annual catches of twenty-seven of these monster mammals from the perilous waters – and ice and icebergs – of Baffin Bay.[100] By the end of the 1870s sealing had assumed greater importance. Seal oil was slightly cheaper than that derived from whales. Demand from the jute industry, the argument goes, sustained much of this activity.

There is certainly much truth in the proposition that the town's whaling fleet benefited from sales to the textile trade. The introduction of gas lighting meant the loss of a major source of demand for whale oil, used in the town's public lamps. Yet there are reasons to qualify other aspects of this much-loved piece of local lore; the 'light bulb' moment when, allegedly, it was realised that by using whale oil for batching jute the manufacture of jute to scale could commence. For one thing, it seems highly likely that oil from whale blubber and sperm oil extracted from the head cavity of the cetacean had been used to soften flax and hemp fibres.[101] We don't have a date for when this began, but the practice certainly preceded the application of these oils to jute, possibly during the 1820s as flax spinners strove to improve the performance and productivity of their steam engine-driven spinning frames. Handloom weavers too applied oil to their webs. Intriguingly, one descendant of William Halley – active as a cloth manufacturer in the 1820s – pinpointed 1826 as the turning point, the year that Dundee Gas Works began to supply the townspeople with the means of lighting their homes instead of whale and seal oil. Desperate to find another market, 'Someone', J. R. L. Halley suggested, 'must' have had the idea that the 'new dry fibre might spin if it were moistened with oil'.[102] This proposition smacks of wishful thinking. It was a long time until jute was spun on any scale in Dundee; flax and hemp were still the principal fibres spun. That from the time of the opening of his flax-spinning mill at Oakbank (Blairgowrie) in 1825–6 James Grimond was placing frequent and substantial orders for hogsheads and pipes of sperm oil from Barret & Co., 'Spermaceti Refiners' in London and elsewhere, including Dundee's Dorothy Whale Fishing Co., is indicative of a need other than to fuel the mill's oil lamps during the winter months. Supporting the argument that it was the flax and hemp trades that were the initial and main users is the fact that demand for whale oil rose markedly during the 1830s, when little jute was being prepared. Three decades later, when more hemp and tow were being spun, what was called the damping process for these fibres required a mixture of whale oil, water and soft soap (for 60 tons of hemp, an estimated 320 gallons of whale oil was required).[103]

It is questionable, therefore, whether the ready availability of whale oil was a decisive factor in determining why Dundee became the UK and world leader in jute production.[104] When attempts were being made to spin jute at Dens Works in 1845, the 'great secret', it was noted later, had been 'in damping the jute thoroughly before you card it' – with water. There was no mention of any sort of emollient.[105] Furthermore, as was explained to Peter Carmichael by his fellow Dundonian Robert Baxter at around the same time, jute could equally well be softened with vegetable oil. This – from varieties of rapeseed including Cobra – would, Baxter assured Carmichael, on the basis of his experience of spinning in Lille in northern France, 'do equally well' and, in France at least, was relatively cheap.[106] Indeed, vegetable and mineral oils were actually more desirable. Fish oils were expensive (and could add £1 to the cost of preparing a ton of jute), more so during those periods of the year when the whaling fleet was necessarily in port or when the fleet was locked in ice. To secure a supply unaffected by price rises in the open market, at least one spinner employed their own vessel in the Arctic fishery.[107]

But price was not the only consideration. As important was that cloth which had been impregnated with whale and seal oil emitted smells which deterred customers, especially purchasers of domestic items such as the Dundee manufacturers' 'very beautiful' carpets. For, as the *Dundee Advertiser* put it, for 'ladies who have tried jute carpets', whale oil 'virtually renders them inadmissible for the furnishing of any dwelling where the inhabitants are at all afflicted with sensitive olfactory organs'.[108] Accordingly, from the 1860s if not earlier, effort was directed towards eliminating whale and seal oils from the batching process altogether. In the autumn of 1863, hopes were high that oil from linseed, shipped along with jute cargoes from Calcutta, could be acquired locally.

There are other, complementary, factors that account for the relative ease with which Dundee's manufacturers managed more or less across the board to shift from flax to jute. The 'great secret' of Dundee's early success in jute, according to a descendant of one of the industry's early pioneers, John Sharp, was that the pre-existing machinery from the established linen industry was readily switched to jute.[109] With some modest adjustments and an upscaling in terms of their strength and scale, jute could be carded, spun and woven on machines with which those working in flax had recently become familiar. With the successful adaptation of power looms in Dundee for jute weaving from the end of the 1840s, the hold of the Bengali weaver households on the global market for gunny bags was loosened, although not lost altogether. In fact, in Dundee too, handloom weaving carried on, with numbers actually increasing in the decade or so following the widespread use of power looms.[110] Only in the 1860s did exports of handmade jute products from Bengal begin to fall sharply – as the limitations associated with traditional manufacturing equipment and methods were exposed.[111] In Dundee, however, technically the move from coarse linen to jute was relatively straightforward. As the knowledgeable Alexander Warden remarked, 'the prevailing character' of Dundee's fabrics remained the same.[112]

JUTE TRIUMPHANT: JUTEOPOLIS

It was the outbreak of the American Civil War in 1861 and the consequent shortage of raw cotton and cotton cloth that provided the real catalyst for lift-off. John Symers, born in 1794 and in his late 60s at this time, had resided and worked as a banker with the British Linen Company in Dundee for most of his adult life.[113] Chairman of the Northern Insurance Company, and shareholder in several other firms, he had experienced Dundee's earlier surges of success (as well as the troughs). But, he declared at the end of 1861, citizens were now 'enjoying in this city a prosperity in trade and commerce beyond anything which has occurred in all my previous recollection'.[114]

Within two years imports of jute had more than doubled, to 75,000 tons.[115] By 1863 the Cox's had established their own jute-baling and -pressing plant in Calcutta – and shipped direct to Dundee in the company's own vessels. Demand for jute, now 'the most important vegetable fibre in the world', apart from cotton, burgeoned, drawing both Dundee and Calcutta more tightly into the globalised market and creating between the two centres a series of business-based cultural associations.[116] The Royal Navy continued to use Dundee-made sailcloth and there was a market too for some other flax goods. Osnaburgs were still part of the product mix. But jute was now king, hessians above all, in a multiple range of widths, types of fabric and qualities, for bags and sacking for guano, seeds, grain, flour and baling for wool and other fibres. Tarpaulin was a Dundee speciality. Eight yards-wide cloth – after being painted – was used as floor covering. Carpets and matting, mentioned earlier, were also important products, renowned for their colour, design and patterns.[117] By the end of December 1863, unusually, not a single mill was on the market.

Imports of raw jute to Dundee rose eightfold between the mid-1850s and 1873.[118] In thirty years, the burgh's population surged by over 61,000. The decade from 1861 saw the fastest growth in Dundee's history, from 91,664 to 119,141, an increase of well over 27,000 people. For the rural poor from the surrounding countryside and post-Famine Irish migrants familiar with flax spinning and to a lesser degree handloom weaving, Dundee continued to offer the prospect of regular employment, along with steady and, in the first years, rising wages and new levels of spending power.[119] Massive investment poured into existing and new factories – 'palatial . . . colossal . . . in . . . magnificence, or comfort, unsurpassed by mills in any town in the kingdom, or of any other country in the world', purred Alexander Warden.[120] The 1860s, architecturally 'the most extravagant decade' of the century, was when most of the mill and factory complexes that would dominate Dundee's industrial landscape in the second half of the nineteenth century and beyond were constructed.[121] By the end of the decade, in the region of £5 million had been invested in mills and weaving factories operated by seventy-two firms, with another £1 million on bleaching works, calenders and other ancillary activities. Often these were on sites that had previously been the locus of smaller works. Leading the way were the Cox's at Lochee, Baxter Brothers at Dens, and Gilroys at Tay Works.

At the height of the boom for what would soon be known as the 'golden fibre', investors elsewhere were drawn towards jute. In 1865 in Glasgow for example, the second city of the empire, several leading businessmen raised £500,000 to form the Glasgow Jute Company, an extension of W. and J. Fleming's long-established Baltic and Clyde Linen Works, on a 10 acre site. Their intention, as with another partnership established in London some months later, was specifically to rival Dundee. The Glasgow company's prospectus boasted of the city's direct shipping links with Calcutta and Bombay (now Mumbai), a large labour pool, cheap coal and an unlimited water supply – claims Dundee would be hard pushed to match.[122] The London Jute Company, also founded in 1865, was even more explicit in declaring its advantage over Dundee, the success of which in jute, it asserted, was 'merely accidental'. Dundee had 'no special facilities . . . over other localities'. Labour was no more abundant than in London, with its plentiful supply of women, boys and girls for work which was 'light, clean . . . and healthy', while demand for jute cloth was greater.[123] On mainland Europe too, from 1861 jute works were established, often behind steep tariff walls, with others in Australia and the United States.[124] Rather more ominous was the emergence of spinning mills and factories in India. Few prior to the mid-1870s, however, lost sleep about the potential of rivalry in the jute trade – in which Dundonians felt they had the superiority – many thousands of miles distant.[125] It was in 1855 that a mill for spinning jute was erected at Rishra, near Serampore in Bengal. The machinery was made in Dundee, by John Kerr of Douglas Foundry. Others followed soon after and, as in Dundee, their owners 'coined money'.[126]

The heady optimism of the period is reflected in the classical pediments that adorned many of the mill and factory frontages, accompanied in some cases by great Italianate bell and water towers. As impressive was the careful fenestration and great bulk of the mills, set off by neoclassical urns at the gable ends or, occasionally, a centrally placed statue.[127]

Symbolically but as a physical fact, above them all, including their 'dwarfish' chimneys, stood Cox's 'gigantic' industrial chimney carrying the smoke from some fifty-eight furnaces and several forges at Camperdown Linen Works at Lochee. All this was concealed within the square 86.2 metres-high, ornamental Italian campanile structure (although the upper section was octagonal). Built in 1865–6 and designed by George A. Cox in conjunction with the James Bryce-trained local architect James Maclaren at a cost of around £6,000, the 'vast tower of variegated [red, white and black] brick' was Dundee's highest edifice. With the brick-work supervised by James Frier from Glasgow, it was an unmissable declaration of Cox's and Dundee's triumph as Juteopolis, about which local journalists (as well as an unnamed 'lady from Edinburgh'), taken by a small steam engine-powered elevator to the balcony near the top when it was completed, waxed lyrical.[128] A year later, the firm had a clock, also in Italian style, built by J. W. Benson of London. Visible from all parts of Lochee and with its four seven-foot-diameter dials, it was the largest public clock in Scotland.[129] Little did those concerned with flamboyant mill-building projects of this kind – Dundee's 'most important contribution to the architecture of the 19th century' – realise that nothing on this scale would be replicated in the future.[130]

Yet what could be dismissed as the biased assessment of a Dundee-centric industry insider like Warden was confirmed by the impressions of an envious American visitor in 1878, intent on discovering the foundations of Dundee's success and then replicating these in the USA. Dundee presented 'an impressive spectacle of manufacturing greatness'. High walls around the town's hundred or so jute mills resembled the 'ramparts of extensive fortifications', while the streets were shaded with 'a forest' of lofty chimneys.[131] By this time Dundee stood head and shoulders above the rest of the UK as far as jute was concerned; both the London and Glasgow ventures, founded when wartime demand for jute was at its peak, had by this time failed, in 1870 and 1878 respectively.[132] For Dundee too, the end of hostilities in America in 1867 meant the end of the town's most opulent era, but with the outbreak of the Franco-Prussian War in 1870 prosperity returned once again, but this time of shorter duration.

In Dundee the flax and jute princes' spectacular earnings prompted another round of ostentatious villa building, an earlier one represented by Reres House, in Broughty Ferry (1849). Dundee's west end attracted mansion building in the 1850s and 1860s.[133] But it was in the fashionable suburb of Broughty Ferry that houses were sufficiently grand and imposing (and their owners' pretensions great enough) to be accorded the title of 'Castle'. Joseph Grimond of Bowbridge Works had created sumptuous Carbet Castle following his purchase of Kerbet House as early as 1850. George Gilroy of Gilroy Brothers' Tay Works had in the late 1860s built the neo-Tudor ninety-plus-roomed Castleroy nearby.

Others purchased estates and erected large mansions in the countryside beyond Dundee, and sometimes further afield, 'conspicuous proofs of the great prosperity which a single industry has created'.

The Cox's were simply one of the more prominent of the town's textile manufacturers to flee to the suburbs (and beyond), although even the proprietors of or senior managers in smaller enterprises followed similar paths, albeit reluctantly at first, as we have seen.[134] William Ogilvy

Figure 2.3 Castleroy, 'the greatest of the jute palaces' (David M. Walker), constructed between 1867 and 1869 for George Gilroy, partner in Gilroy Brothers, one of Dundee's largest jute manufacturers, employing around three thousand workers in the 1870s. © D. C. Thomson & Co. Ltd.

86   THE TRIUMPH OF TEXTILES

Dalgleish, who became chairman of Baxter Brothers and, like his predecessor Sir David Baxter and fellow partners, was one of Dundee's most generous philanthropists, moved first to Mayfield House in West Ferry, and thereafter to Errol Park, some miles to the west of Dundee, and also owned Coulin Lodge in Ross-shire.[135] Alexander Grimond of J. and A. D. Grimond, had a large house in the Perth Road, Dundee's west end, as well as Glenericht Estate, further out in the countryside near Blairgowrie, Perthshire. Similar routes were taken by Alexander J. Buist, long-standing owner of Ward Works, Harry Walker of Caldrum Works and William Halley of Wallace Craigie Works.[136] Frederick Sharp, one of John Sharp's sons, purchased Wemyss Hall near Cupar in Fife, which he had rebuilt by Robert Lorimer as the Hill of Tarvit mansion house. Like several of his contemporaries, Sharp was an assiduous art collector and wanted somewhere to showcase his paintings and other collectibles. This interest in art as well as the encouragement and promotion of contemporary Scottish artists among Dundee's business elite – mainly those involved in textiles in one capacity or other – dated back to 1843, when the Watt Institute had held an unexpectedly popular exhibition. The visit to Dundee of the British Association in 1867, the conviction that galleries and museums could educate and refine the taste of ordinary people, a desire to place Dundee on a par with other culturally aware towns and cities, and undoubtedly the value of art as a potential financial asset, spurred what was to be a lengthy surge of enthusiasm for art collecting, and not only of Scottish works.[137] George Simpson, William Ritchie, John Bell, James Orchar and others boasted eclectic collections, which they hung in their newly built villas in the west end of Perth Road and in West and Broughty Ferry. In order to widen the obvious interest there was in such work among the general public, in 1873 an east wing was added to the Albert Institute, for a permanent art gallery and museum.

In and around the town, civic improvement projects multiplied.[138] Less obvious as a sign of success, but noted by contemporaries, was the fact that at the peak of the 1860s boom the number of couples marrying reached an all-time high.[139]

Notes

1. David Bremner, *The Industries of Scotland* (Newton Abbot, 1969 edn), p. 247.
2. *Aberdeen Press and Journal*, 12 June 1833, extracted from the *Morning Post*, p. 2.

DUNDEE'S EMERGENCE AS A GLOBAL CITY

3. Dundee City Archives, GD/CC/1/1/1, Sederunt Book of the Forfarshire Chamber of Commerce and Manufactures, 1819–1832, 11 December 1830.

4. UDA, MS 120/1/5, 1831–2, James Duncan to James Grimond, 22 November 1831.

5. Gordon Jackson with Kate Kinnear, *The Trade and Shipping of Dundee* (Dundee, 1991), pp. 16–19.

6. *Aberdeen Press and Journal*, 12 June 1833, p. 2.

7. *Caledonian Mercury*, 19 January 1833.

8. Alastair J. Durie, 'Government policy and the Scottish linen industry before c. 1840', in Brenda Collins and Philip Ollerenshaw (eds), *The European Linen Industry in Historical Perspective* (Oxford, 2003), pp. 242–4.

9. Mark Watson, *Jute and Flax Mills in Dundee* (Tayport, 1990), p. 49.

10. *Roscommon Journal*, 23 January 1835.

11. Watson, *Jute and Flax Mills*, p. 13.

12. UDA, MS 66/I/5/6 (4) MS Notes on Bell & Balfour.

13. UDA, MS102/1/1, Peter Carmichael, Reminiscences, 1, p. 177.

14. UDA, MS66/VI/7/12, Harry Walker & Sons, MS Notes by K Bell.

15. UDA, J. R. L. Halley, 'Business in Dundee in the XIXth Century', typescript notes, n.d., p. 7.

16. UDA, MS6/3/3/2, Robert Cock to William Cock, 22 December 1834.

17. UDA, MS11/5/2, Costs journal, c. 1860, 'History of Improvements in Hackling and increasing yield and cleaning Tow', 10 February 1862, p. 59.

18. *Dundee Advertiser*, 23 January 1857.

19. *Reading Mercury*, 18 January 1836; *Fife Herald*, 21 January 1836; *The Scotsman*, 10 February 1836; *Manchester Times*, 15 October 1836.

20. *Fife Herald*, 19 January 1837.

21. *Caledonian Mercury*, 12 December 1836.

22. UDA, Diary, James Cox, pp. 87–9; and section headed '1834 and up', pp. 1–2.

23. *Fife Herald*, 26 January 1837.

24. UDA, Diary, James Cox, pp. 87–9.

25. Calculated from A. J. Warden, *The Linen Trade: Ancient and Modern* (London, 1868 edn), p. 633.

26. W. Hamish Fraser, *Chartism in Scotland* (Pontypool, 2010), pp. 125–9.

27. Watson, *Jute and Flax Mills*, pp. 14–15.

28. Halley, 'Business in Dundee', p. 7.

29. UDA, MS11/5/5 (II), 'Memorandum', March 1926.

30. Halley, 'Business in Dundee', p. 9.

31. UDA, MS102/1/2, Peter Carmichael, II, Life and Letters, 1, p. 24; DCA, GD/CC/2/2/1/1, Baltic Coffee House Minute Book, 1835–48, pp. 96–7.

32. UDA, MS6/1/3/1/1, Wet Letter Book, James Cox, February–October 1840.

33. *Dundee Courier*, 17 September 1863.

34. *Dundee, Perth & Cupar Advertiser*, 11 November 1856.
35. *Dundee People's Journal*, 15 October 1859.
36. *Fife Herald*, 18 June 1857.
37. UDA, MS11/5/42, Instructions for Manufacturing Canvas for Her Majesty's Navy, April 1842, n.p.
38. UDA, Baxter MSS, MS 11/5/42, Notebook, Manufacture of Canvas, Experiments on Spinning, n.d.
39. UDA, MS102/12/4, Letter of Tests of Twisted Canvas, 10 December 1847; Turnbull & Co., Claverhouse, 13 March 1847.
40. UDA, MS11/5/42, Instructions.
41. UDA, MS 11/5/42, Quantity of Sail Cloth required for the fitting of ships of different classes in H M Navy, September 1854.
42. Gordon Jackson with Kate Kinnear, *The Trade and Shipping of Dundee 1780–1850* (Dundee, 1991), p. 30.
43. Bremner, *Industries*, p. 251.
44. Warden, *Linen Trade*, p. 573.
45. Watson, *Jute and Flax Mills*, p. 56.
46. Ibid., p. 627.
47. Ibid., p. 58.
48. *Dundee, Perth & Cupar Advertiser*, 26 February 1858.
49. Bruce Lenman, Charlotte Lythe and Enid Gauldie, *Dundee and its Textile Industry 1850–1914* (Dundee, 1969), p. 1045.
50. *Fife Herald*, 18 June 1857.
51. *Dundee Advertiser*, 23 January 1857.
52. UDA, MS11/5/42, Instructions.
53. Warden, *Linen Trade*, p. 633.
54. *Dundee Advertiser*, 26 December 1856.
55. Enid Gauldie, 'The Dundee jute industry', in John Butt and Kenneth Ponting (eds), *Scottish Textile History* (Aberdeen, 1987), p. 120.
56. Gauldie, 'Dundee jute', pp. 112–25; Jim Tomlinson, *Dundee and the Empire: 'Juteopolis' 1850–1939* (Edinburgh, 2014), pp. 10–11.
57. Karolina Hutkova, *The English East India Company's Enterprise in Bengal, 1750–1850* (Woodbridge, 2019), p. 3.
58. Tariq Omar Ali, *A Local History of Global Capital: Jute & Peasant Life in the Bengal Delta* (Princeton and Oxford, 2018), pp. 21–36.
59. Indrajit Ray, 'Struggling against Dundee: Bengal jute industry during the nineteenth century', *Indian Economic and Social History Review*, 49: 1 (2012), pp. 113–23, p. 117.
60. Tara Sethia, 'Rise of the jute manufacturing industry in colonial India: A global perspective', *Journal of World History*, 7: 1 (Spring 1996), p. 73; Nibaran Chandra Chaudhury, *Jute in Bengal* (Calcutta, 1921), p. 175.
61. Stephen Broadberry and Bishnupriya Gupta, 'Lancashire, India and shifting competitive advantage in cotton textiles, 1700–1850: The neglected role of factor prices', *Economic History Review*, New Series, 62: 2 (May 2009), pp. 279–305.

62. Lawrence James, *The Rise and Fall of the British Empire* (London, 1994), pp. 127–9.
63. H. V. Bowen, *The Business of Empire: The East India Company and Imperial Britain, 1756–1833* (Cambridge, 2006), pp. 240–6.
64. Gauldie, 'Dundee jute', p. 115.
65. *Caledonian Mercury*, 24 January 1801; Hem Chunder Kerr, *Report on the Cultivation of and Trade In, Jute in Bengal* (Calcutta, 1874), pp. 83–4.
66. Tirthankar Roy, 'Trading firms in colonial India', *Business History Review*, 88: 1 (Spring 2014), pp. 15–16.
67. James G. Parker, 'Scottish enterprise in India, 1750–1914', in R. A. Cage (ed.), *The Scots Abroad: Labour, Capital, Enterprise, 1750–1914* (Beckenham, 1985), pp. 191–8.
68. Andrew Mackillop, 'Dundee, London and the empire in Asia', in Charles McKean, Bob Harris and Christopher Whatley (eds), *Dundee: Renaissance to Enlightenment* (Dundee, 2009), p. 168.
69. Alastair J. Durie, *The British Linen Company, 1745–1775* (Edinburgh, 1996), pp. 4–5.
70. Warden, *Linen Trade*, p. 67.
71. NRS CS 96/4030, Letter Book of John Moir, 28 May 1828, p. 148.
72. Sir Joseph Banks, quoted in Ray Desmond, 'William Roxburgh', *Oxford Dictionary of National Biography* (https://doi.org/10.1093/ref:odnb/24233), accessed 2 June 2020, p. 2.
73. Kerr, *Report*, p. 5.
74. H. R. Carter, *Jute and its Manufacture* (London, 1921), p. 2.
75. D. Ritchie, 'Textiles', in A.W. Paton and A. H. Millar (eds), *British Association, Dundee, 1912: Handbook and Guide to Dundee and District* (Dundee, 1912), p. 268.
76. *Manchester Times*, 15 October 1836.
77. Warden, *Linen Trade*, p. 65.
78. Ibid., pp. 619–20.
79. Ibid., p. 78; Bremner, *Industries*, pp. 251–2, 263; *Dundee Courier*, 21 November 1891.
80. Warden, *Linen Trade*, pp. 75–7, 134.
81. UDA, MS66/1/5/7 (I(vii)), Notes on the Jute Trade.
82. Warden, *Linen Trade*, p. 68.
83. UDA, MS66/1/5/7 (1 (vii)), Notes on the Jute Trade, n.p.
84. Warden, *Linen Trade*, p. 72.
85. Bruce Lenman, Charlotte Lythe and Enid Gauldie, *Dundee and its Textile Industry 1850–1914* (Dundee, 1969), p. 14; *Dundee Courier*, 2 September 1880.
86. Warden, *Linen Trade*, pp. 72–4; Christopher A. Whatley, 'The making of "Juteopolis"', in Christopher A. Whatley (ed.), *The Re-Making of*

Juteopolis, Dundee c. 1891–1991 (Dundee, 1992), p. 10; Carter, *Jute*, pp. 142, 186.

87. UDA, MS66/1/5/7 (1 (vii)), Notes on the Jute Trade.
88. Gauldie, 'Dundee jute', p. 122.
89. See Subscriber database, at Macmanus168.org.uk.
90. Warden, *Linen Trade*, p. 594.
91. UDA, MS6/1/3/1/1, James Cox, Wet Letter Book, 1 August 1840, 28 September 1840.
92. UDA, MS11/5/2, Costs journal, c. 1860, p. 59.
93. Warden, *Linen Trade*, p. 633.
94. DCA, GD/CC/2/2/1/1, Baltic Coffee House Minute Book, 1835–1848, 11 May 1842, p. 95.
95. *Dundee, Perth & Cupar Advertiser*, 26 February 1858.
96. Warden, *Linen Trade*, p. 75; Ritchie, 'Textiles', p. 278.
97. Louise Miskell, 'Civic leadership and the manufacturing elite, Dundee, 1820–1870', in Christopher A. Whatley, Bob Harris and Louise Miskell (eds), *Victorian Dundee: Image and Realities* (Dundee, 2011 edn), p. 61.
98. DCA, GD/CC/2/2/1/1, Baltic Coffee House Minute Book, pp. 1–8.
99. Miskell, 'Civic leadership', pp. 57–60.
100. Gordon Jackson, *The British Whaling Trade* (London, 1978), pp. 59, 73, 126–30, 145–7.
101. See entries in UDA. MS11/3/1, Abstract of Quarterly Balances, 1852–1875.
102. Halley, 'Business in Dundee', p. 4.
103. UDA, MS11/5/2, Costs journal, c. 1860.
104. Gauldie, 'Dundee jute', pp. 115–16.
105. Carmichael, Reminiscences, 1, p. 26.
106. UDA, MS102/12/2, Miscellaneous Correspondence to Peter Carmichael, Robert Baxter to Carmichael, 27 January 1845.
107. *Dundee Advertiser*, 12 October 1863.
108. *Dundee Advertiser*, 7 October 1864.
109. Peter Sharp, *Flax, Tow, and Jute Spinning: A Handbook* (Dundee, 1907 edn), p. 203.
110. Chaudhury, *Jute in Bengal*, p. 175; Gordon Stewart, *Jute and Empire* (Manchester, 1998), pp. 40–1; *Dundee Advertiser*, 26 December 1856.
111. Ray, 'Struggling'.
112. Warden, *Linen Trade*, p. 596.
113. *Dundee Courier*, 3 May 1866.
114. *Dundee Advertiser*, 17 December 1861.
115. Halley, 'Business in Dundee', p. 11.
116. Roy, 'Trading firms', pp. 37–8; S. Waterhouse, *Report on Jute Culture and the Importance of the Industry* (Washington, 1883), p. 13.
117. *Dundee Courier*, 10 September 1867.
118. Tomlinson, *Dundee*, pp. 12, 26–7.

119. Brenda Collins, 'The origins of Irish immigration to Scotland in the nineteenth and twentieth centuries', in T. M. Devine (ed.), *Irish Immigrants and Scottish Society in the Nineteenth and Twentieth Centuries* (Edinburgh, 1991), p. 9; Christopher A. Whatley, 'Altering images of the industrial city: The case of James Myles, the "Factory Boy" and mid-Victorian Dundee', in Christopher A. Whatley, Bob Harris and Louise Miskell (eds), *Victorian Dundee: Image and Realities* (Dundee, 2011 edn), pp. 77–9.
120. Warden, *Linen Trade*, p. 621.
121. Watson, *Jute and Flax Mills*, pp. 15–16.
122. David Walker, *Dundee Architecture and Architects, 1770–1914* (Dundee, 1977), p. 18.
123. *Dundee Advertiser*, 22 August 1866.
124. *Dundee Advertiser*, 29 October 1867.
125. Walker, *Dundee Architecture*, p. 18.
126. *Dundee Advertiser*, 13, 22 June 1865; *Dundee Courier*, 22 August 1866.
127. *Shoreditch Observer*, 12 August 1865.
128. Carter, *Jute*, p. 188.
129. Tomlinson, *Dundee*, pp. 39–40.
130. Sethia, 'Rise of jute manufacturing', pp. 77–9.
131. See Waterhouse, *Report*.
132. *Public Ledger and Daily Advertiser*, 18 May 1870; *Dundee Courier*, 1 November 1878.
133. David Walker, 'The man-made landscape', in J. M. Jackson (ed.), *The City of Dundee* (Arbroath, 1979), p. 42.
134. Louise Miskell, 'Civic leadership and the manufacturing elite, Dundee, 1820–1870', in Whatley, Harris and Miskell (eds), *Victorian Dundee*, p. 62.
135. Christopher A. Whatley, 'William Ogilvy Dalgleish', in Anthony Slaven and Sydney Checkland (eds), *Dictionary of Scottish Business Biography 1860–1960: Volume 1: Textiles* (Aberdeen, 1986), pp. 350–1.
136. Miskell, 'Civic leadership', p. 62.
137. Matthew Jarron, *'Independent & Individualist': Art in Dundee, 1867–1924* (Dundee, 2015), pp. 9–31.
138. Waterhouse, *Report*, p. 11.
139. *Montrose, Arbroath and Brechin Review*, 28 December 1866.

3

Entrepreneurial Endeavour, from Angus Flax Merchants to 'Lords o' Juteopolis'

Nearly half a century ago some sagacious Scotchmen engaged in the manufacture of jute. (1883)

It was a Professor Sylvester Waterhouse, of Washington University in St Louis, in a report on jute sponsored by the American Department of Agriculture, who lavished such praise on Dundee's textile entrepreneurs.[1] Although Waterhouse initially wrote up his findings on the jute industry in India in 1876, he supplemented these after visiting Dundee in 1878. His impressions of the town were noted in the previous chapter. Such was the extent of the achievement of Dundee's jute magnates that Waterhouse heralded them as having enriched Scotland but also, by facilitating the movement of bulk goods such as cotton and grain, the commerce of the world. What had been so successfully accomplished in Dundee, he believed, could be done on a still grander scale in the United States. Waterhouse was not alone in his praise of Dundee's manufacturers. Reporting on his sojourn to Dundee in January 1847, the Edinburgh publisher and popular journalist William Chambers had been intrigued and impressed by their single-mindedness. He liked to see 'a town take up a manufacture in earnest, and stick to it so pertinaciously as to gain from it a name', a result he was convinced was due to the sagaciousness, enterprise and 'indomitable spirit of industry' of Dundee's inhabitants.[2] Even closer to home, the *Fife Herald* was of a similar mind: Dundee, now the third-largest in Scotland in terms of population, was 'the principal emporium of the linen manufacture in the United Kingdom'. Wherever commercial enterprise has penetrated, the paper's writer continued, 'the fabrics of Dundee are to be found'. Despite some 'occasional sneering to the contrary', the burgh's success was thoroughly deserved in what was a kindly and liberal community.[3]

Historians, however, have taken a less charitable view – that is when the industry's entrepreneurs have been considered at all. Some have implied that they were 'fortunate', and beneficiaries of favourable market conditions.[4] That is true, but it is far from a comprehensive explanation. Admittedly referring to the period after c. 1850, one of the industry's foremost authorities, Enid Gauldie, concluded that 'there can have been few spheres in life in which ability counted for less than in jute or flax'. Profits, she continued, 'bore hardly any relation to ability or efficiency'; during the boom years of the 1850s and 1860s 'anyone' could buy or rent a decrepit mill and make a fortune.[5] Gauldie's judgements appear to have been endorsed elsewhere, and are compounded by the criticism of the extent to which from the 1870s many linen and jute manufacturers dissipated their capital in speculative trust companies in the United States and elsewhere rather than in their own works.[6]

Yet this may be an unfairly harsh assessment. As we have seen, there were many more failures than successes among Dundee's flax and jute firms. Numerous small fortunes were lost – along with the ignominy of bankruptcy and sometimes necessary flight from Dundee to the debtors' sanctuary near Holyrood, Edinburgh. This was in stark contrast to the relatively few who made vast fortunes from coarse textiles. Thus, while good luck may well have played a part in determining the fates of those businesses that survived the downturns which punctuated the textile trade prior to the 1850s, to succeed was not a straightforward matter. Nor was it later. The relatively short lives of jute companies in Glasgow and London has already been noted, although by this time those in Dundee had become relatively secure; the town's business failure rate was significantly less than Glasgow's or Edinburgh's.[7] Of course, the role of providence shouldn't be denied: the Crimean War and the American Civil War were undoubtedly huge boons for Dundee; the last, according to the *Illustrated London News* as early as 1862, had 'made the fortune of Dundee'.[8] That the price of raw jute had 'scarcely increased' while demand soared had combined to generate the unprecedented profit levels mentioned in the previous chapter. The same had been true of flax, with war the main influencer of the price of raw materials, as well as, often, the price of the finished product. Nevertheless, there are grounds to suppose that it may be premature to dismiss out of hand the judgements of those contemporaries who were more complimentary about the achievements of Dundee's business classes. As was remarked in 1912 during the visit of the British Association to Dundee, in spite of growing competition in jute from Calcutta from 1855, which had many advantages over Dundee, and the emergence of rivals on the European continent, Dundee 'still retains its supremacy as the great centre for jute and linen in Great Britain, and as the chief commercial textile centre in Scotland'.[9]

ENTREPRENEURIAL ENDEAVOUR: ROOTS OF SUCCESS IN NINETEENTH-CENTURY DUNDEE

The origins, characteristics, motivations, abilities and qualities of those individuals who raised Dundee to such an elevated position in the eyes of outsiders – of whom there were many more than those quoted here – and who saw off their rivals elsewhere, therefore merit investigation. Necessarily, we are limited in this regard by the paucity of evidence, but should be wary of generalising from the examples of successful entrepreneurs whose lives in business have been well documented. That a handful wrote detailed accounts of their times – and their successes – in the textile trade is to be welcomed. Equally, caution is required when drawing on such personal, one-sided testimony.

What is striking about those firms that came to dominate Dundee's textile industry during the 'golden age' of the 1860s and beyond is their longevity. Their remarkable prosperity owed much to decisions taken in the preceding decades. In almost every case, they were led by individuals who either had acquired personal experience in the textile trade as merchants or producers, or whose fathers and even grandfathers had roots in the industry going back several decades.[10] In some cases it was both. This is not to imply that they were well endowed financially. It is, however, to suggest that they were well connected and had friends and acquaintances in the flax trade from whom they could seek advice and who could offer support. As we will see, they had other characteristics in common too.

The most telling example of a lengthy pedigree is the Cox brothers at Camperdown in Lochee. The Cock family appear to have come from mainland Europe and settled in Scotland – the Carse of Gowrie between Perth and Dundee, to be precise – at the turn of the sixteenth century. There, possibly led by James Cox (1676–1742), they established themselves as weavers and bleachers along with their farming operations.[11] By the 1770s James's son David was employing some 280 handloom weavers, either directly or on a putting-out basis. In this respect they were simply one household in a district where what some historians have termed 'proto-industry' (defined simply as small-scale domestic manufacture in a rural setting) was commonplace. By the turn of the nineteenth century, however, it was clear that John Cox had risen above many of the rest of his neighbours and was established as a yarn and cloth merchant. He travelled, by foot, to markets in Dundee, Inchture and Perth (20 miles distant), purchasing yarns before putting these out to handloom weavers and then buying up a range of cloth types, widths and weights from weavers 'for miles around' the family home at Foggyley.[12] Cox was the lynchpin in a tight but scattered network of the best spinners, warp preparers and weavers, whose products he sold as far distant as London. To here he periodically travelled by sea in search of custom, as well as obtaining orders for the coarser, unbleached cloth on which he – like many of the rest of Dundee's manufacturers – concentrated from the end of the Napoleonic wars.[13]

The origins of the town's other Victorian textile behemoth, Baxter Brothers, were similar. As early as 1728 the handloom weaver John Baxter (1700–84) migrated from the countryside (the rural township of Tealing in the county of Angus) to Dundee – a not uncommon pattern for those merchant-manufacturers who settled in the burgh.[14] A few decades later his son John was purchasing flax – on credit terms where he could – and then putting it out to be spun by a small army of rural hand spinners before, like the Cox's, he delivered the yarn to country weavers. It was the value added at this stage that encouraged William Baxter, John's son, to build a waterwheel-driven spinning mill at Glamis in 1806 prior to moving to Dens Mill in Dundee in 1822, where he used steam power. Initially he was in a partnership with his son Edward. John Baxter the third, that is John Baxter of Idvies, took responsibility for exporting the family's cloth, thereby connecting what was made in Dundee with market requirements overseas. Edward, however, left the partnership and became a full-time merchant and shipping agent in his own right, his place being taken by his brother David (later Sir David Baxter), who was in no doubt about the debt he owed to his predecessors in providing the platform for the company's nineteenth-century success.[15]

Moving into Dundee – with the advantage it had of its proximity to the Tay, the North Sea and shipping routes to the Baltic and Russia, as well as down Britain's east coast to London, and north and west into the Atlantic – made good business sense once steam-driven spinning became feasible. The costs incurred by inland mills were high, above all for transport. Literally tons of flax and tow had to be carried from Dundee's harbour by horses and carts the several miles inland to the country mills, with the spun yarn – and waste – making the return journey. If the weather was clement, that is; flax was best spun dry, so supplies to the mills were interrupted as merchants were unwilling to risk rain damage which when dried out weakened the flax, while the roads to Dundee were often in a parlous state. Infernal is how one Forfar manufacturer described the road to Dundee in 1814, adding that horses were killed

Figure 3.1 Sir David Baxter. Baxter Brothers' leading partner and chairman during the golden age of Dundee's textile industry. Baxter and his sisters donated the land for the city's largest public park, laid out by Sir Joseph Paxton and opened in 1863. In turn, Baxters' grateful workers subscribed to a statue of Sir David, made by Scotland's leading sculptor at the time, Sir John Steell. © University of Dundee Archives.

and carts broken on it. Much earlier, in January 1795, when frost and a snowstorm had blocked the road, the same man, William Don, reported to an important London customer that in order to be sure of getting his cloth to the quayside at Dundee he had levied and led sixty men on an expedition to cut a passage through.[16] Coal, casks and hogsheads of whale oil which could contain over 60 gallons, machinery including spinning frames, lime and mill furniture had necessarily to be taken along what could be rutted and flooded tracks.[17] A minor inconvenience, but one that could be eliminated if merchants and manufacturers could talk directly with the spinners rather than by letter, was the need – in response to their customers' requirements – for the former to instruct the spinners about what material to spin and whether, for instance, to add another twist. Complaints about poor quality too demanded immediate action.[18]

Blessed with several rivers and streams which could be tapped for water-powered spinning mills, Fife too provided its share of the originators of what would become Dundee's more prominent textile concerns. Indeed, early on some of Fife's spinning mills were well known for the quality of the yarn they put out. Balgonie Mill was 'like a King's Palace for beauty inside and outside', while George Moon of Russell Mill near Cupar was credited with an early breakthrough in carding machinery.[19] Both the father and grandfather of Harry Walker, of Harry Walker & Sons, had run a spinning mill in Fife, at Dura Den, which provided the name for the family's first works in Dundee around 1834. Their Balgay Works would later be one of the town's largest employers of jute workers.[20] Fife was the origin of the firm of Thomas Bell of Thomas Bell & Sons, of both Belmont and Heathfield works, where canvas and later jute were woven. Bell was President of Dundee's Chamber of Commerce in 1854. His father Thomas had moved to Dundee in 1778 and established a shipping and merchanting partnership with Alexander Balfour, also from Fife. Eventually they became flax spinners when they revived Chapelshade Mill, around 1822; both men, who are credited with being among the first in Dundee to spin jute, also became provost of Dundee. The mercantile and industrial experience this provided prepared young Thomas to join with his father in building Belmont Works in 1833, a handloom factory that focused initially on producing canvas floorcloth.[21]

Experience told too in the case of Peter Carmichael, whose engineering and management skills were crucial to the Baxters' success.[22] Carmichael's father James had been a mechanic in a Glasgow cotton-spinning mill and then at Ballindalloch Mills near Stirling. Partly through marriage, he then moved to the aforementioned flax mill at Balgonie in Fife, Scotland's first, and after that to a rope and canvas factory at Limehouse, on the Thames, where he managed the flax-spinning mill. After the Limehouse Mill failed in the post-war depression of 1816, he came to Dundee and leased the then struggling Dens Mill with its 6 horsepower steam engine. As a boy, Peter observed the operations of his father's mill (to which he hoped to succeed) before becoming an apprentice mechanic at one of Dundee's foundries around 1825. Thereafter he spent time in London and then worked for the Scottish-born engineer and entrepreneur Peter Fairbairn in his Leeds foundry, where he saw and worked on machinery being made for the Leeds flax mills, which included Marshalls, the biggest in England. Recognising how valuable his knowledge of flax machinery could be, by December 1833 Carmichael had been invited to become and had accepted the post of manager of William and David Baxter's new mill at Upper Dens.[23]

These though are simply the best-documented examples. William Small, a flax merchant and shipowner, and for a time a partner with Thomas Neish, one of Dundee's pioneers in jute, had been 'brought up to the Cowgate business'. Small was considered knowledgeable enough by the Chamber of Commerce to represent Dundee's flax and jute interests in Paris when the Anti-Corn Law League leader and free trade advocate Richard Cobden MP was negotiating a commercial treaty with France.[24] John Halley, the father of William Halley, later of Wallace Craigie Works,

Figure 3.2 Peter Carmichael, of Baxter Brothers, arguably the most important company in Dundee's textile industry's history. A brilliant engineer, Carmichael was also an able works manager who directed and oversaw the development of Dens Works to become the world's leading manufacturer of linen cloth and canvas.
© University of Dundee Archives.

had been a flax dresser in Perth before relocating to Dundee in 1782.[25] William Halley's foray into textiles had been as the proprietor of a hand-loom 'factory' at Forebank in Dundee, which meant in effect that he had a house which also accommodated a number of looms in the base-ment.[26] His acquisition of Wallace Craigie was in partnership with two other knowledgeable manufacturers, Robert Brough and James Gilroy. Alexander Warden, the industry's chronicler, had come to Dundee from Forfar in 1825, and served an apprenticeship in banking as well as with Balfour & Meldrum, shipping agents and flax importers. Around 1833 he set up his own business as a linen manufacturer, employing handloom weavers before taking a pioneering role in printed jute. A fire destroyed his Ann Street and Nelson Street factory, but as he was underinsured he reverted to his former role as a merchant, this time importing jute.[27] The three original partners of Messrs Malcolm, Ogilvie & Co., founded in 1850, may have been relatively young at the time (their late twenties), but each had amassed relevant experience – respectively as an engineer, in flax and linen merchanting, and as proprietor of a small flax-spin-ning mill. One of them, George Malcolm, had come from a flax-spinning family.[28] By 1864 their factory, Constable Works, had four thousand spindles and 220 looms employing around a thousand workers. But the division of labour by the specialist knowledge and skills that George Malcolm, David Ogilvie and James Cunningham brought to the concern was a significant feature of the larger companies such as Cox's: by such means each contributed what they could best, without in any sense being a drag on the rest. Such allocation of skills among the partners has been viewed as a main reason for the success of J. & P. Coats of Paisley:[29] the model, it seems, was applicable in Dundee too.

Family networks were important too.[30] The right marriage could pro-vide access to vital expertise. Thus both James Cox and Peter Carmichael (of Baxter Brothers) married daughters of James Carmichael, of Ward Foundry, who at the time was Dundee's most eminent machine maker and engineer. Cox was helped by his brother-in-law Peter Carmichael when planning Camperdown Works and did regular business with the firm of J. and C. Carmichael for his machinery requirements. Social links, also noted already, were equally helpful, especially in the pioneer-ing early decades of the nineteenth century when sharing information rather than shielding it from rivals seemed mutually beneficial.[31]

What many of what were to become the foremost concerns also had in common was the experience of failure. This had happened to the Cox's in 1819, when the bleaching works they had established near Lochee were consumed by fire. The silver spoon James Cox believed he had been born with was in such circumstances of little avail.[32] Worse was the depression of 1825–6, during which the family had considered emigration as a way out of their difficulties. John Sharp, considered by some of his contemporaries to have been the main driving force behind the adoption of jute in Dundee, and the proprietor of a modest-sized flax-spinning mill in Ward Road, had gone down during the depression of the mid-1820s, and did so again in 1839.[33] He was sufficiently recovered by the time of his death in 1852 that his son John was able not only to succeed him and expand the business, but also to purchase a Forfarshire estate, Balmuir. In 1842 both William Halley and James Gilroy were among a large number of struggling enterprises: Gilroy's creditors had to settle for one penny for each pound sterling he was owing. Equally, however, those concerned were prepared to learn from what had gone wrong. If there was a common denominator among those businesses that had crashed as trading conditions worsened, it was their reliance on large amounts of credit. The problem was widespread across the country, but in Dundee, wrote the *Perthshire Advertiser* disapprovingly of the wave of bankruptcies that rocked the country in 1826, there was a higher proportion of individuals, 'possessing little real property, but much imprudence', who had borrowed sums of money they were unable to pay back.[34] The safer alternative, although requiring greater patience to succeed, was to limit borrowing and to live frugally, and depend on ploughing back saved profits. According to James Cox, he and his brothers had determined early on 'never on any account . . . [to] begin any work without having money to finish and carry it on'.[35] It is therefore ironic that around 1763, Cox's ancestor, James Cock, 'manufacturer' in Lochee (a burgh to the north of Dundee), had evidently recognised (along with another thirty-five mainly merchants in Dundee) that the town and its interlinked neighbourhood could collectively benefit from the credit facilities and notes of a bank, the Dundee Banking Company, and subscribed £200 to the undertaking.[36]

The Cox's financial rectitude in the mid-nineteenth century, however, was hardly the norm. Following a series of failures in 1857, David Baxter 'boldly and strongly' denounced 'the system of excessive credit as affording temptations to overtrading, speculation and extravagance', to which he believed some of his neighbours had succumbed by borrowing from several banks concurrently.[37] There was truth in the *Perthshire Advertiser*'s observation and a downside to the relative ease with which credit could be obtained from Dundee's banks (of which there were five by the early 1820s), partly facilitated by the appointment of local agents who were also involved in the flax trade. The great benefit of obtaining credit from the banks was that flax importers were able to take advantage of the facility

ANGUS FLAX MERCHANTS TO 'LORDS O' JUTEOPOLIS'

this allowed them to buy the commodity in bulk when it was cheap. In turn the spinners and manufacturers borrowed heavily to expand their businesses and produce great volumes of yarn and cloth at prices their less fortunately situated rivals found it hard to compete with. In the mid-1830s, over a quarter of the flax-spinning firms listed in the Dundee Directory – including some well-known names – were borrowing from the Bank of Scotland.[38] Yet even though the Bank's agents made it their business to know their customers well, this was no guarantee that loans made were secure. The aforementioned John Sharp of Ward Mill was described as 'cautious' and 'keen on saving, even to a fault'; yet he had failed.[39]

Equally important, however, was a level of commitment to their businesses that was manifest in the time, energy and sheer dogged perseverance of the industry's most successful entrepreneurs. Thus Thomas Bell, joint founder with his father of Belmont Works, was credited with being the 'energetic power' of the business. There are too many references of this kind, from a range of sources, to dismiss this merely as Dundee-serving hagiography. It was these qualities that characterised James Cox, who had observed his 'very active and persevering father', who attended closely to his business 'from which he was never absent other than when he went to the main yarn markets'.[40] William Baxter was credited with being one of 'the largest and most successful export merchants during the first half of the nineteenth century'. As with Cox, the parental model was strong, with his son Edward, who 'devoted himself with extraordinary energy to his commercial pursuits', being one of Dundee's most important businessmen in the pre-jute era, not least through the lead he took in effecting the abolition (in 1823) of the restrictive and costly stampmaster regime.[41] On a much smaller scale was the firm of Alexander Moncur of Victoria Works, which turned out a range of high-quality sacking materials and sacks. From very modest beginnings – as a pirn winder – Inchture-born, son of a ploughman and domestic servant mother, Alexander Moncur set up a power-loom factory employing up to 150 people. His success was attributed to 'habits of economy [he saved the capital he needed to set up in business from his earnings as a weaver, supplemented by his wife's income from sack sewing], self denial and industry'.[42] A feature of the dedication of such men to the fortunes of their businesses was the close attention they paid to day-to-day operations. In the first half of the nineteenth century most opted to live close to the works, which meant either the town centre or the inner suburbs. And even when they began to opt to reside further afield from the 1850s, they made sure that transport links were such that they could attend to their business premises every day, even if this meant, as in the case of William

Halley in Carnoustie, travelling by carriage and pair in the morning and returning home in the evening by rail.[43]

There are striking similarities in these respects with the immensely successful Coats and Clark thread-manufacturing families in Victorian and Edwardian Paisley. One reason advanced for the ascendancy of these two dynasties was their adherence to the Protestant faith, with its belief in ethical duty, and a dedication to vocation as a task set by God. Work, according to Calvinists, was 'an absolute end in itself, a calling'.[44] More widely, it has been proposed, commerce and religion were the 'twin poles of cultural life in most Scottish towns', and key elements in the development of Scottish manufacturing, linen in particular.[45] It is intriguing, therefore, that an identifiable sense of seriousness of purpose appears to have prevailed among Dundee's close-knit business class. A 'city of saints' was how one contemporary described Dundee at the turn of the nineteenth century.[46] Most of the thirty leading textile manufacturers in Dundee in the period 1820 to 1870 were affiliated to Protestant congregations, with the Church of Scotland just ahead of the Congregationalists.[47] It is notable how many of the industry's early leaders were either noted for or alluded to the religiosity of their upbringing. Many of the several hundred men who employed handloom weavers were said to have been 'godly', ruling their households 'in the fear of God'; it was from this source that some of the best families in Dundee were thought to have originated.[48]

More specifically, shortly after arriving at Dens, Peter Carmichael wrote on a card, which he kept on his desk, his 'Rules for my Life', which were based on Psalm 15. He only employed 'men with the fear of God in their eyes' for supervisory positions, in the hope they would inculcate habits of 'order, punctuality, diligence and thrift' among a workforce he was convinced was 'noticeably superior'.[49] The Carmichael brothers had been brought up 'in the principle of the gospel'. James, the better-known Peter's brother, was manager of a flax and jute works in Ailly in northern France in which Baxter Brothers were partners. From the outset he had not only attached himself to an existing Protestant congregation but became 'the most faithful and zealous of its members', and a generous benefactor.[50] Indeed, in 1849 Peter commended his brother for providing a religious service for his workpeople and hoped his evangelical actions, including the example of his living a 'blameless life', would 'be a means of bringing many to the knowledge of the truth in Jesus'.

The same seems to have been true of James Cox, who later in his career was active in the United Presbyterian Church, campaigning for instance for improvements in ministers' pay. At Camperdown he and his brothers took a close interest in the works' school, despite objections to Catholic children being 'compelled to learn the protestant catechism, read the protestant version of the scriptures, and hear comments thereon by a protestant teacher'.[51] Similarly, at Dens Peter Carmichael paid weekly visits to the new, larger works school opened on Clement Street in 1858 to satisfy himself that the teachers and monitors (of whom there were fifty-four ten years later) were doing all they could 'to secure good conduct and good manners'.[52] There was no contradiction in being both a committed Christian and a textile entrepreneur. Indeed, Alexander J. Buist and his brother James (later of Ward Mills) were the sons of the Rev. John Buist of Tannadice parish, who provided much of the capital that set James up in business. A. J. Buist became a prominent figure in the United Free Church, forming a congregation in Broughty Ferry around 1862 and setting in motion a campaign for a new church building.[53] There is little in the record to allow us to assess how widespread such values were, and the impact they had on the social environments of the town's linen and jute works. Yet there are proxies, clues to the degree to which the proprietors of textile firms acted out their Christian duty to give generously to their fellow human beings – what the sociologist Max Weber termed 'the social ethic of capital[ist] culture'.[54] The principal indicators are active involvement with their respective churches, charitable donations, philanthropy and a concern for the town of which they were part. We will see in the following chapter that all of these were ubiquitous features of the behaviour of Dundee's textile magnates.

PRODUCTS AND PRICES

The best way to demonstrate how the linen and jute industries' foremost capitalists went about their business is by examining the ways in which they tackled three of the most challenging obstacles to success. First, they had to establish what the markets for coarse cloth were, manufacture what was wanted and identify and win over buyers. Second, the coarse textile trade operated on the tightest of margins. One-sixth of a penny on the selling price was enough to lose an order, while a reduction by the same amount could win one. Price competition between suppliers was intense and costs therefore had to be kept under the closest scrutiny. Thirdly, and related to this, it was in the interests of spinners and manufacturers who wished to maximise their profits to turn out yarn and cloth in large volumes as efficiently as possible. The smaller mills of the early nineteenth century struggled to yield their proprietors profits of any substance for more than short periods.[55]

A determination to satisfy their most valuable customers by adapting to their needs was evident among the more ambitious – and successful – spinners and weaving firms. First though, as just noted, it was necessary to find buyers. Notable is how many of Dundee's spinners and manufacturers had initially found places in merchants' offices, where flax was bought, and cloth sold. Thus, the Grimond brothers, whose father David had set up as a flax spinner in Blairgowrie, spent time with David Martin & Co. in Dundee and even opened their own office in Manchester prior to establishing Maxwelltown Works. Even before the Camperdown Works began building at Lochee, James Cox, having learnt something of 'mercantile work' as a young man in the Town Clerk's office, had begun to build 'connections' with Glasgow warehousing companies, and by 1831 had a list of contacts in Carlisle, Newcastle, Manchester and London. With limits to how much yarn could be made by hand spinners, the next logical step for Cox – taken after inspecting some Glasgow cotton-spinning machinery – was to integrate backwards into machine spinning on frames adapted to deal with heavier linen yarns.[56] This he did with his brothers William, Thomas (who had a background in finance and commercial matters) and George, an engineer, to whom 'the entire control of the works [Camperdown] was given'.[57]

Neither James Cox, the Baxters nor the Carmichaels at Dens were among those merchant-manufacturers in Dundee who had been prepared by using low-cost, part-time spinners and weavers to sell unevenly made or 'indifferent' cloth, and at the lowest prices. Weavers and even some dealers were accused of making up rolls of cloth, normally Osnaburgs, of more than one piece. The best material on the outside concealed inferior and uneven cloth inside, thereby 'destroying' the reputation of the coarse linen manufacture at home and 'more particularly in the Foreign markets'.[58] This strategy brought those concerned into conflict with the local Board of Trustees stampmasters who, after inspection, might at worst seize the offending webs, or otherwise mark them as 'Faulty' in red or black lettering depending on whether the cloth was bleached or not.[59] (Much to the delight of the town's weavers, the stamping system was ended in 1823.) Even so, such were the volumes of yarn and cloth turned out, according to Charles Mackie, a spinner in Dundee during the first half of the nineteenth century, that Dundee was able to take the lead in the British flax trade in the mid-1810s.

The drop in standards, however, was not without precedent; this had been the direction of travel for some time. In 1760 Dundee's manufacturers were accused by the British Linen Company of 'hurting . . . the trade of the Nation' by resisting the Company's attempt to introduce what was called Pomerania linen (which was a degree finer than Osnaburgs) to the district by gathering in British Linen Company banknotes as a means of putting a stop to their business.[60] While further attempts were made to use finer yarns to make better cloth – and there were distinct gradations within the genus – Dundee's coarse linen was deemed perfectly adequate for most colonial uses. And there were, it seems, manufacturers who were content 'with their lot and their manner of life', and who had little interest in expanding their operations or changing current ways of working.[61]

By the end of the second decade of the following century, however, collective concern on the part of some mill spinners, conscious that a 'race to the bottom' would ultimately be ruinous for them all, was sufficiently strong to cause them to discuss the issue and pay greater attention to the quality of their merchandise.[62] Key to the town's future in this respect was the quality of the yarn spun in the new steam-driven spinning mills which, if done successfully, would silence the country spinners who would be unable to compete, burdened with the additional costs of transporting raw flax inland and then back to coastal Dundee.

It is often assumed that coarse textiles were synonymous with poor quality. Not so. This is important; as we have seen, while merchant-manufacturers such as James Moir were keen to obtain for customers the cloth they wanted, it was only material made by his own weavers that he could guarantee would be of the highest standard. This required the manufacturer to seek out the best yarns. And if a merchant or manufacturer wished to target more lucrative markets (as in New York) in which to sell better grades of linen such as diaper, they had to differentiate themselves from the Dundee norm. Indeed, for certain manufacturers in Forfar, some miles inland from Dundee, who were 'loud against the Dundee uneven yarns', a key selling point was that their cloth was distinct from Dundee's, and better.[63] Robert and William Don, Forfar's foremost cloth manufacturers and dealers in the early nineteenth century, went to extraordinary lengths to discredit the Dundee product while improving their own. It was a tactic that paid dividends, in that sales were often maintained when markets for lower grades of cloth fell off.[64] But there were Dundee manufacturers too who boasted that their product was superior, for instance, to the 'deficient' Osnaburgs from Kirriemuir, which was lighter (20 and 22 porter instead of 24) and of lower quality. The Don brothers as well as some Dundee manufacturers added to their range 'Strelitz' Osnaburg, which was slightly wider and used higher-quality yarns, although a tow variant was also made. Lint or tow, Strelitz commanded a higher price and was sought by London dealers who also served the transatlantic market.[65] In a further effort

106 THE TRIUMPH OF TEXTILES

to maintain quality (or the appearance thereof), the way in which cloth from Dundee was packaged was greatly improved too. Prior to the 1820s, bales were light, loosely wrapped (or 'lapped') in the outside sheets of the cloth pieces that had been hand beetled. After experimenting with calendering and press-packing machinery from Glasgow, William Shaw, a Dundee spinner, managed to perfect a heavy steam-powered calenderer which enhanced the appearance of the finished cloth as well as giving the coarse linens 'more body than they really possess'.[66]

Genuine improvement, however, came a few years later. Almost immediately after opening their weaving factory at Dens in 1836, Baxter Brothers were turning out a 'finer class of linens than had formerly been manufactured at Dundee'.[67] While Baxter Brothers and other large houses had their own calendering facilities, by the mid-1860s there were another seven 'public' calenders which could offer a range of finishes that improved the look of the final product without compromising on quality.[68]

Perhaps surprising given Dundee's unflattering reputation as a global centre for the production of utilitarian bagging and sacking materials, was the importance of product innovation, a factor in the industrialisation process generally that can be overlooked.[69] Aspects of this were noted in Chapter 2, sail canvas and coloured carpeting providing two instances that were crucial to Dundee's emergence as the world's main producer of coarse textiles. At the risk of repetition, it is worth noting that it was after seeing a sample of coloured jute carpeting from Abingdon that both James Neish and the Cox brothers began to manufacture this in Dundee, in the latter case using hemp as the raw material. According to James Cox, this 'took amazingly'. In no small part this was due to Cox's efforts to collaborate with and please his customers (he was, he wrote to one of them, 'most anxious' to do so). In order to maintain good relations, he travelled up and down the country, stopping off at the main towns where he paid visits to current and potential buyers, while his engineering-savvy brother William consulted with them about technical issues such as the kinds of yarns, weaves and designs they wanted in carpeting and other products.[70] Of greater moment was 'bedding' for making straw mattresses. This was striped cloth, 54 inches wide and in various qualities and prices, which became a 'great trade' – and even better when a bright cotton stripe was incorporated into the material.[71] At the same time, however, James Cox did not lose sight of the market there was for products such as hop sacking, gently persuading potential buyers that by blending jute into the mix he could reduce his prices, although even then he frequently met with consumer resistance.[72] There were, however, ways to circumvent the problem: in receipt of an order from Jonathan Dudgeon in Liverpool for bagging for cotton, he advised that while the cloth would comprise a mixture of jute, flax tow and black hemp, the end product would 'have the appearance of hemp'.[73]

Complaints were taken seriously. In 1865 one of Baxter Brothers' longest-established customers, Richardson, Lee & Co. in Manchester, complained about and even sent back some pieces of linen cloth which they described as a 'coarse looking, loose and thin fabric'. An investigation was immediately set in train at Dens, and several flaws identified. Among these were 'great carelessness' in both the preparatory and weaving processes – this last due to work being done by gaslight and a large number of 'learner' weavers. The calendering left much to be desired. 'Hard' yarn (which had been bleached and stove-dried during the winter) too was a problem. However, the fundamental issue was a deterioration in the quality of some of the flax they had purchased, an ongoing problem noted in the previous chapter. The solutions adopted included using less of the harsh and poorly cleaned flax which was now coming from Pernau and instead using a higher proportion of mellower flax from Archangel and Ireland.[74]

Crucial to success though in both the flax and jute industries was obtaining the raw material at the lowest possible price. Cost reductions in the spinning and manufacturing processes were of course important and will be discussed below, but to do well in terms of profitability required 'prudent speculation and timely dealing' on the part of buyers. An American observer made the point even more succinctly, identifying 'foresight' and even 'daring' as essential attributes if a spinner was to succeed financially.[75] In this respect, up-to-the-minute, reliable information was key, as in 1834 when news of a poor flax crop in Russia caused those fortunate enough to be able to 'immediately set to buying up all the flax they could lay their hands on'. For 'daring' can be read as gambling of a sort. The *Dundee Advertiser* reported on the 'anxious faces of the importers when a Russian mail came in'. They would crowd round the agent of a Russian firm, who would gladden the hearts of those who had made successful purchases in advance, while others went away empty-handed with the news 'that the quotations were much above their limits'.[76] Buying the right quantity mattered too and demanded that spinners knew or estimated in advance of the arrival of their raw materials how much product they would be able to sell. To hold too much old stock of flax could be disastrous: 'the moment the fresh supplies begin to arrive what remains of the old will be totally neglected', wrote James Buist in 1836.[77] While there were many circumstances in which such a combustible material could catch fire, stored bales of flax and jute were

108   THE TRIUMPH OF TEXTILES

particularly prone to do so, or even spontaneously combust – leading to
the loss of entire warehouses (which were rarely fireproof until mid-century and more prone to fire than mills). Even though prudent proprietors
insured their raw materials, the costs of lost output and sales were not
covered. Nor was the inconvenience of having to re-recruit workers who
were generally laid off immediately following the more destructive mill
fires. Examples abound, with losses amounting to two or three thousand
pounds or as much as the estimated £50,000 or £60,000 worth of flax
and jute that was lost in a conflagration in a large store on the south side
of the Seagate in June 1855, in which had been stored goods belonging
to several owners, including the firms of Paton and Fleming, Neish and
Small, W. Hendry and J. Crichton.[78] Within two years the first of these,
Paton and Fleming, had erected a spacious, purpose-built, stone-walled
warehouse complex – 'not little creditable to their enterprising spirit' –
with iron doors and a frontage to Trades Lane that was 'an architectural
ornament to the town'.[79]

Yet to strike a deal on the current year's harvest too early, when the
price could be high, could also be financially ruinous. So too was to be
left without a sufficient quantity to spin and in this respect the smaller
mills struggled to survive, being dependent on what flax they could store
themselves or hold – at a cost – in warehouses. Yet there were times when
spinners used flax shortages to their advantage, by working shorter hours
and raising their prices for the manufacturers, in effect holding them
to ransom.[80] The way round this was costly – but beneficial. It was to
create vast integrated complexes which contained warehouses and both
spinning and weaving facilities (along with a host of other processes), as
happened most notably at Baxter's multifaceted Dens Works and later at
Cox's Camperdown complex in the 1850s and 1860s on what was ultimately a vast multi-acre site. By adding to warehouse capacity, owners
could buy varieties of flax when the quality was good and retain it for
use in response to the vagaries of consumer demand over a longer period
of time.

Initially, dealing directly with the purchasing agents was the preferred
method for those with sufficient credit. The system was carried on into
the jute era, through resident Scottish agents who bought jute on orders
from Calcutta merchant houses who in their turn were instructed from
Dundee.[81] The jute market was complex and demanded intimate knowledge of the various types of raw jute: the main ones were Uttariya – the
finest, Desi (mainly used in gunny bags), Sirajganj (more easily bleached),
Deora, Daisee and Naraingunge.[82] Purchasers too had to be able to distinguish within these categories the quality of the raw material. For such

ANGUS FLAX MERCHANTS TO 'LORDS O' JUTEOPOLIS' 109

reasons some firms became even more closely linked with India, as for example the enterprising Gilroy Brothers who not only grew jute on land they purchased in Bengal, but also shipped it to Dundee directly in their own vessels, the two largest being the aptly named *George Gilroy* and the *Dundee*.[83] Sometime after 1857, when Bowbridge Works was opened, Joseph Grimond travelled to Calcutta in order to obtain good-quality jute, and subsequently opened an office there and appointed staff who would select and buy the best they could find on the Grimonds' behalf.[84] The larger firms – the Cox's, H. Walker & Sons, John Sharp & Sons, Don Bros, Buist, Malcolm, Ogilvie & Co. and some others – did much the same. Most shipments arrived after September, when the new crop was harvested, and the following spring, after a passage of around 130 days for a sea journey of some 10,000 miles.

There were opportunities to shave costs at the other end of the production process too, when selling yarn or cloth. Traditionally, Scottish linen for export had been sold through middlemen, that is agents based in marketing and distribution centres such as Glasgow, Liverpool and London.[85] This was not only costly given that the agents had to be paid a commission for their services. There was frustration too for Dundee-based manufacturers or merchants who bought local yarns and cloth in response to orders from customers through agents elsewhere. This happened when, for example, agents sold Dundee-made or locally bought cloth at lower prices than anticipated or, keen for a sale that would boost their commission, they sold too quickly just as information might have been filtering through to Dundee of impending improvements in market conditions. Accordingly, negotiations by letter with agents in Glasgow, London and elsewhere (the only option before the invention of the electric telegraph) and their customers who could be overseas, were often tetchy and unproductive. As in June 1825, when John Moir expressed his deep disappointment with the American 'friends' of John Bell in Glasgow, as he had heard from a 'neighbour of mine whose bagging was much inferior in quality [to mine]' that he was able to obtain two-pence more per yard in Charleston.[86] With bulk orders frequently amounting to hundreds if not thousands of yards of cloth, the impact on income and profits could be immense.

It was Edward Baxter who led the way in Dundee in ending the system and dealing directly with buyers abroad. It was an obvious but significant move which, by securing for Dundee's firms the profits that had formerly gone to the factors, was recognised and applauded by his contemporaries.[87] Very soon afterwards Baxter was appointed – by the United States government – as a consular officer, and in 1834 upgraded to US Consul for Dundee. In this capacity he was able to gain inside knowledge of marketing opportunities in the US, along with performing a similar role in Britain and Europe for US exporters.

But to satisfy customer demand and indeed create new markets, innovation was needed on the production side too. In part this meant increasing volumes of yarn and cloth, but also ensuring that the quality of what was made was reputable and uniform. The solution lay in the utilisation of machinery, at most stages of the production process. In general, mechanisation was adopted as a strategy to reduce labour and capital costs.[88] But quality and standardisation were important considerations too. Until the end of the eighteenth century all the flax was prepared, spun, woven and finished by hand. However, for merchants like the aforementioned James Cox who purchased the yarn and then put it and the webs out to the handloom weavers, the situation became increasingly unsatisfactory. While there were many talented hand spinners who could draw fine yarns from the flax, there were others – 'slubber spinners' – whose yarns were thicker and prone to break at the reeling stage.[89] Regardless of the quality of the yarn produced, putting-out merchants had little control over the time a spinner devoted to such work, and how much was made. With literally thousands of women and girls so engaged – as many as four-fifths of Scotland's adult females may have been involved in spinning to some extent – it was little wonder that there were such variations in quality and output.[90] The same was true of the woven cloth, all of which was produced by handloom weavers.

This was a problem faced in the textile trades across the country, whether in cotton or wool or other materials. Cotton spinning was the first to be successfully mechanised. The invention of water-powered flax-spinning machinery by Kendrew & Porthouse in Darlington in 1787 appeared to offer a solution for the flax trade. In fact, in the same year a spinning mill was erected in Inverbervie, several miles to the north of Dundee, fitted out with machinery from England. But it was nearer Dundee, probably in 1788, that the first mill for spinning heavy yarn used in making Osnaburgs was set going. James Ivory, a teacher of mathematics in the town, and his partners converted a corn mill into a mill specifically to spin heavier yarns, and erected housing for its workers in what became Douglastown. Although little is known about Ivory, we can reasonably assume that like many British inventors and innovators he was able to benefit from the prevailing culture of scientific inquisitiveness and the sharing of practical knowledge that was a feature of the Enlightenment period generally. Close observation in order to gain an understanding of why a particular device worked as it did, badly or

ANGUS FLAX MERCHANTS TO 'LORDS O' JUTEOPOLIS'

well, was a feature common to Dundee's technical innovators from the beginning.[91] In Dundee, an 'alert town of ambitious, intelligent people', including 'unusually literate' readers of an array of newspapers and periodicals, there was both a Speculative Society and, from 1811, a Rational Institution, through which up-to-date information was channelled and where ideas were debated.[92] More directly relevant was the opening in 1826 in Dundee of its own mechanics' institute, the Watt Institution. Built in honour of James Watt (d. 1819), rather than a statue (a campaign for which, in London, had sparked interest in Dundee) it was a utilitarian vehicle for the instruction of tradesmen and others largely in practical subjects; notably, at the founding meeting, five of the twenty-three attendees were 'operative flaxspinners'.[93] In a similar mould, and avidly read when they became available shortly afterwards, were *Chambers Journal* and *Tait's Magazine*.

In 1806 an operation similar to Douglastown was begun in nearby Glamis, at the instigation of Patrick Proctor, factor to the earl of Strathmore.[94] Also in the forefront were individuals such as William Brown (of East Ward Mill, in Dundee itself), and James Carmichael, father of Peter Carmichael (later, of Baxter Brothers). But there were lesser-known figures who won admiration too, such as the Rev. James Smith, of the Quoad Sacra Church in Lower Chapelshade. Originally a weaver, Smith managed to set up (around 1806) and operate with some success a crude mill at Gateside in north Fife, while at the same time managing to preach in Dundee every Sunday and write about divinity.[95]

But in virtually every case the pioneer mills failed to live up to the hopes of their proprietors. They tended to be erected by wheelwrights rather than millwrights (then an infant trade) and were poorly laid out internally. Management of machinery and workpeople in what was for most a new and even an alien environment was a major problem – although the challenge of finding the right calibre of individuals who could organise and take the tactical decisions about the day-to-day running of the first mills and the centralised processes that followed was by no means unique to Dundee.[96] We will see later just how important managers and other supervisory staff were for the successful operation of mills, factories and allied premises employing large numbers of people.

PRODUCTION AND PRODUCTIVITY

Above all, however, the problems were technical, flax proving to be too brittle to be drawn out at any length without breaking, or indeed damaging the machinery. The quality of what was spun was variable. So too was the availability of water in the streams alongside which the early mills were located, with lengthy interruptions at certain times of the year, notably during the winter months. Furthermore, it proved impossible to spin tow which, ironically, with demand for yarn growing, gave the hand spinners a new lease of life at a time when their livelihoods looked to be threatened by the machine.[97]

Yet as was noted in Chapter 1, in Dundee itself, steam engine-powered spinning mills were established during the first years of the nineteenth century. This inaugurated a feature of Dundee's industrial development that continued through the rest of the century. It can best be categorised as bold but pragmatic experimentation, and was crucial for the lead Dundee took in coarse linen production as well as for the town's later global ascendancy in jute. Fortunately, almost from the commencement of steam engine-powered spinning, there was a small cohort of men with technical knowledge and experience of managing spinning machinery in the water-powered mills that could be adapted to their urban counterparts.[98] Progress though was far from straightforward, as indicated by the number of failed ventures. As just noted, the supply of mechanics was limited.[99]

In the early days at least, there seemed to be something of a collective approach to the challenges the mill proprietors faced. According to Charles Mackie, proprietors and mill managers were in the habit of visiting each other's premises, so that 'no mill should get before them'; the facility for 'mutual copying' that close proximity allowed, may well have been a contributory factor in Dundee's success in comparison to other parts of the country where linen was manufactured but on a more scattered basis.[100] It was cooperation of this kind that around 1830 heralded 'a new era in spinning', according to one contemporary: namely the successful experiment by one spinner to double the speed of his spinning frames without yarn breakages, the others then following suit.[101] But not at this stage in jute, which despite the attempts to spin with it outlined in the last chapter, could not easily be spun, mixed with other yarns or woven, other than as weft for sacking or carpeting.[102]

The most ambitious spinners, mechanics and engineers, however, didn't restrict their investigations to Dundee, but travelled to the country's other textile towns, as well as to Ireland and France, observing where they could gain access to works or glean information from local sources about how mills and factories were organised, and what machinery was used in them. Leeds was the main attraction, with Marshalls' works – 'the most extensive and best regulated in Britain' – seen as the model for others to follow. Dundee's textile entrepreneurs did patent several devices during the course of the nineteenth century.[103] However, as with other Scottish industrialists of the period, their usual practice was to imitate the best technology and methods from elsewhere and adapt these in accordance with specific local needs. 'Trying to invent is a great mistake', reflected Dens Works' Peter Carmichael. Instead, he chose through scrupulously detailed investigation into imperfect or problematic processes to make what were often minor adjustments to machinery and working practices, the cumulative effect of which was profound. By this means he was able to maintain Baxters as the nation's (and for a time the world's) leading flax and linen producer until his gradual retreat from active involvement in the company in the later 1870s.[104] But in his endeavour to match and even improve on best practice and desire to be at the cutting edge of flax- and jute- manufacturing machinery Carmichael was not alone. The spirit of the age, Alexander Warden reflected, 'is so thoroughly bent on utilitarian improvements that every spinning and weaving establishment in town has made wonderful progress, and . . . [was] applicable to all, even the most unpretending'.[105] Perseverance in improving machinery, often by small unheralded steps, which had eliminated much hand labour, cheapened production costs and improved the quality of the material put out, David Bremner concluded in 1868, was the main reason for the prosperity of Dundee's staple trade.[106]

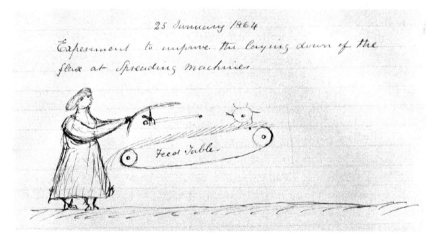

Figure 3.3 Sketch by Peter Carmichael of Baxter Brothers, 1865. This is a rare image of a female flax preparer, drawn using one of the many machines Carmichael either invented or improved. © University of Dundee Archives.

114   THE TRIUMPH OF TEXTILES

This was effected by frequent upgrading of machinery, as in 1862 when at Dens a new spinning mill was proposed. This would increase the number of spindles, but more importantly, reduce the number of spinners required from sixty-seven to twenty-five, with a consequent fall in wages from just over £16 16s (£16.30) a week to £10 16s (£10.30).[107] But there were other, less obvious ways to achieve efficiency gains. An early instance was at William Brown's East Mill. There his chief mechanic was instructed to identify the worst card or breaker (devices used to comb the long, tangled jute fibres as they were taken from the tightly packed bales) in the preparing room and, after minute inspection, to attempt to alter it until it was performing like or better than the best. 'This is the way to carry out improvements', observed Brown, 'and, if persisted, will no doubt be successful.'[108] What this case hints at, is the importance of good managers, mechanics and engineers.[109] Despite this, they too rarely make other than fleeting appearances in the evidence available, as in the case of a Mr Singers who played a prominent role at the Baxters' Dens Works prior to the arrival of Peter Carmichael.[110] When they do, however, more often than not they appear to have been highly regarded, by their employers and, often, those who worked under their direction. Technical ability, including inventiveness, were sought-after attributes. Much later in the century, William Leggatt, who had spent some time at Dens before becoming manager at Manhattan Works, was credited with being one of the country's most respected authorities on jute spinning and weaving, and prior to his untimely early death wrote some of the best-known manuals on these subjects, as for example *The Art of Weaving*.[111] A lifelong Congregationalist, like several of his counterparts, Leggatt shared the religious values held by some of Dundee's employers, noted above. Similar was James M'Glashan, formerly manager at Pole Park Works, at the time of his death in 1885 judged by Dundee's most prominent churchman in the nineteenth century, the Rev. George Gilfillan, to have been 'one of God's gentlemen'.[112]

Not all enhancements, however, were incremental. Severe bottlenecks in aspects of the production process had to be broken through by a combination of technical ingenuity and determination on the part of the burgh's more ambitious textile entrepreneurs. The opening of the first country mills had been met with alarm – and physical opposition – from the female population in Forfarshire, who had created what seems to have been a fulfilling and familiar way of life in which part-time spinning and the culture associated with this was part. Owners and managers had had to overcome this resistance to mill work through a combination of strategies that included monetary rewards, the prospect of regular employment and the transplantation and adaptation within the new workplaces of the paternalistic relationships with employees that had prevailed in the countryside. This was a drawn-out process.

Much more compressed was the struggle with the flax dressers, or hecklers. This was a body of men who separated, cleaned and combed the raw flax (as it was taken from the bales in which it was packaged) to varying degrees of fineness prior to spinning. A crucial operation, carried out by hand, by the 1820s hand heckling had been identified as a serious impediment to the smooth running of what was the increasingly mechanised spinning process, for without the hecklers flax could not be spun. Tightly organised both in Dundee and indeed nationally and used to determining how hard, for how long and at what price they worked, the flax dressers had become 'a dislocating element in the system of spinning'. Aware of their importance in the process, in the words of Peter Carmichael they became 'self-assertive, over-bearing, dictatorial and ready to stand out for their demands', as they did by frequently withdrawing their labour.[113] With spinners' livelihoods dependent upon their ability to obtain good-quality heckled flax – some having their favourite dressers[114] – it was difficult for those masters who were keen to break the hecklers' combinations to cooperate as a body. Only by building a sizeable stock of dressed flax would they be able to hold out long enough to break a strike.[115] It was a dispute in 1827 that induced the first attempt – in Belfast – to heckle by machine, which in 1834 led to another, four months long, strike in Dundee.[116] Two years later, and crucial for Dundee, was the appearance of John Sharp's hemp- and flax-preparing machinery, which he patented at the end of 1836.[117] Although there were limits to what Sharp's machine could do, which meant that the hand-heckling trade carried on for some time, the new device, operated by boys and girls, represented a major breakthrough. It was not the end of the story, however, although with further modifications to their machinery the Baxters were able to start paying off the most troublesome hecklers at the end of 1845 and a year later to dispense with the last of them.[118] For many, however, this was not the end of the road as far as demand for their skills was concerned. More than a hundred of them left Dundee and found employment in France, in the linen and jute works the Baxters had a share in in Ailly.[119] As with the eighteenth-century linen trade, Dundonian skill and knowledge was much in demand. It was mechanics and other workers from Dundee who provided the technical expertise and skills required to get this enterprise built and running – one of the first in France to work with jute.[120]

116   THE TRIUMPH OF TEXTILES

At Dens the deterioration in the quality of tow imported from St Petersburg and the Baltic from the mid-1850s had a 'disastrous' effect on the manufacture of all kinds of cloth, 'from Canvas to the lowest class of tow'. Costs too had risen, with the proportion of waste rising to 24 per cent, although this was an improvement on the 1820s when the proportion of waste in Tay Street Mill, where Charles Gill of Leeds' preparing machine had been adopted, was 40 per cent.[121] The solution, reached after extensive discussions over ways to proceed, was a double set of drawing rollers that would better clean the raw material in which 'seed bolls' had been embedded. Patented in 1860, the effect was almost immediate: during the first two years after its introduction the quantity of waste fell to just over 6 per cent.[122] Not only did this produce a cost saving of well over £9,000 in the course of a year, but with the better yarns more spinning could be done, which raised the annual profit on the spinning operation (1,500 spindles at sixpence each) at Dens by £1,875. This, however, was the case for flax. Even by 1856, heckling was still being done by hand in Thomson's Seafield carpet works, 'no hackling [sic] machine yet invented for jute doing its work so well as the hand hacklers' (of which there were eighty employed). This would quickly change. Not only had Peter Carmichael invented (and patented) his heckling machine some years earlier, but more important for Dundee's jute sector was the availability of James Combe of Belfast's 'automaton-like' 'Patent Intersecting Heckling Machine', specially devised for jute.[123]

Another major constraint for those manufacturers intent on increasing the volumes of the cloth they were able to market was the capacity of the handloom weavers to turn out more cloth, as cheaply as possible. As in other parts of Europe – Ireland, for example – where linen was made domestically, most handloom weavers were either small-scale farmers, rural cottagers or the inhabitants of small settlements who had access to some land upon which to keep a cow and perhaps some other livestock and grow vegetables.[124]

There was less flexibility for the growing numbers of more or less full-time handloom weavers who clustered in the burgh's Bucklemaker Wynd and the Chapelshade, Hilltown and Seagate districts, often using looms handed down by fathers and grandfathers. Here there was a greater concentration of weavers, including those in workshops of various dimensions where masters could more easily supervise their employees who rented looms from them. By around 1830 there were some four hundred 'manufacturers' (also termed 'household weavers') in Dundee who between them had between four and five thousand looms, that is an average of between ten and twelve each, clustered together in houses where the manufacturer also lived, as well as organising the heckling, boiling and starching processes.[125] One such integrated premises was offered for sale in 1819. The house had three bedrooms, a dining room, a kitchen and cellar, a boiling room, two starching lofts, a warehouse and twelve looms. Most had far fewer than this.[126] A handful had more. These included weaving sheds like the handloom 'Factory' belonging to Thomas Webster & Co. in Hawkhill, or William Halley's in Forebank. Over time, however, home working and the smaller weaving shops were abandoned and replaced by weaving sheds or factories, ranging from those housing as few as thirty-six looms to those with three hundred or more.

Even so, there were limits to the gains that could be obtained from such concentration and closer regulation of the weaving process. One of the most irritating issues for employers, albeit it was predictable (and commonplace throughout most of industrialising Britain), was the propensity of weavers and others to stick with their pre-industrial work routine. Even as late as the 1860s, masters of handloom-weaving factories complained but could do little about the fact that many weavers worked only half of Monday and then only hard from Tuesday morning – a continuation of pre-industrial practice. Despite laying down rules for weekday working hours from 6 am until 8 pm, Thomas Sime, the foreman at Ritchie and Simpson's 165-loom factory in Nelson Street, reported to Hugh Seymour Tremenheere's investigators for the Royal Commission on children's employment in 1864 that as they were paid by the piece, 'the workers come as they please'.[127] In addition was the weavers' habit of abandoning their looms in accordance with the agricultural cycle – that is, to sow in the spring and then take a week or two off for the later summer harvest. The temporary absence of 'hands' frustrated James Cox as he attempted to build a solid customer base, apologising in September 1840 that as most of them were out 'at harvest', the promised delivery of an order for sacking cloth would be difficult to honour.[128] The practice was still in evidence more than two decades later, with one English visitor who had visited Dundee to enquire after employment opportunities for unemployed workers from Preston reporting (with a degree of exaggeration) that 'Early in spring, a great many factory hands leave the mills at the setting of the potatoes, and remain out till the harvest is over.'[129]

If such absences from the loom were customary and long-established, other challenges arose from the tensions there were between manufacturers and their weaver employees, the latter digging their heels in by refusing to weave certain kinds of cloth and exerting what pressure they could on their employers through collective action.[130] For their part the manufacturers were squeezing the weavers increasingly hard, exploiting the freer hand they had by being no longer subject to the rules laid down by the stampmasters. The most controversial of the measures they took was to extend the length of the webs they gave out to their weavers. At the turn of the century webs had been 102 yards long; by the early 1830s the lengths had been increased to an average of 130 yards, although not uniformly. Regional and local competition between manufacturers was fierce and had demanded action of the kind taken by the Dundee masters; weavers in rural Perthshire making Osnaburgs may have been putting out as many as 150 yards per piece, while sheetings and shirtings measured around 135 yards.[131] The ell too – the unit by which cloth was traditionally measured (at 45 inches) – had been elongated, with only one firm, Richards & Co. in Baltic Street, being credited with having stuck to the old extent. Payments to the weavers, however, were by the full piece, and not by the yard. And across the board, the prices paid to the weavers were reduced, from around 16s per piece in 1809 to half this by 1833.[132]

The handloom weavers' response, which was to organise resistance through collective action, was troubling but not crippling. The employing manufacturers concerned laid off as many as 1,200 of the offending workers, a good number of which were Irish, and invited 'Industrious and well-disposed men' to come to Dundee and fill their places.[133] Which they did. Quite simply, the handloom-weaver labour market was over-full so that new openings were quickly filled. Thousands – women, who were recruited to weave lighter cloths, as well as men – had been drawn into the trade by the prospect of earning relatively high wages and enjoying the agreeable working conditions that had prevailed during the 'Golden Age' of the 1790s and first decade of the nineteenth century.[134]

But this was not a lasting solution to challenges of the kind that flax spinners had had to face some decades earlier. The answer was the same as had been applied to the hand-heckling trade during the two previous decades: mechanisation. The power loom had been invented by Edmund Cartwright in 1786 and after a lag was successfully employed for linen weaving in Aberdeen, by Sir John Maberley at his Broadford Works in 1824. At this time a power-weaving flat was set up at Dens, but the looms were abandoned shortly afterwards. In part this was due to resistance on the part of the handloom weavers and fears on the part of employers of Luddite-type attacks on their machinery and premises of the kind that had rocked the textile districts in England. There appears to have been a limited appetite for confrontation and change among the manufacturers,

ANGUS FLAX MERCHANTS TO 'LORDS O' JUTEOPOLIS' 119

who in general were 'well-pleased' with their manner of life as small-scale employers (sometimes termed 'wee corks') and standard of living.[135] The fact is too that mechanisation was no straightforward matter. The early machinery, whether for winding, warping, dressing or weaving, was described as 'miserable affairs', each one with its own peculiarities, at worst manifesting as 'a stubborn fit' that required half a day's work to get it to work well.[136] Much if not most was imported to Dundee, primarily from Belfast, Glasgow, Leeds and the other British textile centres. This situation transformed in the early decades of the nineteenth century; as with the other textile towns in Britain, the emergence of local engineering and machinery-making firms such as J. and C. Carmichael and, later, Messrs Low in Monifeith was crucial. But while enormous strides forward were made in making mill and factory machinery in foundries and workshops in and near Dundee, including at some of the largest works such as Baxters, numerous firms elsewhere in Scotland (mainly Glasgow) and the UK provided specific equipment such as high-powered steam engines.[137] Dundee's emergence as a major industrial centre, as with Scotland as a whole, was British made.

Not all manufacturers were satisfied with their lot, however. In 1836 David Baxter broke ranks and made another attempt, this time fairly successfully, aided by John Bruce, an inventive handloom manufacturer in Dundee, and helped by several experienced power-loom weavers under the management of Hugh McGow, who he had managed to attract from Aberdeen. Driven by a 25 horsepower engine, the loom factory, at 150 feet long and 75 feet wide, was 'looked upon as one of the wonders of Dundee'. Within six years the Baxters had managed to introduce yet another game-changing innovation. This was not just by employing females as weavers in a trade that hitherto had largely been a male preserve. Rather, exploiting the trade depression of 1842 and the fact that almost 1,500 weavers in the town were out of work, Peter Carmichael and his colleagues initiated a short-lived negotiation involving both carrots and the heavier stick of dismissal, which resulted in agreement that each weaver – now all female – should be responsible for minding two looms.[138] After Carmichael's patenting of a heckling and rubbing machine (the second he patented in 1846), which further reduced the need for hand labour, by the mid-1840s the looms at Dens were turning out some 60,000 yards of cloth each week.[139] The scorn which the proposal for two-loom working had been met with initially soon turned to admiration – not least as the length of each web or piece was increased to 165 yards and the wage per piece reduced. At the same time, the Jacquard method for changing the shuttle instead of by hand

120   THE TRIUMPH OF TEXTILES

was incorporated. Even more significant was another labour-saving (and de-skilling) device, again invented by Carmichael. This was the self-acting rubbing machine which dispensed with the need for the weaver to rub the web by hand to equalise the warp and tighten the selvedge – 'the principal part of her skill'. A 'most profitable' innovation, one such machine, which cost £60 at most, could with the labour of a single boy treat a hundred looms 'in an infinitely superior manner'.[140]

This though applied to the weaving factory at Upper Dens. Although the cloth produced was of a high standard, it took some time – years – for the technical challenges outlined to be overcome and for power-loom weaving to become the norm elsewhere. Even the Baxters' own facility at Glamis employed 228 handloom weavers, two hundred of whom were women. In 1851 there were more handloom factories in Dundee (sixty-two) than spinning mills (forty three) or power-loom factories (eight).[141] And while the foundation stone for what would become the Cox brothers' consolidated Camperdown Works was laid on 1 January 1850, they continued to employ carpet weavers working in their own homes in nearby Lochee. Change came two years later, but only in that the Cox's added a handloom factory at the Camperdown site, owing to the inconvenience of putting out webs and collecting the finished pieces prior to them being finished at the works' newly installed calender. In 1868 there were seven hundred power looms producing some 14 million yards of sacking each year, but jute carpeting was still being made on three hundred handlooms.[142] Similar was the Grimonds' Maxwelltown Works, erected 1847–8, which specialised in world-renowned jute Brussels carpets; initially this was a vast handloom-weaving operation – and reputedly where conditions were worst as the dye came off so that a weaver 'looks as black as a sheep from it'.[143] In 1861, during a dispute in August, Heathfield Carpet Works advertised for handloom weavers to replace the striking men, with assurance given that those taken on would be trained in 'Three-leaved sacking' and the other heavy fabrics the firm produced.[144] The future, however, lay in power looms, even if growth was slow at first. In 1856 there were only 2,075.[145] A partial explanation for this was the reluctance by buyers to accept cloth woven on power looms; the Admiralty was one of these, as were hosepipe manufacturers.[146] But thereafter the number of power looms multiplied as manufacturers experimented with various kinds of loom, and cloths. The advantages of so doing were easily apparent, with those used in Seafield Works producing more than four times what a handloom could turn out, at a quarter of the expense in wages.[147] Indeed, as demand for coarse cloth intensified with the outbreak of the Civil War in America, there was reckoned to be a shortage of between three hundred and five hundred power-loom weavers in Dundee. Glasgow women were deemed to be the best suited to this role and were encouraged to travel east to secure the available work.[148] During much of the 1860s power-loom numbers multiplied rapidly in Dundee and Forfarshire, with an increase of 53 per cent estimated to have taken place between 1862 and 1864 (5,514 to 8,421). The vast bulk of these – 6,709 – were in Dundee and Lochee.[149] Largely owing to their being located outside the factories, it was difficult to estimate how many handloom weavers there were. With many of them ageing and unable to find alternative employment, and as it suited employers to retain their services for particular types of cloth as there was no risk to their capital, the numbers involved in this dying trade remained stubbornly high.[150] There may have been as many as five thousand in the mid-1860s.[151]

Much more immediate in its effect was a cost-saving measure Carmichael had introduced in 1864. Hitherto Baxters had employed a 'staff of strong men' as porters at the firm's dockside warehouse. Relatively well paid at £2 per week, during the summer while unloading an unusually large number of ships the porters had exercised what they considered to be their traditional right to employ others to assist them. Carmichael though had had enough, and refused to pay the additional expense. Consequently, the porters 'left in an evening without further warning'. Carmichael's response was swift and decisive: it was to order a small 3 horsepower locomotive that could be operated by a 'lad' for 5s a week, thus almost at a stroke reducing wage costs and ensuring there would be no further strikes.[152]

MACHINES AND MANAGEMENT

The technical advances discussed in this chapter are simply the best known. Many others – as hinted by Bremner and Warden and confirmed by the detailed notes on costs and output kept by men like Carmichael – were less well publicised. Even the well-connected insider Alexander Warden was unable to document the improvements in jute spinning that made this a viable yarn; the dates and nature of these 'were unnoted and remain unknown'.[153] But not all processes could be mechanised, particularly during the transition to jute. Reeling and warping, for example, the stage between spinning and weaving, continued to be done by hand, 'the short length of jute yarn on the bobbin not making it desirable to drive the machines by power'.[154]

122 THE TRIUMPH OF TEXTILES

Occasionally too productivity gains were simply the outcome of serendipity. At Dens in 1862, for example, dry rot was discovered in the main weaving shed. The solution was to cover the wooden beams with cast-iron boxes through which air was fanned, thus reducing the amount of rot-inducing stagnant air. A consequent drop in temperature had the unexpected effect of increasing the amount of cloth put out by the weavers – as well as their wages. With no provision previously either for heating or cooling the room, during the summer it had been 'no uncommon thing for many of the girls to turn sick at their work in the afternoon'. But no longer, with the weavers' improved performance, it was concluded, being due to the better ventilation of the space.[155] Until this point, ventilation had rarely been a consideration.[156]

How the mills and factories were laid out was another determinant of efficiency and cost – and ultimately, therefore, profit levels. The older premises which had been adapted and extended served their purpose during the first phase of steam-powered flax spinning in Dundee. But they had their limitations. This was recognised by William Brown, of East Mill. There was a place for 'repairs, enlargements and alterations', he conceded, as long as these were executed in a 'judicious, skilful, liberal and substantial manner'; slight, 'patched up' work, on the other hand, led to 'decay' and distress and even failure for proprietors.[157] But even new premises could present difficulties. These were, observed Charles Mackie, often too small, the ceilings of the flats low and lacking daylight. Tightness of space meant that some machinery was hard to operate.[158]

From the 1840s onwards, however, new works began to replace the older structures. Among the first, around 1850, were Edward Street Mill, Upper Dens, Tay Works and Camperdown. Not only were these larger, more spacious, and better lit (with natural light through big windows and glass roofs) and ventilated. David Bremner commended the Cox's for the height (of 14 to 17 feet), light and ventilation of their rooms at Camperdown.[159] They were also grander and more ornate than their predecessors. Critically, however, more works were also more closely integrated and on one level – the shed system – so that all the processes involved in flax and jute production were housed not necessarily under the same roof, but on the same site, which now occupied several acres. It was not until 1872, however, that the first fully integrated complex of this kind was designed and built: Robertson and Orchar's Caldrum Works for Harry Walker & Sons.[160]

The move towards the shed system was partly necessary owing to the weight of much of the machinery used for jute spinning and weaving. Power looms, which vibrated heavily, were best located on the ground floor, which led in the 1870s to the gradual abandonment of multistorey works, which in Dundee had generally been lower. Four storeys high was the usual maximum (although there were notable exceptions, such as the Gilroys' Tay Works), unlike in cotton.[161] Accordingly, some of the new greenfield locations were on the outskirts of Dundee rather than in the central area, where they had clustered around the main sources of running water. There had been plenty of this at Dens. Not only was there a spring, but the burn itself was dammed and the water stored in ponds. Elsewhere, however, especially to the west, mill owners struggled against nature and with each other as they dug ever-deeper wells to supply their needs.[162]

But as was remarked as the Grimonds' Bowbridge Works, Clepington, were under construction in 1859, 'The economy of labour . . . [was] a guiding principle' when plans were being laid.[163] The example given was the preparing flat where the machines required for the six different processes were placed in parallel lines, with the output from each passing smoothly to the next stage. Technically efficient, such a layout had the additional advantage of providing an ideal space in which managers and overseers could survey and supervise their workers. The need for discipline, as determined by the clock and machines, in the enclosed spaces in which industrial workers performed their various tasks, had been recognised by the first mill owners and managers, not only in Dundee but across industrialising Britain.[164] Working time is a crucial element of economic production; many but by no means all historians believe that the better utilisation of labour was one of the keys to industrial success.[165] William Brown had been in no doubt as to what was required. Mill 'hands' should be kept busy: 'The more closely they are held at their work, the more comfortable they are . . . It is a mistaken humanity to indulge them in ease, idleness or play.' Instructions should be delivered firmly, but fairly, and followed up with reprimands and punishments if disobeyed.[166]

In order to distinguish working life from that of family and community, barriers were created, for example by enclosing workplaces inside high walls, with entry and particularly exits controlled at manned gates. Within the mill and factory complexes – in effect townships within the town – steps were taken to ensure that as much supervision as possible was undertaken, with a hierarchy of controls instituted. In the weaving shed, for example, there were overseers, assistant overseers and 'tenters', men who set up and tuned the looms but who also worked 'as a sub-foreman who exercised authority over the [female] weavers and controlled the pace at which they worked'. Although much attention has been paid to the gendered nature of such controls, males were not exempt from the efforts of employers to impose upon them mill and

Figure 3.4 Mr G. Brown (c. 1865), a mill manager in Baxters' Dens Works. Mill managers played a key role in the development of the textile industry, recruiting, drilling and supervising the workforce. Although greatly appreciated by their employers, some were guilty of abusing those in their charge, although many were regarded with affection by those they managed. © University of Dundee Archives.

factory discipline, although given the peripatetic nature of some of their work, which meant they were less often under a supervisor's gaze, this was more difficult to instil. Even so, at Dens even the night watchmen had to be watched. In July 1864 an 'Inspector of Night Watchmen' was appointed, with strict instructions to take an 'occasional walk' around the premises to ensure that the night watchmen were performing their duties; a regular routine was to be avoided, so that the watchmen would never know 'what hour he may visit them'.[167] With the shed system it became possible – indeed, was planned to be so – for virtually all workers in each department to be observed, and their behaviour, performance and absences monitored.[168]

Notwithstanding the remarkable productivity gains achieved due to the technological advances made since the first spinning mills were erected in and around Dundee, there were limits to what machinery on its own could achieve. Traditional skills such as heckling might have been dispensed with, but the new technologies often demanded different kinds of expertise, without which they were unable to reach the potential their inventors envisaged. Some of the innovations introduced at Dens to improve the heckling process were noted earlier. Also noted were problems arising from a drop in the quality of Russian and Estonian flax during the 1860s. A similar situation had occurred the previous decade, during the Crimean War, which had an adverse effect on the quality of the canvas being produced. On this occasion, however, a shortage of skilled labour was identified as the issue, with the drawings and rovings from the preparing machines getting 'out of order from laps and ends running away'. This, knots and other imperfections in the yarn were due more to this cause 'than apparently from any other'.[169] At Lower Dens at the same time similar problems were encountered, namely a shortage of docile workers (those in post had become 'troublesome') and a 'want of skill in overseers'.[170]

While works' engineers and mechanics made the more substantial contributions to what was an ongoing search for efficiency gains, certainly at Dens according to Peter Carmichael, 'a great deal of success had been owing to the workpeople themselves' who, rather than opposing improvements, made suggestions based on their own observations and experience.[171] The suggestion here is of a more harmonious relationship between Dundee's employers and their workers than has often been portrayed, although admittedly references to industrial strife and social conflict usually apply to the period beginning in the mid-1870s.[172] Allied to this is the broader question of how the working classes fared during the early phases of industrialisation in Britain. It will be seen in the next chapter that in Dundee at least, there are more substantial grounds for optimism on this score than is often assumed.

Notes

1. S. Waterhouse, *Report on Jute Culture and the Importance of the Industry* (Washington, 1883), p. 5.
2. *Chambers Edinburgh Journal*, 167 (13 March 1847), p. 161.
3. *Fife Herald*, 18 June 1857.
4. B. Lenman, C. Lythe and E. Gauldie, *Dundee and its Textile Industry 1850–1914* (Dundee, p. 20).
5. E. Gauldie, *The Dundee Textile Industry 1790–1885* (Edinburgh, 1969), p. xv.

6. W. Stewart Howe, *The Dundee Textiles Industry 1960–1977* (Aberdeen, 1982), p. 7; Nicholas J. Morgan, 'Textiles', in Anthony Slaven and Sydney Checkland (eds), *Dictionary of Scottish Business Biography 1860–1960, Volume I, The Staple Industries* (Aberdeen, 1986), pp. 300–1.
7. M. S. Moss and J. R. Hume, 'Business failure in Scotland 1839–1913: A research note', *Business History*, 25, I (March 1983), pp. 6–7.
8. *Illustrated London News*, 23 July 1862, p. 91.
9. Thomas Woodhouse, 'Spinning and weaving', in A. W. Paton and A. H. Millar (eds), *Handbook and Guide to Dundee and District* (Dundee, 1912), pp. 286–8.
10. Louise Miskell, 'Civic leadership and the manufacturing elite, Dundee, 1820–1870', in Christopher Whatley, Bob Harris and Louise Miskell (eds), *Victorian Dundee: Image and Realities* (2nd edn, Dundee, 2011), pp. 55–6.
11. Alexander Elliot, *Lochee: As it Was and as it Is* (Dundee, 1911), p. 166.
12. UDA, Diary, James Cox, p. 46.
13. Ibid., pp. 58, 62.
14. Anthony J. Cooke, 'Baxter Brothers in Dundee', in A. J. Cooke (ed.), *Baxter's of Dundee* (Dundee, 1980), p. 16.
15. UDA, MS102/1/2, Peter Carmichael, II, Life and Letters, I, p. 258.
16. Christopher A. Whatley, *Onwards from Osnaburgs: The Rise & Progress of a Scottish Textile Company, Don & Low of Forfar, 1792–1992* (Edinburgh, 1992), pp. 57–9.
17. UDA, MS120/1/5, Receipt, John Tyrie for carriage, 10 August 1832; MS120/1/6, David Martin to James Grimond, 25 November 1833, George Renny & Co. to James Grimond, 2 January 1834.
18. UDA, MS120/1/21, John Hadden to James Grimond, 16 October, 1 December 1827.
19. UDA, MS11/5/4, Charles Mackie, 'Reminiscences of Flax Spinning from 1806 to 1866', pp. 32, 48.
20. UDA, MS66/VI/7/2, Harry Walker & Sons, MS Notes by K. Bell.
21. UDA, MS 66/I/5/6/14 (4), Bell & Balfour MS.
22. Gauldie, *Dundee Textile Industry*, pp. xxii–xxiv.
23. Ibid., pp. 3–53.
24. W. Norrie, *Dundee Celebrities of the Nineteenth Century* (Dundee, 1873), p. 364.
25. J. R. L. Halley (ed.), *A History of Halley's Mill, 1822–1980* (Dundee, 1980), pp. 1, 4.
26. UDA, J. R. L. Halley, 'Business in Dundee in the XIXth Century', typescript notes, n.d., p. 3.
27. *Dundee Courier*, 25 February 1892.
28. For biographical details of several of Dundee's linen and jute firms, see the website hosted by the McManus Art Gallery and Museum, Dundee (<https://mcmanus168.org.uk/articles/>).

ANGUS FLAX MERCHANTS TO 'LORDS O' JUTEOPOLIS' 127

29. Kirsten Kininmonth, 'Weber's Protestant ethic: A case study of Scottish entrepreneurs, the Coats family of Paisley', *Business History*, 58: 8 (2016), p. 1243.
30. Miskell, 'Civic leadership', pp. 59–60.
31. Ibid., pp. 57–8.
32. Louise Miskell and C. A. Whatley, '"Juteopolis" in the making: Linen and the industrial transformation of Dundee, c. 1820–1850', *Textile History*, 30: 2 (1999), p. 190.
33. Christopher A. Whatley, 'Frederick Sharp and commercial Dundee', unpublished paper, National Trust for Scotland Open Day, Hill of Tarvit, October 2001, n.p.
34. *Perthshire Advertiser*, 20 April 1826.
35. UDA, Diary, James Cox, pp. 79–80, 92.
36. C. W. Boase, *A Century of Banking in Dundee* (Edinburgh, 1867 edn), pp. xvii–xviii; see too, Charles McKean, Bob Harris and Christopher A. Whatley, 'Introduction to Georgian Dundee', in Charles McKean, Bob Harris and Christopher A. Whatley (eds), *Dundee: Renaissance to Enlightenment* (Dundee, 2009), p. 137.
37. Carmichael, II, Life and Letters, 1, pp. 256–7.
38. Miskell and Whatley, '"Juteopolis" in the making', p. 187.
39. Whatley, 'Frederick Sharp'.
40. UDA, Diary, James Cox, pp. 45–6.
41. Norrie, *Dundee Celebrities*, pp. 372–4.
42. *Dundee Archive and Record Centre* [DARC], DARD GD/X99/10, 'Memoir of Alex Moncur'; *Dundee Courier*, 13 August 1875.
43. Miskell, 'Civic leadership', p. 62.
44. Kininmonth, 'Weber's Protestant ethic', p. 1247.
45. Bob Harris and Charles McKean, *The Scottish Town in the Age of the Enlightenment 1740–1820* (Edinburgh, 2014), p. 400.
46. Mackie, 'Reminiscences', p. 58.
47. Miskell, 'Civic leadership', pp. 56–7.
48. Gauldie, *Dundee Textile Industry*, p. 21.
49. UDA, Carmichael, Reminiscences, I, p. 45.
50. Carmichael, III, Life and Letters, 2, p. 116.
51. UDA, MS6/1/3/2/12, Peter Grant to George Cox, 23 November 1869.
52. Carmichael, II, Life and Letters, 1, p. 198; David Bremner, *The Industries of Scotland: Their Rise, Progress and Present Condition* (Newton Abbot, 1969), p. 260.
53. Whatley, *Onwards*, pp. 102, 110.
54. Quoted in Kininmonth, 'Weber's Protestant ethic', p. 1238.
55. Carmichael, Reminiscences, 1, pp. 79–81.
56. UDA, Diary, James Cox, p. 84.
57. Elliot, *Lochee*, p. 168.
58. *Perthshire Courier*, 8 August 1811.

59. UDA, Diary, James Cox, p. 47.
60. Alastair J. Durie, The *British Linen Company 1745–1775* (Edinburgh, 1996), pp. 122–3.
61. Gauldie, *Dundee Textile Industry*, p. 79.
62. Mackie, 'Reminiscences', pp. 48, 60.
63. Ibid., p. 60.
64. *Fife Herald*, 19 January 1837.
65. Whatley, *Onwards*, pp. 31–62; NRS, CS 96/4030/25, Letter Book of John Moir, 1823–27, 24 February, 14 March 1823.
66. A. J. Warden, *The Linen Trade, Ancient and Modern* (London, 1868 edn), pp. 614–16.
67. Gauldie, *Dundee Textile Industry*, p. 78.
68. Warden, *Linen Trade*, pp. 615–16.
69. G. N. von Tunzelman, 'Technological and organisational change in industry during the early Industrial Revolution', in P. K. O'Brien and Roland Quinault (eds), *The Industrial Revolution and British Society* (Cambridge, 1993), p. 259.
70. Elliot, *Lochee*, p. 168.
71. Diary, James Cox, pp. 80–4.
72. UDA, MS6/1/3/1/1, Letter Book, James Cox, February to October 1840, James Cox to Edward & Griffen, 28 September 1840.
73. UDA, MS6/1/3/1/1, Letter Book, James Cox, James Cox to Jonathan Dudgeon, 2 October 1840.
74. UDA, MS11/5/2, Calculations Book, c. 1864, New Works, No. 2, p. 160.
75. W. A. Graham Clark, *Linen, Jute, and Hemp Industries in the United Kingdom* (Washington, 1913), p. 100.
76. Report reprinted in *The Sun*, 3 November 1834.
77. Christopher A. Whatley, 'The making of "Juteopolis"', in Christopher A. Whatley (ed.), *The Re-Making of Juteopolis, Dundee c. 1891–1991* (Dundee: Abertay Historical Society, 1992), p. 10.
78. See, for example, *Glasgow Courier*, 1 November 1845; *Fife Herald*, 7 June 1855; *Bicester Herald*, 8 September 1865; *Dundee Courier*, 3 December 1866.
79. *Dundee, Perth & Cupar Advertiser*, 19 May 1857.
80. *The Sun*, 3 November 1834.
81. Clark, *Linen, Jute, and Hemp*, p. 13.
82. H. R. Carter, *Jute and its Manufacture* (London, 1921), pp. 13, 17–18.
83. Norrie, *Dundee Celebrities*, p. 407.
84. *Dundee, Perth & Coupar Advertiser*, 28 October 1862.
85. Gauldie, *Dundee Textile Industry*, p. xix.
86. NRS, CS96/4030/149, Letter Book of John Moir, 1 June 1825.
87. *Roll of Eminent Burgesses of Dundee, 1513–1886* (Dundee, 1887), p. 248.
88. Von Tunzelman, 'Technological and organisational change', pp. 256–7.

89. Mackie, 'Reminiscences', p. 18.
90. Alastair J. Durie, *The Scottish Linen Industry in the Eighteenth Century* (Edinburgh, 1979), pp. 75–7, 159.
91. Mackie, 'Reminiscences', p. 20.
92. Charles McKean, '"Not even the trivial grace of a straight line": or Why Dundee never built a New Town', in Whatley, Harris and Miskell (eds), *Victorian Dundee*, pp. 7–8.
93. Dundee, County of Forfar, *New Statistical Account*, XI (1845), pp. 46–7; James V. Smith, *The Watt Institution Dundee 1824–49* (Dundee, 1977), pp. 1–9.
94. Ian McCraw, 'The Glamis Mill and Baxters', in Cooke (ed.), *Baxter's*, pp. 6–11.
95. UDA, MS 11/5/14, History of Flax Spinning, p. 38.
96. Sidney Pollard, *The Genesis of Modern Management* (London, 1968 edn), pp. 11–16.
97. Mackie, 'Reminiscences', pp. 20–38.
98. See John R. Hume (ed.), *Early Days in a Dundee Mill* (Dundee, 1980).
99. Mackie, 'Reminiscences', p. 20.
100. Pollard, *Genesis*, p. 116.
101. Mackie, 'Reminiscences', p. 68.
102. Warden, *Linen Trade*, p. 75.
103. Lenman, Lythe and Gauldie, *Dundee and its Textile Industry*, pp. 47–9.
104. Miskell and Whatley, '"Juteopolis" in the making', pp. 179–84.
105. Warden, *Linen Trade*, p. 644.
106. Bremner, *Industries*, p. 248.
107. UDA, MS11/5/2, Calculations Book, c. 1864, p. 96.
108. Quoted in Miskell and Whatley, '"Juteopolis" in the making', p. 183.
109. Miskell and Whatley, '"Juteopolis" in the making', p. 185.
110. Gauldie, *Dundee Textile Industry*, pp. xxv–xxvi, 54.
111. *Dundee Courier*, 14 December 1897.
112. Ibid., 3 April 1886.
113. Gauldie, *Dundee Textile Industry*, p. 61.
114. UDA, MS120/1/4, John Hadden to James Grimond, 3 February 1829.
115. Hume, *Early Days*, pp. 60–2.
116. Gauldie, *Dundee Textile Industry*, p. 62.
117. *The Sun*, 8 November 1836.
118. Carmichael, Reminiscences, I, p. 73.
119. Carmichael, II, Life and Letters, 1, p. 30.
120. Fabrice Bensimon and Christopher A. Whatley, 'The thread of migration: A Scottish–French jute works and its workers in France, c. 1845–c. 1870', *Journal of Migration History*, 2: 1 (March 2016), pp. 120–47.
121. Mackie, 'Reminiscences', p. 53.
122. UDA, MS11/5/2, Calculations Book, c. 1864, 'History of improvements in hackling for increasing yield and cleaning tow, 10 February, 1862', p. 59.

123. *Dundee, Perth & Cupar Advertiser*, 11 November 1856; *Dundee People's Journal*, 15 October 1859; Gauldie, *Dundee Textile Industry*, pp. 131–3.
124. Brenda Collins and Philip Ollerenshaw, 'The European linen industry since the Middle Ages', in Brenda Collins and Philip Ollerenshaw (eds), *The European Linen Industry in Historical Perspective* (Oxford, 2003), pp. 18–19.
125. Halley, 'Business in Dundee in the XIXth century', typescript, n.d., p. 3.
126. Carmichael, Reminiscences, I, pp. 90, 92, 180.
127. *Royal Commission on the Employment of Children in Trades and Manufactures not Regulated by Law* (1864), p. 230.
128. Cox, Letter Book, 21 September 1840.
129. *Dundee, Perth & Coupar Advertiser*, 28 October 1862.
130. Whatley, *Onwards*, pp. 43, 50–1.
131. UDA, MS 120/1/4, William Smith to James Grimond, 15 February, 22 March 1830.
132. *Perthshire Advertiser*, 21 March 1833; *Perthshire Courier*, 12 June 1834; *True Sun*, 4 July 1834.
133. *Inverness Courier*, 25 June 1834; *Dublin Weekly Register*, 12 July 1834.
134. Norman Murray, *The Scottish Handloom Weavers, 1790–1850* (Edinburgh, 1978), pp. 8, 40–2, 168–76.
135. Carmichael, Reminiscences, I, pp. 252–5; Murray, *Scottish Handloom Weavers*, pp. 17–18, 68.
136. UDA, MS11/5/2, Calculations Book, c. 1864, 'Notes on Power Loom Factory Work & Wages', 16 May 1862, pp. 82–5.
137. Lenman, Lythe and Gauldie, *Dundee and its Textile Industry*, pp. 43–56.
138. Gauldie, *Dundee Textile Industry*, p. 84; Carmichael, Reminiscences, I, pp. 270–1.
139. Carmichael, Reminiscences, I, p. 47.
140. UDA, MS11/5/2, Calculations Book, c. 1864, 'Notes on Power Loom Factory, Work and Wages', 16 May 1862, pp. 82–5.
141. Miskell, 'Civic Leadership', p. 47.
142. Bremner, *Industries*, p. 265.
143. *Royal Commission on the Employment of Children*, p. 231.
144. *Dundee Courier*, 13 August 1861.
145. *Edinburgh Evening Courant*, 27 December 1856.
146. Lenman, Lythe and Gauldie, *Dundee and its Textile Industry*, p. 46.
147. *Dundee, Perth & Cupar Advertiser*, 11 November 1856.
148. Ibid., 3 October 1862.
149. Warden, *Linen Trade*, p. 657.
150. Murray, *Scottish Handloom Weavers*, pp. 74–5.
151. *Dundee Courier*, 12 September 1864.
152. Carmichael, II, Life and Letters, 1, p. 291.
153. Warden, *Linen Trade*, p. 78.
154. *Dundee, Perth & Cupar Advertiser*, 11 November 1856.

ANGUS FLAX MERCHANTS TO 'LORDS O' JUTEOPOLIS' 131

155. UDA, MS11/5/2, Calculations Book, c. 1864, 'Ventilation of the Large Weaving Room', p. 67.
156. Bremner, *Industries*, p. 263.
157. Hume, *Early Days*, p. 16.
158. Mackie, 'Reminiscences', p. 20.
159. Bremner, *Industries*, p. 264.
160. Mark Watson, *Jute and Flax Mills in Dundee* (Tayport, 1990), p. 75.
161. Emma M. Wainwright, 'Dundee's jute mills and factories: Spaces of production, surveillance and discipline', *Scottish Geographical Journal*, 121: 2 (2005), p. 127.
162. Carmichael, Reminiscences, 1, pp. 231–2.
163. *Dundee People's Journal*, 15 October 1959.
164. Sydney Pollard, *The Genesis of Modern Management* (London, 1965), pp. 213–31; E. P. Thompson, 'Time, work-discipline and industrial capitalism', *Past and Present*, 38 (1967), pp. 56–97.
165. For a brief introduction to these issues, see Hans-Joachim Voth, *Time and Work in England 1750–1830* (Oxford, 2000), pp. 1–16.
166. Hume, *Early Days*, pp. 20–1.
167. UDA, MS11/5/2, Calculations Book, New Work No. 2, n.d., p. 145.
168. Wainwright, 'Dundee's jute mills and factories', pp. 134–7.
169. UDA, MS11/5/42, 'Notes on Spinning 3lbs Tow, Upper Dens, December 1855'.
170. UDA, MS11/5/42, 'Notes on Preparing of Flax for Spinning Canvas Yarns at Lower Dens Mills, December 1855'.
171. UDA, MS11/5/2, Calculations Book, c. 1864, p. 85.
172. William M. Walker, *Juteopolis: Dundee and its Textile Workers 1885–1923* (Edinburgh, 1979), pp. 20–1.

4

Dundee's People and the Headlong Chaos of Industrial Transformation

A 'starving, turbulent population'?

Notwithstanding the productivity gains achieved through mechanisation, the expansion of textiles production in nineteenth-century Dundee required a vast increase in the numbers of people to work in the industry. Fortunately, there was a deep enough pool of available labour in both Scotland and Ireland from which recruits could be drawn. Indeed, many people actively sought employment in what during the industry's boom periods were labour-hungry warehouses, workshops, mills, factories, calenders and engineering works, while others managed to find employment as outworkers in handloom weaving, sack sewing and a range of ill-paid part-time tasks.

Almost from the time of the industrial revolution itself, contemporary commentators such as William Cobbett, Charles Dickens and Karl Marx's co-author Friedrich Engels, and then historians like the Hammonds and the Webbs, and later Edward Thompson, have portrayed the industrialisation process in 'relentlessly dark colours'. A negative experience, the onset of the machine age was 'unforgiving in its grinding down of the independent labourer of old.'[1] Received wisdom – or tradition – has it that Dundee's textile workers were particularly harshly exploited, presumably after having left behind them a countryside idyll. Largely young, and female, they endured, it has been argued, poor if not abysmal working conditions, including low wages, chronically inadequate housing provision and a host of related social ills. The late William Walker was characteristically blunt: Dundee was 'a large manufacturing centre of physically retarded children, overworked women and demoralized men'.[2] And there is much substance in this compressed depiction of the lives of Dundee's labouring people.

However, it can be argued that Walker's assessment oversimplifies the realities of working-class life in Dundee. There are reasons to believe, as Emma Griffin has found – based on working-class autobiographies (mainly, it must be conceded, from England) – for viewing the lived experience of industrialisation in a much more positive light. Rather than harking back to the good old days of impoverished country living, she proposes, ordinary people welcomed the opportunities created by the industrial revolution – not least the availability of more and regular work, much of it full-time – and consequently increased spending power.[3] Instead of servile submission to the will of their social superiors, there was now an element of choice in their life decisions, more personal liberty. While the last decades of the eighteenth century and the first seven decades of the nineteenth century – that is, Dundee's transition from what was primarily a port town to a major manufacturing centre – were no bed of roses, there were buoyant periods within this time frame when employment was full, wages high and the town flourished. We should be cautious though. It was largely upon male testimonies that Griffin's optimism about the human impact of industrialisation is founded. Dundee's textile trade was dominated by women workers. Yet despite the trials and tribulations many endured, the fact is there was considerable variation in the experiences of females in Dundee, depending on their occupations, domestic roles, relationships, living conditions and social and political involvement.

Worth noting too is that notwithstanding the classification of Dundee as a 'women's town' at the turn of the twentieth century, there was an identifiable male presence, even in the linen and jute industries as well as in ancillary occupations. It is true that labour relations in the final decades of the century were fractious and punctuated by strikes. Prior to this, however, while there were periodic employer–employee disputes, the workplace environment for many was imbued with paternalism – a model of industrial relations that in part was based on mutual respect and some shared values and interests between employers and employed, but which has been little examined in the Dundee context.[4] Beyond the workplace too, there were bouts of unrest and sporadic radical uprisings, which the authorities were keen to suppress – and appear through various interventions to have done so successfully, to the extent that social relations were more harmonious than might be assumed.

PEOPLING THE INDUSTRIAL CITY

Natural population increase would not have sufficed in satisfying the need for workers in the textile and allied industries. In common with

134 THE TRIUMPH OF TEXTILES

Table 4.1 Population of Dundee, 1755–1891

Date	Number
1755	12,477
1793	23,500
1801	26,804
1811	29,616
1821	30,575
1831	45,355
1841	62,873
1851	78,931
1861	90,568
1871	119,141
1881	140,239
1891	153,587

manufacturing towns elsewhere in industrialising Scotland, it was migrants who met this surging demand for labour.

The near 90 per cent increase in population for the period 1755 to 1793 was largely due to the growth and concentration of the linen industry in Dundee, outlined in chapter 1. Across Scotland it was the textile towns that grew fastest and continued to do so until the 1830s.[5] Indeed, it was in the previous decade that Dundee's population grew faster (48.3 per cent) than at any time in the town's history. But notwithstanding assumptions to the contrary, none of this owed anything to jute.[6] The rate in the 1830s – 38.6 per cent – again pre-jute, was slightly slower but still exceeded that of any other important Scottish town.[7] By 1851 Dundee had risen to third place in Scotland's urban league. *Chambers Journal* was unequivocal as to the cause. It was the increase in the number of mills (of which there were thirty in 1832) that accounted 'for the rapid increase in the population of Dundee'. Three mills under construction in 1836 would add another thousand workers, 'besides great numbers of individuals connected with other departments of the manufacture, and multitudes of tradesmen who are equally necessary for supplying these with articles of subsistence and with professional service'.[8] This assessment finds support in employment statistics for 1841. Not surprisingly, but a pointer to just how dependent the town's fortunes were on its staple trade, the proportion of the population employed in textiles and clothing (just over 50 per cent) was higher in Dundee than in any of

DUNDEE'S PEOPLE AND INDUSTRIAL TRANSFORMATION   135

Scotland's other three main towns. Marginally higher than Glasgow and Aberdeen was the figure for employees in food, drink and tobacco – 5.3 per cent. Dundee's working people had to be fed and at least some of their comforts supplied.[9]

The significance, then and in the future, of how many people were employed in textile production is difficult to overstate. Of the total population of just over 78,000 in mid-century, up to 25,000 were directly employed in the textile industry. The majority of these were women; indeed, women accounted for around half of the town's employed population, a higher percentage than any of the other large Scottish towns.[10] Seventy-five per cent of the jute labour force was female. By the end of the century, almost one-third of the city's females were employed in the mills and factories, with the figure for married women (over 24 per cent) being substantially higher than Glasgow (6.1 per cent) or Edinburgh (5.6 per cent).[11] In 1851 male workers accounted for over a quarter of the textile workforce.[12] In 1861 men and boys comprised 32.5 per cent of the workforce at Dens.[13] They shouldn't be overlooked, or employed simply as a useful foil by which to contrast on an impressionistic basis the treatment and experiences of their female counterparts. Males could struggle too.

The incorporation of jute into the town's textile portfolio and its subsequent rise to prominence continued the pattern of population growth, although at a slower pace. That is until the 'golden decade' of the 1860s, when almost 29,000 incomers (a 31.5 per cent increase) had swelled the town's populace to over 119,000 by 1871. By 1881 the number had risen to over 140,000. In twenty years, driven by jute, Dundee had grown by 50,000 people.[14] There had been a fivefold increase since the turn of the century. The 'great increase in strangers', in the opinion of the town council in 1867, was Dundee's 'peculiarity'.[15] Not entirely; inward migration accounted for much of Scotland's urban growth in this period. It was the social mix and the economic conditions unique to jute in particular that made Dundee different.

Most of the new arrivals came from rural Angus and elsewhere in Scotland's east coast hinterland, moves made easier as the process of agricultural improvement went on apace. During the first decades of the nineteenth century, landowners and tenants continued to create larger, more productive farms and dispensed with smallholders and cottars, so creating a pool of largely redundant men and women in the countryside.[16] If there was less of this consolidation of farming units in the counties to the west and north of Dundee than the Lothians and Borders, and only a limited influx of displaced Highlanders – and checks therefore on

136   THE TRIUMPH OF TEXTILES

how much labour was available – there was another source of industrial workers: Ireland. This migrant stream into Scotland had begun
towards the end of the eighteenth century. It was from the later 1820s
and above all during the later 1840s in the wake of the Irish potato
famine that what had been a trickle became a flood. These were desperate times in both Dundee and Ireland. Peter Carmichael was troubled in
October 1847 at having to lay off 'old servants' at a time when the cost
of basic provisions was soaring. Yet, he noted, 'the misery of the poor in
Dundee . . . was aggravated by the influx of bands still poorer from fam-
ine-stricken Ireland'. Uncannily, the previous autumn he had witnessed
at first hand wasted potato fields, 'not a green leaf to be seen and the
odour very obnoxious'.[17] Such was the flight from Ireland that by 1851
the proportion of Irish-born migrants residing in Dundee was 18.8 per
cent, higher than anywhere else in Scotland, and in the UK second only
to Liverpool.[18] Some 15,000 Irish-born migrants had settled in Dundee
by this date.[19] By 1865 – the peak of the jute boom – there may have been
25,000 if the children born of Irish parents are included, although the
numbers tailed off thereafter.

The binding agent was flax and linen. Rural dwellers who engaged
in handloom weaving from the countryside south of Belfast had been
linked with Dundee through their use of yarn spun in Dundee's mills;
this trade route was an important conduit through which information
flowed. A few handloom weavers had crossed the Irish Sea and negotiated their way through Lowland Scotland to take up employment in
Dundee in the early nineteenth century. Indeed, in 1834 the weavers'
union actively discouraged their Irish counterparts from being tempted
by the offer of another five hundred jobs by Dundee's employers, partly
on the grounds that several hundred Irish weavers already in the town
had been 'thrown idle' for refusing to sign away their rights to associate
collectively.[20] With improvements in cleaning flax, from the later 1820s
increasing amounts of this from Ireland were being brought to Dundee,
as were migrants from counties such as Cavan and Monaghan (most of
the Irish who settled were from Ulster), although accents from all Irish
counties were eventually to be heard, suggesting that Dundee's pull was
island-wide.[21]

Opportunities for flax preparing and hand spinning in the domestic setting in the north-west and western counties of Ulster had been
drying up, and consequently peasant farming became more precarious.
But with demand for workers preferably with some familiarity with flax
intensifying in Dundee, emigration offered a way out of a deteriorat-
ing situation at home.[22] It was the prospect of employment in Dundee

allied to depressed conditions in Ulster that accounted for the departure of several of the 'best skilled and most industrious' handloom weavers from Drogheda in 1858.[23] As this indicates, the move to Dundee was neither random, nor necessarily due to desperation, but rather to considered judgements about where the best prospects lay. 'Wherever there was a want of hands', noted one of the local newspapers in 1856, those already resident in Dundee 'informed their friends over the Channel, and a new importation occurred.'[24] For Irish males, or a few of them, there was the additional prospect of promotion to foreman, possibly as they were better able to supervise their own people. Disproportional (but unsurprisingly so) was the sex ratio, 67.4:100, reflecting the need among Dundee's textile firms for females, mainly in the preparing and spinning departments but also as cleaners and in other menial employments. In 1871 there were twice as many Irish females than men in Dundee.[25] Overwhelmingly too, the new arrivals were younger, more so than the indigenous population. It was those in their teens and twenties, with their sisters and less often brothers, and a parent or parents, or in the company of friends, who tended to be the most likely to leave and seek a life furth of Ireland. Lucy Paterson, later of the Lochee branch of the Irish Ladies' Land league (founded in 1881), was typical, arriving in the 1860s with her mother and five siblings, and starting work at Camperdown while in her early teens.[26]

THE CHANGING WORLD OF WORK: HAND SPINNERS AND THE FIRST SPINNING MILLS

For the labouring classes, the period from the later eighteenth century when Dundee emerged as Scotland's flax- and linen-producing centre to the early 1870s when jute reigned supreme encompassed dramatic change. The nature and timing of this, though, was far from uniform. The most obvious feature of the new world of work was the appearance of workshops, mills, factories and other centralised workplaces. These required new forms of discipline – both as internalised by the workers themselves and as exercised by owners, managers and overseers. Task orientation, a feature of pre-industrialised work where labour and social life were intermingled, became a thing of the past.[27] As was outlined in chapter 3, more so than beforehand, with employers paying for their employees' time rather than a product, work was more closely supervised. Clock time – announced by bells, whistles and 'knocking up boys' – who wakened workers from their beds – determined the start, finish and length of the working day, which in the first mills were at least twelve

138   THE TRIUMPH OF TEXTILES

and a half hours and sometimes longer, with around ninety minutes in total for breakfast and dinner breaks.

Payment by the piece was designed to ensure that workers put in maximum effort, although many – like spinners – were paid by the hour. Otherwise, they were relieved only when boilers broke down, coal or water supplies were interrupted, or machine parts gave way. All lost time – at market days, for instance, but also for repairs – William Brown advised, was to be made up. Hands were to give 'regular and strict attendance' and be 'held strictly at their duty'; 'bad ones' (workers) were to be 'quickly got rid of and replaced with good'.[28] Another disciplining agent was the extent to which ordinary people – most of whom as we have seen were migrants to Dundee – were dependent on money wages. Removed from the rural world with which they had been familiar and that had sustained them, they were no longer able to produce any of their own food, other than perhaps by poaching game. Exceptions were handloom weavers and few tradesmen whose attachment to the land was such – perhaps through country-dwelling relatives – that they were prepared to leave Dundee at key periods during the agricultural cycle and engage in farm work.[29]

We should, however, resist the temptation of painting an overly rosy picture of life prior to the era of urban mills and factories. Even so, there is a sense in which the amalgamation of industriousness in agriculture and even more so at the spinning wheel or loom offered a greater degree of personal autonomy – some control over the allocation of time and the ranking of priorities – than would be the case within only a few years. Albeit seasonal, and influenced by the weather, it was a situation which gave both spinners and weavers some control over the production process, in that they could determine how long to spend at the wheel or loom respectively and how hard to work at it. Indeed, as we saw in chapter 3, despite worsening material rewards, handloom weavers appeared unwilling to surrender the relative freedom they had retained to determine when and what effort they devoted to loom work, well into the 1860s. Yet their options were restricted: as they aged, alternative work opportunities reduced, while there were limits to the numbers of assisted passages the Colonial Land and Emigration Commissioners were prepared to support (married couples were preferred), despite the formation of the Handloom Weavers and Flax Dressers Emigration Association in 1852.[30]

Yet the existence of a palpable sense of satisfaction among domestic spinning communities tends to support the scanty evidence there is that as elsewhere in early industrialising Britain, there was fierce resistance to

DUNDEE'S PEOPLE AND INDUSTRIAL TRANSFORMATION   139

the dislocation threatened by the intrusion of spinning mills. This opposition, outlined in the previous chapter, seems to have taken the form of arson, with those women affected by the introduction of mill work regretting the loss of their way of life, fearing (it was rumoured) that younger spinners would be denied the opportunity of finding a marriage partner. There was concern too about the injuries that might result from working with the water- and steam-driven spinning frames. Above all, those involved were anxious about the threat mills posed to their skill-derived status – and income. Over time, those who were left behind suffered a sharp fall in wage rates as more mills were opened.

Consequently, the first proprietors of spinning mills in and around Dundee had little choice but to tread carefully in order to entice females – who were more desirable than males, as they were experienced in spinning yarn – into their premises. We noticed some of the steps taken to ease the transition from home working to the mill in chapter 1. Another was wages, which, according to William Brown, should not be 'squeezed down to the utmost' but kept up to ensure a supply of 'good hands'.[31] And initially at least, there was some negotiation over wages and terms of employment. In February 1829 John Lindsay agreed with James Grimond of Oakbank Mill in Blairgowrie that he and his three daughters would work for Grimond for a year. Lindsay would be paid ten shillings weekly for whatever work he was asked to do, with an increase of a shilling should the price of spindles rise. His three daughters were to be employed as spinners for six shillings a week, 'or whatever wages are current in the place'. The family were also to be provided with a house and eight falls (around 44 metres in length) of garden ground, presumably for vegetables, for two pounds for the year.[32] The first mill spinners were not simply passive victims in a system driven by market forces that was heavily weighted against them. One of the earliest incidences of collective action being taken comes from Grimond's Mill in Blairgowrie, to the north of Dundee. Early in November 1826 Johanne Mackay had evidently led her colleagues out of the mill in some kind of protest. Although at first Mackay protested her innocence, demanded in the justice court that Grimond prove she was the leader and refused to go back in, within a few hours, perhaps the next day, she had bound herself not only to return to work but also to complete her engagement.[33] Not a victory, but a warning shot to employers that there were limits on their authority.

And notwithstanding the demands of the new work regime, some masters recognised and continued older customs, in part to maintain good relations with their workpeople as well as to retain the most

Figure 4.1 Evocative view of the interior of an unknown Dundee spinning mill, assumed to be from the 1850s but may be later. Hand winding wheels or 'muckle wheels' and other hand tools are to be seen in the foreground. The female spinners are seated. Behind them to the left are several males, amongst whom are an overseer and some mechanics and other tradesmen. The sole female amongst the men may have been a supervisor. © Dundee Industrial Heritage.

Figure 4.2 Postcard depicting female spinners, late nineteenth century. Dressed in their work clothes, on their hands are palm protectors, while round their waists are tool belts. The woman fourth from the left has a whistle around her neck, which suggests she may have been a supervisor. Cards like this may have been sent to family and friends, possibly in Ireland. © Dundee Industrial Heritage.

DUNDEE'S PEOPLE AND INDUSTRIAL TRANSFORMATION 141

proficient of them. At Glamis Mill, for example, the proprietors laid on new year balls.[34] Similar gestures – pints of whisky included – were on offer elsewhere, above all at new year. Consciously perhaps, by restricting the amount of liquor consumed, masters were able to exert some control over the proceedings, in hopes that work would not be long interrupted.[35]

But with demand for cloth buoyant in the early 1830s, mill owners could do little to resist the spinners' pressure for higher wages. Not only was the pool of available workers shallow, they were also reputed to 'know their value'.[36] In the light of what would happen in the spinning departments later in the century – relatively low wages and frequent disputes with employers – more positive contemporaneous accounts of the spinners' circumstances in the better years of the 1830s and up until the 1860s, admittedly mainly written by outsiders and some local employers, cannot be dismissed out of hand. In 1836 William Chambers, the observant Scottish publisher and writer, reported that such were the wages of the young women in Dundee's mills they were able to save or, more likely, spend as much as six shillings on dresses, 'of which they are fond', and other pleasures. (Although it was believed that there were some 12,000 depositors with the Dundee savings banks in 1831, factory workers were far outnumbered by domestic servants.[37]) Girls, the writer of an article for *The Builder* claimed in 1865, were 'in the ascendant over men in money and wages'.[38] Furthermore, and possibly with an element of wishful thinking (although not necessarily), the same writer noted that as mill workers gathered in groups on the town's streets during the summer months, those present bore 'the appearance of perfect satisfaction with their circumstances'. Furthermore, and pleasing for observers, they conducted themselves, in general, 'without any offence to the most rigid notions of decorum'.[39] In June 1836, encouraged by the town's spinning masters, some one hundred of them evidently felt themselves to be in sufficiently 'easy circumstances' to join with three hundred men from Dundee's mills and associated trades in a steamboat excursion along the river Tay, where they visited Scone Palace, Kinnoull Hill and other attractions.[40]

Admittedly a couple of years earlier, the town's ministers had seen things slightly differently, commenting in the *New Statistical Account* on the substantial numbers of working women (mainly spinners) who were recognisable by being 'wrapped in coarse plaids'. Silk cloaks and bonnets suggestive of greater gentility were a rarer sight.[41]

Regardless of how they were dressed, unsurprisingly, also noticeable was the youthfulness of the mills' workforce.[42] The prevailing belief was

142 THE TRIUMPH OF TEXTILES

that females would not become 'expert spinners if they do not commence before being twelve years old' – and many were younger than that when entering mill employment. Thirteen-year-old Rosanna Logan was six and a half when she began work in William Boyack's mill, while her colleague Jesse Douglas, also thirteen, may have been even younger.[43] More than half of the three thousand or so employees in the spinning mills in 1830 were aged between ten and eighteen.[44] Later in the same decade, children under eighteen (most were between thirteen and eighteen) accounted for 43 per cent of what was then a workforce of 5,798 persons.[45]

Further justification for measured optimism about the fortunes of the town's workforce comes from the early 1850s, when, for example, spinners' wages rose from a typical six shillings and sixpence weekly in 1850 to seven shillings and sixpence in 1856 – an increase related to the boom conditions created by the Crimean War. For the preparers in the low mill – feeders, rovers and 'enders' – the upturns were even more substantial, proportionately, rising from five shillings for feeders to six shillings and ninepence. The mills' preparing departments were places where little skill was required, and therefore attracted widows, deserted women and those driven by poverty to find any kind of paid work. Often it was among the Irish that such conditions were met, so most of this category of work was done by Irish recruits. But with conditions improving in Ireland once recovery from the immediate effects of the famine had begun, the flow of migrants to Dundee had slowed, although not immediately: in March 1849 two parties from Ireland arrived – forty in one group, fifty in the other – by sea, from Leith.[46] Wages rose accordingly. Such was the intensity of demand for Dundee products at the height of the Crimean War that over two years (1854 to 1856), with the rapid expansion of mill and factory capacity in terms of spindles and looms respectively, over five thousand more workers were taken on.[47] It was at times like this that owners became acutely aware of the importance of recruiting and retaining the best workers. This had been highlighted at Dens in 1855 when the workers had been 'scarce and troublesome', while it also became evident that the overseers were below par. The situation was made worse by 'the total cessation of immigration from Ireland'. Poor management and the scarcity of skilled hands was 'causing the [heckling] machines to get out of order from laps and ends moving away . . . more knotty, uneven, small places being found in the yarn from this cause than apparently from any other'.[48]

There were downsides, however. The apparent abandon of the mill workers on the streets may have owed more to their release from the lengthy daily grind than to any undue fondness for mill work.

Ann Mackay, a twenty-four-year-old spinner in one of J. and W. Brown's spinning mills, articulated what may have been a widespread dilemma. She was pleased to be earning six shillings a week in 1833; however, 'she would not work in a spinning mill but for the high wages'.[49] And for good reason.

But there were few alternatives, and over the following decades a mill and factory culture developed which was marked by a palpable workplace pride. Spinners, it was said, 'gloried' in their work, and often demonstrated a strong identification with the firms which employed them.[50] It is notable that on the grand procession that preceded the opening in 1863 of Baxter Park (on land donated by the textile magnate Sir David Baxter), images of women workers were displayed on banners those marching carried, while a song celebrating the event referenced 'The mill lassies, all looking so fine/With their mantles and bonnets, and trig crinoline.' Females too were among the 16,731 subscribers who funded the statue of Baxter by Sir John Steell, then Scotland's most eminent Victorian-era sculptor, which was unveiled at the same time.[51] Whatever the hardships endured during the early stages of Dundee's transition to an industrial powerhouse, there is evidence of an element of satisfaction among working people with their new environment, and much civic pride. For some at least, the transition from country to town was eased by the links maintained with family and friends who they visited at weekends and at harvest time. Others moved into the town in steps, as in the case of the parents of the manufacturer Alexander Moncur, referred to in chapter 3. There is no doubt that as in much of industrialising, urbanising Scotland there was a lingering nostalgia for the countryside – the world the town's migrants were losing touch with. But the reality of so many lives in mid-Victorian Dundee was of relative prosperity. A visitor from Edinburgh even contrasted the evidence of 'idle opulence' in the capital city's Princes Street with the bustle of Dundee, a place where 'either rich or poor . . . seemed to have something to do and be doing it'.[52] This included 'comely matrons' and 'industrious millworkers', whose faces 'lighted up', observed one newspaper correspondent in 1868, on their work-free Saturday afternoons.[53] Attractions included circuses, shows, theatres, public houses and, especially popular, shops selling clothes and shoes.[54] Evening 'promenading' was another much-enjoyed habit, although rarely after nine o'clock other than on Saturday nights when things got 'rough' and out of hand. Was not the city, asked James Myles, a local artisan with literary pretensions, 'brimfull of interest', vastly more so than 'silent woods, sunny dells, and moss-covered ruins in the country'?[55]

144 THE TRIUMPH OF TEXTILES

Contrary to what is often assumed about the character of the town's female workers, preliminary investigation suggests that it may have been females who were unable to obtain mill and factory work who were more likely to turn to crime or engage in antisocial activities. In one sample year, 1845, for example, most female mill workers who appeared in High Court precognitions did so as witnesses rather than as suspected thieves or prostitutes.[56] Adding to this hypothesis are figures that show that of those women whose cases were heard in the Magistrates Court in 1860, 325 had no trade (compared to 302 for males); furthermore, there were more weavers (190, though this could include males) among this cohort than mill workers (fifty-two).[57] More of them than might be assumed may even have absorbed the advice – exhortations – of employers, managers and overseers about the importance of self-respect and domestic 'duties'; up to a thousand mill workers formed the largest part of a tightly packed audience assembled in the Corn Exchange for such a lecture in May 1862.[58]

However, to achieve the degree of control over their workforces that was necessary if their capital outlays on plant and machinery were to pay dividends, employers during the early decades of the century could be uncompromising in their management styles. The other side to William Brown's apparent generosity over wages was his conviction that 'bad ones' (workers) should be 'got rid of'. For those retained, it was 'mistaken humanity to indulge them in ease, idleness or play'.[59] The evidence presented in May 1833 to the Royal Commission on the Employment of Children in Factories suggests that this stance was widespread. While there were few outright condemnations of their employers on the part of the mill workers the commissioners interviewed, managers and overseers were identified as having beaten younger workers with slaps or their fists, as well as using a leather strap or tawse. Such practices carried on beyond mid-century; one fifteen-year-old shifter in 1859 was awarded five pounds in compensation after having been hit on the head and pushed into a spinning frame by her male overseer. Her victory, however, was only partial, with no blame being attached to the firm, Gilroys, in whose mill the assault had occurred, or to the overseer, while the pursuer's 'proneness to hysteria' was suspected of having exaggerated the extent of the harm done.[60] The even darker aspect of such abuses of power were the occasions when distressed mothers of illegitimate and unsupported children had cause to apply to the Sheriff Court to pursue fathers who were often mill managers, foremen or craft workers who had failed to acknowledge their role in the process of conception – as 'on

DUNDEE'S PEOPLE AND INDUSTRIAL TRANSFORMATION   145

the common stair in Brown St, Westport, Dundee'.[61] Absences other than through illness brought severe repercussions, with those caught spending a few hours at Broughty Ferry beach or a day at the races brought back forcibly if they were spotted. There was overwhelming evidence of the harmful effects of long days spent standing in the mills: swollen legs, ankles and feet were universally complained of by women and girls, along with headaches and breast pains. Hoarseness was 'so common among mill workers that they may be found out to be such when talking in the street'.[62] This was the result of working in the heavy stour thrown off by flax and jute and having to shout above the relentless rattle of the steam-driven machinery; those employed in wet spinning, enveloped in hot steam and walking over wet floors all day, were also more prone to colds and other discomforts. Industrial injuries could be horrific. On his visit in 1833, Sir David Barry and his colleagues saw some fifty self-nominated workers from Dundee's mills, most of whom had suffered some kind of industrial injury: several had lost one or more fingers, or lower arms by amputation. Most injuries were caused by unguarded machinery.[63] Mary Herries, for example, was twelve years old and had been in Boyack's mill for a year; she had lost her 'fore, middle, and ring fingers of her right hand . . . [the driving gear] not being fenced off'. Respiratory diseases resulting from the inhalation of dust and oil fumes, such as chronic bronchitis and 'mill fever', were a common cause of admission to Dundee's Royal Infirmary, opened in 1855, partly with funds collected and donated by textile workers.[64] Their contribution was acknowledged with a day's holiday on 22 July 1852, then the foundation stone had been laid. Although there was little amelioration for the spinners' and weavers' lungs and vocal cords, means were found by the workers themselves to limit how much shouting they did, although on the streets they showed less restraint.[65] Signs and symbols had by mid-century become a regular means of communication between workers and their supervisors, 'human language . . . [having become] almost inaudible amid such a deafening concert of discordant sounds'.[66]

Tiredness – exhaustion is the more accurate term – was deemed to be no excuse for slowing down. Even though John Urquhart, an overseer at Kinmond's mill, readily conceded that a thirteen-hour day was too long, he admitted that when he found females or boys sitting down or even sleeping, he would give them a 'lick' with the back of his hand on their back and shoulders. But perhaps the most notorious and nationally known instance of harsh treatment of their workers by a textile firm occurred in October 1845. This was when six spinners (the youngest of whom, reportedly, was only thirteen years of age) at Baxters' works who had asked for and been refused a pay rise of 3d that had apparently been granted to others in the mill, left their work for the afternoon – effectively on strike. The following day, having returned to their employment, they were interviewed under duress and subsequently jailed by the Justices in the Bridewell or House of Correction for ten days, with hard labour.[67] The case – perhaps the first of its kind in Britain – not only raised the ire of several Dundonians (including the relatives of the accused, who had been refused admission to the courtroom), but was also the subject of heated debates in the House of Commons led by the Radical, Chartist-supporting Thomas Duncombe MP.[68] Subsequently Scotland's Lord Advocate insisted that such trials should be conducted in open court. The case, however, may have been exceptional, at least in the context of Dens. Baxters were judged to be one of Dundee's more benign employers. Peter Carmichael had found the evidence from Dundee to the Factory Commissioners 'painful'. The firm then moved to the front of the campaign for a shorter working day, after having grudgingly accepted that legislation governing working conditions was necessary; otherwise, rival employers would ignore any informal agreements between them and continue to drive their workers hard and long. Carmichael's preference was for a reduction to sixty-six hours a week – but no fewer.[69] And there was to be no softening of his position on state interference in working conditions. Forty years later, as moves were made for a nine-hour working day, he feared for the future of textile manufacturing; 'the child unborn may rue the day', he wrote of the proposal he elsewhere condemned as 'an act of confiscation disguised as philanthropy'.[70]

By mid-century twelve hours per day was the norm, with not much less than two hours for breakfast and dinner. Countering any suggestion that they were quiescent or unable to organise collectively is the fact that females from some thirty-nine works in Dundee petitioned Parliament in April 1850 about their working conditions and in favour of the Ten Hours Bill; elsewhere in the country it was largely males who led the campaign.[71] In the 1870s, however, there was a further reduction in hours, with work on Saturdays ending at 9.30 am (with the usual weekday start of 6 am) rather than 1 pm.[72] Mill and foundry workers were present in their thousands at a rally on Magdalen Green in favour of the Reform Bill in 1866.[73] Mill workers participated too in local politics, as in the general election of 1868 when, arm in arm, they marched through the streets singing abusive songs about the Conservative-inclined secret ballot supporter J. A. Guthrie, displaying instead the colours of the Liberal George Armitstead.[74]

WORKPLACE TRANSITIONS: HECKLING AND WEAVING

Thus far, our attention has largely been focused on the spinning mills, which from the outset comprised a mix of younger women and children (who were piecers and shifters respectively), along with a few males mainly in better-paid supervisory positions and as mechanics. Even more traumatic, however, was the transition to the centralised workplaces of the heckling and weaving processes. We know already that the flax dressers, or hecklers, of whom there were between three hundred and four hundred, tried to stand firm in defence of their handicraft skills and pre-industrial workplace practices that included periodic 'pint' or drink breaks.[75] Through combination and strikes in 1822 and 1827 they managed to resist the introduction of machinery long after its use had become commonplace in the rival textile town of Leeds. Nevertheless, and after a prolonged war of attrition and through the efforts of the Ward Road spinner John Sharp to mechanise the process (alluded to in the previous chapter), the balance of power eventually shifted.[76] From 1836 the job of flax dresser in Dundee became increasingly precarious, a consequence that resulted in numbers of them seeking work in other parts of the country, in northern France where during the 1840s linen and jute works were being established, and to emigrating to the British colonies.

Over a relatively short period of time, handloom weaving, a comparatively well-paid, high- status, largely male-dominated handcraft, was reduced to become a chronically poorly paid occupation that despite falling wages continued, as we have seen, to employ thousands of men up to and beyond the 1860s. Some customers – the Royal Navy, for example – preferred hand-woven canvas. Hand-woven carpets too were much sought after, which helped maintain the wages of weavers in factories where these were made at a higher level than those working alone or in small workshops, and on sacking and similar cloths that could be manufactured on power looms. Increasingly though, handloom weavers working alone or in small numbers in workshops became appendages of the power-loom weaving factories, called upon only during periods of peak demand.

As in so many other Scottish municipalities it was the well-read, radically inclined handloom weavers who mainly filled the ranks of the radical societies that were active during the early years of the French Revolution. The Dundee weaver George Mealmaker was a leading figure in the clandestine United Scotsmen movement later in the 1790s. On the other hand, led by the town's propertied classes, large numbers of weavers joined the loyal volunteers as fears of a French invasion grew

148   THE TRIUMPH OF TEXTILES

and the earlier enthusiasm for the Revolution cooled. Despite Dundee's reputation at the time, as well as subsequently, as a hotbed of radicalism, recent research has concluded that militant support for the Friends of the People and the authority-alarming planting of Trees of Liberty during 1792 was confined to a 'committed minority' which had shrunk by the end of the 1790s.[77] In accounting for this apparent passivity, the part played by the town's staple trade seems to have been significant. Wartime demand for sailcloth and plain brown linen was high, and exports were still dependent upon the government bounty. With wages at high levels for much of the time, Dundonian weavers and their dependants experienced a reasonably comfortable war. Certainly, their situation contrasted well with their Irish and continental rivals.[78] Marching armies and battles had devastated competitor regions such as Saxony, Silesia and Westphalia; recovery was slow or even non-existent, with linen production 'doomed by the widespread use of cotton'.[79]

Following Napoleon's defeat, the (mainly male) handloom weavers' incomes had plummeted; in Dundee, then and later, the end of a period of conflict was good for neither masters nor men (or women). While a handloom weaver prior to the battle of Waterloo in June 1815 could earn twenty shillings for a standard length of cloth, by winter this had been slashed to five shillings. With the demobilisation of the armed forces came the return of youths and younger men from military service in search of work, which further diluted the labour market in what were a catastrophic few years (c. 1812–20) for weavers across the country.[80]

Little could be done to resist the downward pressures on the handloom weavers – a Scotland-wide phenomenon.[81] Not only was the work in weaving irregular everywhere, but it was also the practice of Dundee's manufacturers, exposed in 1834, to extend the length of the ell, and the webs, sometimes without giving notice to the weaver, thereby exacerbating tensions in the weaving trade. Conscious that the manufacturers were intent on making individual agreements with their weavers, the Dundee and Lochee Weavers Union had been formed in 1833. But as with its counterpart in Paisley, it was to little avail. Over one thousand of their number were turned out as the manufacturers sought to replace some of them – as we have seen – by inviting weavers from Ireland to take their places.[82] The employers usually held the whip hand. No progress had been made by 1849, when at a meeting of the weavers Peter Findlay moved that an approach be made to the town's MP George Duncan (who was sympathetic to the weavers' plight) to broker an arrangement with the manufacturers for a 'fixed standard of length of the different fabrics, to be acted upon for the future'.[83] The Dundee manufacturers of plainer cloths – requiring less skill than fancier work – also managed to pay lower wages than those in the surrounding towns. By 1851 handloom weavers at the bottom end of the trade were earning only around fifteen shillings a fortnight (less winding costs of over a shilling), during which a weaver was expected to have woven three sacking webs. Furthermore, at this point the length of webs had increased still further, to as many as 89 yards for lighter-weight sacking.[84] Some weavers it was reported were at their looms for as many as eighteen hours a day. In Dundee as elsewhere, competition between small-scale – or 'small cork' – manufacturers was intense and kept wages low.[85] Periodically the weavers fought back, as in October 1846 when they attempted to obtain better terms (6d a piece on canvas, the best-paying work) by 'blockading' selected workplaces, on this occasion 'Mr Bell's' factory on Perth Road.[86]

The financial circumstances and living conditions of the handloom weavers altered in accordance with the state of the market for their services and the fact that there were too many of them for the work available, despite the existence of emigration schemes – not their collective actions. From princes of the occupational league table, within a couple of generations they were on the way to being paupers. At its worst, their situation was dire. By the 1860s the trade was on its last legs, although the war in America provided short-term relief; indeed, in January 1865 there was more or less full employment, certainly in linen, 'unprecedented at this time of year'.[87] Yet with the civil war in North America having encouraged further investment in power looms, it was these that would be kept going when the war ended, the *Dundee Courier* predicting that 'the hand-loom will be stopped, and the poor weaver will be made to feel in want and wretchedness the evils of that hopeless competition which it has been so long his fate to maintain'.[88]

The formation of the weavers' union was simply one example of resistance on the part of one group of textile workers. In his evidence to the Factory Commissioners in 1833, David Baxter had not only stated his objections to state interference over working conditions but also asserted that working people needed little protection. In the workplace he argued it was the masters who were the slaves. This was clearly an exaggeration. However, it does hint at some irritation about the capacity of working people to exercise constraints on the efforts of Peter Carmichael and his counterparts at other works to act entirely with a free hand when introducing machines and processes designed to shave costs – mainly those of labour – and to loosen the grip of their employees on established ways of working. Progress in this direction in Dundee had been partly delayed by news of attacks on cotton mills including loom breaking in Manchester during the depression of 1825, and anxiety in 1837–8 and 1841–2 over the Chartist threat, which in Dundee had a physical force dimension.[89] But while anxieties on the part of the authorities had resulted in the recruitment of the shore porters and 755 special constables to protect the mills from a threatened attack, Chartism in Dundee was something of a damp squib, culminating in the locally renowned but much-mocked mainly handloom weavers' march to Forfar.[90] The lower orders in Dundee represented less of a danger than they did in Glasgow and other industrial cities. At Dens, therefore, Carmichael carried on with his cost-cutting innovations. It became apparent that two of the more efficient power looms brought over from Glasgow might be worked by one woman. Success, however, was not immediate. The woman he asked to trial the new arrangement – his best weaver – refused

Figure 4.3 Handloom weaver, mid-nineteenth century. By this time most jute was woven on power looms operated by women, but some specialist types and widths of cloth continued to be produced on handlooms in loomshops like this one, usually at pitifully low rates of pay. © Libraries, Leisure and Culture, Dundee.

to return to work the following day, claiming that the other hands had threatened her. She was immediately dismissed. Carmichael, determined not to be beaten, then approached two of the other girls and, after commending them for the high quality of their work, induced them to try the two-loom method. With the dismissed weaver reinstated, the other weavers 'were quieted and soon reconciled to the system'.[91] As noted in the previous chapter, from the outset the power loom was made the preserve of females – but now designated as operatives, machine minders or even 'hands', rather than skilled craftspeople. Although weaving was no longer considered a skilled occupation, there was an informal apprenticeship system. Ironically, while it took longer to train a spinner, weavers eventually earned more – although an attraction of the former was that full wages could be earned at a younger age than in weaving.[92] However, with the introduction of the power loom, it was calculated in 1864 that 'one girl . . . can mind two looms running more than twice the speed . . . and earn double the wages twenty years ago'. What was more, those wages were high, or could be for the best weavers – as much as sixteen shillings weekly at the Seafield Works in 1856.[93] This points to another difference between the spinners and the factory weavers, the former's wages being determined by the pace of work set by the machine, while the latter were pieceworkers whose earnings were largely dependent upon how much effort they put in.[94] This gave the weavers a certain sense of superiority, but more important perhaps was the greater cleanliness of the weaving factories compared to the stour-filled mills. Accordingly, the power-loom weavers were able to dress better, with hats and gloves, in their apparent aspiration for working-class respectability – and tradesmen husbands.[95] Observers were inclined to contrast the 'tidy steam-loom lassie[s]' who 'cultivated the social values to a marvellous degree, their ways and means considered', with the 'low morals' of the spinners, although there were those who thought that compared to domestic servants the mill girls were 'not so bad after all'.[96]

Dismissal was a crude but effective tool on other occasions when workers had failed to cooperate; at the end of 1845, exploiting a downturn in trade, Carmichael – who admitted to employing an iron hand 'sheathed in a velvet glove' – paid off the hecklers who 'stopped our flax frames in the old mill'.[97] We saw in the previous chapter that in his dealings with the porters, he continued to apply his 'iron hand' as required. There were, however, limits to what Carmichael or indeed Baxters could do in the face of competition from rivals in Dundee, let alone elsewhere. In 1864 the firm was forced to raise the weavers' wages – even those of 'learners' and the less able performers – as twenty-seven of the best had given notice that they would leave Dens, 'saying they could make more wages at other works on one loom'.[98] Prior to this, in a fashion that would typify industrial disputes in Dundee's textile industry for decades to come, the weavers had at their dinner hour 'clubbed in the street and made noises instead of going to their work . . . [and] were encouraged by the workmen and by others passing by'.

Carmichael continued to meet with frustrations, as in November 1864 when he, fellow partner William Ogilvy Dalgleish and two managers met with a three-man delegation of mechanics who wished to reduce their weekly working hours to fifty-seven. In his journal, Carmichael recorded the five reasons he and his colleagues had given to deny the request (including a comparison with the many longer hours worked in parts of Europe), followed a short time thereafter by a brief additional note: 'Most of the mills . . . in Dundee having given in to the 57 hours we agreed to commence on 21st cur.' Soon afterwards, in 1866, he faced a 'tyrannical' campaign by Dens Works' masons for a nine-hour day, which led him to think that the best 'check' on such behaviour would be to import workpeople from northern Europe. Such a step though would be so unpopular in Dundee that few of his fellow employers would 'care to incur the odium'.[99]

INSIDE AND BEYOND THE MILLS: SKILL AND SUFFERING

Mention of the masons leads to the role of males in the mills and factories. All of the owners were men, as were the managers, discussed in chapter 3. It was only at the level of the spinning flats that women are to be found in supervisory positions – as shifting mistresses who, armed with a whistle and strap, managed the child shifters.[100] However, all the traditional craft occupations were male domains. The larger integrated works with their own foundries, machine making and repair facilities employed fairly significant numbers of such men. At Dens, for example, in 1862 there were 187 'Mechanics etc' on the firm's payroll, along with a further forty-seven 'sundry' tradesmen – masons, blacksmiths and founders and their apprentices.[101] The list included foremen, who usually had a background in one or other of the crafts. The most common trade was fitter, who along with joiners were to be found in most departments. Less numerous were draughtsmen (two with one apprentice), pattern-makers (three), wood and iron turners (eleven with eight apprentices) and blacksmiths (two). There were twenty labourers. Few firms were large enough to employ many workers such as these, so it was at the twelve or so engineering firms that were going in Dundee in the 1860s where most artisans associated with textiles were to be found. Invariably they were paid more than the mill and factory operatives, especially during boom periods when new works were being erected, or older ones extended. Skilled workers were important assets, not easily replaced. Peter Carmichael complained in the early 1850s that 'mechanics' were hard to recruit, with many of them leaving Dundee for better-paid work in the Clyde shipbuilding industry or pulled by the prospect of a new and better life in Australia and Canada.[102] It was only reluctantly that employers paid such men off and fought hard to find alternative work for them in the mills and factories. It was among this section of the working class that the values associated with respectability are most clearly to be seen. Hard work, self-knowledge and self-improvement, thrift, religiosity, modest alcohol drinking, sobriety and 'rational' recreation that included reading and learning were among these. The diary of one such individual, John Sturrock, a millwright or mechanical engineer, of Lilybank Foundry, reveals in extraordinarily vivid detail the accuracy of this generalisation in the Dundee context.[103] Disapproving of the excesses of the town's mill girls – in fact, of any uncontrolled excess, especially if alcohol was involved – he made sure that his Saturday evenings were spent well away from thoroughfares like the Perth Road, and instead went into the country or stayed in his lodgings, reading and writing.

It is unlikely, however, that such an elevating prescription for wholesome living was either heard or welcomed by another category of workers – one to which little attention has been paid by historians. This was the raggle-taggle army of thousands of mainly women who sewed the coarser woven jute cloth into sacks.[104] Sack sewing was an occupation virtually unique to Dundee.[105] Outworking, however, of which it was a variant, was commonplace in Britain's industrial towns and cities, and coexisted with factory production. For employers the advantages were low costs (the home workers bore these by paying for their workspace and simple equipment) and flexibility. Workers from what was a surplus labour market could be taken on and laid off as required.[106] Sack sewing then was just one of the so-called 'sweated trades' which horrified late-Victorian and Edwardian investigators.

For some Dundonians too, this form of exploitation was a cause of concern, shame even, the obverse of the manifestations of prosperity we have noted elsewhere, in part owing to the high visibility and obvious poverty of the sewers. Although they were to be found 'in almost every house' in Dundee's poorest districts, the greatest concentration was in the Hawkhill, to the west, and close to the Scouringburn, both areas the location of huddles of weaving factories. Most of the work was carried

154   THE TRIUMPH OF TEXTILES

out in the sewers' own homes – or, more often, single rooms – although a few were employed in factories, as in Alexander Moncur's in Watt Street in the 1850s. Abysmally paid, by the piece, the sewers were sometimes the wives of handloom weavers whose dire circumstances have already been described. Later in the century there were reports of males – presumably despairing of finding any other kind of remunerative employment – trying their hand with needle and thread.[107] But for no more money than women.

For a bundle of sacks that involved some 84 yards of sewing, in 1874 female sewers were paid one shilling and threepence (from which they had to purchase the thread as well as pay for heat and light); a decade or so later the pay rate had been reduced to less than half.[108] This was after the sewers had collected and carried home from the factory or warehouse a heavy and cumbersome bundle of brown sacking that weighed an average of 60 pounds; they then returned the finished product, not uncommonly the next day, having sewn long into the evening or night. As by mid-century handloom weavers' wages were barely sufficient for a household to survive on, and typically not even this, the meagre monies earned from sack sewing made an essential contribution to family budgets – although this could be in addition to other scraps of paid employment. Many of the sewers, however, lived alone, as widows, or deserted or battered wives –'the poorest and most unprotected of the poor'.[109] They were assisted by an 'immense' number of children, not infrequently as young as six years of age.[110] Much of the sewing was carried out in the evening, as this was when the work became available at the factory or warehouse gate. Witnesses were struck – horrified – by the conditions in which the sewers lived and worked: dark rooms that smelled 'offensively' of oil, jute and tar.[111] Often the sewers suffered from chronic conditions such as asthma and bronchitis, which prevented them from working in the mills – easier employment if it could be obtained. The work itself could be crippling: one unnamed woman testified that some kinds of sacks had to be 'held in a certain way . . . and that the lifting and stretching of these . . . made her arms so stiff at night that she could not bend them herself but had to get her children to lift them for her'. By and large, however, such individual suffering was hidden from public view. It was the sight of bow-backed females struggling to carry their heavy loads through Dundee's streets that elicited both pity and protest from contemporaries. A combination of the two responses is to be found in one local unknown poet's lines on the sewers' plight. After describing their conditions – no payment even of the ninepence they earned for fifty sacks for any not tightly sewn – 'E Lindsay' concluded 'The Sack-Sewers of Dundee' with the lines:

Many a one would gladly throw
Sacks down upon the way,
If it were not for starvation,
So near their homes today.
Ye rich, that move through plenty,
Just think of poor Dundee,
And a penny throw the sack-wifies
When that you do them see.[112]

Before this (1879), a 'Don Juan' had in a letter to the press called for the town's employers to deliver the sacking material to the sewers' homes – a call to relieve the women's physical burden that had been made some fifteen years earlier by a George O'Farrell. 'Don Juan' though had made the barbed comment that while Dundee's employers were 'very philanthropic in speech', they could benefit both 'humanity and . . . the sad wives of Dundee' by acting as he had proposed. Such was the distressing nature of the sewers' circumstances that they were tempted to pilfer some of the cloth with which they had been entrusted. An example is Mary M'Kay, who was accused of receiving several bundles of jute to sew into sacks between November 1878 and January 1879. Instead of returning them to the factory, she sold them. Her plea that her husband was unemployed, and two children were ill (one had died a few days before her arrest) was rejected by the Sheriff: she was sentenced to five months in jail.[113] But it was by no means only sack sewers who were driven to take desperate measures, which cut little or no ice with the judiciary. In March 1867 thirty-year-old Helen Henderson, a power-loom weaver, abandoned by her seducer, had left her new-born child, to which she had given birth 'at the foot of the Law somewhere', clothed in a white flannel petticoat, in 'well lighted' Tay Square. She was accused of child murder. Although the Sheriff was prepared to accept that at the time of the offence Henderson had been 'not in her right mind', and despite glowing references from her current and previous employers, he accused her of having forgotten 'the maternal interest of her sex'. She was sentenced to three months' imprisonment.[114]

As conditions worsened in Dundee from the early to mid-1870s, numbers of the sewers found themselves suspected of 'overlaying', that is carelessly and perhaps 'wilfully' (the term used by Charles Templeman, Dundee's Police Surgeon and later Medical Officer of Health) suffocating

156   THE TRIUMPH OF TEXTILES

their infant children while breastfeeding, in bed or otherwise. A typical case was the sudden 'Suspicious Death' of seven-week-old Betsy, daughter of Anne Smith, a sack sewer residing in Couper's Land, the child having been injured during 'a scuffle' the previous Sunday.[115]

But it was not only among the sack sewers that such tragedies occurred: spinners too were incriminated. Very occasionally, a man was implicated. Mary Ann, the daughter of James Clancey, a labourer, of Miller's Pend in the Scouringburn, was found dead in bed in August 1879; the 'supposed' cause was overlaying.[116] The reasons for the incidence of such deaths are hard to pin down, not least as contemporaries appear to have been unwilling to investigate too deeply behind sparse announcements of the kind just noted, or to prosecute. 'About five o'clock yesterday morning William Atwal, a child of four months old, son of Mary Atwal, sack sewer, Ramsay's Pend, Scouringburn, was found dead in his mother's arms', was how the *Dundee Evening Telegraph* reported the incident, other than noting that while the infant's health had been 'delicate', there was no obvious cause of death.[117] Such was the veil of official disinterest, or perhaps the discomfort of civic shame, that deaths were most commonly registered on the word of the mother, without a doctor's certificate giving a cause of death. These included overcrowding in single rooms, drunkenness, neglect of infants by working mothers and high levels of illegitimate births. This last had been a challenge for Dundee (and Scotland) for some time and early on had been associated with mill workers (above all, accounting for sixty-one out of 158 such births in one district of Dundee in 1857) but also other textile workers, both power-loom and handloom weavers.[118] However, such factors were not unique to Dundee and are insufficient to explain why infant suffocation rates in Dundee were 'staggeringly disproportionate' (almost five times higher than in Glasgow in the 1880s, for example). Nor do they account for the fact that so many of the deaths occurred on a Saturday night. SIDS (Sudden Infant Death Syndrome) will undoubtedly have played a part, but there was a suspicion in the mind of the late historian of Dundee's working class, William Walker, that so desperate were the circumstances of those involved that in an unknowable number of cases infant homicide may have been a factor too, allegedly as the mother or parents sought short-term material relief through insurance payments.[119] But explanation too must surely include the wretched condition of many women's bodies, exhausted from their labours, and deprived of the kinds of nourishment vital to sustain infants in early life. Many returned to work within days of their confinement. Dundonian mill worker males

DUNDEE'S PEOPLE AND INDUSTRIAL TRANSFORMATION 157

who survived through to adulthood were notoriously physically inferior compared to young men elsewhere and were at the time they began work. They were also shorter, lighter and punier (in terms of chest size) than other men in the city.[120]

The greater concern for contemporaries, however – of which overlaying was part – was Dundee's high infant mortality rate. Again, in this regard Dundee stood out – or did later in the century. Earlier, in 1841 both Glasgow and Edinburgh were worse, suggesting that in subsequent decades there had been a distinct deterioration in the conditions in Dundee in which the very young struggled to survive.[121] Overcrowding and insanitary conditions inside and outside the home were clearly partly to blame. The relatively high rate for Dundee, however, was also attributed to the fact of female employment but even more so to the deleterious impact this had on home life. Paid employment, it was argued, led to women neglecting their role as wives and mothers. Dundee's women workers – or many of them – were seen as dissolute, coarse, aggressive and overly masculine in their behaviours. Intervention, tardy at first, became more noticeable from the 1880s, with policies and strategies introduced by the state nationally, while Charles Templeman and Dundee Social Union and others campaigned locally for what has been described as 'constant medical supervision'.[122] House visitations, the provision of clean milk (infected milk, and the low numbers of women who breastfed, were seen as significant contributors to the infant mortality problem) and restaurants for working mothers were the most visible efforts to intervene, but it would not be until the interwar years of the twentieth century that the situation began to improve.

SOCIAL RELATIONS IN DUNDEE DURING THE 'GOLDEN AGE'

In reflective mode later in life, Dens Works' Peter Carmichael conceded that 'a great deal of the success [of Baxter Brothers] has been owing to the workpeople . . . they are so far from opposing improvements as is often the case in other towns'. Carmichael may have forgotten earlier difficulties, but his benignity was not without foundation. In 1873 he had become aware that the town's calender workers – 'lappers' who finished the cloth and tied up the webs prior to dispatch – had formed an 'association' that met weekly on Saturday evenings and among other things noted which employers paid best. Mechanisation was Carmichael's response, ultimately perfecting an 'apparatus' which pressed and tied the cloth in a manner 'superior to what was ever done by hand'.

158   THE TRIUMPH OF TEXTILES

By linking 'the men on to the machines' the process was speeded up, one consequence of which was that they accepted what they had previously refused – to be paid by the piece. Indeed, so enamoured were they with the new device that some of them pointed out defects in the machine and offered suggestions for improvement. A little thing like this, Carmichael reflected, 'is very cheering in the din and strife'.[123] It revealed a change that had taken place in Dundee some decades earlier, and that marked industrial relations – and those between the classes – until the 1870s.

After the workplace struggles of the 1820s, 1830s and 1840s and the recent surges in support for Chartism – the last, faintly, in 1848 – working-class leaders advocated discussion and conciliation as an alternative to class war. Key was the notion of respectability, as working people, led by the skilled artisans, strove to win the approval of employers as well as middle- and upper-class society. In their turn, Dundee's employers adopted a strategy of class bridge-building, recognising that labour had legitimate needs. So too did civic leaders (who included business owners) and the middle classes, whose philanthropic activities were widely supported. Where possible, confrontation was replaced by liberal consensus. Ongoing concerns about the morals and habits of the working classes and fears that the rottenness at the lower levels could taint those more easily led astray, ensured that there was a powerful reforming edge to such efforts.[124] Key was education. Many firms established works schools. The benefits of education, however, were mutual: Peter Carmichael, for whom ignorance was a 'disgrace', railed against what he saw as the inadequate attainment levels of his apprentice mechanics – most had only basic writing and reading skills and knew only 'the simpler rules of arithmetic'.[125] They should, he urged, read more and learn more, though he was aware that the challenge was United Kingdom-wide. Although not deemed a priority by most of the other textile firms whose main products were bagging and sacking, he was one of those who advocated a school of design for Dundee, 'no town in the empire of the same size' being 'deficient' in this regard.[126] Genuine concern for their workers was demonstrated by the Cox's too, with James Cox, for example, recording his pleasure when 'any of the mill girls at Camperdown Linen Works consulted me how they should lay out their little savings to the best advantage'; even better was when they took his advice.[127]

Few opportunities were lost at least to attempt to inculcate approved attitudes and habits among the respective works' employees. Another was the practice of some proprietors to organise events for new year and other celebratory occasions. On 1 January 1864, for example, Messrs J. & A. D. Grimond held and attended a soiree in the Corn Exchange Hall for their Bow Bridge workers. Hung above the platform was a large flag depicting the works, which had been on display at the opening of Baxter Park, a visual statement of what viewers might read as a shared enterprise and recollect as a harmonious day. After tea, those present sang the hundredth Psalm, following which Mr Butchart, the works manager, addressed the company, 'recalling to mind the great benefits which all classes had enjoyed during the past year'. He expected all concerned would 'deplore' the American war, 'the primary cause of their present prosperity', but urged his listeners to 'be gratified that so much good had been done to the town.'[128] For his efforts, Butchart was rewarded with three cheers, before song singing and dancing commenced. Similarly, at a soiree held for the workers at O. G. Miller's East and West mills, the initials 'O G M' were prominently displayed, while Mr Mackintosh the manager chaired proceedings, and 'gave a very useful address, appropriate to the occasion'. More explicit in their messages were speakers at the soiree for Messrs Ritchie & Simpson's Ward Street mill workers and their weavers at Hawkhill and Maxwelltown. These included Mr Sime, a mechanic, on 'Leisure Hours and how to improve them', and the Rev. Dr James M'Gavin, who gave an address on 'How to Earn and Spend a Penny'.

The paternalist ethos this example illustrates permeated Dens Works. The 'iron hand' of discipline was clothed in the velvet glove of 'an approving smile', praise for work well done and 'by and by the looked-for advancement'. The partners' concern for their more loyal employees is palpable, as in 1854 when job losses seemed inevitable, even of those workers who had trained at Dens Works and 'are much attached to it'.[129] Sir David Baxter, for long the leading partner in Baxter Brothers, left in his will substantial sums of money for the firm's managers, deputy managers, overseers and clerks, several of whom had been employees for twenty, thirty and even more than forty years; Donald Mackintosh, manager of the heckling department, may have been the longest serving of them. Those at lower levels too were rewarded, with eighty men in the heckling and spinning departments, for instance, sharing £600 between them.[130] Baxters' paternalism owed much to the firm's unique position as Dundee's largest linen manufacturers and virtually monopoly supplier of canvas and sailcloth to the British government, which partly but by no means wholly shielded them from the sharper fluctuations in the jute trade which was increasingly exposed to international competition.

But paternalism as an ethos was neither confined to Baxters or Cox's, but prevailed through many of the town's various works. J. & W. Brown, of East Mill, and Brown & Miller were in the habit of holding socials

160   THE TRIUMPH OF TEXTILES

at which tea, cakes and other foodstuffs were served, and at which both owners and workers were present. A near neighbour of Baxters, Pearce Brothers, of Lilybank Foundry in Princes Street, adopted measures such as paying an unexpected wage increase, and organising a supper to celebrate the completion of a particular contract. In their turn the employees organised a soiree (November 1865) to thank the company for its decision to pay wages weekly rather than fortnightly. As was seen in chapter 3, similar events were held for those managers and foremen who were held in particularly high regard by those who had worked under them. Striking is the apparent authenticity of such tributes. Ellen Johnston, the power-loom weaver poet, was frequently chosen by her fellow workers to sing or recite poems on their behalf on works outings or for a foreman of whom they were particularly fond.[131]

But the fruits of industrial success (and the seeds, it was recognised, that would maintain this) were widely spread. As early as 1850 it was acknowledged that several of the town's leading employers had 'exerted themselves in the promotion of schemes of benevolence for the exclusive benefit of working men, with a view to increasing their comforts and elevating their characteristics'. Part of a 'cultural offensive' common to Britain's industrial towns, the hope was that measures taken, which included the provision of coffee and reading rooms, model lodging houses, ragged schools and allotments, would result in a 'better feeling ... between the different ranks of society' and thereby 'assuage popular discontent, and increase the general happiness of the community'.[132] 'You cannot coop up hordes of human beings in narrow pestilential closes, hemmed in on all sides with whisky shops, and pawn shops', raged the moderately reformist *Dundee Advertiser*, without regard to their social condition. 'If amusements are not provided', the people would amuse themselves, and sometimes 'without much consideration for public order and quiet'.[133] This was very much what lay behind Sir David Baxter's gift to the people of Dundee of the 36-acre park named after him – the fourth of Scotland's great urban parks to be laid out.[134] Seen later by Sir John Leng, newspaper proprietor and one of Dundee's two MPs, as a turning point in Dundee's history, the opening, by Earl Russell, a former and future Prime Minister, was attended by as many as seventy thousand people – roughly equivalent to three-quarters of the town's population. An indication of the degree of social harmony that then existed were the banners carried in the procession that preceded the opening. Prominent were those that celebrated Queen Victoria, industry, empire, free trade, and the poets Robert Burns and Lord Byron. What this points to is the consensus on a range of subjects that united masters and working men and women. In addition to those listed were a tangible Scottish patriotism, and pride in place, including Dundee's history, such as the Wishart Arch where the Protestant reformer George Wishart was believed to have preached. Other common causes included rights of way around Dundee, access to land and, above all, the need for public – *people's* – parks, although there was less enthusiasm for these among Liberals who had landed friends and interests.[135] There were, however, limits to how far working people were prepared to behave as their social superiors hoped. Demand on the part of the public caused Baxter Park to be opened on Sundays, this after several weeks when 'several thousands of people [had] issued from the narrow lanes and closes of the town' and forced their way in. Worse was what some ministers described as the 'levity, carnal mirth, and profanity' which, they claimed, further besmirched the sabbath.[136]

Baxters were one of those companies that thought and acted beyond their own works – although with around four thousand workers in their employment at any one time, it would have been difficult to have restricted all their paternalistic measures solely to Dens. These may well have emanated from Peter Carmichael's awareness of the social conditions with which the company's workers struggled. An outbreak of cholera late in 1853, for example – the third of the century – he called 'God's judgement against filth'. Equally, however, recognising that the root cause was the town's wholly inadequate sewerage system (as had been the water supply until recently), he raged against his fellow townsmen, including the town council and the Free Church which had declared a fast day to pray for relief, on the grounds that no one would 'allow his pocket to be touched'. Indeed, he felt so strongly that he declared himself ready to live under a despotism if that was what was required to bring about 'the purification of the towns and the education of the people'; verily, he wrote, 'our present liberty is licentiousness'.[137]

The Cox's too assumed for themselves a wider social mission. This culminated in James Cox's election, after being urged to do so by a delegation of working men, to Dundee town council, and elevation in 1872 to provost. During his period of office, he claimed, 'many great works were finished . . . and many more begun'.[138] Perhaps the greatest of the first of these – which actually preceded Cox's provost-ship, but which he supported – was the Albert Institute, today the city's McManus Art Gallery and Museum.

Within days of the death of Queen Victoria's husband and Consort, Prince Albert, in December 1861, across the nation discussions were begun as to how 'Albert the Good' could be commemorated. In Dundee, as in other manufacturing towns, he was admired in particular for his interest in and promotion of industry and the industrial arts: Albert had been one of the organisers of the spectacular Crystal Palace 'Great Exhibition of the Works of Industry of all Nations' in 1851 and was a champion of the British empire upon which so much of Dundee's success depended. He had also supported causes that chimed with the liberal values of many leading Dundonians – as, for example, the abolition of slavery. Although initial thoughts were for a statue of Prince Albert, what was eventually proposed in Dundee was an institute dedicated to science, literature and the arts, with no less a designer being appointed than the pre-eminent Gothic architect Sir George Gilbert Scot.[139]

The launch of such an ambitious proposal came at an opportune moment in Dundee's history. For one thing, as the subscription lists were opened the town was entering its greatest-ever period of prosperity. Indeed, it was in September 1863 that the term 'Juteopolis' was first applied to Dundee, in part owing to the number of firms which were now importing raw jute directly from Bengal, in their own ships, but also to the belief that only in Dundee was jute (as opposed to mixed fibres) manufactured for products ranging from coarse bagging to carpets that outshone even the brightest from Kidderminster.[140] Secondly, as the editor of the *Dundee Courier* put it in January 1862, when 'persons of taste' visited the town they were 'sure' to ask the question, 'Where are your monuments?'. The answer had to be that there were none – unlike in Edinburgh and Glasgow, both of which were awash with statues and other civic embellishments, and elsewhere.[141] Dundee's first public statue was not unveiled until 1872 – of the former radical MP, George Kinloch – almost four decades after a committee had been formed to raise a monument of some kind to him.[142] For some Dundonians, including most of the leading industrialists and merchants and those who provided services for them as bankers or lawyers, this was a matter of some embarrassment. While few observers failed to be impressed by the town's industrial and commercial endeavours, a widespread perception was that Dundonians were obsessed with 'the enterprise of money making'. These were the words of the Rev. Archibald Watson, who in a somewhat exaggerated speech at a meeting held to discuss the proposed institute in November 1863, had alleged that in 'no town in the world' had 'so little been bestowed in acquiring public treasures of beauty and literature'.[143] Mill and factory chimneys there were in abundance, but what for a visitor, he asked rhetorically, was there beyond 'weaving and spinning, and forging, and building ships, and making money, and eating and drinking'? In other words, art and socially elevating architecture were largely absent. So too was a public library or museum 'worthy of our numbers, or wealth, or . . . our intelligence', wrote one writer of a letter to the local press, in support of this proposal from the recently elected provost, Charles Parker, who was determined to advance Dundee's claim to be recognised as a leading Scottish town, in this regard in the form of its own fitting memorial to the late Consort, rather than one shared with the nearby counties or even Edinburgh.[144] So as the subscription lists for the proposed institute were opened, now with the added aim of hosting in it the prized annual meeting of the British Association, as many as 327 of the town's businessmen – and a few female relatives who had inherited money – pledged support by buying £10 shares in what was the Albert Institute (Ltd), with a proposed capital of £20,000. In the vanguard were Sir David and Edward Baxter (£1,000 each) and individual family members, the Grimonds, Gilroys, George Armitstead (£500), a flax merchant, shipowner and later MP for Dundee, and others from the linen and jute industries and related trades like engineering.[145] At the other end of the scale were subscriptions of £5 – half shares – from members of the lower middle classes, shopkeepers for instance, the Rev. George Gilfillan and even Mr R. Powell, a waiter from Lamb's Temperance Hotel. It was the contributions such as these which earned the praise of outsiders, who were impressed not only by the strength of support there was for the Institute but also the 'great liberality of the less highly favoured'.[146] Late in 1867 the doors of what would be one of Dundee's finest buildings were opened, on what had been one of the burgh's most objectionable sites – the Meadows, an 'obnoxious conglomeration of bunks, pig-sties, and slaughter houses'.[147] With the striking David Bryce-designed Royal Exchange and the High School already in close proximity, the town, it was hoped, would replace the older merchant hub in the Cowgate with a new commercial centre ('not surpassed by any town in the kingdom'), leading off from which following the Improvement Act of 1871 was the new, wide and impressive Commercial Street which cut through a cluster of medieval structures and opened an airway to the sea.[148] In addition to the Kinloch statue, the erection of others, of the local pioneering engineer and inventor James Carmichael, in 1876, and Robert Burns in 1880, is suggestive of an effort to begin to match Glasgow's 'Pantheon of Heroes' in George Square.[149] If these high aspirations were to be disappointed, that they were held is nevertheless indicative of the enormous positivity and ambition of the town's mercantile and civic elite in its Victorian heyday.

Part of the motivation for the Institute had been that, in common with civic leaders elsewhere in industrial, urbanising Scotland, in Dundee there was growing concern about the apparent irreligiosity of the town's working classes – or sections thereof.[150] Hence Provost Parker's advocacy of free library provision – reading being regarded as an antidote to the wayward habits of the working classes – and his promotion of the Institute's function as a public library and reading room. Not everyone was like the millwright John Sturrock, who regularly attended two or more church sermons on a Sunday, and read the cloying *Sunday Magazine* with its advice if ill to 'lie meek, and humble, and still', to sing hymns and accept your fate, if 'the Master calls for you'.[151] Among the artisan class, of course, Sturrock was not alone; across urban Scotland skilled workers formed the majority of working-class church memberships.[152] This was no less true in Dundee. Throughout much of the Victorian era, most of the elders, managers and trustees of the energetic Rev. George Gilfillan's School Wynd secession church, which had for many decades attracted large attendances, were from the working classes, albeit mainly from the ranks of the skilled and semi-skilled. Shopkeeper-craftsmen, artisans, textile workers as well as small-scale manufacturers all featured at one time or another, although by the 1870s the social status of the management group had risen somewhat to include mill managers and others of similar standing. James M'Glashan was one of these. However, Gilfillan's appeal, based on his understanding of working-class life and aspirations, was much broader. An indication of the charismatic Gilfillan's reach and influence among ordinary people was his funeral procession to Balgay cemetery in August 1878, 'a genuinely communal event', watched by over fifty thousand people, including operatives from nearby Camperdown Works.[153] Indicative too of the pull of evangelical religion – or 'millenarian yearning'[154] – are the large crowds which in this and previous decades had attended camp meetings in Barrack Park to hear revivalist preachers. These included the enormously popular temperance reformer James Scrymgeour, a layman member of the Church of Scotland and afterwards a Methodist who spoke at services of and for other denominations too.[155] The power of such men's oratory held their audiences spellbound long into the evening. Scrymgeour's legacy as an ardent campaigner against drink, and friend of the poor in Dundee, was a factor in his equally passionate temperance reformer son Edwin's election as a town councillor in 1905 and much later, in 1922, as one of the town's Members of Parliament.[156] Others acted to provide church accommodation. Following the lead of Glasgow – 'Gospel City' – in 1873 William Ogilvy Dalgleish of Baxter Brothers was in the forefront of a move to establish a Free Church Buildings Society. Most of the burgh's existing churches, it was pointed

DUNDEE'S PEOPLE AND INDUSTRIAL TRANSFORMATION 165

out, were within a radius of a quarter of a mile from the centre. Yet, 'New streets and tenements with a teeming population' were 'springing up in the outskirts – east, west, and north – at a distance of from one to two miles from the centre of the town.' The shops had followed their customers, Dalgleish argued, and so should the churches, otherwise 'spiritual destitution' followed when the populations of towns like Dundee swelled with newcomers; there was a risk too that those rehoused from the squalor of the burgh's medieval core would find excuses for not attending Sunday sermons and lose the churchgoing habit.[157]

Notes

1. Emma Griffin, *Liberty's Dawn: A People's History of the Industrial Revolution* (New Haven and London, 2013), pp. 10–20, 241–7.
2. William M. Walker, *Juteopolis: Dundee and its Textile Workers 1885–1923* (Edinburgh, 1979), p. 85.
3. Griffin, *Liberty's Dawn*, p. 245.
4. See William Knox, 'The political and workplace culture of the Scottish working class', in W. H. Fraser and R. J. Morris (eds), *People and Society in Scotland, Volume II, 1830–1914* (Edinburgh, 1990), pp. 138–66.
5. T. M. Devine, 'Urbanisation', in T. M. Devine and R. Mitchison (eds), *People and Society in Scotland, Volume 1, 1760–1830* (Edinburgh, 1988), p. 36.
6. Michael Flinn et al., *Scottish Population History from the seventeenth century to the 1930s* (Cambridge, 1977), pp. 466–7.
7. Louise Miskell and C. A. Whatley, '"Juteopolis" in the making: Linen and the industrial transformation of Dundee, c. 1820–1850', *Textile History*, 30: 2 (1999), p. 177.
8. Quoted in the *Manchester Times*, 15 October 1836.
9. Figures listed in Devine, 'Urbanisation', p. 40.
10. Eleanor Gordon, *Women and the Labour Movement in Scotland 1850–1914* (Oxford, 1991), p. 20.
11. Walker, *Juteopolis*, p. 86.
12. Calculated from B. Lenman, C. Lythe and E. Gauldie, *Dundee and its Textile Industry 1850–1914* (Dundee, 1969), p. 11.
13. UDA, MS 11/5/2, Census of the Workers at Dens Works, 4 April 1861.
14. W. A. Graham Clark, *Linen, Jute, and Hemp Industries in the United Kingdom* (Washington, 1913), p. 170.
15. *People's Journal*, 25 May 1867.
16. Malcolm Gray, 'The social impact of agrarian change in the rural lowlands', in Devine and Mitchison (eds), *People and Society*, pp. 57–62.
17. UDA, Peter Carmichael, II, Life and Letters, 1, pp. 30, 81.
18. Flinn et al., *Scottish Population History*, p. 456.

19. Niall Whelehan, 'Saving Ireland in Juteopolis: Class and diaspora in the Irish Ladies' Land League', *History Workshop Journal*, 90 (Autumn 2020), p. 77.
20. *Dublin Weekly Register*, 12 July 1834.
21. *Perthshire Courier*, 20 October 1825; *Perthshire Constitutional and Journal*, 14 August 1835; Richard B. McCready, 'Irish Catholicism and nationalism in Scotland: The Dundee experience, 1850–1922', *Irish Studies Review*, 6: 3 (1998), p. 247.
22. Brenda Collins, 'The origins of Irish immigration to Scotland in the nineteenth and twentieth centuries', in T. M. Devine (ed.), *Irish Immigrants and Scottish Society in the Nineteenth and Twentieth Centuries* (Edinburgh, 1991), pp. 8–12.
23. *Newry Herald*, 27 April 1858.
24. *Dundee, Perth & Cupar Advertiser*, 26 December 1856.
25. Walker, *Juteopolis*, p. 121.
26. Whelehan, 'Saving Ireland', p. 81.
27. E. P. Thompson, 'Time, work-discipline and industrial capitalism', in E. P. Thompson, *Customs in Common* (London, 1993 edn), pp. 358–9.
28. John R. Hume, *Early Days in a Dundee Mill* (Dundee, 1980), p. 14.
29. Christopher A. Whatley (ed.), *The Diary of John Sturrock, Millwright, Dundee, 1864–65* (East Linton, 1995), p. 8.
30. *Dundee, Perth & Cupar Advertiser*, 9 July 1852.
31. Hume, *Early Days*, p. 14.
32. UDA, MS120/1/4, Agreement, James Grimond and John Lindsay, 2 February 1829.
33. UDA, MS120/1/2, Johanne McKay to James Grimond, 2 November 1826.
34. UDA, MS 11/1/3, Glamis Mill Account Book, 1806–15, p. 63.
35. Diary, James Cox, p. 62; UDA, MS 120/1/1, Grimond Collection, 'List of hands engaged from Whit to Mart 1824'.
36. UDA, MS120/1/6, James Grimond to James Watt, 8 October 1832.
37. Carmichael, Reminiscences, 1, p. 190.
38. Reprinted in the *Dundee Courier*, 27 November 1865.
39. Reported in the *Manchester Times*, 15 October 1836.
40. *Perthshire Courier*, 23 June 1836.
41. Charles McKean, Bob Harris and Christopher A. Whatley, 'An introduction to Georgian Dundee', in Charles McKean, Bob Harris and Christopher Whatley (eds), *Dundee: Renaissance to Enlightenment* (Dundee, 2009), pp. 138–44.
42. Carmichael, Reminiscences, 1, p. 177.
43. Royal Commission on the Employment of Children in Factories: Second Report, Minutes of Evidence (1833), p. 28.
44. 'Parish of Dundee', in *New Statistical Account, XI, County of Forfar*, pp. 4–5.

DUNDEE'S PEOPLE AND INDUSTRIAL TRANSFORMATION   167

45. House of Commons Papers, Return of Mills and Factories, 1837–8; Number of Persons Employed in Cotton, Woollen, Worsted, Flax and Silk Factories of UK, pp. 330–1.
46. *Dundee, Perth & Cupar Advertiser*, 23 March 1849.
47. Ibid., 26 December 1856.
48. UDA, MS11/5/42, Notes on Spinning 3 lbs Tow, Upper Dens, December 1855.
49. Royal Commission on the Employment of Children in Factories, p. 26.
50. Christopher A. Whatley, 'Altering images of the industrial city: The case of James Myles, the "Factory Boy", and mid-Victorian Dundee', in Christopher A. Whatley, Bob Harris and Louise Miskell (eds), *Victorian Dundee: Image and Realities* (2nd edn, Dundee, 2011), p. 79.
51. Whatley, 'Altering images', pp. 80–1.
52. *People's Journal*, 28 September 1860.
53. Ibid., 18 April 1868.
54. Whatley, 'Altering images', pp. 97–8.
55. James Myles, *Rambles in Forfarshire, or Sketches in Town and Country* (Dundee, 1850), pp. 17–18.
56. Margaret Knight, 'She Devils: Women and Crime in Dundee, 1842–1852 (unpublished MA dissertation, University of Dundee, 1994), pp. 10, 19–38.
57. *Dundee Advertiser*, 5 June 1861.
58. *People's Journal*, 24 May 1862.
59. Hume, *Early Days*, pp. 14, 20.
60. *Dundee Courier*, 8 March 1981.
61. For this and other cases, see, for example, National Register of Archives, SC45/1/12, Dundee Sheriff Court, 1863–4.
62. Royal Commission on the Employment of Children, p. 25.
63. Ibid., pp. 16–18.
64. For example, *Dundee, Perth, and Cupar Advertiser*, 18 October 1853.
65. Whatley, 'Altering images', p. 79.
66. *Dundee Courier*, 27 November 1865.
67. House of Commons Papers, Warrant on Which Various Persons were Apprehended in October 1845 at Dundee (1846), pp. 1–4.
68. See, for example, *Dundee Courier*, 3 March 1846; *Morning Post*, 3 April 1856.
69. Carmichael, Reminiscences, 1, pp. 178–9.
70. Carmichael, III, Life and Letters, 2, pp. 78–9.
71. *Glasgow Herald*, 22 April 1850.
72. Gordon, *Women and the Labour Movement*, p. 146.
73. Aileen Black, *Gilfillan of Dundee, 1813–1878* (Dundee, 2006), p. 74.
74. Whatley, 'Altering images', p. 80.
75. William Brown, *Reminiscences of Flax Spinning* (Dundee, 1962), p. 25.

168   THE TRIUMPH OF TEXTILES

76. Dennis Chapman, 'The combination of hecklers in the east of Scotland 1822 and 1827', *Scottish Historical Review*, 27: 104 (October 1948), pp. 156–62; A. J. Warden, *The Linen Trade, Ancient and Modern* (London, 1868 edn), p. 658.

77. Bob Harris, 'How radical a town? Dundee and the French Revolution', in Charles McKean, Bob Harris and Christopher A.Whatley (eds), *Victorian Dundee: Image and Realities* (Dundee, 2011 edn), p. 206.

78. Miskell and Whatley, '"Juteopolis" in the making', pp. 177–8.

79. Ibid., p. 176.

80. Norman Murray, *The Scottish Handloom Weavers 1790–1950: A Social History* (Edinburgh, 1978), pp. 64–75, 226.

81. Murray, *Scottish Handloom Weavers*, pp. 42–8.

82. *Dublin Morning Register*, 9 July 1834.

83. *Dundee, Perth & Cupar Advertiser*, 9 October 1849.

84. Ibid., 16 December 1851.

85. Murray, *Scottish Handloom Weavers*, pp. 67–8.

86. *Northern Warder*, 1 October 1846.

87. *Dundee Advertiser*, 12 January 1865.

88. *Dundee Courier*, 12 September 1864.

89. Murray, *Scottish Handloom Weavers*, pp. 228–33.

90. Whatley, 'Altering images', p. 83.

91. Carmichael, Reminiscences, 1, pp. 270–1.

92. Gordon, *Women and the Labour Movement*, pp. 157–8.

93. *Dundee, Perth & Cupar Advertiser*, 11 November 1856.

94. Gordon, *Women and the Labour Movement*, p. 157.

95. Ibid., pp. 156–61.

96. Whatley, 'Altering images', p. 79.

97. Carmichael, II, Life and Letters, 1, p. 29.

98. UDA, MS11/5/2, Calculations Book, New Work, No. 2, p. 144.

99. Carmichael, II, Life and Letters, 1, pp. 327–8.

100. Gordon, *Women and the Labour Movement*, p. 151.

101. UDA, MS11/5/2, Number of Mechanics etc, October 1862.

102. Carmichael, II, Life and Letters, 1, p. 179.

103. Whatley, *Diary of John Sturrock*.

104. Lythe and Gauldie, *Dundee and its Textile Industry*, p. 58.

105. *Royal Commission on the Employment of Children in Trades and Manufactures not Regulated by Law* (1864), p. 230.

106. Alice J. Albert, 'Fit work for women: Sweated home-workers in Glasgow, c. 1875–1914', in Eleanor Gordon and Esther Breitenbach (eds), *The World is Ill-Divided: Women's Work in Scotland in the Nineteenth and Early Twentieth Centuries* (Edinburgh, 1990), pp. 158–61.

107. Walker, *Juteopolis*, p. 91.

108. Myra Baillie, 'Mary Lily Walker of Dundee: Social Worker and Reformer' (unpublished MA thesis, McMaster University, 1996), p. 30.

109. *Dundee Courier and Argus*, 14 October 1864.
110. *Royal Commission on the Employment of Children*, p. 231.
111. *Dundee Courier*, 15 August 1873.
112. 'The sack-sewers of Dundee', in Kirstie Blair (ed.), *Poets of the People's Journal* (Glasgow, 2016), pp. 149–50.
113. *Dundee Courier*, 12 March 1879.
114. *Dundee Advertiser*, 16 March 1867.
115. *Evening Telegraph*, 11 February 1879.
116. *Dundee Courier*, 22 August 1879.
117. *Dundee Evening Telegraph*, 8 February 1873.
118. *Dundee, Perth & Cupar Advertiser*, 2 March 1858.
119. William M. Walker, 'Infant suffocation – Historical myth?', *Scottish Economic & Social History*, 8 (1988), pp. 56–72.
120. Walker, *Juteopolis*, pp. 104–6.
121. Flinn, *Scottish Population*, p. 379.
122. Emma Wainwright, '"Constant medical supervision": Locating reproductive bodies in Victorian and Edwardian Dundee', *Health & Place*, 9 (2003), pp. 163–74.
123. Carmichael, III, Life and Letters, 2, p. 49.
124. Whatley, 'Altering images', pp. 82–9.
125. Carmichael, II, Life and Letters, I, p. 143.
126. *Dundee, Perth & Cupar Advertiser*, 25 March 1853.
127. UDA, Diary, James Cox, '1834 and up', bundle headed '1866'.
128. *Dundee Advertiser*, 1 January 1864.
129. Carmichael, II, Life and Letters, I, p. 197.
130. Carmichael, III, Life and Letters, 2, pp. 33–4.
131. Judith Rosen, 'Class and poetic communities: The work of Ellen Johnston, "The Factory Girl"', *Victorian Poetry*, 39: 2 (Summer 2001), p. 218.
132. Patrick Joyce, *Visions of the People: Industrial England and the Question of Class, 1848–1914* (Cambridge, 1991), p. 59; James Myles, *Rambles*, p. xiii.
133. *Dundee Advertiser*, 7 June 1853.
134. Whatley, *Diary of John Sturrock*, p. 19.
135. Whatley, 'Altering images', pp. 80, 92–4.
136. Dundee Public Library [DPL], Lamb Collection, 103 (9), Rev. J. MacPherson, 'A Word to the People of God in Dundee on the Opening of Baxter Park on the Sabbath-Day' (1863); *People's Journal*, 21, 28 February 1863.
137. Carmichael, II, Life and Letters, I, p. 158.
138. UDA, Diary, James Cox, notes (1866) in folder.
139. Charles McKean and David Walker, *Dundee: An Illustrated Architectural Guide* (Edinburgh, 1993), pp. 43–4.
140. *Dundee Courier*, 17 September 1863.
141. *Dundee Courier*, 7 January 1862.

142. Christopher A. Whatley, 'Contesting memory and public places: Albert Square and Dundee's Pantheon of Heroes', in Whatley, Harris and Miskell (eds), *Victorian Dundee*, pp. 176–87.
143. *Dundee Advertiser*, 27 November 1863.
144. *Dundee Courier*, 31 January, 17 and 27 February 1862.
145. Jim Tomlinson, 'The Subscribers' (https://mcmanus168.org.uk).
146. *Dundee Advertiser*, 30 December 1863.
147. *Dundee Advertiser*, 10 December 1863.
148. Rob Duck and Charles McKean, 'Docks, railways or institutions: Competing images for mid-nineteenth-century Dundee', in Whatley, Harris and Miskell (eds), *Victorian Dundee*, pp. 166–8.
149. Whatley, 'Contesting memory', pp. 173–4.
150. Callum G. Brown, *Religion and Society in Scotland Since 1707* (Edinburgh, 1997), pp. 102–3.
151. Whatley, *Diary of John Sturrock*, p. 10.
152. Callum G. Brown, 'Religion, class and church growth', in W. Hamish Fraser and R. J. Morris (eds), *People and Society in Scotland, Volume II, 1830–1914* (Edinburgh, 1990), p. 321.
153. Black, *Gilfillan of Dundee*, pp. 34–72.
154. Walker, *Juteopolis*, pp. 25, 270–6.
155. *Dundee Courier*, 25 April 1887.
156. See John Kemp, 'Red Tayside? Political change in early twentieth-century Dundee', in Whatley, Harris and Miskell (eds), *Victorian Dundee*, pp. 217–38.
157. *Dundee Courier & Argus*, 14 March 1873.

5

The Darker Side

Industrial Dundee: a 'very dangerous place to live'?

Notwithstanding the evidence there is of widespread religiosity, or at least of a search for spiritual sustenance, also identified in Dundee was a disturbing undercurrent of 'vulgarity, domestic discomfort, misery, and vice', much of it 'springing out of our present prosperity'. Thus, in spite of full employment and better wages brought about by the American Civil War, there was an increase in drink and disorderly cases from 1,425 in 1863 to 1,804 the following year.[1] Just prior to this, in 1862, there were reckoned to be between six hundred and seven hundred shebeens in Dundee – unlicensed drinking dens, some of which were also brothels, the bulk of which were operated by women such as Jane Brown or Lawson, Hawkhill, Mary Smith, Tyndal's Wynd, and Isobel Thomson or Davidson, Fenton's Close, although some couples and a few men were also proprietors.[2] Most shebeens were small, catering for ten or a dozen customers, although as was observed at the time, this meant that there were probably as many as seven thousand of these. It was a matter of some satisfaction then, when the 'New Club' or 'monster shebeen' in St Margaret's Close was shut down in 1862.[3] Along with profuse amounts of alcohol, the 'Club' offered its male patrons (of all classes) gambling, 'scientific' boxing, 'worrying' of cats and dogs, and the aforementioned brothel services. Yet the following year, instigated by sailors, a riot involving 'the lowest rabble of the town' broke out in an effort to stop the police closing other shebeens.[4] With the help of the Public Houses Amendment (Scotland) Act, however, and the diligence of the Shebeen Court, progress was made, so that by 1865 the number had been reduced to one hundred and fifty. Even so, what one of the town's temperance advocates ('Anti-Bacchus') described as 'dens of iniquity', and a 'disgrace

172   THE TRIUMPH OF TEXTILES

to the town and immediate cause of desolation and ruin', continued to flourish.[5]

This less salubrious aspect of Dundee's social life, however, preceded jute and can be dated back at least to the early concentration of textile manufacturing in the town. The English traveller Henry Skrine had visited Dundee in 1793. He had been impressed with what he saw from afar and the pleasant approach. Once in the centre, however, he found it 'an irregular and unpleasant place', and oppressively malodorous, its inhabitants 'unusually coarse in manners', many 'strangely huddled together . . . conveying an appearance of unbounded population exceeding that of our most crowded English towns'. This was not simply the biased account of a Scoto-phobic Englishman. In his generally positive report on Dundee for the *Statistical Account* of the 1790s, the Rev. Robert Small listed a number of 'disadvantages and defects', which echoed Skrine's observations. These included lanes and streets that were 'uncommonly narrow' (when elsewhere in Scotland's towns, street widening and straightening was going on apace; Dundee moved more slowly, and in a distinctive direction, eschewing the contemporaneous New Town movement).[6] Dwellings were too tightly packed and overcrowded, 'many possessing only single rooms'. Open spaces, for walks and play, for young and old, were wanting.[7] Inadequate room for the living and, with the 1564 Howff graveyard on the northern edge of the burgh full to overflowing, 'too little room for the dead', was Small's succinct assessment. Even three decades later, gas lighting was far from generally available, and even though 'excellent' water was being distributed from the burgh's nine 'ancient' wells in pipes, as late as the mid-1840s it was still being sold on the streets by carters who had brought water in from the countryside for those less fortunate. Many mill proprietors had had to sink wells in order to provide water for their steam engines – a cause of disputes between neighbouring mills – while fires, a constant threat, were hard to extinguish.[8]

No one was spared from virulent diseases such as smallpox and typhus, from which even the linen and jute magnate James Cox contracted and suffered from in 1837 and 1851 respectively.[9] Three of his children died of scarlet fever. It was after this that he moved his family away from Dudhope Crescent on the outskirts of the burgh, first to a detached property, Clement Park in Lochee, and later, in 1878, to a country mansion near Meigle, Cardean.

It was in April 1842 that the Circuit Court judge Lord Cockburn, from the vantage point of a sitting in Perth where there had been a record number of cases brought before him, most from Dundee, vented

THE DARKER SIDE

his disgust about the town and 'its steam engines, precarious wealth, its starving, turbulent population, its vulgar blackguardism'.[10]

Cockburn was right about the precariousness of Dundee's economy – as we have already seen in relation to the linen industry's businessmen in the first half of the century. But early on too, perceptive observers of the pattern of boom and slump which characterised the textile trade were wary of the consequences of a growing population dependent for its subsistence upon money wages. A 'serious matter' was that any 'deviation from prudence in a few merchants and manufacturers' might, 'in a moment', lead to the curtailment of work, 'so as to produce wide-spread misery'.[11]

Even during the better times of the later 1840s and beyond, there was a bleaker side to Dundee's social life, outside the reach of paternalistic exhortations and interventions. These could do little about periodic unemployment, industrial injury, sickness and old age.[12] The homes of thousands were 'miserable, wretched, dark, and dirty', not least – it was alleged – owing to a factor that distinguished Dundee from Scotland's other cities and large towns: the ready availability and attraction of work for women, including those who were married. The percentage of married women in work was almost certainly higher than the official figure of just under 25 per cent.[13] Such women, it was argued, should be attending to their domestic duties.[14]

Ominously too, the headlong speculative rush into mill spinning had attracted migrants to the town in search of the promised work; but incomers needed to be housed. And such accommodation as had been available was now fully inhabited. If a single works was being built or expanded, as at Dens in the mid-1830s, much of the demand for additional housing could be met. With the construction of the new mill at Dens the nearby ground of Wallace Craigie was feued and 'an extensive suburb' created along with a new road running through it – Princes Street.[15] But larger surges in the numbers of works premises simply exacerbated a problem that had been identified in the previous century, had become more apparent in the 1830s, was an issue in the 1840s and 1850s when 'a great want' of housing was reported, and a crisis thirty years later. Between 1841 and 1861, only 568 new homes had been built. By the time hard comparative data became available, it was clear how bad the situation had become. Although the scale of Glasgow's housing problems was greater than Dundee's, as the twentieth century opened, Scotland's two leading industrial cities were vying with each other as to which had the highest proportion of their families living in one- and two-roomed houses. Dundee won, with 71.8 per cent in this category,

174   THE TRIUMPH OF TEXTILES

but Glasgow had more single ends and Dundee's working people more often were able to find two rooms.[16] Paisley, a better comparator as another textiles-dominated town of similar size to Dundee, outdid them both, however, with 37 per cent of families living in one room.[17] Even so, the statistics do little to conceal the appalling circumstances in which so many Dundonians were accommodated, and the extent of overcrowding by lodgers within two-room houses, which so many commentators noted and deplored.[18]

'A Townsman' was only one of many critics of the housing situation in 1865, as the textile industry boomed as never before. Dundee, he asserted, was in this regard a disgrace, and becoming 'a very dangerous place to live', with waves of diseases such as smallpox, typhus, cholera and other fevers periodically striking the town's inhabitants and killing large numbers of them. Poor housing was only part of the problem: water closets were a rarity, and sewage disposal was messy, inadequate and the stench pervasive – and was the primary cause of the periodic outbreaks of typhus and typhoid from which the town's population suffered. Some areas were worse than others; in 1847, for example, a doctor familiar with typhus and its causes observed that he had 'never found typhus fever to be absent' from the Scouringburn. 'For years past Dundee had been confessedly the dirtiest town in Scotland', admitted Neish, the jute pioneer who also campaigned for cleaner streets, that is, better paved and free of human waste – the right to and responsibility for the disposal of which was leased to a private scavenging contractor.[19] Making matters worse was the practice particularly among the inhabitants of the Hilltown of keeping pigs (a common 'domestic accompaniment' according to 'C.C.H.', in a column headed 'Bonnie Dundee' written for *The Builder* magazine), although it was in Millar's Wynd off Perth Road that William Brown was accused of allowing his tenants to keep twenty-three of the animals.[20] Their purpose, it was understood, was to 'meet the half-yearly or yearly wants' that occurred largely among the Irish, although this allegation was countered by the observation that 'Sandy may [also] be met with an occasional grunter in his safe keeping'.[21]

Whatever their source, the odours of urine and excrement were compounded in the shoreside and central districts with that of boiling whale oil. Many streets and most passages and closes were unpaved, while over the town there was often a pall of sooty smoke that emitted from the numerous works' chimneys.[22] It was only in 1869 that the burgh took on responsibility for the supply of clean water – as the Dundee Water Commissioners – and it was only in 1876 that the Chamber of Commerce felt able to pronounce the problem resolved.[23] A handful of the owners

THE DARKER SIDE   175

of the town's linen and jute works had built or were erecting housing for their employees – Kinmond & Luke and the Gilroys found praise locally. Others were wary; indeed, it was not until the mid-1860s, and then reluctantly, having decided early on not to provide their workers with housing, that Baxters felt obliged to act on the grounds of 'necessity and humanity'. Inspired by brick-built workers' housing in Glasgow, they decided to do likewise, putting up some eighty small houses, with two rooms each ten feet square – a fact that caused Peter Carmichael to wonder where the occupants said their prayers.[24] There were, though, tensions with the 'double relationship of master and landlord', and fairly soon the policy of letting the houses to the best and most reliable tenants was adopted, whether or not they were company employees.

However, unable to keep pace with the sudden influxes of migrants to a town where low wages meant there was a limit to what rents could be charged, private builders were unwilling to risk their capital in speculative ventures. They preferred, implied 'Townsman', to build palaces for the employers of labour rather than build for the employed.[25] Others were more strident, demanding that the mill owners should 'come forward with a scheme for the erection of houses' to provide accommodation for 'the many hundreds and thousands of operatives they have brought to the town'. Less concerned about a housing shortage was 'A. B.', who while conceding that ventilation was a problem in the 'narrow lanes to be found in the bowels of the ancient royalty', pointed to 'large blocks and long ranges of streets of dwelling houses for the use of the working classes' from Blackness Toll in the west of Dundee, through the Scouringburn to Maxwelltown in the east.[26] It was, he asserted, the tenants of such properties who were largely responsible for Dundee's episodic fevers, and 'the dirty habits common to a certain class of immigrants, who have been encouraged to take up their abode amongst us'. This was plainly a reference to the Irish, whose 'vile slang and immoral habits' had, it was alleged, 'seriously injured the general character of the poor population of Dundee' – and Scotland. They had, wrote James Myles, an observer of and writer on early industrial Dundee, 'like the Goths and Vandals of old, deluged all the manufacturing towns of modern civilisation'.[27] Unscrubbed floors, rotten straw for bedding, boulder stones for seats and wooden panelling being torn down for kindling were among the charges directed at the Irish settlers.[28] Accordingly, Roman Catholic priests were urged by the editor of the *Dundee Advertiser* to embark on a campaign against 'rags and dirt', as a means of reducing anti-Catholic feeling which from the 1830s until the 1870s was endemic in Lowland Scotland.[29]

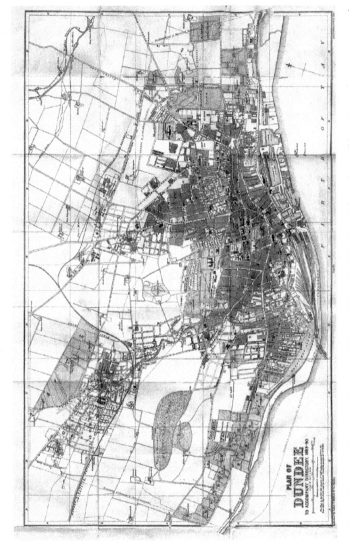

Figure 5.1 Map of Dundee, late nineteenth century. Most of Dundee's industrial works and housing were compressed within a central area some two miles along the river and extensive docks, and one and a half miles northwards. New middle-class housing was extending up the slopes of the Law. The grander detached mansion houses of the textile princes are to the west, cut off from the Tay by the Dundee and Perth (Caledonian) railway line. © University of Dundee Archives.

THE DARKER SIDE

This was not the first attack on the Irish in Dundee. Rioting aimed at 'forcing them [the Irish] to leave the Town' broke out in the early summer of 1830, in part owing to fears among the labouring classes about wage reductions and the loss of employment, as well as a 'foolish dread of Popery' (there was by this time a resident Roman Catholic priest in Dundee), while more formally, on the top of the Law hill, 'pugilistic combats' were fought by the 'champions' of Ireland and Scotland.[30] Nor would it be the last. There was a strong Protestant presence, evidenced by the formation – unusually in one location – of branches of both the Protestant Association and the Protestant Operative Association. Resentment about the influx of poor Irish migrants resulting from the potato famine heightened tensions in the town. In July 1848 a provocative march of Orangemen, decorated with sashes and various insignia, had on their way through the Hilltown – heavily populated by Irish migrants – on the way to their lodge in Murraygate, been met with a hail of stones, thrown principally by Irish Catholics.[31] It was Roman Catholics who were accused some time afterwards of attempting to break up the open-air sermons at Barrack Park, in response to which the town's Orangemen came to the defence of the preachers: that individuals on both sides were suspected of carrying knives and pistols led to the temporary suspension of the proceedings.[32]

Yet partly, or perhaps even largely, as there was such a high preponderance of females among the Irish population in Dundee, while there was a visceral Protestant antipathy towards them and the Roman Catholic religion, including its liturgy ('a piece of the merest trumpery that I ever saw', opined the aforementioned, intelligent, consciously self-improving John Sturrock), the sectarian divide was less conspicuous than in the west of Scotland. What appears to have kept the Irish apart from much of the rest of Dundee's working class was the well-organised priesthood of the Catholic Church, led from the 1840s through to 1862 by Fermanagh-born Stephen Keenan, and in the provision made for Catholic worship, in St Andrew's Church in the Nethergate, and, in 1866, the Immaculate Conception, St Mary's, Lochee, where there was a high concentration of Irish migrants and their children. Not much more than a decade later there were four Catholic churches in Dundee, along with six schools.[33] But there is evidence too to suggest that members of the Irish migrant community maintained close bonds through attachment to their country, if not the county, they came from. Where they were accommodated maintained bonds too; they frequently boarded in rooms rented from their countryfolk. Collectively too they met as workers, as at Camperdown and other works where they were concentrated, and as supporters of

178   THE TRIUMPH OF TEXTILES

the Irish land agitation.[34] Yet the hostility referred to here was not universal. The Irish had their defenders in Dundee, such as the writer of a letter to the *Advertiser* who pointed out that 'neither brothel-keeping nor brothel visiting is an Irish custom'; and, to counter the charge that Irish Catholics were particularly malodorous, suggested that 'if you congregated together as many poor, who are not Roman Catholics, the most fastidious Protestant nose could not distinguish them'.[35]

There were comparatively quiet areas and streets in Dundee where the middle classes and respectable working men like John Sturrock could walk undisturbed. But in the industrial parts of the town a very different atmosphere prevailed, not least as within the 'thickets of houses' just mentioned, large steam-powered works were being squeezed in. Oaths and 'obscene talk' were commonplace, especially among the young, many of whom, being in work and with a degree of independence, were apparently beyond parental control. The 'multitudes' of young people employed in the low mills, observed 'A.B.', not only suffered physically due to their being confined all day in a dust-filled environment, but, with no parental guidance or time for self-improvement, were 'in ignorance of every moral virtue'.[36] Others had no regular employment – even in 1850 it was estimated that there may have been between seven thousand and eight thousand destitute children on the streets of Dundee. Often these were boys who had been employed as 'half-timers' in the mills – mainly as bobbin shifters – and who were made redundant when they reached the age when they would expect adult wages.[37] Indeed, in the low mills, where much preparatory work was done, more boys were employed than girls – 151 as opposed to eighty at Dens in 1861, for example. Others had never been in any kind of employment, regular or otherwise.

The most dissolute among them were described as 'Arabs'. The term, used in many British towns, referred to boys who were poor – paupers, often fatherless, or the sons of broken or alcoholic fathers (or, less often, mothers) who spent much of their days on the streets, frequently in gangs, and resorted to beggary and theft and other criminal acts to survive. They could be very young. John Logan, the son of a weaver and whose mother was confined in Dundee's lunatic asylum, was nine. He, his father and his other siblings lodged with Mary Ramsay and her family of four – that is, ten people – in a single room in Alexander Street. Both Logan's father and Ramsay were alleged to be 'drunken and dissipated characters'. Consequently, John disappeared for weeks on end, running about the streets 'in company with suspected thieves', and was accused of several acts of 'malicious mischief'. Arrested on 15 May after having

THE DARKER SIDE

been found asleep on a stairway, two days later he was committed by the Police Court to Baldovan Industrial School, a corrective institution.[38]

Incarceration for some, though, was preferable to life on the streets and the descent into criminality. Some even appealed in the courts to be sent to the *Mars* training ship – one of a number of training ships in Britain – that was anchored in the river Tay off Wormit from August 1869, a floating reformatory for orphans and delinquents.[39] Thus, in October 1876 fourteen-year-old Patrick Moncrieff, unable to find work and whose mother despaired of keeping him from 'bad boys', notably a well-known gang in Blackness Road, persuaded the presiding baillie to commit him to the *Mars* until he was sixteen – and possibly block his pathway to crime.[40] At that stage, all being well, he might be set on a career in either the Royal Navy or the merchant marine, or learn a trade. And at the same time would be housed, clothed, clean, fed (simply), have a place to sleep (in a hammock) and be educated, albeit under strict military-like conditions with a God-fearing, monarch- and empire-celebrating backcloth, and known for the period of his confinement only by a number.[41]

BREAKING DOWN AND SUNDERING APART

The outbreak of the Franco-Prussian War in 1870 brought about another period of prosperity for Dundee. It was welcome, as the benefits of the boom years of the American Civil War had been wearing thin. By 1867 depression was setting in. From 1868 short-time working in the mills and factories was becoming more common, as was unemployment, although not widespread.[42] Yet from 1869 jute imports had begun to recover. In 1873 more jute was imported than ever before: almost 140,000 tons, compared to the 48,000 tons which were recorded for 1867. Indicative too of the strength of the recovery, as during the heady days of the 1860s, wages rose – those of the low mill spinners advanced five times between March 1870 and the middle of 1874.[43] This last, however, had to be fought for at some works. Gilroys, John Henderson and Sons, and Malcolm Ogilvy had refused to pay. The result was a remarkable action begun in March 1874, when 'hundreds' of 'young lads and girls' left their respective mills, demanding that they receive the extra shilling a week more too.[44] This large-scale movement of the younger workers transcended discussions between mainly adult males in supervisory positions and their employers that had begun in 1871 about extending mealtimes, the effect of which would have been to reduce the length of the working week from sixty hours to fifty-seven.[45] Serendipitously,

Figure 5.2 Demolition of Whitehall Close, showing the warren-like living conditions in parts of central Dundee – the medieval inheritance that endured long into the nineteenth century. © Libraries, Leisure and Culture, Dundee.

the combination of respectable male-led negotiation and the apparently spontaneous walkout of the young mill workers was successful: across the town, wages were increased by 5 per cent and hours were reduced.[46] What seems to have been a more militant turn among Dundee's workers had been foreshadowed the previous year when an unprecedentedly wide range of employees either went on strike or threatened to do so. Bakers, cabmen, hecklers, horseshoers, policemen, shipbuilders, shoemakers, slaters, tailors and others all sought wage increases – a halfpenny an hour in the case of hourly paid workers.[47] The town's domestic servants had been active too, not in search of higher wages, but respect from their employers, and improved working and living conditions – a campaign that upset Victorian notions of propriety and respectability and attracted attention as far away as New York.[48]

This activity, however, was sporadic and uncoordinated. The mood and character of industrial relations in the linen and jute industry changed dramatically in early December 1874 when, as orders began to dry up, the town's textile firms resolved to reduce wages by 10 per cent. This, they argued, was preferable to laying off large numbers of their workers. One firm, however, J. and W. Scott of Mid Wynd Works, under pressure from their workers who refused to accept the reduction, rescinded their decision. The result was 'a scene . . . which probably never occurred at any period of its former history'. This was an industry-wide strike as over an estimated twenty thousand or more linen and jute workers – notably the younger ones – left their places of work without warning. They paraded through the streets, several carrying 'banners manufactured of staves and planks, to which were attached pieces of old cloth'. At some mills where production had carried on stones were thrown, while 'large droves' mainly of women marched along the streets chanting and singing. Their chief target was the Cowgate, where much business was carried on by flax and jute merchants and manufacturers, with the first day of the strike culminating on the High Street, where 'young girls' assembled and became involved in a scuffle with the police.[49]

But such behaviour was short-lived. The 'Great Strike in Dundee', as it was termed by intrigued journalists and newspaper editors around the country, lasted only a few days. While male operatives and others in the better-paid supervisory positions who were focused on shorter hours debated whether they should accept a lesser wage reduction, and favoured negotiation with the masters, it was clear that the women strikers would accept no compromise. A shorter working day was welcome, but their opposition to wage cuts was non-negotiable.[50] The employers, who were divided as to how to act, caved in, with most, including the biggest jute firm, Cox's, agreeing to withdraw the reduction notices and to maintain wages at their original level. A few tried to settle for 5 per cent.[51] But the workers' victory was temporary. The power-loom weavers at J. K. Caird's Hawkhill Works, for example, resumed their strike action after learning that their wages were to be reduced after all, after which Cairds locked out their dressers, tenters and sack sewers until 4 January.[52] Others followed: on 7 December, 'nearly all the mill and factory workers' were on strike.[53] This had hardly ended when in 1875 a number of firms announced a second reduction of 10 per cent. By the end of July a further major strike was under way, and by early August some thirty-seven works were shut down – more than half of the town's total.[54] Several, however, remained open, including some of the largest – Camperdown, Dens, and Bowbridge, for example – their owners not having announced a further wage cut. It was in jute that losses were being made, and while some firms could bear this, most felt unable to do so. At Dens and as a linen manufacturer, Peter Carmichael felt sanguine about his own firm's position, but worried about the consequences for the town as a whole of a 20 per cent fall in workers' incomes over the coming winter.[55]

It was hardly surprising, then, that for those on strike, despite a well-organised relief committee, financial support from other textile

Figure 5.3 Scouringburn feus. The housing on the left dates from the later eighteenth century, when flax spinning and weaving began to be concentrated in the district and nearby Hawkhill. In the nineteenth century, streets like this became closed in, overshadowed by tall tenements. © Libraries, Leisure and Culture, Dundee.

towns and the determination of the workers to stand their ground – reflected in a massive rally on Magdalen Green at the start of August – the absence of earnings forced a gradual return to work. The strike was called off early in September, although with a partial win for the workers – the reduction was 5 per cent.[56]

But the mood in the industry – and beyond the workplace – had markedly altered. Walking to the station in December 1874, Carmichael had sensed a darkening mood among the people he passed. This new-found anger can be heard in the words of David Bruce, a Lochee blacksmith who had spoken at a mass meeting there in support of the striking workers in Dundee. In his speech – much cheered by the six or seven thousand people present – Bruce questioned the reality of the apparent harmony based on a sense of common purpose that existed between many employers and their workers in the 1860s. 'If trade was so bad as some employers

THE DARKER SIDE

believed', declared Bruce, 'why did they not in their personal establishments show some sign of retrenchment?'[57] Bruce then made reference to the great suburban villas built by the textile magnates – the much-resented post-1850s flight from the burgh of Dundee by merchants and manufacturers who had formerly resided locally, in close proximity to the bulk of their workers. They had been warned: in 1865, drawing attention to the increasing overcrowding in parts of Dundee, and the absence of amelioration, a concerned inhabitant urged that 'Those who erect substantial mansions for their own accommodation' should be aware of the consequent physical and mental deprivation of 'large portions of our population'.[58] Ostentation and competitive display between the newly rich flax and jute merchants and manufactures became commonplace, as did the sight of carriages conveying the suburban dwellers and those living further out, as at Balruddery (where one of the owners of Logie Works moved to), to and from their works.[59] The bitterness and sense of resentment revealed in Bruce's speech was captured too in a poem printed in the local press during the strike itself, one of several at the time, which highlights the heroic role of working women in the dispute.[60] Written by 'Auld Betty', 'The Lassies o' Bonnie Dundee' points to the role of 'Sir Avarice' in suggesting to the jute lords that 'The factory lassies . . . [who] gae sae braw' could well endure a second wage reduction. The first of these 'aff them we easily drew', so another was proposed and agreed by the 'sma' fry' owners who flocked around Sir Avarice, 'like dirt flies aboot a pigstye'.[61] Spared from Auld Betty's critique were the 'big three' aforementioned firms who had 'scorned fae their workers to wrench a bawbee'. This would not have applied a year later. Dens too was suffering, worse even than the jute firms, so that Carmichael had no idea 'from day to day if we can keep our workers'. He blamed the emergence of competition from the India mills, but also United Kingdom legislation reducing the working day to nine hours, referred to earlier.[62]

It was not until towards the end of the decade that trade picked up again. In October 1877 Peter Carmichael, increasingly despondent about the industry's future, wrote that 'I have never seen such a prolonged depression': stocks were accumulating, prices were 'at zero', and wages remained high. In this regard he was far from pleased that a strike in Forfar against proposed wage reductions there had ended in arbitration, in which the arbiter, Thomas Thornton, had found in favour of the workers.[63] Worse was that the agent for the latter, David Petrie, was said to be 'triumphant and ready for another contest'.[64]

The preparedness of Dundee's maidservants in 1872 to challenge their employers and demand better treatment, the first time females in that

184 THE TRIUMPH OF TEXTILES

occupation had ever taken such steps, points to the existence of a potent spirit of resistance in late-Victorian Dundee. In the mills too and among the female power-loom weavers there is clear evidence of collective firmness in the face of perceived injustices.[65] Paternalism had little purchase in this fracturing environment. Benefactions designed to improve the quality of life in Dundee, and to elevate the town's standing architecturally and culturally, which hitherto had been widely applauded, became a matter of some sensitivity. Their civic generosity and reputation as decent employers notwithstanding, even the Baxter family were unable to avoid the obloquy that was directed against the textile industry's leading figures. In 1880 Mary Ann Baxter, heir to the vast fortune of William Baxter, the founder of Dens Works, decided to lead a subscription for a place of higher learning in Dundee. Earlier, she had joined with her brother David and sister Eleanor in funding Baxter Park. In 1881 her donation of £130,000 was the largest portion of the Baxter family's endowment of what became University College, Dundee.[66] No matter how commendable her financial support, it would not necessarily be universally welcomed. Peter Carmichael did so but was aware too of the bigger issue of the gulf in the circumstances of men like himself and the great majority of the population of Dundee. He was acutely aware that while Dens during the 1860s had been a 'gold mine', the biggest nuggets had gone to the partners. Even before the amount of the Baxter donation for University College was known, he articulated his concern about the 'probable discontent likely to arise amongst the workpeople as to their share in such vast wealth, which makes it difficult for those who have to guide . . . affairs in these bad times'.[67] His late-in-life reflection that he and his brothers had been 'the greatest warriors' in the cause of global peace through commerce, 'the civiliser of the world', was a cause of immense personal satisfaction. Yet the last years of his life (he died in 1891) would be spent observing, commenting upon and deploring conflicts much closer to home. Dundee from the 1870s was an industrial city in turmoil.

Notes

1. *Dundee Advertiser*, 21 March 1865.
2. Ibid., 27 October, 22 December 1862.
3. *Dundee Courier*, 7 April 1862.
4. Christopher A. Whatley, 'Altering images of the industrial city: The case of James Myles, the "Factory Boy", and mid-Victorian Dundee', in Christopher A. Whatley, Bob Harris and Louise Miskell (eds), *Victorian Dundee: Image and Realities* (2nd edn, Dundee, 2011), p. 90.
5. *Dundee Courier*, 1 January 1867.

THE DARKER SIDE

6. Charles McKean, '"Not even the trivial grace of a straight line" – Or why Dundee never built a new town', in Whatley, Harris and Miskell (eds), *Victorian Dundee*, pp. 1–28.
7. *Old Statistical Account*, VIII (1793), Dundee, County of Forfar, p. 243.
8. UDA, MS102/1/1, Peter Carmichael, Reminiscences, 1, pp. 236–7.
9. UDA, MS56/2/5/2, James Cox Diary, section headed '1834 and up', p. 2.
10. *Circuit Journeys by the Late Lord Cockburn* (Edinburgh, 1975), p. 163.
11. *Manchester Times*, 15 October 1836.
12. Whatley, 'Altering images', in Whatley, Harris and Miskell (eds), *Victorian Dundee*, p. 89.
13. Eleanor Gordon, *Women and the Labour Movement in Scotland 1850–1914* (Oxford, 1991), p. 142.
14. *Dundee Courier*, 15 August 1873.
15. Carmichael, Reminiscences, 1, p. 184.
16. John Butt, 'Working class housing in the Scottish cities 1900–1950', in George Gordon and Brian Dicks (eds), *Scottish Urban History* (Aberdeen, 1983), pp. 247–9.
17. Gordon, *Women and the Labour Movement*, p. 143.
18. William M. Walker, *Juteopolis: Dundee and its Textile Workers 1885–1923* (Edinburgh, 1979), p. 120.
19. *Dundee Courier*, 12 January 1847.
20. Ibid., 26 November 1866.
21. Ibid., 27 November 1865.
22. See Alex Mair, 'Public health', in J. M. Jackson (ed.), *The Third Statistical Account of Scotland: The City of Dundee* (Arbroath, 1970), pp. 386–407.
23. B. Lenman, C. Lythe and E. Gauldie, *Dundee and its Textile Industry 1850–1914* (Dundee, 1969), p. 9.
24. Carmichael, II, Life and Letters, 1, Peter Carmichael to Mr Peebles, 31 October 1865.
25. *Dundee Advertiser*, 24 November 1865.
26. *Dundee Courier*, 2 December 1865.
27. James Myles, *Rambles in Forfarshire, or Sketches in Town and Country* (Dundee, 1850), p. 25.
28. *Dundee Courier*, 1 December 1865.
29. *Dundee, Perth, and Cupar Advertiser*, 23 December 1853; Elaine W. McFarland, *Protestants First: Orangeism in 19th Century Scotland* (Edinburgh, 1990), p. 99.
30. UDA, Diary of Thomas Handyside Baxter, 6 June 1830.
31. *Glasgow Courier*, 22 July 1848.
32. *Dundee Courier*, 25 April 1887.
33. William W Walker, 'Irish immigrants in Scotland: Their priests, politics and parochial life', *Historical Journal*, 15: 4 (1972), p. 656.
34. Niall Whelehan, 'Saving Ireland in Juteopolis: Class and diaspora in the Irish Ladies' Land League', *History Workshop Journal*, 90 (Autumn 2020), p. 82.

35. *Dundee, Perth, and Cupar Advertiser*, 23 December 1853.
36. *Dundee Courier*, 2 December 1865.
37. See Walker, *Juteopolis*, pp. 100–6.
38. *Dundee Courier*, 17 May 1883.
39. Walker, *Juteopolis*, p. 104.
40. *Dundee Courier*, 24 October 1876.
41. See Gordon Douglas, *We'll Send Ye Tae the Mars: The Story of Dundee's Legendary Training Ship* (Newport, 2019 edn).
42. Lenman, Lythe and Gauldie, *Dundee and its Textile Industry*, p. 31.
43. *Dundee Courier*, 15 December 1874.
44. *Edinburgh Evening News*, 10 March 1874.
45. Gordon, *Women and the Labour Movement*, pp. 172–9.
46. Ibid., p. 174.
47. *Belfast Weekly News*, 10 May 1873; *Dundee Courier*, 11 March, 15 July, 10 October 1873; *Irish Times*, 25 March, 15 July 1873; *Edinburgh Evening News*, 14 October 1873.
48. Jan Merchant, '"An insurrection of maids": Domestic servants and the agitation of 1872', in Whatley, Harris and Miskell (eds), *Victorian Dundee*, pp. 112–33.
49. *Newry Telegraph*, 12 December 1874.
50. *Dundee Courier*, 11 December 1874.
51. Ibid., 12 December 1874.
52. Ibid., 16 December 1874.
53. Carmichael, III, Life and Letters, 2, not paginated.
54. *Dundee Courier*, 3 August 1875.
55. Carmichael, III, Life and Letters, 2, not paginated.
56. *Dundee Courier*, 7 September 1875.
57. Ibid., 3 August 1873.
58. *Dundee Courier and Argus*, 2 December 1865.
59. Carmichael, II, Life and Letters, I, pp. 105–6.
60. Kirstie Blair (ed.), *Poets of the People's Journal: Newspaper Poetry in Victorian Scotland* (Glasgow, 2016), pp. 127–32.
61. *Dundee Courier*, 14 August 1875.
62. E. Gauldie, *The Dundee Textile Industry 1790–1885* (Edinburgh, 1969), pp. 214–16.
63. *Dundee Evening Telegraph*, 8 October 1877.
64. Carmichael, III, Life and Letters, 2, not paginated.
65. *Dundee Courier*, 14 August, 7 September 1875.
66. Gauldie, *Dundee Textile Industry*, p. xxxiii.
67. Carmichael, III, Life and Letters, 2, p. 162.

6

Calcutta Bites Back: The One-industry City under Duress

Of late, the jute mills of India have been dangerous competitors. (1883)

In January 1897 Bailie Doig urged the citizens of Dundee to support the drive for money to help relieve the catastrophic famine in India. 'Dundee had benefitted to a very large extent from her connection with India. Indeed, the upbuilding of the city had been very largely the outcome of their connection with India.'[1] Large sums were raised from this and other local appeals, both in 1897 and in response to the famine which followed in 1900.[2] But some in the city saw this disaster in another light. Two weeks after Doig's appeal, 'Johnny', a correspondent in the 'Weekly News' column of the *Dundee Courier*, noted how the plague would benefit Dundee if competition from Calcutta was cut off, and went on to say that 'It looked as if in contemplation of such an Eastern calamity that the Cowgate [the centre of the Dundee jute business district] was quite jubilant the other day'.[3]

These divergent responses to the tragedy in India illustrate some of the complexities of Dundee's relationship with Calcutta. As we have seen in chapter 2, raw jute from Bengal was the foundation of Dundee's rise to becoming Juteopolis. In the middle of the nineteenth century, myriad other connections between the two cities were established. From the 1850s, capital, machinery and labour, mainly supervisory and managerial, went from Dundee and district to the fast-developing Calcutta jute mills, which were displacing some of the long-established domestic manufacture of jute in India. But the consequence of this development was growing competition for finished jute products between Dundee and Calcutta in world markets. This competition was recognised but brushed aside at the time of the 1867 British Association meeting in Dundee: 'There are also several large works for the production of the same class

188   THE TRIUMPH OF TEXTILES

of goods in Calcutta, and these places compete with Dundee in the home markets, as well as in foreign countries. Dundee has several disadvantages to contend against when competing with these places, but she also has various compensating advantages which enable her to hold her own against all competitors, and jute fabrics can nowhere be better or cheaper made than in this town.'[4] But from the 1870s Indian competition was taken increasingly seriously, doom-mongers asserting that 'If factories in India were held and managed similarly to those in Dundee – say with an expert commercial manager and a mill manager working together – then the words "Dundee to Let" which went the round of the papers the other day as a joke, would be no joke indeed.'[5] But there was never unanimity about how serious the challenge from Calcutta really was, in part because of the belief in some quarters that the jute employers opportunistically used the supposed threat as a weapon to resist wage increases in their industry, an argument first aired locally in the mid-1870s.[6]

Against this background, this chapter explores the dynamics of the complex relationship between Juteopolis and Calcutta from the 1870s to the First World War. It looks at the ways in which Dundee helped establish and shape the Calcutta mills, but also at how Dundonians sought to comprehend the life of India, and these foreigners whose activities came to be seen as so consequential for their own lives. In particular, we ask how and with what effects did Dundee's jute employers respond to the challenge of competition that increasingly seemed to threaten the very existence of Juteopolis.

THE CALCUTTA JUTE INDUSTRY

The pioneer jute mill in India was established by an Englishman, George Acland, in 1855, but the Dundonian role began later that decade with the 'Borneo Jute Company' (later the Barnagore Jute Manufacturing Company).[7] This first company was managed by Thomas Duff, who later became a major figure in the Dundee–Calcutta connection as head of an eponymous managing agency.[8] The managing agency form, where manufacturing and mining companies were sponsored, sometimes partly owned, and managed on behalf of a holding company in Britain, was ubiquitous in Scottish-Asian economic relations in the nineteenth century, the biggest and most famous being the Glasgow firm of James Finlay.[9] Maria Misra summarised the position: 'By the late nineteenth century there were about sixty significant managing agency houses, of which a dozen had capital assets of between £100,000 and £2 million. Most British private direct investment in India in the colonial period was represented by the Managing Agencies, and by 1914 they controlled capital of over £200 million in India.'[10]

It should be emphasised that how these agencies operated means that we cannot think of the role of Dundee companies in the growth of the Calcutta jute industry as akin to twentieth-century style industrial multi-nationals like, say, Timex or Ford, with 'branch plants' in foreign countries. No Dundee jute company followed this model. The nearest any came was with Cox Brothers' jute- pressing facility, focused on the supply of the raw material. William Cox was responsible for this initiative, because of his dissatisfaction with the 'cumbrous and expensive arrangements for buying in London and Liverpool'.[11] Generally, what grew up was a set of much more fragmented and often informal connections.

Investment from Dundee was important in the early years of the Calcutta industry, but its role is often exaggerated. As Gordon Stewart, the premier historian of the Dundee–Calcutta connection, notes, '. . . after the first flush of investment from Scotland, and notwithstanding the continuing supply of Scottish expertise, the Calcutta mills were funded with general British and Indian capital. The favourite destination for Dundee overseas investment in the middle and late decades of the nineteenth century was not India but the United States.'[12] Jute employers held extensive American investments both as individuals and through their companies. For example, Cox Brothers had an extensive portfolio across a range of sectors of the US economy.[13] An estimate from 1912 suggested Dundonians had investments in the local Trusts dedicated to foreign investment (and which generally drew funds from middling groups rather than 'jute barons') six times the value of Dundonian holdings in Calcutta jute mills.[14]

There was considerable scepticism in Dundee about the benefits of investing in Calcutta jute mills. In 1880 the *Dundee Advertiser*'s special correspondent in Bengal published a series of articles collected in book form as *The Jute Mills of Bengal*, offering a negative assessment of investment prospects for European investors in Indian manufacturing.[15] Such scepticism about investment in India was a common trope in the rather dismissive attitude commonly adopted in Dundee at this time to the fledgling rival, despite the occasional concerns over competition from that source: 'You know we have always avoided them and discouraged anyone from having anything to do with them. They are managed on principles altogether different from the Works here.'[16]

These responses to what was happening in Calcutta were a blend of cultural assumptions and simple economic calculations. The first of these may be partly explained by an ingrained sense of Dundee superiority,

190 THE TRIUMPH OF TEXTILES

with clear racist/Orientalist overtones.[17] Some of the complexities of Dundonian attitudes to India are very much on display in the letters home from India of Edward Cox in the early 1870s. Much of the tone was dismissive: 'The natives of India are great rogues as I have often already told you. Every native cheats. I do not believe there is one honest man in 1,000 of them' and 'Well! These natives are horrid wretches. Upon my word one's blood often boils with rage at them, nasty, unfeeling, inhuman wretches.' Further, 'Naturally they are a race, intellectually and physically our inferior.'[18]

Cox defended the Raj as a bringer of peace and low taxes, and, as a strongly religious man, also as part of God's purpose, anticipating British departure but only when 'the beneficent purpose, which the Ruler of Nations has in keeping us here, is accomplished'. He believed that Hinduism was 'fast dying out' and that conversion to Christianity, and contact with Europeans along with the railway and the telegraph 'are daily disseminating light and truth on every side'.[19] But this imperial attitude went along with a clear-eyed and reflective view about Indian views of the British. 'We are not at all loved by the natives – I mean we English [sic], and it is said that on passing us they sometimes grind their teeth or spit on the ground to show their spite. It is, I think, quite natural, and if some black fellows took our country and imposed their laws upon us, no doubt we should seize every opportunity to throw off their yoke – and quite right too.'[20]

Alongside such attitudes, economic calculation about Dundee–Calcutta competition overwhelmingly emphasised the differences in jute wage costs between the two countries as the fundamental factor. This became a central issue in debates in Dundee about the fate of the industry and is returned to in detail below.

While Dundee was not the dominant source of capital for Indian jute, machinery exported from Dundee was central to the growth of the industry. Along with Kerr's from the Douglas Foundry, pioneer suppliers in the 1850s, there followed exports from Carmichael's at the Ward Foundry, James Low at the Monifieth Foundry, Urquhart Lindsay at the Blackness Foundry, and Robertson and Orchar at the Wallace Foundry.[21]

Accompanying the machinery, and often with intimate knowledge of its workings, came skilled mechanics as well as supervisors and managers. For a century, even after Indian independence, Scots from Dundee and district were to make their way to Calcutta to find pay levels and status far beyond what they were likely to achieve back home.[22] In Dundee, a distinct group of middle-class villa owners, and participants in investment trusts, emerged from those having a period of employment in Calcutta, 'where a mechanic could quickly become a works manager, or a clerk could become a manager'.[23] One visitor from Dundee eulogised the life of the European mill assistant, who known in Dundee as 'Sandy Thomson' in Calcutta becomes 'Alexander Thomson, Esquire' and has several servants, pays no rent and gets free medical attendance.[24] Tony Cox has argued that these migrants brought with them a distinctive approach to running jute manufacturing, forming a 'nexus' of oppressive managerial styles between the two industries. Certainly, the Scots in the Calcutta mills were able to operate a management regime which yielded only reluctantly to any pressure from workers for improved wages and conditions, especially if that involved accepting the presence of trade unions.[25] Many of the foremen and managers had received training at the Dundee Institute of Art and Technology; indeed, Calcutta was the destination of a majority of those who undertook this training.[26]

DUNDEE AND BENGAL JUTE

The Dundee jute industry was wholly dependent on the price and quality of raw jute from Bengal. This led to recurrent concerns about possible alternative sources elsewhere in the empire. In the early 1890s the Chamber of Commerce had backed the colonisation of Uganda (taking direct control from the East African Company) in order to encourage the growth of jute.[27] In the 1900s the collective body most concerned with the importing of raw jute, the Jute Importers Mutual Protection Association (JIMPA), became enthusiastic about the prospects for jute in West Africa, notably in Sierra Leone, with the idea that seed from Bengal could be used to begin this cultivation.[28] None of this activity appears to have had significant effects. Climatic and topographic conditions, along with the flexibility of Bengali peasant production, seem to have given the region a decisive competitive edge in producing and selling raw jute in the pre-1914 years.

How much of a sphere of action did Dundee have on the question of raw jute? Economically this trade was vital to the survival of the Dundee industry, not only in the obvious sense that there was no alternative source of supply, but also because the price of raw jute was crucial to the industry's profitability, making up more of the final price of output than wages.[29] As historians of Dundee have noted: 'the industry really made its profits before manufacture began, by speculating in the fluctuating raw jute market, where accurate forecasting of supply was virtually impossible'.[30] As a result, much attention was paid in Dundee to all those factors likely to affect this supply, from monsoon conditions in the subcontinent, and the organisation of production and distribution of the raw product in Bengal, to the costs of shipping. These issues were the source of continuous comment in the pages of the *Advertiser* and *Courier* in Dundee.

While JIMPA had the most direct involvement in raw jute imports, the Dundee Chamber of Commerce (DCC), dominated by representatives of jute companies, also intervened occasionally on this issue, as it did on other matters affecting the city's biggest industry.[31] JIMPA's main activities were concerned with the establishing and policing of contracts for raw jute. Key issues concerning the quality of the jute involved the application of quality marks, the 'watering' of the product and other sources of deterioration. The watering issue was especially problematic, as the harvesting of jute in the countryside required an initial softening by 'retting': the application of water to make possible the separation of the useable fibre.[32] Some moisture was therefore inevitably present in the product delivered in Dundee. JIMPA believed that because raw jute was bought by weight, they were being taken advantage of by excessive moisture content being included in the bales (a bale weighed around 400 lb). So concerned were they on this issue that deputations were sent to the India Office in London, and representations also made to the Lieutenant Governor of Bengal.[33]

The authorities responded in conciliatory terms to such complaints but argued that the manufacturers could do more to help themselves. When the Lieutenant Governor visited Dundee in 1904, he responded to claims from the Chamber of Commerce that the 'price of jute has risen fabulously' even though the crop size was allegedly at a peak, by arguing that the problem was that the peasant was not getting the benefit of rising prices, and that Dundee manufacturers should get in touch directly with the peasant, and cut out the middleman.[34] Some official action was taken in India. An enquiry in 1904/5 noted that laboratory experiments on jute had been previously pursued, but that now more action needed to be taken. The enquiry focused on the problem of watering, in the belief that this had become recently much more severe with the sharp rise in price of raw jute. The aim of the research was to establish standards, with a view to possible legislation on the matter.[35] In addition, a few experimental jute farms were established to try and improve quality.[36]

On matters of jute quality, JIMPA also sought the cooperation of the Calcutta Baled Jute Association, the main representative body of raw jute exporters. It was joint pressure between the two bodies that initiated the enquiry noted above.[37] JIMPA also sent the Association monthly reports on ship damage, and later agreed to send samples of raw material of appropriate quality to be used to set a standard for future supplies.[38] Quality concerns also led to JIMPA to try and tighten contractual conditions, a process which was resisted by the jute balers on the grounds of the penalties for non-compliance being excessive.[39] Another major issue for JIMPA and also the DCC was the forecasting of jute supplies, with obvious implications for prices.[40] The Bengal government supplied such forecasts from 1887, based on acreage sown and expected yields, but the quality of these forecasts was often decried in Dundee. In 1904, for example, the forecasts seem to have been particularly adrift, and improvements were promised, but the issue recurred in 1910 and then in 1911, with further representations to government authorities in Bengal.[41]

The great bulk of the jute trade within India was handled by Indians, with a complex hierarchy of traders between the peasant grower and the arrival of the material in Calcutta. At the core of this hierarchy were credit relations, many of them based around long-standing indigenous commission agencies and the use of bills of exchange.[42] There was a sharp separation between the formal banking arrangements used at the top of the hierarchy by the big agencies and the informal networks which operated at village level – the latter, as already noted, being characterised by highly disadvantageous terms for peasant producers. The predominant group in the middle and top part of this hierarchy of traders were increasingly Marwaris (originally from Marwar, a region in Rajasthan in North-west India), Hindus who became a dominant element not only in the raw jute trade but eventually in jute factory manufacturing via shares in managing agencies.[43] An important measure of their growing role in the raw jute trade is the fact that when the jute balers' association was founded in 1892 it was dominated by Europeans, but by 1903/4 a majority were Marwaris.[44]

A sophisticated market for raw jute grew in Calcutta, with hedging and futures markets being established by 1905/6.[45] However, there was no Indian presence in the shipping of raw jute from there: 'the only important shipping and steamer companies controlled by Indians before and after the First World War were registered in Bombay'.[46] From the time of the first direct carriage of raw jute from Calcutta to Dundee, on the *Selma* in 1840, the trade was in the hands of the British merchant marine.[47]

A key participant in the international trade in raw jute was the Greek firm of Ralli Brothers, which was a purely trading concern, unlike managing agencies with their manufacturing interests. Ralli's had a range of interests in India, including a large role in the huge business of importing cotton piece goods from Lancashire. But 'as the leading exporter of

194 THE TRIUMPH OF TEXTILES

cash crops it built up an unparalleled upcountry organisation for buying raw produce'.[48] Alongside grain, cotton, groundnuts and oilseeds, from the 1870s Ralli's built up a significant jute-trading infrastructure, with offices in five of the principal jute markets in Bengal, two warehouses and a showroom in Dundee, and an office in London. In this role Ralli's combined the advantage of ready access to the London money market with working closely with native merchants in Bengal to limit credit risks in purchases, though the company seems to have been staffed largely by Greeks rather than employing Indians directly.[49]

How did the jute get from the peasant farm to the Dundee mills? Most jute, whether bound for the Bengal mills or for export, was transported to Calcutta. After the building of the Assam to Bengal railway in the 1870s, some was diverted to Chittagong for export, but this usually counted for no more than a small percentage of the material that made its way to Dundee: by 1913/14 only six out of forty-five ships arriving that year were from Chittagong.[50] When the first jute arrived from that city in 1878, local opinion in Dundee anticipated that this would become the primary port of embarkation, leading to the belief that this would cheapen transport of the raw material. But this ignored the strength of the merchanting route through Calcutta;[51] so despite claims that Calcutta was 'one of the most costly ports at which a cargo can be loaded', the predominant pattern of jute movement remained Calcutta to Dundee.

Sailing ships were increasingly challenged by steamships, especially after the opening of the Suez Canal in 1875, with sailing times falling sharply. But steam did not immediately replace sail in the raw jute trade, because while freight rates overall were coming down, steam was initially more expensive than sail.[52] What told against sail in the long run was not only the longer passage, which meant capital tied up in the raw material for longer, but the greater likelihood of quality deterioration during the sea voyage round the Cape.[53]

From the 1850s onwards, most jute came into Dundee directly from Calcutta, though London and Liverpool had a small share in the trade.[54] But while raw jute mainly came directly to Dundee, London or Glasgow were major ports for exporting jute manufactures, sent by railway from Dundee. Thus Dundee as a port had a heavy imbalance of imports over exports, and was especially reliant on the one import of raw jute (see Fig. 6.1), along with flax to feed into the still important linen industry in the city.[55] Other imports from Calcutta included linseed, castor oil, oil cake, bones, guano, saltpetre and tea, though Dundee never gained a significant share of this last (huge) trade.[56] There were strong trading links with the USA, with exports of both jute and linen manufactures

Sources: Bruce Lenman et al., *Dundee and its Textile Industry*, p. 105; T. Woodhouse and P. Kilgur, *The Jute Industry: From Seed to Finished Cloth* (London, 1921), p. 22.

Figure 6.1 Total raw jute production and Dundee imports, 1851–1911.

and imports of grain figuring heavily.[57] Because of the imbalance in trade into the port, many ships left Dundee empty, going coastwise to pick up a cargo of coal for transport to coaling stations on the route back to Asia.[58]

Unlike in the case of Glasgow, the local economic network only involved a limited number of shipping lines, and these were largely confined to sailing ships. Dundee was the home of David Bruce and Company's Dundee Clipper Line, which had eleven sailing ships built for the jute trade between 1874 and 1878. Barrie's Dundee–Calcutta Line, later known as the Den Line, was another significant local shipowner. Initially this line was also based on sailing ships (including *Juteopolis*, a steel-hulled sailing ship built by W. B. Thompson in Dundee and delivered in 1891), but from the 1890s made the transition to steam.[59] However, it was difficult for a relatively small owner to compete in the long-distance steam shipping business.[60] This business was affected by the fact that steamships not only got larger but also faster, so that the increase in effective capacity outpaced the simple rise in tonnage; and from the 1870s that capacity rose faster than demand.[61] This put considerable downward pressure on freight rates.[62] The result was the formation of cartels by the shipowners (called 'conferences') to try and limit competition by price-fixing and controlling the entry of ships into the business. The first of these was the UK–Calcutta conference in 1875,

196   THE TRIUMPH OF TEXTILES

which was made up of seven major British lines, none of them based in Dundee.[63] So most jute came into Dundee in the ships of shipping lines based elsewhere in the UK. In the early twentieth century the lines involved were the Brocklebank and the City lines, with P&O entering in 1908 (tramp shipping was also involved in this trade).[64]

The desire to expand imports of jute was the main driver of harbour improvements in the period after 1850. How far the pace of harbour improvement slowed the growth of the local industry is unclear, though harbour provision was a frequent source of complaint at the DCC. Certainly, the town lacked a deepwater quay until the 1880s, though the new Camperdown dock opened in 1865 and the Victoria and East Graving in the 1870s.[65] But landside improvements in handling were also important in lowering costs, with hydraulic jiggers reducing ship turn-round times to as little as thirty hours by the 1880s.[66]

COMPETING WITH CALCUTTA

Faced with increased competition from Calcutta, Dundee's jute employers pursued a number of strategies, with varying degrees of success. They sought to hold wage costs down and resist improvement in conditions, using the threat of Calcutta competition as a weapon to persuade workers to lower their expectations. They looked to diversify their product range, to move 'upmarket', where Calcutta competition would be reduced if not avoided. And they acted collectively to try to change policies in India and London in ways that would improve their competitive edge.

The argument that competition from Calcutta should frame the discussion of workers' wages and conditions became a persistent theme of employers' statements from the 1870s. For example, in 1873 when James Cox, currently the Provost of Dundee, addressed a meeting about the viability of a nine-hour day, he stressed the growing scale and competitiveness of the Calcutta industry, and noted, 'I have an interest myself in certain works there, and can speak from knowledge of the cheapness of labour there.'[67] Pressure for shortening the working day was persistent in these decades. In 1891, when J. H. Walker, a jute employer, gave evidence on behalf of the Chamber of Commerce to the Labour Commission, he was asked about the viability of an eight-hour day. His response was stark: 'it would be the ruin of the jute industry in this country, and my firm would be quite prepared to go to India at once'.[68]

Similar arguments were deployed in relation to wages. In 1895, when the DDFMOU pressed for a 10 per cent wage increase, they were met with an employers' response that even a 5 per cent increase 'meant the imperilling of the position of Dundee as a jute manufacturing centre' because wages in Calcutta were 'merely nominal in comparison with those paid in Dundee'.[69]

Competitive pressure on wages because of competition from Calcutta was a weapon for Dundee's jute employers in bargaining with their workers, and one the employers deployed with opportunism and enthusiasm. But undoubtedly such competition was an important factor in determining that jute was a low-wage industry, judged by the standards of other industries in Scotland and the UK at this time. It was not the only factor. Labour supply in Dundee was plentiful, with few attractive alternatives, especially for women – domestic service was the other large-scale opening but was spurned by many women as more confining and restricting than labour in the mill. As will be seen in chapter 7, low wages relative to much of the rest of Scotland form an inescapable context for the social and political world of Dundee after 1870.

Alongside wages, raw jute was the biggest cost to jute employers, and as already noted, much energy went into seeking to secure cheaper and better-quality supplies. But as well as action on costs, the employers also sought to diversify their products. Jute is a coarse fibre, and this put limits on its uses. The greatest growth of demand for jute products in the late nineteenth century was for sacks and bagging to carry the trade in food and raw materials which was at the centre of the 'first great globalisation' of this period. In these products Dundee struggled to compete, as the basic machinery and largely unskilled labour required for such production was readily available in India. To break out of the competitive cage, Dundee had to find products where there was greater requirement for skill, both in design and production, so that substantial added value was possible beyond the processes of spinning and weaving plain cloth. One area of considerable success in this regard was carpeting – not fitted carpeting, which is a twentieth-century invention, but rugs. Carpets woven from jute were produced almost as soon as the raw material was introduced to Dundee, with James Neish employing both hand and mechanical looms for this purpose at Heathfield Works from the 1840s.[70] In that same decade another floor covering, linoleum, pioneered by Nairn's of Kirkcaldy, also provided an important source of demand, as backing for this product shifted from flax to jute.[71] In time other companies moved into this type of output.[72] These products were for both home and export markets; for example, in the 1880s Cox's was selling yarns for carpet making in the USA and seeking to appoint an agent in Paris for the sale of 'carpets and mattings'.[73]

Local press commentary tended to talk up the possibilities of diversity in jute goods. In the 1880s it was argued that 'The trade in Jute

Carpets, Rugs &c, is receiving increased attention, and has shown further development during the year in new styles both of printing and weaving. Many manufacturers are becoming alive to the fact that there is a large field in Jute goods outside of ordinary Burlaps, and specialities are being more favourably entertained than formerly.'[74] In the following decade the boosterish message continued: 'It was early discovered that jute could take on a brilliant dye, and this led to carpet-weaving – one of the earliest products, and one of the most successful – and at the present time the world is pretty well laid with Dundee carpets.'[75]

Product diversification drawing on the benefits of Dundee from a relatively sophisticated workforce were spelt out in characteristic terms early in the twentieth century: 'Dundee is more and more becoming the home of the manufacture of special widths and weights, and this is, of course, aided by having the services of intelligent work people, while Calcutta mills are saddled with the fact that the ordinary Indian worker can turn out good cloth once he has just one particular weight to attend to, but once he has to change often from one to another he finds himself in difficulties. Dundee is hard to kill . . . there is every hope that Dundee will at least maintain its present status . . .'[76]

From the jute owners' point of view, switching as far as possible away from a concentration on low-value goods was imperative. Letters from Cox Brothers to their selling agents are full of requests for more focus on newly developed products. In 1884 Edward Cox worries that 'the old standard things like paddings and tarpaulins may be easier for you' but there were no profits in these lines. Household textiles such as bed and table covers were urged on the agent, Cox writing, 'You may think I am pushing you rather hard lest I tell you our trade was *never* anything like what it is at present nor the prospects so bad. You must get alive to the fact therefore that we must get out of the old grooves as far as possible, or at least, if we can, get into new ones.'[77]

These developments did not mean Dundee completely abandoned the 'traditional' products, such as sackings, partly because the product could be cheapened by technical change, with, for example, sack-sewing machines being introduced from the 1880s.[78] An itemisation made after the turn of the century makes this clear, and also the diversity of products even within this category: 'when Calcutta prices of narrow twilled sackings are surveyed the wonder is that Dundee scrapes anything out of the heap at all: but home trade with its grain, cement, potato and coal bags; the Central [American] States with their coffee and sugar bags; the Levant with its bags for soap, nuts and other produce; and the West Coast of South America with its rice bags, made up with brattice and packsheet for home and sackings for various purposes abroad, quite a repository of acceptable work for twilled looms.'[79] Dundee also seems to have been more competitive in yarn production than in finished products, and built up the output of products of unwoven yarn, such as cords, twines and ropes.[80]

Often related to product changes were changes in the technologies deployed in the jute industry, which were far from static in this period. For example, the rise of linoleum incentivised the production of wider looms, eventually reaching eight yards in width.[81] There are no 'heroic' figures like Peter Carmichael in technological change in jute in the late nineteenth century; change was incremental and spasmodic. But it was aided by close continuing relationships between the manufacturers and the machinery builders, most, but not all, local. Indeed, the close interconnections between different parts of the jute industry – machinery production, raw material purchase and preparation, spinning, weaving, printing, merchanting – helps to explain how Dundee could to a degree fight back against foreign competition. The city and its surrounds formed a classic case of what the famous nineteenth-century economist Alfred Marshall called an 'industrial district', where geographical closeness, facilitating exchange of knowledge and cooperative as well as competitive relations between firms in a single industry, gave a large boost to efficiency.

Undoubtedly Dundee was losing ground to Calcutta in the simpler products sold in world markets. Dundonians had conceitedly referred to Calcutta as the 'Dundee of India' but by 1913 it was clear which industry dominated the global market, and their relative importance can be seen in the employment figures; in 1911 Dundee's 34,000 jute workers compared with Calcutta's 200,000 plus. But right up until the First World War, Dundee producers still dominated the British market for jute products. In 1912 £2.7 million out of £5.9 million of Dundee production was consumed at home, compared with products to the value of £0.8 million imported, overwhelmingly from Calcutta.[82]

In looking beyond wage and product issues to trying to exert political pressure to change the basis on which Dundee met foreign competition, especially from India, Dundee's jute employers faced a range of constraints. Attempts to somehow move away from the free trade regime which underpinned Britain's integration into the world and imperial economy were for a long time inhibited by their own commitment to free trade. As emphasised elsewhere in this book, in the middle decades of the nineteenth century Dundee was an overwhelmingly Liberal city, and a key part of that Liberalism was support for free trade.

The employers' adherence to that doctrine was unproblematic when in 1869–71 they successfully pressed for the abolition of tariffs on British jute goods imported into India.[83] But from the 1880s, like many industrial employers in late-Victorian Britain, Dundee's jute capitalists became increasingly sympathetic to protectionism. Part of this was about changing political allegiances, especially over the issue of Irish Home Rule in the 1880s: 'The Home Rule controversy lost the Liberals the support of almost all the local lairds and business magnates like the Baxters, Buists, Coxs, Grimonds and Dons . . .'[84] As Liberal Unionists or Conservatives, these employers moved towards less liberal political positions, including especially a diminishing enthusiasm for free trade.

There was much complaining about the way in which protection in Germany and elsewhere in Europe had eroded Britain's share of world markets, but the real competitor to Dundee was Calcutta. However, the relevance of protection to the competition from Calcutta faced by Dundee jute manufacturers was limited. Unlike in the cotton industry, where India was the key market for British exports, the problem for Dundee jute was not the threat of lost markets from protection of the Indian home market, but the loss of markets elsewhere in the world. In these circumstances the only protective device which gained much support was for an export duty on raw jute which would only be paid by non-empire purchasers – a measure which would aid Dundee vis-à-vis Europeans but not in the competition with Calcutta. In this schema, the export tax would be matched by an excise duty on Indian purchases of the raw material so as not to increase Calcutta's competitive edge, but as critics pointed out, by raising prices such a proposal would potentially reduce total demand for the commodity, to the disadvantage of the peasant producer. No such policy was introduced, but Dundee reacted angrily in 1910 when it was proposed that there be an export duty (without an excise duty) to raise revenue for the improvement of Calcutta.[85]

From the 1880s to 1914, the protectionist turn in employer sentiment led to periodic talk of movement away from free trade, but there was little clarity on what could plausibly be done beyond the preferential excise duty. Despite this shifting sentiment, the Chamber of Commerce was wary of getting directly involved in the political contention over free trade. In 1902 a special meeting decided against protesting about the newly imposed registration duty on corn, which many free traders saw as beginning down the slippery slope to protection.[86] But in 1904 this reticence diminished, following Joseph Chamberlain's initiative in reopening the fiscal question, and setting up a Fiscal Commission. Early that year the first protectionist motion got through the DCC, though this reiterated support for the principle of 'unrestricted free trade', before going on to support 'freedom of action in fiscal negotiations'.[87] Most of the discussion was on European competition. The political impossibility of getting direct restrictions on Indian competition was clearly recognised, though the possibility of addressing that issue through Factory legislation was held out by some as an alternative response. Thus, one opponent of protectionism asked whether 'any responsible statesman [was] prepared to propose that the Mother Country should be protected against the competition of its own great dependencies' before going on to deplore the impact of the British Factory Acts in increasing Dundee's costs. He also pointed out that Chamberlain had said little about jute, but 'they might take it that he had no idea of favouring them at the expense of Calcutta'.[88]

Action on regulation of the Calcutta industry by strengthened legislation on such matters as hours of work had emerged as another route for Dundee to try to lessen Calcutta's competitive edge from the 1880s. Following the pioneering British pattern, India had introduced Factory Acts in 1881, but these were notably less restrictive than those in Britain. But pressure from Dundee's jute employers for strengthening the Indian protective legislation raised a host of complications, both ideological and political. These complications emerged very clearly from debates in the DCC in 1894. More conservatively inclined employers attacked the City's Liberal MPs (John Leng and Edmund Robertson) for their perceived hypocrisy in supporting factory legislation at home but not in India, and urged that Dundee electors should put pressure on the two to take action. In response, Leng sought to depoliticise the issue, and advocated allying with Lancashire to bring pressure to bear: 'He did not think it would be difficult to show that the factories in this country were placed at a most serious disadvantage in comparison with the factories founded in India, a part of the British dominions, by British men, and worked under British management for British interests. Why they in India should have such immense preponderating advantages over them in Dundee or their friends in Lancashire, seemed to him utterly unreasonable.'[89] This position put Leng in seeming alliance with his political opponents, the local Liberal Unionist party, who favoured toughening Indian factory legislation, though as suggested below, his position remained equivocal.[90]

Sensitive to public opinion on this matter, other speakers insisted any such action would be motivated entirely by philanthropic motives. The Lord Provost, after reminding his listeners that the British Factory Acts 'were brought into operation on the grounds of humanity', went on to add, 'and that was one of the grounds on which they should approach the

Secretary of State for India'. While recognising that 'the Indian factory system was most injurious to industry here', he proclaimed, 'they did not want protection' and the grounds for action were that 'the worker in India were [sic] fellow-citizens under the Crown'.[91]

Another contributor made the link between ownership of the Dundee mills and Factory Acts. He argued that unlike a situation where capital was invested in a foreign country, where the investor was reasonably subject to the laws of the country invested in, in the Calcutta case the jute mills 'had not been established by the natives of that country, but by the people of this country – people who were amenable to the laws of the United Kingdom; and their property ultimately depended on the protection of the British force, supported by taxation in this country.'[92]

Readers of the Dundee newspapers were made well aware of the Calcutta response to Dundee's agitation on the Factory Acts. The *Courier* of 27 March 1895 quoted *The Englishman* newspaper published in Calcutta, summarising the chairman of the Indian Jute Manufacturers' Association (IJMA), George Lyell, in recent comments he had made on the idea of applying the British Factory Acts to India: 'conditions of labour in India, and especially on this side of India, are so wholly different from anything obtaining in Dundee as to make a common law, or system of work, impossible of operation in the two cities'. Lyell went on to argue that if, under pressure from home, shorter hours were to be insisted on in India, 'then Indian manufacturers will exact, and must exact, more labour from each individual than they have hitherto done; the result will be that pressure from home, so far from reducing Indian competition, is likely to make that competition more and more effective.'

Further attacks on the Dundee jute owners were reported in the local press through 1895. In October an article from the Calcutta newspaper *Capital* was reported as suggesting that the Dundonian proponents of tougher Factory Acts for India had given up the pretence that their motives were philanthropic: 'The motive was shown to be as pure and unsophisticated as Keiller's marmalade.' Later the same month the Elgin Mills company in Cawnpore was reported as saying that 'working in the leisurely manner usually followed by women and children in India, the maxima of 11 and 7 hours respectively, with compulsory intervals now ruling, are in comparison with English rules, certainly not too great'. A similar theme was evident in the comments of Messrs Dyer of Simla, who argued against assimilation of Indian to British rules because 'the native of India, they say, prefers working lazily for a rather longer number of hours, instead of more briskly for a shorter period, and the existing system is no doubt better suited for the Indian climate and people'.[93]

In the wake of this controversy, Leng visited India in 1895/6 and published a series of letters in the *Advertiser*.[94] He argued that the biggest advantage of Calcutta in competition with Dundee was much lower wages (somewhere around one-sixth of Dundee levels, he suggested at this point). But this, he claimed, did not translate into lower living standards for Indian workers, because of the much-reduced demand for clothing in the Indian heat, low food prices (especially for the prevalent vegetarian diet) and 'nominal' rents. Citing some illustrative family budgets, he argued that wages in Calcutta were such that a family of five, all working in the industry, could meet all their needs and save up to 40 per cent of their income.[95] Similarly, Leng argued that the shift system worked in the Calcutta mills fitted with the local norms: 'the habits of the natives, consequent on the greater heat during nine months of the year, their weaker constitution, the distance in some cases of their dwellings, and their love of bathing led them to prefer working in what may be described as alternating shifts, so that they might work at two different parts of the day with a pretty long interval between'.[96] His conclusion was that Dundee could not hope to compete in the basic products of bags and sacking, but could prosper by combining movement 'upmarket' to more sophisticated products, and by searching for new, less coarse and more versatile fibres than jute.[97]

These themes were reiterated when Leng returned to Dundee and addressed the DCC. He stressed the advantages of Calcutta: 'The astonishing cheapness of native labour, wages being on average less than one-fourth what they are here, and although one-third more hands are required, and the cost of European superintendence is heavy, the low wages bill on the aggregate tells immensely in favour of Indian mills'.[98] He linked this to the argument that the Factory Acts were largely irrelevant to the competition issue. While accepting that the Indian Act conferred a greater 'elasticity of working' than in Scotland, he went on: 'I am satisfied that the Indian method of working by shifts is adapted to the climatic conditions and the habits of the people, and is not open to attack on humanitarian grounds, since the hours any of the women and children are employed not only do not exceed but are often fewer than in our own mills.'[99]

Leng linked the genesis of the Calcutta industry in Dundee to a view that 'it would not benefit Calcutta, as the phrase is, to wipe out Dundee, from which its own vitality has been and is being largely drawn'. More practically, he argued Dundee could survive by developing the finer end of the jute business, but alongside this advocated developing the use of a different raw material, rhea. But more generally he urged energy and perseverance in seeking out new commercial opportunities. There is no clear evidence on how this talk was received by the industry in Dundee, though one respondent noted that while Leng spoke of energy and perseverance, 'unfortunately, energy and perseverance alone will not suffice to do away with the stubborn facts'. Leng was undoubtedly increasingly out of step with the growing protectionist views of the DCC. Shortly after Leng's address, it received a long-delayed response from the India Office, saying that the Government of India was not prepared to modify the Factory Acts. This, for the time being, seems to have closed the matter.[100]

Estimates of how much lower wages were in Calcutta were commonly linked to stories about how Indian lifestyles meant that such low wages actually delivered a high standard of living to 'native' workers. In one of his letters, Leng suggested that Calcutta wages were somewhat less than a quarter of those in Dundee, and said that, 'It is most incredible of all that the wages they receive are considerably in excess of their requirements, and that they can, if they choose, and most of them do, save as much in some months work at the mill as enables them to go home and live at ease for a considerable time, until they have spent their money, and return to work for more.'[101]

The high standard of living on low wages was explained by Leng as a result of the climate, reducing the need for shelter, clothing and food. But beyond that, he argued, 'the habits of their lives are the results of centuries of experience. Their wants are few and easily supplied . . . they have never been used to working steadily eight, nine, ten hours a day, or day after day, week after week. Short spells of work and long intervals of rest are what they and their fathers before them have been familiar with. The, to them, comparatively high wages of the mills are necessary to compensate them for an unpleasant change of habits.'[102]

This analysis, in which any objection to low wage competition is undermined by stressing how in Indian conditions such wages bought high standards of living, is common in contemporary European representations of Calcutta. It was strikingly evident in another, distinctive, 'report back' to Dundee from India – that by two women journalists, Marie Imandt and Bessie Maxwell, sent on a tour round the world – published by the *Courier* in 1894. This is distinctive in its gender dimension – not only were the journalists women, but when they reported on conditions in Indian industry they put special emphasis on the women workers.[103] The first relevant report was from Bombay: 'Dundee working girls work for a few shillings a week. Rents are high and coals dear, a great deal of clothing is needed merely to keep out the cold. At prayer meetings these girls give their substance to send to India to convert the heathen. Why? These heathen, the very poorest of them, have a thousand things our starving people at home do not have.'[104]

Assertions about the superiority of workers' living conditions in India over those in Scotland were also made in the journalists' reports from Calcutta. Imandt explicitly drew this comparison from a woman's point of view, arguing that, 'When I declare that women working in Calcutta for 1 rupee 8 anas (2d) a week, there will not be wanting those utterances of amazement will involve visions of women starving in Dundee on 8 shillings. To draw a parallel is not possible for those who have not seen the two sides of the question. It is scarcely conceivable, but true, that circumstances forge a chain mighty enough to render the woman 1r. 8a. a week, happier, more comfortable, and in some ways even the superior to the 8s Dundee woman'.[105]

While equivocating on the Factory legislation issue, Leng, as a Liberal MP, remained adamantly opposed to protectionism. At the key debate at the DCC in 1904, he stressed that Britain had no overall trade imbalance problems, although 'a few particular trades were not as prosperous as they once were'. Changing patterns of production were normal: 'one fails and another prospers. One rises and another decays.' The problems of jute were down to local conditions, and in the case of jute the problem was clearly Calcutta. 'The mills on the Hooghly, several of which have been built by Dundee capital, and most of them planned, engined, spindled, and loomed by Dundee engineers, financed and directed from Panmure Street, within a few yards of this Exchange – these Dundee-owned and managed mills have been the chief invaders of Dundee markets, and in a sense the most formidable dumpers of cheap jute goods in competition with those made in Dundee mills.' He went on to ask whether 'any responsible statesman [was] prepared to propose that the Mother Country should be protected against the competition of its own great dependencies?'[106] Here Leng was bringing out the obvious point that the basis of trade with India was set by the imperial context.

Despite the vote in favour of retaliation in 1904, the DCC seems to have been wary of being embroiled in the political arguments about protectionism. In September 1905 it agreed to 'sit on the fence' on the issue in the run-up to the 1906 general election.[107] That election took place in exceptionally buoyant conditions for the Dundee jute industry; this may have reduced the intensity of concern about Indian competition, and the Factory Act question was notably absent from election contention.[108] By contrast, the 1908 by-election in Dundee, which brought Winston Churchill in as the Liberal MP, was fought in much worse economic conditions, and the issue of free trade figured particularly prominently in the political debate. The Liberal Unionist candidate, Sir George Baxter, head of one of the largest jute and linen companies, sought to make the protectionist case, though his biggest emphasis was on the Irish Home Rule issue. Strikingly, in talking about the industry's difficulties he focused attention on European not Indian competition, the latter clearly a much more intractable problem.[109]

The depth of worries about Calcutta competition, and the willingness to seek political solutions, was partly a function of the state of the industry. It is no coincidence that serious attention to trade protectionism and regulation of factory conditions was strong in the mid-1880s and early 1890s when the trade cycle pushed Dundee into a trough of inactivity. Something similar was at work after the turn of the century; the industry recovered after 1908, but it was not until 1912 that boom conditions temporarily returned. These immediate pre-war years were notable, in Dundee as in much of Britain, for a much greater degree of industrial unrest than had previously been usual, as discussed in chapter 7. While jute was never the epicentre of labour discontent in the city, there were major disputes, and industrial relations issues seem to have gained much greater prominence in the concerns of the jute employers as a result. Protectionist pressure and agitation for reform of the Indian Factory Acts were in abeyance.

But Indian issues still stimulated debate. It had long been perceived in Dundee that cooperation and price-fixing among Calcutta manufacturers would reduce competitive pressure.[110] But some regarded this cooperation as inhibited by activity in the raw jute market. A highly racialised account of this activity appeared in the *Advertiser* in 1911, in an article titled 'Marwaris and the Jute trade', which explicitly attacked that group. They were alleged to have been 'gradually tightening their grip' on the raw jute trade, and their speculative activity was said to have 'upset all industrial calculations'. These remarks were made in the context of considerable instability in the Calcutta industry, including mill closures, which led some to say: 'Good to Dundee may come out of the evil to Calcutta.'[111] So the love-hate relationship continued, reflecting the conflicts inherent in Dundee's combination of reliance upon but competition with India.

CONCLUSIONS

Pontificating about the extent and seriousness of competition from Calcutta was a staple of public discourse in Dundee from the 1870s.

Estimates about how big the impact of this competition was partly linked to political positioning, whether it be over wages or free trade. But these estimates also varied with the state of the trade cycle, with Dundee subject to sharp cycles of activity throughout this period. Thus, in the 'good times' in 1898 it was averred 'that there has been a remarkable recovery of tone cannot be denied, and in optimistic moments the "bogey" of Calcutta competition is even referred to with a suspicion of humour'.[112] But five years later, 'there is no denying that Calcutta has taken all the most important markets from us'.[113]

The evidence from profit levels in the industry suggests there was considerable exaggeration in statements about the problems facing the industry. Lenman and Donaldson show that in the so-called 'great depression' period from the early 1870s to the mid-1890s, 'the balance sheets of many jute and linen firms remained remarkably healthy'. In the following years up to 1914 they suggest not much changed, with profits boosted somewhat by the Boer and then the Russo-Japanese wars.[114] The concentration of jute production in Dundee, which aided its efficiency, simultaneously reduced the political significance and hence bargaining power of the city – the town had two (non-marginal) parliamentary constituencies, whereas Lancashire's famously assertive cotton lobby was linked to between sixty and seventy much more politically volatile seats. But in any event, imperial politics told against much influence being exerted from Dundee. For an imperial politician the interests of a small city weighed little against those of one of India's most important (and politically well-organised) industries.[115]

The fightback against Calcutta competition was more effective when it focused on changing the product mix. Dundee-made carpets and linoleum backing, homeware and other higher-quality products could find markets where the Indian producers were absent or insignificant, especially in the home market.[116] Dundee jute was in many respects a highly efficient industry, where the localisation of the industry provided many economies of scale. But the global market was dominated by sacking and bags, and while Dundee retained niches within this market, it could not compete across the board. While productivity was lower in Calcutta, the difference in wages was even greater. Last, but far from least, the search for competitiveness meant the Dundee jute economy was largely low-wage; fortunes could be made, and there were well-paid supervisory, managerial and technical jobs such as millwrights, but for the bulk of the jute workers in mill or factory, low pay (by contemporary industrial standards) was the norm.

Notes

1. *Dundee Courier*, 27 January 1897. On these famines, see Mike Davis, *Late Victorian Holocausts: El Niño Famines and the Making of the Third World* (London, 2001).
2. The Fund supported by Doig raised £5,556; the national 'Mansion House Fund' raised over half a million pounds: *Dundee Courier*, 13 May 1897. In 1900 a broadly similar sum was raised locally, but the MHF raised only £300,000, far less than the competing fund for the widows and orphans of soldiers killed in the Boer War: *Dundee Courier*, 3 March, 22 October 1900. Cox Brothers gave £500: UDA, MS86/11/1/1 Minute Book, 29 January 1897.
3. *Dundee Courier*, 13 February 1897.
4. 'Local industries of Dundee', in British Association, *Meeting of the British Association in Dundee September 1867* (Dundee, 1868), p. 11.
5. Communication from 'An Indian Shareholder', *Advertiser*, 22 June 1877.
6. Letters to the *Dundee Courier*, 31 August 1875; Tony Cox, *Empire, Industry and Class: The Imperial Nexus of Jute, 1840–1940* (Abingdon, 2013).
7. D. R. Wallace, *The Romance of Jute* (Calcutta, 1909), pp. 12–18; the first jute factory was supplied with machinery from Kerr's of Dundee.
8. Alexis Wearmouth, 'Thomas Duff & Co. and the Jute Industry in Calcutta, 1870–1921; Managing Agents and Firm Strategy' (unpublished PhD dissertation, University of Dundee, 2015).
9. Blair Kling, 'The origins of the managing agency system', *Journal of Asian Studies*, 26 (1966), pp. 37–47, points out that the form originated in India.
10. Maria Misra, *Business, Race and Politics in British India c. 1850–1960* (Oxford, 1999), pp. 3–4.
11. UDA, MS66/XI/6/2, 'Documents relating to the property of the Camperdown Pressing Company Limited' (Camperdown was the name of the Cox's factory in Lochee, Dundee); William Cox Obituary, *Dundee Year Book (DYB)* 1894, p. 85. For Cox's, see https://mcmanus168.org.uk/ Messrs. Cox Brothers, Manufacturers.
12. Gordon Stewart, *Jute and Empire* (Manchester, 1998), p. 20; for Dundee's investments in the USA, see Claire Swan, *Scottish Cowboys and the Dundee Investors* (Dundee, 2004).
13. UDA, MS86/11/1/1, Cox Brothers Minute Book 1896, 1897.
14. C. Marshall, 'Dundee as a centre for investment', in *British Association 1912, Handbook and Guide* (Dundee, 1912), p. 356.
15. *The Jute Mills of Bengal* (Dundee, 1880), p. 3.
16. UDA, MS86/11/2/1, Cox Brothers Letter Book, Thomas Cox to Henry Cox, 14 January 1881.
17. Stewart, *Jute and Empire*, passim.
18. UDA, MS/5/5/2/1/1, Letter from Edward Cox to his father, 3 January 1872; letter to James Cox, 29 February 1872; letter to John Keith, 3 April 1872.

CALCUTTA BITES BACK

209

19. UDA, MS/5/5/2/1/1, Letter from Edward Cox to his aunt, 7 January 1872; UDA, MS6/5/2/3, Edward Cox to George (?) McAlister, 2 April 1872.
20. UDA, MS6/5/2/1, Letter from Edward Cox to his mother, 21 November 1871.
21. B. Lenman, C. Lythe and E. Gauldie, *Dundee and its Textile Industry, 1850–1914* (Dundee, 1969), p. 27; A. Fulton, 'Mechanical engineering', in *British Association 1912*, pp. 299–303.
22. The classic, extended account of this world relates to the 1930s and 1950s: Eugenie Fraser, *A Life on the Hooghly: A Jute Wallah's Wife* (Edinburgh, 1989).
23. Lenman et al., *Dundee and its Textile Industry*, p. 39.
24. *DYB 1894*, 'The Calcutta jute mills', pp. 100–1.
25. Cox, *Empire, Industry and Class*, passim.
26. Isobel Menzies and Dennis Chapman, 'The jute industry', in H. A. Silverman (ed.), *Studies in Industrial Organization* (London, 1946), p. 246.
27. *Dundee Advertiser*, 23 November 1892.
28. JIMPA, *Annual Report* 1904, 1905, 1906. When in the 1850s the problems of continental flax production were shifting the city towards jute, the DCC tried to persuade the new imperial government to encourage the growing of flax in India. DCA: DCC, GD/CC/4/3, AGMs 1858, 1859, 1860 and 1861.
29. The same was true for the Calcutta industry, though of course mills there did not face the added complication of the costs of shipment to Europe: Glasgow University Archive (GUA), 91/11/6/1, Finlay Muir 'Draft history' 1886/90 section, p. 8; Amiya Bagchi, *Private Investment in India 1900–1939* (Cambridge, 1972), p. 271.
30. Lenman et al., *Dundee and its Textile Industry*, p. 40; see also Stewart, *Jute and Empire*, pp. 44–5, 51–4.
31. UDA, MS 83/1/1-3, *Annual Reports* of the Jute Importers Mutual Protection Association (JIMPA) 1892–1917; DCA, GD/CC/4/3-9, Minutes of Dundee Chamber of Commerce, 1856–1918.
32. This was the process which gave women a significant role in jute cultivation.
33. UDA, MS 83/1/3, JIMPA *Annual Report* 1906.
34. *Dundee Courier*, 4 September 1904. The Dundonians were also assured that the Indian government was pursuing the expansion of flax growing, given concerns about over-reliance on Russia.
35. R. Finlow, 'General Report on Jute in Bengal for 1904–05', Government of Bengal (Calcutta, 1906), pp. 2–5.
36. UDA, MS 83/1/3, JIMPA *Annual Report* 1903.
37. Finlow, 'General Report', p. 1.
38. UDA, MS 83/1/3, JIMPA *Annual Report* 1900, 1908, 1909.
39. JIMPA, *Annual Report* 1901.
40. *DYB 1882*, p. 22 for criticism of the DCC on this issue.

41. JIMPA *Annual Report* 1904, 1910, 1911.
42. Rajat Ray, 'The bazaar: Changing structural characteristics of the indigenous section of the Indian economy before and after the Great Depression', *Indian Economic and Social History Review*, 25 (1988), pp. 263–318.
43. Gijsbert Oonk, 'The emergence of indigenous industrialists in Calcutta, Bombay and Ahmedabad, 1850–1947', *Business History Review*, 88 (2014), pp. 48–57; Tirthankar Roy, *A Business History of India: Enterprise and the Emergence of Capitalism from 1700* (Cambridge, 2008), pp. 49, 95–8; Omkar Goswami, *Industry, Trade and Peasant Society: The Jute Economy of Eastern India* (Delhi, 1991), p. 85.
44. Oonk, 'The emergence', p. 53.
45. Goswami, *Industry*, p. 85. The JIMPA protested at 'Bhitar Bazar' as this involved 'gambling in jute': JIMPA, *Annual Report* 1914. The idea that the 'problem' in jute was speculative middlemen was an important trope in Dundee discussions.
46. Bagchi, *Private Investment*, p. 263, fn 7.
47. Nick Robins, *Scotland and the Sea: The Scottish Dimension in Maritime History* (Barnsley, 2014), p. 251. The voyage took 156 days.
48. Ray, 'The bazaar', p. 312.
49. Ibid., pp. 283, 285–6, 310, 312.
50. GUA, UGD131/1 32/1, Ellerman Lines, 'Direct jute imports Calcutta and Chittagong to Dundee'.
51. *DYB* 1878, p. 24; Tariq Ali, *A Local History of Global Capital: Jute and Peasant Life in the Bengal Delta* (Princeton, 2018), pp. 72–3.
52. The last sailing ship arrived with jute in 1905, but none had arrived in the previous three years: GUA, UGD131/1 32/1, Ellerman Lines, 'Direct jute imports Calcutta and Chittagong to Dundee'. Kathryn Moore, 'Maritime trade', in James Coull et al., *Scottish Life and Society* (Edinburgh, 2008), p. 518, suggests the prevalence of whaling and jute imports may have slowed the introduction of steamship building in Dundee, compared with Glasgow.
53. Oliver Graham, *The Dundee Jute Industry, 1828–1928* (unpublished manuscript, St Andrews, 1930), p. 73.
54. Alexander Warden, *The Linen Trade: Ancient and Modern* (London, 1867), p. 633; *DYB* 1878, p. 19.
55. In the decade of the 1870s, the value of imports ran at four to five times the value of exports: *DYB* 1879, p. 56.
56. *DYB* 1878, p. 25. Tea imports in that year amounted to 354 chests.
57. *DYB* 1879, p. 34; *DYB* 1896, p. 38.
58. *DYB* 1886, p. 31. A poignant example was the *Bonanza*, which sank near Barry in 1873 while en route from Dundee to Newport in South Wales to pick up coal to be taken to the Cape of Good Hope. The ship was 20/64th owned by the Dundonian merchant and shipowner J. B. Anderson: <https://mcmanus168.org.uk/>. The availability of return cargoes was probably a major influence in sustaining a minority of raw jute imports into

ports other than Dundee, because in such ports export cargoes were more likely.

59. Robins, *Scotland and the Sea*, pp. 98, 251–2. These steamers usually had Scottish officers and Indian crews.
60. Only one jute manufacturer seems to have been directly involved in the ownership of shipping, George Gilroy, but this was a short-lived connection: Obituary, *DYB* 1892, p. 66.
61. B. M. Deakin, *Shipping Conferences: A Study of their Origins, Development and Economic Practices* (Cambridge, 1973), pp. 15–21.
62. A. Angier, *Fifty Years Freights* (London, 1920).
63. Deakin, *Shipping Conferences*, pp. 23–4.
64. GUA, UGD131/1 32/1, Ellerman Lines, 'Direct jute imports Calcutta and Chittagong to Dundee'.
65. William Kenefick, 'The growth and development of the port of Dundee in the nineteenth and early twentieth centuries', in Christopher A. Whatley, Bob Harris and Louise Miskell (eds), *Victorian Dundee: Image and Realities* (2nd edn, Dundee, 2011), p. 35; *Dundee Advertiser*, 17 August 1875.
66. Graham, *The Dundee Jute Industry*, p. 75.
67. *Dundee Courier*, 13 May 1873.
68. Labour Commission, 'The state of the jute industry', in *DYB* 1891, p. 131.
69. *DYB* 1895, pp. 83–4.
70. Mark Watson, *Jute and Flax Mills in Dundee* (Tayport, 1990), p. 210. Heathfield was the 'nursery ground' for the carpet industry: *DYB* 1897, p. 91.
71. Lenman et al., *Dundee and its Textile Industry*, p. 27, based on D. Bremner, *Industries of Scotland* (Edinburgh, 1869).
72. See, for example, the discussion of the Grimond company's switch in this direction: *DYB* 1884, pp. 64–6.
73. UDA, MS 66/II/2/1, Cox's Letter Book, Edward Cox to Stoddard Lavering, Bradford, 11 August 1886; letter to Humphries and Son, Kidderminster, 30 June 1888.
74. *DYB* 1882, p. 23.
75. *DYB* 1897, p. 91.
76. 'Review of jute trade', *Dundee Courier*, 26 December 1905.
77. UDA, MS 66/II/2/1, Cox's Letter Book, Edward Cox to William Shaw (London), 17 July 1884.
78. *DYB* 1886, p. 68. We should not always take at face value claims, such as by Walker to the Labour Commission 1891, that 'the sack trade has largely been transferred to India': *DYB* 1891, p. 125.
79. *DYB* 1903, p. 29.
80. *DYB* 1906, p. 17; T. Woodhouse, 'Spinning and weaving', in *British Association 1912*, p. 286.
81. Woodhouse, 'Spinning and weaving', p. 287.

82. *DYB* 1912, p. 59. The picture is complicated by a large re-export trade, with Indian goods imported and then marketed via UK merchants; see also *DYB* 1903, p. 173.
83. DCA, DCC, GD/CC/4/4 Minutes 1869.
84. Donald Southgate, 'Politics and representation in Dundee 1832–1963', in J. M. Jackson (ed.), *The Third Statistical Account of Scotland: The City of Dundee* (Arbroath, 1979), p. 298.
85. DCA, DCC, GD/CC/4/9, AGM 1910.
86. DCA, DCC, GD/CC/4/8, Minutes, 22 April 1902.
87. DCA, DCC, GD/CC/4/8, Minutes, 15 January 1904. The vote was 92 to 45. For a broad view of local jute employers' opinions on protection, see 'The protectionist revival', *DYB* 1903, pp. 160–76.
88. DCA, DCC, GD/CC/4/8, Minutes, 15 January 1904, speech by J. C. Buist.
89. Report of DCC meeting, 26 December 1894, in *Dundee Courier*, 27 December 1894. A few weeks later, Leng was quoted as having told his constituents that on this issue 'it was necessary that change should be made': *Dundee Courier*, 10 January 1895.
90. *Dundee Courier*, 29 January 1895.
91. Report of DCC meeting, 26 December 1894, in *Dundee Courier*, 27 December 1894.
92. Ibid.
93. *Dundee Courier*, 11 October 1895.
94. John Leng, *Letters from India and Ceylon, including the Manchester of India, the Indian Dundee and Calcutta Jute Mills, 1895/6* (Dundee, 1896); see Stewart, *Jute*, pp. 73–4 for the conduct of this visit.
95. Leng, *Letters*, pp. 57–9.
96. Ibid., pp. 63–4.
97. Ibid., pp. 111–16. Leng argued that the most important reform to working conditions would be to ban Sunday working, a point he pressed in the House of Commons: *Hansard* (Commons), Vol. 37 col. 1217, 27 February 1896; also Vol. 40 cols 1580–5, 18 May 1896.
98. DCA, DCC GD/CC/4/8, Minutes, 7 April 1896. This speech is reproduced in *DYB* 1896, pp. 91–4. An attack on Leng's failure to support assimilation of the Indian Factory Acts was published in the *Dundee Courier*, 9 April 1896. On the same day Leng wrote to the paper stressing that, contrary to the claims of a previous correspondent, 'I have not one penny of interest in any Calcutta mill.'
99. *DYB* 1896, p. 93.
100. DCA, DCC GD/CC/4/8, Minutes, 25 June 1896.
101. Leng, *Letters*, p. 57.
102. Ibid.
103. Susan Keracher, *Dundee's Two Intrepid Ladies* (Dundee, 2012).
104. *Dundee Courier*, 24 June 1894 (this article is not included in Keracher's collection).

105. *Dundee Courier*, 16 July 1894, quoted in Keracher, *Dundee's Two Intrepid Ladies*, pp. 56–7.
106. DCA, DCC, GD/CC/4/8, speech by Sir John Leng, 1904.
107. DCA, DCC, GD/CC/4/8, Minutes, 29 September 1905.
108. *DYB* 1906, pp. 14–25. After the election, the *Dundee Courier* carried an editorial calling for assimilation, on the grounds that, 'It is in the cause of humanity that factory laws have been framed, and humanity has quite as strong claims in India as in other parts of the British Empire', but this comment was occasioned by a speech by the Lieutenant Governor of Bengal, not local politics: 4 September 1906.
109. Jim Tomlinson, 'Responding to globalization? Churchill and Dundee in 1908', *Twentieth Century British History*, 21: 3 (2010), pp. 257–80.
110. The IJMA had sought to raise prices and profits by short-time working and other forms of cooperation since the 1880s, though with variable success; Stewart, *Jute and Empire*, pp. 55–60.
111. *Dundee Advertiser*, 3 January 1911; see also *DYB* 1909, p. 16.
112. *DYB* 1898, p. 5.
113. *DYB* 1903, p. 163.
114. Bruce Lenman and K. Donaldson, 'Partners' incomes, investment and diversification in the Scottish linen area', *Business History*, 13 (1971), pp. 7, 11–12.
115. Jim Tomlinson, 'Churchill's defeat in Dundee, 1922, and the decline of liberal political economy', *Historical Journal*, 63 (2020), pp. 980–1006; Jim Tomlinson, 'The political economy of globalization: The genesis of Dundee's two "united fronts" in the 1930s', *Historical Journal*, 57 (2014), pp. 225–46.
116. *DYB* 1903, p. 164.

7

The City Divided, c. 1876–1918

Ye rich, that move through plenty/Just think of poor Dundee.

In 1911 Dundee experienced 'rioting and scenes of disorder unparalleled in the modern history of the community', with three hundred troops from the Black Watch mobilised in response to a request by the Provost, who alleged that the dockers and carters were causing trouble 'totally beyond control of police, even with contingents from other towns, to protect life and property and the peace of Dundee'.[1] In the days that followed there was small-scale sporadic violence in the city, but by the following weekend a settlement to the underlying dispute between dockers, carters and their employers had been found, and peace returned. Over the following two years there was no recurrence of such dramatic events, but significant labour unrest periodically erupted, including, in 1912, the biggest and most organised strike in the jute industry yet to have taken place.[2]

These events conjure up a picture of a city very different from that of the mid-century, when cross-class consensus and social stability seemed to be the norm – even if that period had itself followed one of considerable unrest in the 1840s, especially at the time of the Chartists.[3] This contrast should not be exaggerated. Dundee in the 1910s was not on the brink of revolution, and despite passing scares as in 1911, for most Dundonians life remained orderly and calm most of the time. On the other hand, the city was undoubtedly much more divided, and active, articulated discontent was much more widespread than in the mid-Victorian years.

This chapter examines why there was such a transformation. It seeks answers in the changing economic structure and performance of the city, and the social conditions that the peculiar economy of Juteopolis

THE CITY DIVIDED

underpinned. It also looks at political changes – not just the changes in political allegiance (though these were undoubtedly important), but the related shifts in the beliefs and understanding of the city's inhabitants. Divisions were grounded in changes in the city, but also changes in how many people viewed their world.

JUTE: APOGEE AND AFTER

The rate of expansion of Juteopolis reached its apogee in the 1850s and 1860s. While output and employment in the industry continued to increase into the twentieth century, the rate of increase slowed down from the 1870s, constrained, above all, by the competition from Calcutta discussed in chapter 6. The city's population growth rate also slowed down. Whereas up to the 1870s population trends were dominated by immigrants from Ireland and the Scottish countryside, along with rapid natural increase, in later decades emigration was also a marked feature, as cheap transport opened up opportunities for affordable movement to North America and Australasia.[4]

Understandably, most Dundonians' awareness of the economy arose not from the (unavoidably opaque) long-term trends at work, but from the sharp experience of the cycles which so dominated the pattern of the city's economy. Even in its most rapidly growing phase the jute industry had been subject to marked variations in activity, not least because of the impact of wars, but these fluctuations now became increasingly regular, and all the more significant for being superimposed on a slowing expansionary trend.

In this way the jute economy of the later nineteenth century imposed on many of the city's inhabitants lives of financial insecurity and periodic if not chronic hardship. This is not to suggest that economic conditions were worsening in all dimensions. By one key metric, real wages, there was some improvement. This improvement was not driven by rising money wages, which broadly fluctuated with the cycle of activity; one important chronicler of the city calculates that there were nine increases and ten reductions in piecework wages in jute between 1878 and 1906.[5] Instead, improving real wages came largely from the substantial fall in the price of food, experienced throughout Britain from the 1870s to the 1890s, at a time when food purchases dominated most household budgets (the ending of this trend may help to account for accelerating unrest after the turn of the century).

That the free-trade policy, pursued since the 1840s, had encouraged cheap food imports and so yielded a major benefit to Dundee wage workers, helps us to understand the continuing enthusiasm of the city's inhabitants for free-trade Liberalism, returned to below. But on a day-to-day basis workers and employers could only negotiate over *money* wages, and much of the most overt division in the city arose from the fact that, as already suggested, money wages changed frequently but without any strong movement in any direction. Contention over money wages thus yielded much battling between workers and employers, but no sustained outcomes for either.

If money wages were the centrepiece of economic struggles, rising real wages mattered; they allowed gradual improvement in the lives of many. But this improvement was at best a partial offset to the harms wrought by the fragility and insecurity of the jute economy: '. . . the pattern of interrupted time and lengthy unemployment thereafter were more significant determinants of health and poverty than a declining cost of living index'.[6] Health and poverty are important matters returned to in the next section, but a different kind of economic change also had important social consequences.

A feature of the fast-expanding jute industry of the middle decades of the nineteenth century was the openings it provided for economic and social mobility. 'Rags to riches' stories, while perhaps always exaggerated, were certainly a feature of this period. One dimension of this was the number of handloom weavers or their sons, who, squeezed out of that activity by mechanisation, became owners of mills and factories.[7] Of course, even in the best of times overexpansion could be merely the precursor to subsequent collapse and bankruptcy, as happened with the Crimean War and its aftermath.[8] But in the later decades of the century increased international competition encouraged amalgamation, generating economies of scale, which in turn made it more difficult for new people to enter the industry.[9]

The ownership structure of the mills solidified with a small number of interconnected families dominating the industry, the most prominent being the Coxs, Baxters, Grimonds, Cairds, Dons and Buists. From the 1880s this entrenchment was further enhanced with a common shift from partnerships to limited-liability companies, but where family control was largely retained.[10] Some idea of the extent of concentration in the industry is given in Table 7.1. This suggests that the top eight companies spun just under half of the raw jute used in the city. (Note that Baxter's, a very important company in the city, is not separately identified in this table as it used only five hundred bales weekly; but Baxter's, more than any other big producer, maintained a very large linen production.)[11]

THE CITY DIVIDED

Table 7.1 Structure of jute spinning, 1908

	Estimated bales per week
Cox Brothers	2,300
J. and A. D. Grimond	1,500
James Scott and Son	1,400
Gilroy, Sons and Co.	1,250
John Sharp and Sons	1,200
J. K. Caird	1,150
Malcolm Ogilvie and Co.	1,100
Harry Walker and Sons	1,100
12 establishments	500–1,000
16 establishments	250–500
9 establishments	0–250
Total for all establishments	24,980

Source: Data from Lenman et al., *Dundee and its Textile Industry*, pp. 114–15.

The pressures on the jute industry did not lead to a significant diversification of economic activity in the city – for good or ill it remained Juteopolis: employment in the city had become 'dangerously lopsided'.[12] The pattern was not helped by pressure on other sectors. Dundee shipbuilders were hit by the growth in ship size, which concentrated activity on the larger Scottish centres, above all on the Clyde.[13] Whaling, another industry tied to Dundee's port, was in rapid decline in the last decades of the nineteenth century.[14] Contemporaries sometimes exaggerated the lack of employment opportunities for men in the city. Lennox claimed this lack explained the relatively high level of military recruitment from the city: 'Female labour is the best recruiting sergeant in Dundee. It prevents the employment of men in civil life. In fact half of the men who join the army are forced to enlist by the successful competition of their mothers and sisters.'[15] However, the jute industry was slowly increasing the share of men in its workforce as it moved 'upmarket' to products requiring more skilled and hence male labour (a trend much stronger after the First World War). But it is undoubtedly the case that male job opportunities in the city were circumscribed, and much of the expansion that occurred in male employment was in poorly paid, often casualised activities, such as in the docks and carting where much of the unrest of 1911 originated.

After the great burst of mill expansion in the 1850s and 1860s, much less was done in the following decades to expand the capital base of the city's economy. Both the jute companies and their owners put most of the profits from jute into investment in overseas ventures, especially in North America, with Dundee becoming famed for capital flowing into

218   THE TRIUMPH OF TEXTILES

cattle ranches and railways. Foreign stocks dominated the listings when
Dundee got its own stock exchange in 1879.[16]

A 'WOMEN'S TOWN'?

Alongside the designation Juteopolis, Dundee was commonly referred
to as a 'women's town', reflecting the predominant role of women in
the jute industry. Eleanor Gordon's pioneering study suggested: '. . . the
female labour market was comprehensively dominated by jute which
employed between three-quarters and two-thirds of Dundee's working
women in the years 1871 till 1911 . . . Dundee was therefore a women's
town: women outnumbered men in the town by 3 to 2; they formed over
43 per cent of the total labour force; and 54.3 per cent of women aged
over 15 were employed.'[17] The Dundee Social Union (DSU) *Report* of
1905 (an important pioneering work on social conditions inspired by the
famous work of Booth and Rowntree in London and York respectively)
argued that 'Without women's labour the city would sink to the level
of a small burgh: as a manufacturing centre it would possibly cease to
exist.'[18] So the evolving role of women is central to our understanding of
the economic and social condition of Dundee in this period.

The DSU *Report* argued that the employment of so many women arose
directly from the competition with Calcutta: 'It is chiefly because labour
must be cheap in the jute works that women's labour is employed.'[19] But
women's labour had predominated before competition from Calcutta
arose, and the employment of women in textiles on a large scale is a
global phenomenon, a good example being their widespread employment in the Lancashire cotton industry. However, jute *did* have exceptional features. Whereas women's employment in cotton spinning has
historically been very common, including in Lancashire, in Dundee they
also dominated the other large employment sector, weaving. Only in the
highly skilled and numerically smaller components of the industry, such
as calendering and dyeing, or as mechanics, did men predominate. Men
also overwhelmingly dominated in supervisory and managerial roles: in
that respect Dundee conformed only too well to Victorian patriarchal
norms.

For many contemporary commentators the feature that was most
concerning was the large role of married women and mothers in the
industry (unmarried mothers were a small minority). While it was recognised that in the case of widowed or deserted women such employment
might be inescapable, the prevalent view was that it was highly regretta-
ble that women should be in this position. 'The married woman is often

the principal, sometimes the sole, wage earner, and in many works she is preferred for her experience and steadiness. The obligation to support a family and also to bring it up is an unnatural condition of life, which leads to the usual consequences – broken-down mothers in early life, and ill-nourished, rickety, children, who develop into weedy unhealthy men and women.'[20]

The story of a distinct pathology arising from the employment of married women in jute focused especially on infant mortalities – deaths within one year of birth.[21] Such deaths were a scourge in this period, and undoubtedly by later standards these were extraordinarily high: the 1893–1902 annual average in the city was 176 per thousand (a century later the figure was around five per thousand). The Dundee level in the 1890s was above that of other Scottish cities; the next worst in these same years was Glasgow with 149 per thousand.[22] But the striking fact to modern eyes is how high such mortalities were across the country, rather than the gap between cities. This suggests it was mainly common, national factors at work, rather than those peculiar to Juteopolis. The DSU sought to boost their case for a direct link from mothers' employment to high infant mortality in the city by their own study which showed rates of mortality at 59 per cent among working mothers, compared with 42 per cent among the non-working.[23] But *both* these figures are so high as to throw doubt on the usefulness of the comparison. The *Report* itself recognised other factors might be at work in accounting for Dundee's especial problems: 'Many of the new recruits among spinners coming from outside the city are said to be of very poor physique, drawn from an ill-nourished and unsuccessful class who have failed to find employment elsewhere.'[24]

The contemporary focus on the damage allegedly caused by women's employment alerts us to the highly gendered assumptions which underpinned contemporary attitudes to thinking about social conditions in the city. Clearly, for most commentators, married women's employment was an 'unnatural condition of life', and one to be avoided if at all possible. For the DSU the answer to many of the city's ills was more and better paid *male* employment, and this was also the common view among leading women trade unionists. When the pioneering woman union leader Mary McArthur came to the city in early 1906 to help found the local trade union for textile workers, she resisted the idea that married women should be excluded from the union. Instead, she suggested, its aim should be to raise male wages in order to make married women's employment unnecessary.[25]

220   THE TRIUMPH OF TEXTILES

Plainly, for most contemporaries, the desirable norm was the male-breadwinner household, with wives and mothers safely dependent on their husbands.[26] But we know there were many obstacles to such 'normality': widowhood and desertion were frequent occurrences, and illegitimate births added to the number of families without a father in the household. From that perspective, the employment of mothers in jute was an important route to some kind of economic independence for many women who would otherwise have been dependent largely on charity or the Poor Law. But plainly working mothers were also common among those who lived with their husbands. Indeed, the male-breadwinner household may have been 'normative' but it wasn't the statistical 'norm' in Dundee. While the precise statistical representativeness of the DSU *Report* is unclear, its data on households and employment is striking. In the western (mostly working-class) part of the city in 1904, of 1,728 employed married men, nine hundred had working wives, the great majority in textiles.[27]

The simple explanation for this pattern was that wages generally in the city were so low that the double-income household (not typical in Britain generally until after 1945) was powerfully attractive, however much at odds with prevailing norms. This data also suggests the largely mythological status of the idea that in Dundee 'kittle-boiler' men, who stayed home and did domestic duties while their wives worked, was a common occurrence. Only just over 10 per cent of the men in this survey were unemployed, and this would have been typical for an industrial city at this time.

Overall, we need to be careful in thinking about Dundee in this period as a 'women's town'. The pattern of women's employment was undoubtedly unusual, but to see this as pathological, as most contemporaries did, is problematic. Working-class mothers everywhere struggled to enable their children to thrive, and in the face of available alternatives, for many women the jute industry offered welcome opportunities, however poor the wages. It also offered opportunities to single women. Households consisting of pairs or larger numbers of such women are another type of non- 'male breadwinner' household quite common in the city.[28] Such households were likely to be relatively affluent, a point supported by the dietary given for one such by the DSU. 'Miss X and her friend are weavers earning 14s a week . . .' They have a 'very neat and pretty room . . . they have meat and potatoes, rice or stewed fruit everyday . . . On Saturdays they have 2d pies for lunch and fish for tea.'[29] This was far superior to most of the dietaries of other types of household.

Figure 7.1 Caldrum Works Dinner Hour, early twentieth century. Younger, presumably fitter, males are at the forefront of this dinner-time exodus. However, female workers are to be seen – well-dressed weavers wearing hats while less status-conscious spinners are bare-headed. © University of Dundee Archives.

Another striking feature of the situation of young women in Dundee was how relatively few of them were domestic servants. Across the UK such employment was by far the largest employment sector for women. But Census estimates show that in Dundee for the period 1871 to 1911 the proportion of women domestics averaged less than 10 per cent, with Glasgow, the city in Scotland with the next lowest proportion, averaging over 20 per cent, and Aberdeen and Edinburgh much higher.[30] This limited employment has usually been accounted for by the small size of the servant-employing middle class of Dundee – a 'demand-side' explanation for the low numbers.[31] But there may also have been 'supply-side' factors at work, with many young women preferring employment in the mill or factory to being a servant. While mill and factory work was regarded by many as a low-status female occupation, it at least offered a degree of independence from the suffocating nature of most 'indoor' domestic work.[32]

Emphasis on the 'women's town' aspect of Dundee can lead to misunderstandings about the employment structure of the town.[33] While women predominated in textiles, there were always more men than women at work in the city. In the 1911 Census the figures were 47,374 occupied males to 38,836 women, of whom jute workers made up 11,042 and 23,368 respectively.[34] These figures make clear that large numbers of men were employed in textiles, and while it was sometimes suggested that males were all made redundant when they became entitled to adult wages at age eighteen, this is a considerable exaggeration. For example, in Cox's in 1912 1,018 men over eighteen were employed, compared with 241 full-timers under eighteen.[35] While wages for men in jute were poor by national standards, they did monopolise the better-paid jobs. They also, of course, monopolised the generally high-wage jobs in such sectors as engineering and shipbuilding, which were important employers in the city. Skilled workers in these trades were paid 35–40 shillings (£1.75 to £2) per week, compared with around 8–12 shillings for a woman worker in jute.[36]

SOCIAL CONDITIONS

Nevertheless, there is no doubt that low average wages in jute depressed social conditions in the city.[37] Nowhere is this more evident than in the case of housing. There is no single satisfactory measure of housing problems, but the scale of overcrowding in the city is rightly seen as vital. For Dundee at the beginning of the twentieth century these numbers are extraordinary. The 1901 Census data showed that over 64 per cent of families lived in one- or two-room dwellings, with almost 50 per cent living in a ratio of more than two persons in a room – the highest levels among Scottish cities. This overcrowding went along with appalling sanitary conditions; the Sanitary Inspector for the city reported cases where a property with 177 persons had no sanitary accommodation, while another with 346 people had four privies.[38]

The enormous scale of Dundee's housing problems in the late nineteenth century is not hard to understand. In the early twenty-first century Britain is widely thought to have a major housing problem, despite billions of pounds spent on Housing Benefit and the provision of social housing to try to bridge the gap between market-determined rents and wage levels. In the nineteenth century government did almost nothing (beyond slum clearance) to address this gap, which was particularly pronounced in a low-wage city like Dundee. Pressure on the housing market was exacerbated by the fact that residential building had not kept pace with the growth of the workforce in the peak years of expansion in the 1850s and 1860s.[39]

THE CITY DIVIDED

Table 7.2 Prices in Dundee, 1893 compared with 1847

	1893	1847
Loaf	4.5d	10d
Sugar	2d	8d
Tea	2s	5s
Soap	3d	8d
Meat	10d	8d
Rent	£9 10s per year	£6 10s per year

Source: *DYB* 1893, p. 171.

Reporting on conditions in Dundee for the Royal Commission on Labour in Scottish Industries in 1893, Margaret Irwin provided this striking table on price changes over the previous decades. The precision of these figures is unknown, but the broad thrust is clear. While food prices (except meat) had shown substantial falls, rents had increased by close to 50 per cent. Furthermore, rents in Dundee, like other industrial cities in Scotland, were significantly above their English equivalents.[40]

So Dundee was characterised by wages below and rents above the national average. This combination was sustained by the slow growth of housebuilding. In the middle decades of the century Dundee saw a boom in mill-building, but no parallel boom in buildings to house the mill workers. While the rate of population growth slowed after 1871, there was a huge backlog of overcrowding and insanitary provision to make up. These housing conditions contributed significantly to the very high infant mortalities already noted, especially through poor sanitation.

There was very limited response to these problems. Particularly before the 'New Liberal' reforms after 1906, most governmental response depended upon local authorities. Their level of activity depended both on their political will and on the resources available, those resources being almost entirely local, before so much of local government finance was centralised in the twentieth century. Until small inroads by the Left from the 1880s, local government in Dundee was dominated by representatives of the middle class, partly because of the restricted franchise, which linked voting to property ownership. Although at times jute employers played an important role in local politics, the typical councillor or member of the various elected Boards was a shopkeeper or small merchant, the kinds of people with a very direct interest in keeping local taxation low. This structure mitigated against upward pressure on local 'rates', the property taxes which financed most local government expenditure.

One way of enhancing the revenue base of the city was to extend its boundaries. After much contention this was done in 1913, with the incorporation of Broughty Ferry, albeit the quid pro quo was a political over-representation of that prosperous area, home to many 'jute barons'. The distributional aspect of this enlargement was nicely captured in a contemporary poem:

The piper took in our toon
And our toon, our toon
The piper took in our toon
An' jined it to Dundee

Said he 'Ye've lived too lang at ease
Noo pay the taxes if you please
I'll gie ye're money bags a squeeze
Ye're pairt noo o' Dundee[41]

The expansion of local initiative was evident in some respects, for example in town planning after the 1871 Improvement Act expanded the scope of local responsibility. This led eventually to some demolition of the pestilent slums in the centre of the city, but nothing was done to provide alternative accommodation for those displaced. Much of the focus of city planners was on creating a grand central pattern of wide streets and monumental buildings, though little beyond the demolitions was done in preparation of such schemes before 1914.[42]

Our knowledge of Dundee's social conditions in these years comes not only from the investigations of the DSU. Alongside this philanthropic approach was evidence gathered by those whose interest in popular welfare came from concerns about Britain's *military* strength, and who worried that poor conditions for the urban working class were producing a large number of men unfitted to defend the empire. In Dundee this approach was taken by David Lennox, a lecturer in forensic medicine at St Andrews, but also a Recruiting Medical Officer.[43] Lennox used data from the military recruiting office to suggest that 17–35 year-old male 'millworkers are 1.4 inches shorter, 9.94 lbs lighter and 1.1 inches less in maximum chest measurement than any other class of men in the city. Compared with the artisan population in the rest of the country they are 2 inches and with the general population 4 inches less in stature.'[44] Lennox's discussion was strongly laced with contemporary eugenicist assumptions about 'race deterioration'

THE CITY DIVIDED

and many of his arguments are highly tendentious. Nevertheless, his data strikingly capture an important measure of the scale of deprivation in Dundee.

THE CHANGING POLITICS OF THE CITY

Between the 1870s and 1914, Dundee underwent profound political changes. Much discussion of this understandably focuses on the theme of 'the rise of labour', especially of trade unions and broadly socialist political forces.[45] But the city was also becoming more politically divided because of the strengthening of conservatism, most obviously among the jute employers.

In seeking to understand the complex dynamics of the 'rise of labour' in Juteopolis we should start with the role of women, the majority of the jute labour force. William Walker, the pioneer historian of labour in Dundee's jute industry, questioned the narrative of the 'rise of labour' by emphasising the division between the respectable weavers and the 'mill-girl' in spinning, the latter being seen as a vehemently unrespectable figure who constantly disappointed male trade unionists with her undisciplined behaviour. These women, he claimed, were 'instinctively committed to a rigorous hedonism' which might on occasion draw them into anti-boss attitudes but provide a weak foundation for any sustained workplace organisation.[46] 'Unruly, raucous, and madcap, the mill-girls were the despair of reformers and an embarrassment to employers and workers alike.'[47] But Walker is careful not to collapse the story of the slow development of trade unions among jute workers into some kind of inherent resistance to trade unions among women. While he emphasises that trade unionism did not become strongly entrenched among them until after the First World war, he notes that it was, if anything, even slower to grow among the mass of male jute workers. Indeed, he argued, 'the reversal of male and female economic roles was complete enough to promote a model of masculinity among females which, when appropriate conditions appeared, encouraged a propensity to organize'.[48]

The approach of Walker's traditional, institutionalist labour history may be contrasted with that of Eleanor Gordon, whose Marxist-feminist approach provides a bracing counterpoint. She is sceptical about the hold of Victorian domestic ideals among the Dundee working class, and her key aim is the 'rediscovery of women in the world of work and making visible the forms of workplace resistance'.[49] While agreeing with Walker that women were not docile in the face of their poor conditions, Gordon disputes the idea that the key division was between the 'respectable' and 'unrespectable' workers. In her view, the 'pivotal distinctions of earnings and authority clove the jute workforce into a slam group of relatively well-paid men and the mass of mainly female workers'. For her the key divide was of gender, though she recognises that in 'popular consciousness' the distinction that mattered was between spinners and weavers. This division had 'concrete foundations' in the separation of workplaces, payment levels and systems (hourly versus piece wages), between mill workers and weavers.[50]

Where Walker shows a Victorian sympathy with nineteenth-century male trade unionist impatience with the 'unruliness' of the 'mill-girl', Gordon celebrates this female behaviour, seeing it as a commendable manifestation of hostility to the jute employers, but also to the stultifying embrace of respectable male trade unionism. For her, 'respectability' was a damaging 'false consciousness' which worked to disadvantage women. By implication, those who sought to build up formal trade union organisation among female jute workers were misguided about where the true interests of women lay.[51]

These highly divergent interpretations help us understand the complexities of the relationship between women in the jute industry and trade unionism. In the light of all this, it is unsurprising to discover that right up until the First World War membership of trade unions among Dundee's jute industry was generally low and subject to significant fluctuations – and ambiguous in its ideological and political affiliations. There were long-standing, but very small, unions among the jute industry's craftsmen such as calenderers and tenters. But among the mass of the workforce the first sustained organisation, the Dundee and District Mill and Factory Operatives Union (DDMFOU), was founded by a clergyman, Henry Williamson, in 1885.[52] Williamson told of the instigation of its founding in characteristic terms: 'when walking down Lochee road in those days it seemed to me that never a week passed without presenting at some part of the route the same sad familiar scene – a band of tousle-haired lassies with the light of battle in their eyes . . . discussing with animation and candour the grievances that had constrained them to leave their work . . .' In his view, such strikes were rarely successful, with the workers going back without redress to their grievances, but with real financial loss to themselves.[53] He felt the need was for an organisation among the 'lassies' that would discourage what he saw as their reckless and self-defeating propensity to strike. This, it should be emphasised, was not a wholly eccentric view of what a union of women textile workers should aim to do, and fitted with the condescending attitude towards these women which, as noted above, is echoed in the work of Walker.[54]

THE CITY DIVIDED

What was to prove the largest and most resilient union for jute workers, the Dundee and District Union of Jute and Flax Workers (DDUJFW), was founded in 1906 and grounded in a very different view about the role of unions. Much of the impetus came from the efforts of the Women's Trade Union League and its Secretary, Mary Macarthur. Though, unlike Williamson's union, the DDUJFW was not aimed primarily at women, its membership was always predominantly female, and this was reflected in its rules. These provided that half of its officials were women, and when it was founded, its provisional committee had fifteen women and ten men.[55] Before 1914 the Union never organised more than a fraction of eligible workers, men or women, but relative to what had gone before it institutionalised women's and, more generally, unskilled trade unionism in the jute industry. It was by most standards a 'moderate' union, but it did not see its role to discourage strikes in principle, and organised an important walkout at Cox's in 1911, and a broader, very substantial strike in 1912, a significant part of the 'great unrest' of the Edwardian years.[56]

The Union, it might be noted, also offered support to women in the broader sense of backing for the suffragette movement.[57] The issue of votes for women was an important political divide in Dundee in the early twentieth century, not least in opposing some on the Left to Churchill as one of the city's MPs, given his, at best, equivocal position on this topic.

If we are seeking for the history of trade unionism in Dundee generally, most of the narrative would concern industries other than jute. Despite the numerical preponderance of jute workers, the most important unions were in engineering. These were male-dominated, predominantly artisan trades, where possession of a skill gave a capacity for (at least occasionally) effective bargaining that workers in jute largely lacked.[58]

In many Scottish cities and towns, Trades Councils played an important role in the development of nineteenth- and twentieth-century trade unionism and were often an important instrument of political action by labour. In Dundee, the first Trades Council was founded in the 1860s, very much the product of contemporary Liberal artisan politics. The Council's closeness to Liberalism was long to remain powerful, even as the Council was reconstituted later in the century. But we should not assume that such Liberalism did not involve a willingness to fight hard for union rights. In 1874, for example, mass demonstrations organised by the Council took place to protest against the Conservative government's Criminal Law Amendment Act, which would have undermined union collective action. This protest was supported by the Liberal MP James Yeaman.[59] Fifteen years later, this alliance between the city's Liberals and the Trades Council was evident when the latter nominated John Leng, owner of the *Dundee Advertiser* and a prominent Liberal, to parliamentary candidature, even if with a rather grudging tone; the Secretary of the Council argued that 'Now we have failed to obtain a working man to represent us, I think our next best thing is to get an employer in whom we have confidence, and I think in Mr Leng we have that gentleman.'[60]

Such an alliance helped to sustain Liberal parliamentary dominance in the city down to the general election of 1906. Such dominance was a feature throughout the history of Juteopolis. Between the first Reform Act of 1832 and 1865, the new single-member constituency of Dundee was only contested four times in nine general elections, and only in one case (1847) was there a Conservative candidate (Gladstone's elder brother), with the most common return 'unopposed Liberal'.[61] These elections were based on a very narrow franchise: in 1832 the electorate was 1,622 voters out of a population of 45,335.[62] The MPs elected in the three decades after 1832 can be broadly described as aristocratic and Whig, though this did not mitigate against the strength of support for free trade, manifested especially in the wave of enthusiasm for the Anti Corn Law League in the 1840s.[63] For example, Ogilvy, first elected in 1857, was a conservative figure: 'He made up for the sterility of Whig principles and their essential irrelevance to the problems of an impoverished industrial community by practical benevolence as a landlord and philanthropist.' In that election he beat the well-known merchant George Armitstead (who could hardly speak English). Oglivy was unopposed in 1859 and 1863 and continued as a winner with Armitstead in 1868, when Dundee became a two-member constituency.[64]

But from the late 1860s, the dynamics of Dundee's politics (and its Liberalism) changed with the expansion of the franchise. The Reform Act of 1868 immediately increased the electorate sixfold, and between 1865 and 1880 there was an increase in the number of Dundee's eligible voters of 11,527, almost 400 per cent, to total 14,566 in 1880.[65] This gave a much greater weight in the electorate to the respectable artisan class, and their politics therefore became central to the parliamentary politics of the city.[66]

Expanding the franchise continued to be a popular rallying cry, uniting Liberals and many working-class groups. A report on demonstrations in Dundee in favour of the 1884 Reform Act suggested there were between sixteen thousand and seventeen thousand attendees, '3,000 from the Liberal Association, 10,500 from the various trades and 3,000 from the mills and factories in Dundee'.[67] When John Leng stood in Dundee in 1889 and won the seat which he was to hold until 1906, his platform included payment of MPs, triennial parliaments and adult suffrage as well as free education, land nationalisation and legal regulation of working hours. As Walker suggests, 'It is quite certain that no Labour candidate in 1889 would have confronted the Dundee electorate with a bolder programme.'[68]

Given the 'advanced' nature of Dundee's Liberals, for many years, and despite the urging of a growing number of labour and socialist voices calling for a break with the Liberals and a shift to separate labour representation, the artisans as represented by the Dundee Trades Council were unmoved.[69] The Trades Council sponsored candidates in the town council elections in 1890, and two were successful, but served for only a short period. However, the majority of the Trades Council at this time saw its role as promoting working-class candidates, not establishing a separate working-class political party. This, of course, is part of the complex story of 'Lib-Lab' politics which evolved across Britain in the 1890s.[70] In Dundee this story is particularly opaque because of the multiplicity of organisations and the difficulty of distinguishing their precise politics. Southgate talks of a 'Radical and Labour Party' being in existence in 1892, and in the same year a branch of the Scottish Labour Party (SLP) was founded.[71] In that year also there was the first Labour candidate in a general election, a London tailor, James Macdonald, sponsored by the SLP and his union (though the Dundee tailors did not support him). The Independent Labour Party (which absorbed the SLP in 1893) wanted to put up the famous union leader Tom Mann in this election, but the seamen's union persuaded the Trades Council against this.[72] In 1889 the Trades Council had been reported as 'staunchly Gladstonian', and in 1892 the majority was opposed to an independent Labour candidate, and this may help to explain the tiny number of votes, 354, that Macdonald received, compared with over eight thousand votes for the two Liberal candidates.[73] Supported by the Independent Labour Party, Macdonald stood again in 1895, receiving 1,313 votes, though he again failed to secure endorsement from the Trades Council. Because Dundee was a two-member constituency, we can observe the combinations of votes cast, and these show that of those who voted for Macdonald and used both votes, more supported a Unionist than a Liberal by a majority of 570 to 444.[74]

In 1906 Dundee was, along with Glasgow Blackfriars, the first constituency in Scotland to elect an avowedly Labour candidate, Alexander Wilkie, a Fife-born shipwright and trade unionist based in Newcastle. While Wilkie's election was undoubtedly significant for the idea of separate Labour representation, its importance in any other respect is arguable. Clearly Labour was gaining strength in the city, but Wilkie's campaign was helped by the strong financial support of his union, which enabled him to spend twice as much as any other candidate, and to deploy 'novel and sensational electoral methods' which made his candidature 'vulgarly attractive'.[75] On the other hand, he was, of course, fighting a constituency where the levels of poverty and patterns of housing tenure reduced the size of the working-class electorate substantially. In 1900 only 50 per cent of adult males in Dundee had the vote, the lowest proportion of any substantial town in Scotland.[76] While there has been debate about how far such disqualifications affected the social composition of urban electorates at this time, it is difficult to see in Dundee how this could not have disadvantaged the potential working-class Labour voter.[77] Certainly Unionists thought so, given the considerable efforts they put into resisting the electoral registration of lodgers (the most contentious category) supported by Labour. For example, in 1907 Labour put in 182 claims for registration on behalf of lodgers, but 172 were rejected after Unionist objections.[78]

Wilkie's election addresses focused attention on his claims to be an authentic representative of working-class Dundonians, not on policy differences with the Liberals.[79] The ambiguity of his position is encapsulated in the newspaper report on his first public meeting: 'His socialist friends complained that he was not a socialist, now his liberal friends complained that he was one.'[80] In parliament he strongly supported the Liberal government, and in policy terms he seems to have had no noticeable differences with Liberalism. In 1910 he was effectively supported by the Liberals, when they decided not to stand a second candidate against him, the debate on this being settled by arguments about his loyalty to the Liberal cause.[81] This loyalty was demonstrated very clearly in the by-election of 1908, where Wilkie refused to support the idea of running a Labour candidate against Churchill (see below).

Hence Wilkie's electoral success does not in itself support the notion of a clear upwards trajectory to Labour politics in Dundee before 1914.[82] Claims for a notable shift to Labour in pre-war Dundee are perhaps most plausible when based on what happened in municipal politics, rather than parliamentary elections.[83] Also strongly qualifying the 'rise of labour' narrative is the success of Winston Churchill as Liberal candidate in the Dundee by-election of 1908. That election was occasioned by the retirement of the sitting Liberal MP, which was followed by the candidacy being offered to Churchill as soon as his defeat in Manchester Northwest was announced, he having had to resign that seat on promotion to the Cabinet as President of the Board of Trade.

Churchill's initial address to the electors of Dundee set out his agenda in the following terms: 'Upon the maintenance of our free trade system, upon the Temperance cause and its conflict with the organized forces of the Liquor Trade, upon the hope of a Concordat in Education . . . upon the Land Reform in town and country, upon South Africa, upon Ireland I vow myself entirely unrepentant.'[84] Churchill set out the issues of the campaign in detail in a number of set-piece speeches which were subsequently published as a pamphlet under the title 'For Liberalism and Free Trade'.[85] In the first of these speeches, Churchill acknowledged the current 'set-back in our commercial activities', but argued this did not alter the basic case for free trade, and that protection would 'allow people for

Figure 7.2 Striking workers, 1912. Strikes in the jute industry became increasingly common from the 1870s. Although these were serious industrial conflicts, contemporary descriptions of strikers – who were overwhelmingly young and female – suggest that there was a light-hearted element at marches and meetings, with chanting, singing and making loud noise to intimidate employers, foremen and blacklegs being commonplace. © University of Dundee Archives.

private profit to impose taxation upon bread and meat' and 'will cheat and starve your children'. He went on to stress the importance of free trade to cheap food, and to say that 'some day' the taxes on sugar and tea imports would be abolished like those on bread and meat. He also attacked tariff reform as bringing about a reversal of the long-running trend towards more tax being raised from direct as opposed to indirect sources, which meant shifting taxes on to the poor.[86]

In this speech there was no explicit attack on the Labour party, though an implicit one on Labour's Right to Work Bill as the solution to unemployment; though Churchill held out the possibility of some counter-cyclical public works, such as afforestation, to provide jobs for the unskilled. However, the next speech was explicitly aimed at drawing a dividing line between Liberalism and socialism. This involved a broad ideological critique of socialism, albeit couched generally in moderate tones as an appeal to the need for a combination of collectivism and individualism, rather than socialism's abolition of the latter.[87] His speech to businessmen addressed in most detail the protectionist issue, including retaliatory tariffs. He explicitly argued against retaliating against Germany, stressing how German tariffs were much lower than those imposed by the USA or Russia, and how, apart from the unlikelihood of retaliatory tariffs yielding significant economic benefits, they would 'cause ill-will between great and friendly peoples, who have no quarrel, and no reason to quarrel'.[88] In his eve-of-poll speech Churchill again focused on free trade: 'You know what would be the result of a Tory Tariff reform victory . . . corruption at home, aggression to cover it abroad; the trickery of tariff juggles; the tyranny of a wealth-fed party machine; sentiment by the bucketful – patriotism and Imperialism by the Imperial pint, an open hand at the public exchequer, an open door at the public house – Dear food for the millions, cheap labour for the millionaire . . .'[89]

Churchill's own account of the election stresses the split into an anti-Tory and anti-Labour phase: 'At the end of the first week when the Liberals had been marshalled effectively against the Conservatives, it was time to turn upon the Socialists.'[90] But the attacks on the socialists were accompanied by a recognition of the supportive role of Labour MPs in the Commons for the Liberal government.[91] On the whole, the tone of the speeches was much more virulently anti-Tory than anti-Labour. Churchill clearly sought to make free trade the key issue of the campaign, evidenced not only by the speeches noted above, but other smaller-scale statements during the campaign.[92] Churchill's belief that free trade would resonate among the Dundee electorate is plausible given both that it was an issue on which Labour and the Left agreed with him, and one with obvious material benefits for many in the city. To emphasise: in a city where wages were generally low, cheap food was the key to most people's living standards.

While Churchill sought to put free trade at the centre of the election debate, Sir George Baxter, the Unionist candidate, and the chairman of one of Dundee's biggest linen and jute firms, focused less attention upon it, even though his party leader, Balfour, saw it as the key issue.[93] This presumably reflected recognition of the appeal of tariff-free cheap food among Dundee's electors, and the absence of a compelling argument on how protection would help the jute industry. Baxter presented tariff reform as the second most important issue, his election address putting it behind the question of Ireland.[94] However, later he said: 'He stood chiefly because he was determined that the people of Dundee, amongst whom his life's work had been spent, and especially the working classes of the city, should at least have the opportunity of expressing their opinion upon a fiscal system which, in his view, was gravely detrimental to their interests.'[95] Despite this assertion, Baxter's position on tariff reform during the election was circumspect. In his election address he wrote: 'The frequent Unemployment of willing workers is in my view largely due to the want of such reform, and the Leader of the Unionist party has given the strongest pledges that reform would involve no increase in the cost of living . . .'[96] He attacked the dumping of cheap goods from overseas, but as a prospect in times of slump rather than an actuality.[97] The specific focus in his pronouncements was on retaliation against Germany, hence Churchill's gibes about Unionist approaches to that country.

In relation to the question of Indian competition, Baxter was notably vague. When asked about the imposition of a levy on raw jute exports he said he was not sure, because 'we would need to take the Indians with us on that'.[98] In a speech on 5 May he focused entirely on tariffs as the problem causing the industry's difficulties.[99] Two days later he argued that 'had they in Dundee had fair play, equal competition and equal terms they would have increased the trade enormously. Of course, he knew all about the competition with Calcutta, but apart from that altogether in his own time they used to export great quantities of jute manufactured goods to foreign European countries . . .' At the same meeting, when asked whether 'the conditions of jute workers in the East were as good as the conditions of jute workers at home', he accepted that 'not only had the Dundee manufacturers to compete against tariffs, but he had to compete against countries whose people were not working under the same beneficial conditions and Factory acts as the workers of this country'.[100]

While the 1908 election showed the continuing strength of Dundee Liberalism, it is important to note the growth in long-run strength of conservatism compared with its weakness in the city before the 1880s. As noted above, in the mid-Victorian years Dundee had been subject to a striking Liberal hegemony. But, as in so much of provincial Britain, that hegemony was fractured at the parliamentary level by the Irish Home Rule controversy of the 1880s, leading to the emergence of Liberal Unionism as an ally of the Conservative (and Unionist) party.[101] This defection of significant sections of the industrial capitalist class from formal allegiance to the Liberal party is perfectly captured in Dundee by the case of Baxter, the candidate in 1908. His father had been a Liberal MP for another Scottish constituency. The younger Baxter broke with the Liberals over Home Rule in the 1880s, and became a Liberal Unionist, along with other prominent local jute capitalists like Alexander Buist, Edward Cox, Joseph Grimond and John Don, putting themselves alongside those with an existing Conservative allegiance, such as James Cox and William Dalgleish.[102]

Before the rise of Liberal Unionism, a Conservative candidate, John Gloag, received a derisory 573 votes in 1874, but in 1885, after the founding of a Conservative Association three years earlier, John Jenkins received 5,149 (35 per cent of the vote). While support for Unionism and Conservatism thereafter waxed and waned, in all the general elections to 1914, Unionist candidates typically received around two-thirds of the vote of the Liberal and Labour (that is, Wilkie) victors.[103] At the parliamentary level, therefore, Liberalism prevailed, but at that level and more broadly it was being increasingly challenged both from the Right and the Left. At its broadest, we can see this as a result of a weakening of the Liberal world view, which reached it apogee at the same time as Juteopolis also reached its peak, roughly in the quarter century after 1850.

RICHES AND POVERTY

Juteopolis was a highly divided city in the forty years before the First World War. There were sharp contrasts in levels of wealth, income, health and social well-being. While many households lived on the margins of survival, a few others accumulated great wealth. The Cox family featured five times in the annual list of the top ten estates confirmed in Scotland between 1876 and 1913, with amounts ranging from George Addison Cox £218,499 to Thomas Hunter Cox £435,792.[104] But there were also increasing divisions in how the city's inhabitants saw the world.

THE CITY DIVIDED   235

This is most straightforwardly registered in the growing political divide between Left and Right, between socialists and Conservatives. For the time being the Liberal centre held. But some of the ideas that had been associated with the dominant Liberalism of the middle decades of the nineteenth century were under serious challenge. That Liberalism had commonly been paternalistic in its beliefs about the relations between the classes. It believed that property owners and employers knew what was best for their employees, and that they owed a duty to those less well-off to shape their lives in order to improve them. Such views were not just held by the propertied themselves. In 1868 the Dundee Working Men's Association and the Trades Council organised a campaign to persuade the town's leading manufacturers to stand for election to the local council. The *Advertiser* reported that this showed 'how good a feeling exists between employers and employed, the latter are now looking to the former to set aside business considerations and assist in giving new dignity, weight and influence to the Council'.[105]

Paternalism went along with philanthropy, and Dundee in the 1860s especially was the home of spectacular examples of the rich spending money for the benefit of the poor, the most famous example being Baxter Park.[106] Of a similar character was the Albert Museum (now the McManus), funds for which were donated by large numbers of the city's 'middling classes' to provide instruction and improvement for the mass of the city's inhabitants.[107]

Paternalism and philanthropy went along with a widespread belief that the ills of society – poverty, unemployment, intemperance, sexual immorality – were the result of character defects, to be corrected, at least in the short term, by stern treatment, seen as the most likely way to bring about moral rearmament.[108] This was a world of class collaboration between masters and working men (and even more, working women), with the masters setting the terms of collaboration. Self-organisation among 'respectable' workers was acceptable as long as its aims were conciliatory and non-antagonistic. Characteristically, the suggestion of a trade union among jute workers in 1875 was welcomed by the Liberal *People's Journal* as a basis for cooperation with the employers on joint action on the reform of the Indian Factory Acts.[109]

This world view was undermined from the 1870s by a variety of factors, summarised for Scotland by Richard Rodger: 'If economic theory, social investigations and philosophical debate were from the 1880s undermining the unanimity of character deficiency as an explanation of poverty, a faltering industrial performance and declining military capability accelerated the process.'[110] Rodger is in line with many other historians in seeing the wave of social investigations of this period as both responding to and shaping new attitudes to poverty which eroded the ideas of mid-century Liberalism. In the case of Dundee, the role of 'social investigations' by the DSU is instructive. The DSU was in part a continuation of the long-established philanthropic tradition, founded in the 1880s to improve housing, and was also replete with the paternalism (especially towards working-class women) that commonly accompanied such philanthropy. But the 1905 *Report* made it very clear that the social problems it focused upon, housing and infant mortalities, were largely the result of the workings of the jute industry labour market, rather than deficiencies in the character of Dundee's poor. The *Report* was not intended as a political document, and indeed explicitly did not deal with 'remedies for the evils disclosed'. Like other contemporary enquiries, it hoped 'that the larger reforms required should spring from a public opinion enlightened by data gathered from any enquiries prosecuted along similar lines'.[111] The DSU seems to have been much more influential in Dundee than the national body, the Charity Organisation Society, whose central purpose was to regulate charitable giving to restrict support for the 'undeserving'.[112]

Class collaboration was not all a matter of 'false consciousness'; most obviously, free trade and cheap food benefited both the jute employers *and* jute workers. But ideas of class collaboration in jute became harder to sustain in the face of 'faltering industrial performance', when Indian competition pressed the employers into a competitive cage, from which they found it hard to escape. This determined them that they would never recognise the trade unions in the industry (though they favoured the DDMFOU wherever possible), and when in 1912 they were forced into the acceptance of the idea of a 'Standing Joint Committee' for the industry they did not make good on the promise.[113] Where jute employers had responded sympathetically to the famous factory reformer Joseph Mundella's call for a nine-hour day in the early 1870s, they strongly resisted the pressure for an eight-hour day from the 1880s.[114]

More broadly, from the 1880s, when the employers moved away from support for free trade, this went along with a broader ideological movement. Free trade was never just about the price of commodities, but also about pacific and cooperative international relations. Support for free trade was integral to the mid-nineteenth-century Liberal world view.[115] For some the shift to Conservatism meant not just a search for possible protectionist devices against competitors in the jute industry, but a more pessimistic view about the world and ideas about the mutual benefits accruing from international trade and cooperation. In turn, we can see this more pessimistic stance affecting attitudes to relations with the jute workforce, with less belief in a natural community of interest between employer and employee. Some employers remained paternalistic in attitude, but this was increasingly challenged by union activity on one side and international competition on the other.[116]

As we have seen already, 'declining military capability' was also a concern in Dundee, with the case of Lennox, the military recruiter, noted above. This eugenically informed concern with popular health also indicated a shift away from the predominance of liberal ideas, which did not regard popular welfare through the lens of international and imperial rivalries, towards a more conservative vision. Philanthropy continued but was less evidently aimed at the social and cultural improvement of the workers. John Caird, the biggest jute philanthropist in the last decades of the century, gave most of his money for medical provision (the Royal Infirmary, maternity and cancer hospitals) and to propaganda for free trade.[117] His philanthropy did not attract the widespread acclaim, nor the erection of a celebratory statue, that had accompanied Baxter's spending in the 1860s.[118]

The old Liberal hegemony had been intimately related to pervasive religious belief. In Dundee this relation is nicely illustrated by the life and work of George Gilfillan, the city's most famous nineteenth-century clergyman.[119] He was active in many of the standard liberal causes from the 1840s to the 1880s, embracing the anti-slavery movement, the liberal internationalism of Garibaldi, and closer to home the Anti-Corn Law League, the nine-hours movement and generally the material and moral improvement of the working class. He became a close ally of the MP John Leng; Leng's 'joint promotion with Gilfillan of the cultural education of the urban population was viewed by both men as a key strategy and pre-condition for achieving the social and political advancement of the working classes'.[120]

But, as his biographer suggests, 'in the last two decades of the nineteenth century, Gilfillan's faith in benevolent progress and the Liberal ascendancy were challenged in Dundee by many new voices. The leadership of demands for political rights and social welfare passed to trade union organizations . . . and to rising socialist parties.'[121] The point is not that religious adherence declined in Dundee in this period, but that Gilfillan's particular brand of liberal social activism no longer fitted the mood of the city.

Dundee's two most prominent religious figures of the years after Gilfillan's death in 1878 were Henry Williamson, founder of the DDMFOU, and William Walsh, successor to Gilfillan as leader of the Gilfillan Memorial Church, Labour party supporter, and author of *Jesus in Juteopolis.*[122] In very different ways they illustrate Callum Brown's argument that, 'In the late Victorian and Edwardian periods (c. 1880–c. 1914), the role of the churches in social policy entered a crisis.'[123] Williamson had many of the same liberal views as Gilfillan, and the purpose of his union was conciliation and the inculcation of responsible attitudes into the 'mill-girls'.[124] He did not hold those he represented in great estimation: 'The fact is that the general public of Dundee have no idea of the dense ignorance of a large proportion of the working people of the city.'[125] Once the DDUJFW was established in 1906, his union quickly lost ground – especially after appealing for an early return to work in the 1912 strike – soon becoming little more than a burial society.[126] Walsh's book offered a very different understanding of Dundee than that offered by Gilfillan or Williamson. The meliorist optimism of mid-century was replaced by a much less comfortable, in places almost apocalyptic, pessimism about the city and its inhabitants. When, in Walsh's novel, Jesus visits Juteopolis, his call for a minimum wage and profit sharing is so unwelcome to the city's inhabitants that he is unceremoniously thrown in the Tay.

CONCLUSIONS

On the eve of the First World War, Dundee was enjoying a sharp cyclical upturn in the jute industry: 'The year 1913 has been in many ways the most outstanding and remarkable that has ever adorned the pages of the history of the trade.' But that boom was accompanied by continuing labour turmoil, the year designated as 'a year of industrial unrest', with 'crisis after crisis, and strike after strike'.[127] While the unrest was by no means confined to jute, in that industry 'No general strike has taken place, but the great body of employees were disaffected . . .'[128] Disaffection was also evident on the part of women, including when in that same year suffragettes disrupted the granting of the Freedom of the City to Prime Minister Asquith.[129]

Division and disaffection were endemic in the city by 1913. Liberal Scotland had not died, any more than Liberal England.[130] That death was to be postponed until after the war. But Dundee was certainly a much less Liberal place than it had been in 1870. The language of class antagonism was commonplace, and faith that this antagonism could be resolved amicably very much in retreat. Dundee was not alone in this regard; class-based ideologies were growing across Britain, causing ideological and political crisis not only for Liberals but also Conservatives.[131] But in Juteopolis these new tensions were especially acute because the staple industry could no longer offer either expanding opportunities or

THE CITY DIVIDED   239

economic security. The city had become trapped in a pincer movement between ever-rising competition on the one side, and a rising unwillingness to accept the dictates of the 'market' on the other.

Notes

1. *Dundee Year Book (DYB)* 1911, p. 105.
2. William Walker, *Juteopolis: Dundee and its Textile Workers 1885–1923* (Edinburgh, 1979), pp. 178–84; M. Forrester, 'Dundee and its Textile Industry: The 1912 Strike' (MA dissertation, Dundee University, 1988).
3. Anonymous, *Memoranda of the Chartist Agitation in Dundee* (Dundee, 1889).
4. Jeanette Brock, *The Mobile Scot: A Study of Emigration and Migration 1861–1911* (Edinburgh, 1999) notes an especially large outflow from Angus between 1891 and 1901 (in which county Dundee was by far the most populous town), pp. 124, 133.
5. UDA, MS134/1, D. Lennox, 'Working-class life in Dundee for twenty-five years 1878–1903' (1928), table 38.
6. Richard Rodger, 'Employment, wages and poverty in the Scottish cities 1841–1914', in George Gordon (ed.), *Perspectives of the Scottish City* (Aberdeen, 1985), p. 41.
7. Examples from the 168 website <https://mcmanus168.org.uk/> include Alexander Easson and George Graham.
8. Bruce Lenman and Enid Gauldie, 'The industrial history of the Dundee region from the eighteenth to the early twentieth century', in S. Jones (ed.), *Dundee and District* (Dundee, 1968), p. 169.
9. Ibid.
10. *DYB* 1901.
11. A. J. Cooke, *Baxter's of Dundee* (Dundee, 1980).
12. Rodger, 'Employment, wages and poverty', pp. 40–1; B. Lenman, C. Lythe and E. Gauldie, *Dundee and its Textile Industry, 1850–1914* (Dundee, 1969), p. 37.
13. S. G. E. Lythe, 'Shipbuilding at Dundee down to 1914', *Scottish Journal of Political Economy*, 9 (1962), pp. 219–32.
14. Gordon Jackson, *The British Whaling Trade* (London, 1978), pp. 130–40.
15. Lennox, 'Working-class life', p. 71.
16. Claire Swan, *Cowboys and Dundee Investors* (Dundee, 2004); Charles Munn, *Investing for Generations: A History of Alliance Trust* (Dundee, 2012). There was also investment elsewhere in Scotland; for example, in his letters home from India in 1871/2 Edward Cox continually worried about his investments in Edinburgh tramways: UDA MS 6/5/2/1-2.
17. Eleanor Gordon, *Women and the Labour Movement in Scotland 1850–1914* (Oxford, 1991), pp. 141, 142.

240 THE TRIUMPH OF TEXTILES

18. Dundee Social Union (DSU), *Report on Housing and Industrial Conditions in Dundee* (Dundee, 1905), p. xi.
19. Ibid., p. xii.
20. Ibid., p. xii; see also C. Templeman, 'Child Mortality in Dundee', a lecture delivered under the auspices of the Society for the Prevention of Cruelty to Children (Dundee, 1898). Templeman was the city's Medical Officer of Health.
21. *DYB* 1903, 'The working poor of Dundee', pp. 146–9.
22. DSU, *Report*, p. xii.
23. Ibid., pp. 73–4.
24. Ibid., p. xiii.
25. *Dundee Advertiser*, 14 March 1906, 4 April 1906.
26. Emma Griffin, *Bread Winner: An Intimate History* (New Haven, 2020).
27. Calculated from DSU, *Report*, p. 45.
28. Mary Walker, 'Work amongst women', in A. Paton (ed.), British Association, *Handbook and Guide to Dundee and District* (Dundee, 1912), p. 73.
29. DSU, *Report*, p. 41.
30. Rodger, 'Employment, wages and poverty', p. 29. There was apparently a sharp fall in this proportion in Dundee between the 1841 and 1851 Census.
31. A. M. Carstairs, 'The nature and diversification of employment in Dundee in the twentieth century', in Jones, *Dundee and District*, p. 322; for Dundee's class structure, Nicholas Morgan and Richard Trainor, 'The dominant classes', in W. Hamish Fraser and R. J. Morris (eds), *People and Society in Scotland Vol. II 1830–1914* (Edinburgh, 1990), p. 106.
32. Jan Merchant, '"An insurrection of maids": Domestic servants and the agitation of 1872', in Christopher A. Whatley, Bob Harris and Louise Miskell (eds), *Victorian Dundee: Image and Realities* (2nd edn, Dundee, 2011), pp. 112–33.
33. DSU, *Report*, p. xiii.
34. Census of Scotland 1911, Vol. II, table XXVII.
35. Walker, 'Work amongst women', p. 70; UDA MS66/II/10/27, data on Census of Production at Camperdown, 1912.
36. A. Bowley and G. Wood, 'Wages in the engineering and shipbuilding trades', *Journal of the Royal Statistical Society*, 68 (1905), pp. 119, 121.
37. Jute everywhere was associated with low wages, setting aside the case of Calcutta. When John Leng visited the USA in 1876, he noted how the jute industry in Oakland, California was overwhelmingly staffed by poorly paid Chinese immigrants (two heads of department were from Tayside): John Leng, *America in 1876* (Dundee, 1877), pp. 168–70.
38. DSU, *Report*, pp. 1–2, 7.
39. Commenting (sarcastically?) on the situation, the Rev. William Walsh (also a councillor) noted, 'It is noticeable that the Municipal rulers of Dundee singularly advanced and successful as they are in various Municipal

THE CITY DIVIDED   241

enterprises, have not hitherto seen the necessity of embarking upon any scheme of Municipal housing': William Walsh, 'The dwellings of Dundee', in British Association, *Dundee Handbook and Guide 1912* (Dundee, 1912), p. 93.

40. Rodger, 'Employment, wages and poverty', p. 42.
41. J. R. L. Halley (ed.), *A History of Halley's Mill* (Dundee, 1980), p. 24.
42. Charles McKean, '"Beautifying and improving the city": The pursuit of a monumental Dundee during the twentieth century', in Jim Tomlinson and Christopher Whatley (eds), *Jute No More: Transforming Dundee* (Dundee, 2011), pp. 70–81 for a characteristically waspish assessment of these ideas.
43. UDA, MS134/1, D. Lennox, 'Working-class life'.
44. Ibid., p. 66.
45. John Kemp, 'Red Tayside? Political change in early twentieth-century Dundee', in Whatley, Harris and Miskell, *Victorian Dundee*, pp. 217–38; Kenneth Baxter and William Kenefick, 'Labour politics and the Dundee working class c. 1895–1936', in Tomlinson and Whatley, *Jute No More*, pp. 191–219.
46. Walker, *Juteopolis*, pp. 17–31, quote at p. 22.
47. Ibid., pp. 22, 30–1, 45.
48. Ibid., pp. 36, 49.
49. Gordon, *Women and the Labour Movement*, pp. 1, 5.
50. Ibid., p. 156.
51. Ibid., pp. 209–10.
52. Walker, *Juteopolis*, pp. 149–98.
53. *People's Journal*, 14 October 1922, cited in Walker, *Juteopolis*, p. 149.
54. For example, the *Dundee Courier*, 20 October 1875, welcomed the creation of the East of Scotland Mill and Factory Workers Protective Association as a way of reducing strikes.
55. DCA, GD JF 1/1 1, *Jute and Flax Workers Guide* (hereafter, *Guide*) March 1906, April 1906; Walker, *Juteopolis*, pp. 200–2.
56. Walker, *Juteopolis*, pp. 144–7, 178–84.
57. DCA, GD/JF/1/1, DDJFWU General meetings, 30 October 1906 and 30 October 1913.
58. *DYB* 1889, 'History of Dundee trade societies', pp. 92–102.
59. *Dundee Courier*, 5 January 1874. Yeaman later moved to the Conservatives, losing under that banner in 1880.
60. *DYB* 1889, 'The Dundee parliamentary election, 1889', p. 113.
61. Michael Dyer, *Men of Property and Intelligence: The Scottish Electoral System Prior to 1884* (Aberdeen, 1996), pp. 51, 53.
62. Donald Southgate, 'Politics and representation in Dundee 1832–1963', in J. M. Jackson (ed.), *The Third Statistical Account of Scotland: The City of Dundee* (Arbroath, 1979), p. 290.
63. Southgate, 'Politics', p. 290.

242 THE TRIUMPH OF TEXTILES

64. Ibid., pp. 292–93.
65. Dyer, *Men of Property*, pp. 111–12.
66. Non-artisan enfranchisement was limited by the city's overcrowding, as to vote if you were a lodger (which many young male workers were) required payment of rent of £10 per annum, and that you did not share a room: Michael Dyer, *Capable Citizens and Improvident Democrats: The Scottish Electoral System, 1884–1929* (Aberdeen, 1996), p. 24.
67. *British Daily Mail*, 22 September 1884.
68. Walker, *Juteopolis*, p. 255.
69. DCL: LHC, J. Handy, 'The Rise of Labour in Dundee 1885–1910' (unpaginated typescript, 1982); Kemp, 'Red Tayside?', pp. 158–61.
70. For the national picture, see Duncan Tanner, *Political Change and the Labour Party* (Cambridge, 1990), pp. 19–96.
71. Southgate, 'Politics', p. 300; Handy, 'Rise'.
72. Iain Hutchison, A *Political History of Scotland, 1832–1924* (Edinburgh, 1986), p. 181.
73. David Howell, *British Workers and the Independent Labour Party* (Manchester, 1983), p. 150; Walker, *Juteopolis*, pp. 261–4.
74. Walker, *Juteopolis*, pp. 265–9; Southgate, 'Politics', p. 301.
75. *Dundee Advertiser*, 10 February 1906, 17 January 1906; Kemp, 'Red Tayside?', p. 162.
76. Dyer, *Capable Citizens*, pp. 21–2.
77. If we make the extreme (but not absurd) assumption that all those excluded from the franchise were working class and combine this with the 1911 data suggesting 20 per cent of the city population were working class, the enfranchised working class would have outnumbered the middle class by only 60 per cent to 40 per cent in the electorate c. 1908.
78. *Dundee Advertiser*, 21 October 1907.
79. LSE Archive, *Parliamentary Representation of Dundee. Reports of Public Meetings. Addresses by Councillor Alexander Wilkie* (Dundee, 1906).
80. *Dundee Advertiser*, 5 January 1906.
81. *Dundee Advertiser*, 6 November 1909, reporting a Liberal meeting which agreed by a large majority not to run a second candidate.
82. Howell, *British Workers*, p. 134.
83. Kemp, 'Red Tayside?', pp. 153–67. Local government politics in many ways had a separate dynamic, not least because the franchise was substantially different, included some women, and had a working-class majority: ibid., p. 153.
84. Churchill College, University of Cambridge Churchill Archive CHAR 5/1, 'To the Electors of Dundee', 30 April 1908; see also *Scotsman*, 1 May 1908.
85. Dundee, no date. Copy in CHAR 9/31/66.
86. *For Liberalism and Free Trade*, pp. 7, 8, 11.
87. *Dundee Advertiser*, 5 May 1908.

THE CITY DIVIDED 243

88. Winston Churchill, *For Liberalism and Free Trade* (Dundee, 1908), p. 23.
89. Ibid., p. 29.
90. Winston Churchill, 'Some election memories', *Strand Magazine*, LXXXI (1931), p. 244.
91. *The Scotsman*, 8 May 1908, Churchill responding to questions from Labour Councillor John Reid.
92. For example, speech at Lochee, 3 May 1908: *Dundee Courier*, 4 May 1908.
93. *The Scotsman*, 9 May 1908.
94. *The Times*, 4 May 1908.
95. *The Scotsman*, 1 December 1908.
96. DCL: LHC, '1908 Election', 'To the Parliamentary Electors of Dundee', p. 3.
97. *The Scotsman*, 29 April 1908.
98. *Dundee Courier*, 1 May 1908.
99. *Dundee Advertiser*, 6 May 1908.
100. *The Scotsman*, 8 May 1908.
101. These separate parties came together to form the Scottish Unionist Association in 1913: John Ward, *The First Century: A History of Scottish Tory Organisation 1882–1992* (Edinburgh, 1982), p. 24.
102. Southgate, 'Politics', p. 298; on Dalgleish, see Sydney Checkland and Anthony Slaven (eds., *Dictionary of Scottish Business Biography, Vol. I, The Staple Industries* (Aberdeen, 1986).
103. Southgate, 'Politics', pp. 294–6.
104. R. Britton, 'Wealthy Scots, 1876–1913', *Bulletin of the Institute for Historical Research*, 58 (1985), pp. 78–94.
105. Louise Miskell, 'Civic leadership and the manufacturing elite. Dundee, 1820–1870', in Whatley et al., *Victorian Dundee*, p. 45; *Dundee Advertiser*, 24 November 1868.
106. Of course, philanthropy is not confined to the well-off: in Dundee, as elsewhere, the working class were often generous contributors relative to their income: Lorraine Walsh, *Patrons, Poverty and Profit: Organised Charity in Nineteenth-Century Dundee* (Dundee, 2000), pp. 41–5.
107. <https://mcmanus168.org.uk/entries/>
108. Rodger, 'Employment, wages and poverty', pp. 26–8.
109. *People's Journal*, 11 September 1875.
110. Rodger, 'Employment, wages and poverty', p. 28.
111. DSU, *Report*, p. vii. There is some evidence that the severity of the mid-1880s recession, which stimulated much debate about unemployment, had earlier shifted understanding of the causes of social distress: DCL: LHC Lamb Collection 197(37), John Leng, 'What are the best methods of dealing with the unemployed?'. Paper read at charity and Poor Law conference', 29 April 1886.
112. Walsh, *Patrons*, pp. 58–9.

244   THE TRIUMPH OF TEXTILES

113. Walker, *Juteopolis*, p. 309.
114. On Mundella's Bill, *Dundee Courier*, 13 May 1873; on the eight hours issue, see chapter 6. At the Dundee Trades Council the threat to shift jute production to India if an eight-hour day was introduced was described as 'incredible claptrap': *Dundee Courier*, 10 December 1891.
115. Anthony Howe, *Free Trade and Liberal England, 1846–1946* (Oxford, 1997); Frank Trentmann, *Free Trade Nation* (Oxford, 2008).
116. Christopher Whatley, *Onward from Osnaburgs: The Rise and Progress of a Scottish Textile Company, Don and Low of Forfar, 1792–1992* (Edinburgh, 1992), pp. 143–54.
117. *DYB* 1912, 'Caird's benefactions', p. 89.
118. Later he was memorialised in the Caird Hall, the largest civic building in Dundee, opened in 1923.
119. Aileen Black, *Gilfillan of Dundee 1813–1878: Interpreting Religion and Culture in Mid-Victorian Scotland* (Dundee, 2006).
120. Black, *Gilfillan*, p. 47; Gilfillan published extensively in Leng's *Advertiser* and especially the *People's Journal*.
121. Black, *Gilfillan*, p. 108.
122. William Walsh, *Jesus in Juteopolis* (Dundee, 1906).
123. Callum Brown, 'Religion', in A. J. Cooke et al., *Modern Scottish History 1707 to the Present. Vol. 2: The Modernisation of Scotland, 1850 to the Present* (East Linton, 1998), p. 148.
124. Gilfillan had derided the attempts by maidservants to improve their conditions in 1872: Black, *Gilfillan*, p. 78.
125. *Dundee Courier*, 13 June 1891, comment at meeting of Dundee Trades Council.
126. Walker, *Juteopolis*, p. 148. Burial insurance was extremely popular: the Dundee Burial Society had 16,481 members and the Lochee Funeral Society 5,616 in 1902: Lennox, 'Working- class life', p. 247.
127. *DYB* 1913, pp. 16, 50.
128. Ibid., p. 17.
129. Ibid., pp. 73–9.
130. George Dangerfield, *The Strange Death of Liberal England* (London, 1966).
131. Ewen Green, *The Crisis of Conservatism* (London, 1995).

8

The City and the First World War

[Dundee] is in the strongest position in jute commodities that has ever been experienced. (1915)

After eighteen months of war, the *Dundee Year Book* noted of 1915: 'Dundee can hardly hope to have another year of such unmixed prosperity'.[1] But such prosperity continued: for 1916 the summary was '. . . a year of richest prosperity to the staple trades of Dundee and district'.[2] These comments suggest that, after an initial dislocation, the impact of the First World War on Juteopolis was to be akin to the historic pattern, when successively the Crimean, American Civil, Franco-Prussian and Boer wars had all boosted Dundee's industrial activity: 'there has never been a war without a good demand for jute goods'.[3] But the First World War was not like earlier wars. While the demand for jute products hugely expanded, this time supplies of the raw material and labour for the industry were constrained by the necessities of 'total war', and this enlarged the opportunities for Dundee's competitors in Calcutta. As a result, the war's impact was much more damaging in its effects, with some short-term benefits to both employers and workers, but much larger long-term costs.

To examine these effects this chapter first outlines the overall effects of the war on the jute industry. It then looks at the shift within the industry's workings that followed, notably the strengthening of labour and the increased role of the state. It pays particular attention to the impact of the war on women, whose predominance in the industry was enhanced by the war, and who, starting from a very low base, began to have a bigger say in the working of the city. Finally, we assess the impact of the war on international competition in jute, how Calcutta's position was immensely strengthened in these years, and Dundee's permanently weakened.

WAR AND JUTE

As with so many British industries, the initial effect of the war was great uncertainty and significant disruption. Eventually, it was largely the demand for sandbags that drove the wartime boom, with production rising from less than a quarter of a million per month to over 40 million in the course of 1915 as the war became characterised by static trenches surrounded by extraordinary numbers of such bags.[4] This initial boom was succeeded by a period of continuing strong demand but increasing constraints on supply, both of raw jute and of labour. Raw material imports, which had averaged 200,000 tons per annum in the last pre-war decade, rose to 295,000 in 1915, but then fell back to a low of 82,000 in 1917.[5] This fall followed the imposition of controls aimed at limiting demand for shipping.[6] The shortage of shipping in turn led to a more than threefold increase in freight charges for raw jute in 1915, contributing substantially to the rise in price of the raw material, whose cost to the user more than doubled in the two years from mid-1915.[7]

The reductions in raw jute imports followed opposition by the jute employers to a government suggestion of a possible complete cessation of raw jute shipments. They pointed out that imports were down to 24,000 tons a month in 1917 and to 16,000 in January 1918, and said that no exports were going out.[8] Stocks were down to 45,000 tons. They claimed that they needed 13,000 tons a month for sandbags and sacks for foodstuffs, and 3,000 for other military needs.[9]

In November 1917 the *Advertiser* was talking of 'the most acute crisis that the jute trade has ever had to pass through' as exports were banned and raw material supplies cut.[10] But in truth the crisis was one that could be borne with some equanimity by the jute employers, given the strength of demand and the resultant high prices and profits that accrued. Limited availability of manufactured products was the result of cuts in raw material supply, with over 16,000 spindles (out of a pre-war total of 267,000) made idle in the first round of reductions in spring 1918. Eventually cuts to raw jute supply reached around one-third.[11] But as discussed in the next section, the impact on the jute workers was minimised by short-time working.

Demand outstripping supply meant profits shot up.[12] Table 8.1 shows the story for Cox Brothers. A similar pattern is evident in the profits of Don and Low, which show a peak in the immediate post-war boom in 1919/20, before an extraordinary collapse to barely more than 1 per cent of the previous year's level in the slump of 1920/21.[13] Even allowing for inflation, and the Excess Profits Duty that was eventually imposed,

Table 8.1 Cox Brothers' pre-tax profits, 1912–19

Year	Pre-tax profits (£)
1912	90,540
1913	104,278
1914	75,165
1915	48,068
1916	169,217
1917	188,942
1918	211,738
1919	348,643

Source: UDA MS66/II/2/6, Cox's Letter book, Ernest Cox to S. Copley, 16 July 1919.

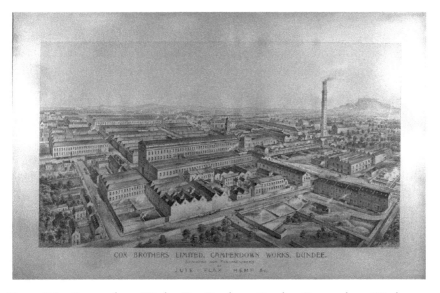

Figure 8.1 Camperdown Works, Cox Brothers, Dundee. Camperdown Works came to dominate Lochee, a suburb of Dundee. It was the biggest jute mill and factory in the world. Like Baxters' Dens Works, Camperdown was a fully integrated plant that was linked to Dundee's docks by railway. Towering over the works was the Stack, an Italianate chimney that broadcast the Cox's dominance in the jute industry. Like the High Mill, the clock tower and some workers' housing, the Stack still stands, a fitting monument to Dundee's industrial past. © University of Dundee Archives.

248

THE TRIUMPH OF TEXTILES

the war was clearly enormously favourable to the owners of jute companies, and in the immediate post-war years many took advantage by floating their companies at temporarily highly inflated values, consolidating much of the industry into two amalgamated firms: Jute Industries Limited (which included Cox's), controlling around a third of the industry's output, and Low and Bonar, which acquired Baxter Brothers in 1924.[14]

The London government also sought to control the distribution of the products of Calcutta's jute mills. In October 1915 exports of hessian bags and cloth from India were prohibited except for the British market, and the sevenfold increase in bag exports to that market from Calcutta between 1914 and 1915 gives a sense of the scale of the boost to Dundee's competitor brought about by wartime conditions.[15] The prices and profits of the Calcutta industry were magnified by problems in increasing supply, especially in the face of the difficulties of getting new machinery (mainly imported from Britain), with the number of looms rising by less than 3 per cent between 1914 and January 1919. Profits were also helped by the fact that the supply of workers proved much more elastic than the supply of machinery, so the Calcutta jute workers obtained little of the bounty that accrued to the wartime industry.[16]

The Calcutta industry was unconstrained by problems of raw material or labour supply, and it expanded its production and exports substantially, with a striking impact on profit levels. The ratio of net profit to paid-up capital was 58 per cent in 1915, 75 per cent in 1916 and 73 per cent in 1918.[17] When at the war's end the Dundee jute owners offered to cooperate with those in Calcutta, the nature of their suggestions 'reflected the city's continuing obtuseness about Calcutta's primary position in the world jute trade'.[18] But this primacy was no longer in doubt – the balance of power in international jute markets had moved permanently against Dundee.

THE RISE OF LABOUR

For most of the history of Juteopolis the employers had the upper hand in bargaining with their workers. Even in boom times, they were usually able to readily recruit all the labour required, albeit with some (usually temporary) wage increases. But the war brought about a much more sustained shift in bargaining power in favour of the workers. This was true both for men, given the demand for their services in the armed

THE CITY AND THE FIRST WORLD WAR   249

forces, but also for women, where alternative job opportunities opened up, especially in munitions (both locally and further afield) but also in other occupations where manpower was stripped out to feed the army's insatiable desire for bodies.

The first clear evidence of the wartime change in circumstance came with an agreement early in 1915 between the newly formalised employers' organisation, the Association of Jute Spinners and Manufacturers (AJSM), and a joint committee of local trade unions. That the employers were willing to enter into a formal agreement with unions was evidence of changing times, given their previous disdain for any type of recognition of such bodies. In response to these changing circumstances, an advance of wages of 5 per cent in February and the following month a 'full-time bonus' of 2 shillings per week was agreed, as long as workers put in the full fifty-five hours a week expected, an arrangement intended to last for the duration of the war.[19] There was also joint agreement in November that year that both sides should seek to resist conscription of workers from the industry.[20]

In October the workers' joint committee put in a claim for a further wage increase of 10 per cent, for the bonus to be made permanent, and for work to cease on Saturday at 10 am. As discussed further below, the changing wartime labour market brought about an unprecedented role of state agencies in Dundee's wage bargaining, and on this occasion that agency (the Committee on Production) ruled against the workers.[21] But this was far from settling the matter. By January 1916 the joint committee was pressing for a wage increase of 15 per cent, in the face of accelerating wartime inflation. Rejection of the demand led to a strike from the end of March to early June. The strike was a short-term failure. But it seems also seems to have marked a turning point in jute trade unionism's fortunes in the city. Membership of the biggest union, the Dundee and District Union of Jute and Flax Workers (DDUJFW), which was only 5,000 in early 1916, rose rapidly to reach 9,000 in early 1917, nearly 16,000 by the end of that year, and peaking at almost 20,000 by the end of the war.[22]

Organisation of the strike also gave increased impetus to the activities of the DDUJFW, evident in the publication of the *Jute and Flax Workers Guide*, which became an important medium of union agitation.[23] Also notable was the 1916 strike's impact on greatly weakening that hangover from old-fashioned Victorian 'collaborationist' trade unionism, the DDMFOU, after it withdrew prematurely from the dispute.[24] From now on the DDUJFW was the unchallenged core of jute trade unionism in the industry, though other much smaller unions, such as the callenderers and tenters, survived.

The failure of the 1916 strike was partly due to the financial weakness of the unions, plus the fact that demand for jute goods had not yet reached its peak. The employers were also still willing to use the threat of future Calcutta competition as a reason for not paying wage advances.[25] The dispute led to interventions by both the Lord Provost, Don, and then by the Labour MP, Wilkie, but neither to any avail. The mood among the workers was undoubtedly becoming more militant. The role of Don was undermined by the fact he was himself a jute owner.[26] Wilkie was also a figure who seems to have lost some authority among the city's trade unionists by his strong support for the war and conscription, the latter stance leading to his repudiation by the Trades Council in February 1916.[27]

A further significant dispute broke out in early 1917, when the DDUJFW called for an increase of 3 shillings per week for time workers and 15 per cent for piece workers based on 'the further increased cost of living which makes it necessary that an advance in wages should be granted to meet the enhanced prices of the necessities of life'.[28] An award of 3 shillings and 10 per cent for men and 2 shillings and 7.5 per cent for women was given by the government arbitration, but this did not resolve the issue. Young workers, whose increase was smaller, seem to have been especially unhappy. The arbitrator thought 'the younger generation, who seem to be rather a law unto themselves in Dundee, are kicking a bit'.[29]

A messy series of disputes followed, with a number of small-scale strikes leading to wider shutdowns, and allegations from the Union of a lockout. The Union never made the company- specific strikes industry-wide, and they eventually petered out. But continuing rumbling discontent was evident through the year. 1917 was, of course, a year of worker unrest throughout much of war-torn Europe, and though no revolutionary movement appeared in Dundee, there were a variety of points of discontent. Rising inflation was at the core of much worker unhappiness, especially as it affected food prices and rent, issues returned to below. The DDUJFW was certainly agitated by these issues, but there were others directly related to the wartime labour market. An important issue was opposition to the call-up of jute workers. The Union was unsuccessful in getting the sector declared a protected occupation (which would have prevented conscription) but the Ministry of Munitions emphasised that because of the importance of jute the Union could intervene with the War Office if supplies were threatened by the military call-up.[30]

THE CITY AND THE FIRST WORLD WAR   251

Opposition to the mobilisation of jute workers is not necessarily evidence of general attitudes to the war. In August 1916 the Union refused to support the holding of a peace conference in Dundee.[31] At its most extreme, a call for support for quasi-revolutionary movements such as the Workers and Soldiers Council in Glasgow was allowed to 'lie on the table' in August 1917. But the tide of political opinion is perhaps suggested by the fact that in April 1917 the Union was opposed to granting the Freedom of the City to Lloyd George, and in October there was support for the idea that there was a need for 'Workers to capture the town council'.[32] Also significant was the by-election in August, forced by Edwin Scrymgeour in defiance of the electoral truce, when Churchill became Minister of Munitions.[33] Scrymgeour was a prominent local councillor, an outspoken pacifist and prohibitionist, who had stood unsuccessfully in all previous Dundee elections back to 1908. Churchill won a convincing victory by 7,302 votes to 2,036, albeit on a turnout of only 43 per cent.[34] The election debate focused on the war, with Scrymgeour's advocacy of a negotiated peace leading Churchill to compare him with Lenin.[35] Though Scrymgeour was a socialist, he got no support from the official Labour party, locally or nationally, while Churchill was able to claim the support of both Unionists and Labour.[36] In his view, 'every vote for Scrymgeour is a vote for a shameful peace'.[37] On the other hand, Scrymgeour, who got a respectable 28 per cent share of the vote, undoubtedly did articulate the opposition to Churchill among elements of the labour movement in Dundee.[38] Most importantly, he was supported by John Sime, Secretary of the DDUJFW, the single most important trade union figure in the city. For Sime, Churchill was 'one of the last men who will do anything for the working classes, unless they compel him by vigorous action to do so', and he cited as an example Churchill's failure to support the case for having jute declared a protected occupation.[39]

At the end of 1917 relations between employers and workers in jute entered a new phase as the government introduced restrictions on the shipping made available for raw jute imports, necessitating a reduction in spinning in the city. A major conflict soon emerged between the two sides on how to respond to this restriction. The employers favoured stopping machinery and at least temporarily dismissing some of the workers. The unions took the view that the better response was to move to short-time working, with compensation for the hours lost. Pursuing this view, Sime invoked government intervention.

The employers argued that in the face of a general shortage of labour, it was inappropriate to move to short-time working and deny other uses to jute workers, suggesting 'the impropriety of deliberately and unnecessarily placing 20,000 to 25,000 workers on short time, when everyone ought in the national interest to be working full time and to the utmost of his ability'.[40] The union view was that the vast majority to be affected would be women workers for whom there was not much demand elsewhere, and that very few men of military age would be made available for mobilisation into the army. Sime suggested that the labour market for women was currently slack, with many firms in Dundee paying off 'girls', and with the local munitions factory having a waiting list for employment. He also made emotional claims about how those thrown out of work if the employers had their way would be the widows and orphans of soldiers killed in combat.[41] The union position was boosted by a ballot among union members, which showed 10,181 favouring short time, and only 1,377 'stoppage of work'.[42]

The numbers likely to be affected by short-time working seem to have been greatly exaggerated by the employers, and the Ministry supported the union view about such working as the best response. Their political concern was expressed clearly by one official who defended the Ministry's decision, arguing that 'we considered that to throw a lot of workers out of employment at the present time would certainly result in grave discontent and provide an excellent breeding ground for pacifist and other undesirable germs and would also be followed by demand for the payment of subsistence by the State'.[43]

Despite this ministerial pressure, the employers were reluctant to concede, and did not deal with all the output reduction by short time. In response to the laying off of several hundred workers, the unions negotiated with the employers a 'War Benefit Scheme' that gave money to those rendered unemployed directly as a response to the cut in raw jute supply between December 1917 and March 1918. Though the numbers affected were small, this was a striking innovation in labour relations in the industry.[44]

Also highly novel was that as an outcome of this crisis the Union secured a cut in the working week (from fifty-five to forty hours), with compensation to the workers for lost time. This arrangement lasted until almost the end of the war, but in September 1918 the employers announced that with the ending of government restriction the industry would revert to a fifty-five-hour week. There was bitter resistance to this, above all because it meant the reintroduction of Saturday morning working, widely regarded as the bane of manual workers' lives. As the war ended the industry was entering a period of rancorous dispute on this

THE CITY AND THE FIRST WORLD WAR   253

issue, which continued into the peace, until the workers were defeated in March 1920 – a potent symbol of the loss of the wartime gains they had made.[45]

The unsurprising consequence of this level of demand for labour was upward pressure on pay levels, with strikes as employers tried to resist labour's claims, though conceding an underlying upward trend in nominal wage levels.[46]

THE RISE OF STATE INTERVENTION

The enhancement of labour's bargaining position during the war relied not only on labour market conditions, but also active intervention by the state. This, of course, was motivated by the government's desire to sustain production of jute products for the war effort. This intervention also spurred the employers into more formal organisation, resulting in the AJSM, with the aim of better coordinating their responses to state initiatives.

The primary role of the state was to act as conciliator and arbitrator in wage and other disputes in the industry. In doing this, conciliators like Sir George Askwith sought to find a 'middle way' between the demands of workers and the willingness to pay of the employers. The war did see very substantial increases in money wages in jute. Detailed figures for Don and Low's in Forfar show that such wages more than doubled across the manual grades, and this is likely to have been the typical pattern in the industry.[47] Real wages did not rise in the same way because of largely matching rises in prices. In bargaining, workers and unions mainly focused on price changes when making their claims, even if they were aware that the strong demand in the industry was causing a notable increase in profits.

In Dundee, as elsewhere in the country, allegations of profiteering were commonplace during the war, but little was known at the time about how profitable the jute firms were. Responses to perceived profiteering focused attention on prices charged by local suppliers of food. When the city council set up a committee on profiteering in September 1917, it was argued that 'one-half of the Committee be composed of ladies. To make it a success, they wanted good, practical housewives from various sections of the community.' The report on this in a local paper was headed 'Ladies wanted. Better anti-profiteers than men'.[48] While there was general recognition of booming profits in the industry, this was not something that could be addressed at the local level, but jute companies, like all others, were subject to Excess Profits Duty, as the national government intervened to head off discontent driven by perceptions of profiteering.

The desire to conciliate workers led to some decisions by state arbitrators that left employers distinctly unhappy, most notably the decision on short-time working. But this does not mean the decisions always favoured the workers. For example, the January 1916 rejection of the unions' wage claim was justified by Askwith and his fellow arbitrators with reference to the 'imperative need for economy in all forms of expenditure and consumption both public and private' and to 'the measures already taken to tax or limit the profits of undertakings'.[49] More equivocal was the role of the state regarding the issue of equal pay for men and women. The agreement between unions and the AJSM in 1915 seemed to embody a version of this principle, but the 1916 wage agreement arbitrated by the Board of Trade gave wage increases differentiated by gender.[50] It was a frequent source of union complaint that some employers were not giving equal pay, but given their own awards, its perhaps unsurprising that the arbitrators were evidently unwilling to get involved.[51]

While in some cases state agencies put unwelcome pressure on employers, it was also clear to some of those employers that in a tight labour market they needed, if possible, to improve the attractions of working in the industry. Apart from wages, this meant improvements in welfare provision, most notably nursery places for some of the many employed mothers.

One legacy of the state's wartime role in Juteopolis was the creation of a Trade Board to regulate wages. Trade Boards were originally introduced in 1908 and were a key feature of the New Liberal legislation of the 1906–14 period, in which Winston Churchill played an important part. The question of creating a Trade Board in jute was raised at the time of the original legislation. One aspect of the drive for that regulation was the especially weak position of women workers, and the women's trade union activist Mary McArthur had made the case for a Trade Board in jute to protect workers who sewed sacks, who were usually women: 'Mr Churchill, it was to be hoped, would not forget the jute workers, for not only was the jute trade one of the lowest paid of the staple trades of the Kingdom, but there was also a considerable amount of sack-sewing, which was even worse paid than the jute trade.'[52] There is no evidence that, at this time, the unions in jute pressed for a Board.[53]

The scope of Trade Boards was widened during the war, and the legislation was extended in 1918. Where the original law had been fundamentally concerned with the level of wages, hence the use of the term

THE CITY AND THE FIRST WORLD WAR   255

'Sweated Industries' to describe affected sectors, the extension, in line with early post-war thinking, focused on the degree of organisation of an industry.[54] The idea of a Trade Board in jute resurfaced in August 1918, when Sime said he was surprised at the idea, given the high level of unionisation in the industry, but welcomed the proposal.[55] The matter was under active discussion by the AJSM by November 1918, and its initial stance was surprisingly favourable, seeing it as a way of regulating wages at a time of exceptional industrial unrest.[56] Employers were assured by the Board of Trade that a Trade Board did not involve suggesting jute was a sweated industry, and further reassurance was offered that a minimum wage would not be set until conditions had settled down.[57] The Board was established at the end of 1919, and set the first minimum wage in June 1920, coinciding almost exactly with the peak of the post-war boom.[58]

While the jute employers were generally wary of state intervention in 'their' industry and supported the Trade Board idea only on a highly contingent basis, they strengthened their demand for a greater state role in international trade relations. Nationally, the war had led to a considerable strengthening of protectionist sentiment, and this was also evident in Dundee. For example, the pre-war idea of a preferential export duty on Bengal's raw jute was revived at the Dundee Chamber of Commerce in 1916.[59] This proposal was returned to by the jute employers as the war drew to a close, in evidence given to the government-appointed committee on the position of textiles after the war.[60] Such plans had clearly been given a fillip by anti-German sentiment, as Germany had been a major jute manufacturer before 1914. This strategic approach to trade was to feed into what came to be called 'Safeguarding', the idea that certain industries should be protected because of their centrality to war-making.[61]

Also, in the last months of the war a committee was set up jointly by the AJSM and trade unions to look at ways 'to expand the industry after the war'.[62] This was the first time that the two sides of the industry had come together in such a way, though as noted above, this joint endeavour was far from suggesting harmonious industrial relations in the industry, where a significant strike was occurring in the later months of the war over the length of the working week.[63] It was against this background that the campaign for the December 1918 election was fought. Churchill stood on the Coalition ticket, 'the 'Coupon', and was not opposed by the Unionists.[64] This meant that protectionism as a response to the industry's expected post-war crisis played little part in the election debate, given Churchill's position as a committed free trader.

THE RISING ROLE OF WOMEN

The nationwide impact of the First World War on the employment and broader role of women has long been a staple of historical debate. In Juteopolis the situation was distinct, in that unlike in any other place in Britain, women made up most of the workforce in the staple industry. If we want to assess the changes in women's employment during the war, we can begin with the data from the Censuses of 1911 and 1921. This, however, is not an ideal source: first, there is a change in categories used between the two census dates, which explains the inescapable complexity of Table 8.2. Second, by 1921 Britain had entered a major economic slump, so we need to be aware that there is a cyclical as well as a trend element in making this comparison. This cycle was especially sharp in jute, so we need to be especially careful in assessing what the pattern was in this industry.

Table 8.2 brings out the great diversity of women's occupations before the war, though the quantitative predominance of jute and textiles generally is unambiguous. The data for intercensal change suggests a rise in the number of women in domestic service, the second most important category in 1911. As noted in chapter 7, before the war this sector had employed a relatively small number of women in the city, compared with other parts of the country, partly because jute offered a more attractive alternative. After the war, the slump, in combination with pressure from the authorities to suspend benefit from those who refused this work, seems to have led to an increase.[65]

There were big increases in some 'white blouse' occupations, most strikingly in nursing and teaching. This registered the acceleration of a pre-war trend, but one which of course was to be central to women's employment and social mobility over the next century. Similarly, the rise of the number of women clerks was not new but seems to have been accelerated by the war, with its tendency to proliferate 'paperwork' of all kinds. Also in line with experience elsewhere was a small increase in women's role in the engineering industry, where having gained a foothold before 1914, wartime growth was never entirely rolled back. There were wartime reports of 'girls' having jobs in the city's Caledon shipyard, but no numbers or details were given, and this must have been a small-scale and temporary phenomenon.[66]

Finally, though this is an area where the changing definitions make the trends especially hard to pin down, it seems that the retail sector continued to expand across this decade. Of course, some of this may have been the result of the slump, with women and men moving into this

THE CITY AND THE FIRST WORLD WAR

Table 8.2 Women's occupations in Dundee, 1911 and 1921

	1911	1921
Jute workers	23,368	22,969 (textiles)
Flax and linen	834	
Canvas/sailcloth	371	
Bleaching, printing, dyeing	203	
Indoor domestic	2,155	2,545
Charwomen/cleaners	381	758
Grocers	213	2,421 shop assistants, 790 proprietors or managers
Wigmakers/hairdressers	128	
Milk/dairy	136	
Drapers	540	
Clothiers/outfitters	910	
Tailors	319	
Dressmakers/milliners	273	
Greengrocers	110	
Shopkeepers (not otherwise specified)	210	
Bread/biscuit/cake makers	152	695 (makers of food, drink and tobacco)
Jam making	356	
Chocolate makers	127	
Costermongers/street sellers	61	
Commercial clerks	984	2,278 (clerks, not civil service or local authority)
Engineering and machinery making	20	106 (metals)
National government	69	142 (public administration and defence)
Schoolmasters, lecturers	512	711
Nurses, midwives	312	440
Total enumerated	74,712	93,636
Total occupied	36,836	38,850

Source: Census, Scotland 1911 and 1921.

258   THE TRIUMPH OF TEXTILES

sector as jobs in jute and other manufacturing shrank – a point which applies with especial force to 'costermongers and street sellers'. Within this sector we know nothing about changes, though it would be interesting to know if bakers, a traditional male preserve (and strongly trade unionised employment), were affected. Note that the total activity rates of women fell, presumably largely as a result of the recession in 1921.

Not revealed by the Census are the jobs where, in the classic pattern, women were (sometimes reluctantly) recruited into pre-war 'men's jobs', only to be largely ejected at the war's end. This was evident in Dundee in the case of tram conductors, where twenty-one women, mostly rural domestic servants, not from Dundee itself, were taken on in March 1917.[67] Their employment led to complaints about their rudeness to passengers.[68] There was a similar shift in railway clerks, with perhaps seventy jobs given to women in the war (out of 135), but with the number falling back to ten out of 268 by 1920.[69] Another important innovation, albeit on a very small scale, was the introduction of women police.[70]

The best, if partial, information for jute arises from a detailed census in some firms related to a dispute over whether to use short-time working or cuts in jobs in response to reductions in imported raw materials in 1917. Table 8.3 shows that total employment peaked in 1917, before raw material controls cut back output. It also shows the unsurprising pattern of loss of men focused on the military age group, while the strongest recruitment of women was among younger age groups.

Table 8.4 suggests that pre-war there was relatively little gendered *horizontal* division of labour, but the most striking wartime change was how in what had been the largest male preserve, calendering, women were able to make a major advance.[71]

Overall, these two tables suggest a clear displacement of men by women in the jute industry; the Union estimated the proportion going

Table 8.3 Gender composition of jute workers in Bowbridge Works, 1914–18

	Male under 18	Male over 18	Proportion by gender	Female under 18	Female over 18	Proportion by gender
Oct 1914	131	229	28%	120	569	72%
April 1915	105	199		123	572	
April 1916	109	150		140	554	
April 1917	150	118		151	626	
May 1918	123	101		151	574	
Nov 1918	109	95	22%	171	549	78%

Source: Dundee University Archives, MS66/IV/8/27, Grimond papers, 'Numbers employed in Bowbridge Works (1907–1919)'.

THE CITY AND THE FIRST WORLD WAR

Table 8.4 Employment at Cox's, 1914 and 1917

	July 1914	April 1917 = peak
Batching	92	134
Preparing	498	503
Spinning	572	552
Bleaching/dyeing	8	18
Calendering	1	67
Labourers	0	7
Total women	2,056	2,296
(Total men)	1,314	765

Source: UDA MS66/II/10/29, Cox's 'Census of labour, April 1917'.

from 75 to 80–90 per cent.[72] This displacement took place despite employers' claims about the irreplaceability of men workers, and that substitution had gone as far as possible, a case they made at Munitions tribunals.[73] Similar views were put forward by Sime, who pressed for jute to be classed as a protected occupation, saying that so many men were being taken away that 'machinery has had to be put off, with the result that female workers are being thrown idle'.[74]

After the initial dislocation, demand for labour in jute was strong, the numbers employed peaking in the spring of 1918. In competition with jute, wages in the new munitions factories were attractive to women workers, though the numbers in the city were always small compared with those in textiles. The National Shell Factory recorded 325 women employed in October 1918, but this may have been past the peak. On 1 March 1918, 544 women and 143 men were recorded at work on shells in Dundee.[75] In addition, Acetone employed perhaps forty women. The jute employers were wary of their female workers 'voting with their feet' by leaving their employment for more attractive jobs in munitions. Baxter's, for example, was complaining about this pattern at the end of 1917.[76]

The supply of labour was added to by an influx of workers into Dundee from other parts of Scotland, most notably two thousand 'fishergirls' from the east coast, where fishing was disrupted by the war. They filled some of the jobs in munitions. Their presence was responded to with hostility from some members of the DDUJFW, who attacked them as 'ill-mannered womanhood' and as 'blacklegs', but others defended them. A letter sent by some of these girls in response to such hostility said 'our proud spirits rebel against those who call us unwomanly and ill-mannered as we feel we are as good as any of our Dundee fellow-workers'.[77]

Responses to women in munitions were also mixed. They were referred to in the *Guide* as 'aliens', but Sime was keen to encourage unionisation among them.[78] The *People's Journal* carried suggestions for the provision of 'golfing evenings for weary heroines' in the munitions industry.[79] The impact of munitions on the local labour market was complex; partly offsetting the inflow, the city also saw women leaving to find munitions work in England.

One of the key historical roles for trade unions was to act as a transmission mechanism, facilitating their working-class members in finding wider social and political roles. We can see this happening for women members of the DDUJFW during the war both in politics, in relation to the expansion of the role of the state, or in relation to 'civil society' organisations. As before the conflict, wartime membership was predominantly female, and their role in the Union was entrenched from its foundation, with a mandatory 50 per cent of committee members. This rule was kept to during the war.[80] Undoubtedly the key role in the Union continued to be played by Sime. But women's role expanded as the Union increased in size, with, for example, both the vice-chair and treasurer being women from May 1918, and it became usual for delegations to be equal in gender terms.[81] Jeanie Spence, the vice-president, chaired many of the Union's wartime committee meetings.

In 1915 there were three women and two men delegates to a Labour Representation Committee (LRC) meeting to protest at the increased cost of living.[82] Both representatives to the LRC appointed in May 1918 were women, so even before achieving the franchise, parliamentary politics on the Left were being influenced by women's actions. Trade unions were a key route into Labour party politics, and a branch of the Women's Labour League was formed in September 1917.[83] The evidence suggests that women were perhaps less well represented when issues were explicitly those of industrial relations rather than those with wider connotations. For example, in the negotiations on hours women made up only one from four in the DDUJFW, one from three among the calenderers, and zero out of four from the power-loomers.[84]

The expansion of the state, especially in labour matters, gave opportunities for women, usually again via the trade unions, to expand their roles; for example, by appointment as advisers to the local Dundee labour exchange, when a women's advisory committee was created.[85] Or as four out of fourteen employee members of the Jute Trade Board when it was created in 1919, with two on the (smaller) reconstructed Board in 1921.[86]

It is easier to find evidence of women's enhanced role than it is to show that this role led to a higher priority being given to women's interests.

THE CITY AND THE FIRST WORLD WAR

One argument used against conscription by the Union was that it would increase women's unemployment, but this could be regarded as purely opportunist rhetoric.[87] The DDUJFW argued for equal pay, and this was formally agreed in July 1915, but the employers said it didn't apply to wartime increases.[88] This led to protests over differential rises in 1917.[89]

PRESSURE FROM BELOW

A whole new arena of activity was opened up when the war eventually led to a national scheme of consumer control and rationing, under a Ministry of Food.[90] This arose as a central government response to widespread discontent over the cost of living, and to nationwide political agitation. But this national policy was underpinned by widespread local action, encouraged by the War Emergency: Workers' National Committee (WE: WNC); action that was substantial in Dundee, especially in the areas of food and rents.[91]

Some of this early consumer-oriented agitation was closely linked to the DDUJFW. For example, in February 1915 three women and two men were appointed as delegates to the LRC to protest at the increase in the cost of living.[92] A 'Special Committee' concerned with food supply and prices had been established in late 1916 and met with representatives of traders and the LRC.[93] Its discussions ranged widely, covering not only food but also key commodities like coke. Much of Dundee's food came from local sources, so that, for example, discussion on relaxing the controls governing pig and poultry keeping noted there were 147 piggeries in the city, with 804 pigs.[94] It is notable that from the beginning Councillor Edwin Scrymgeour, later a victor in the 1922 election, was highly active in this area by, for example, pressing for relaxation of game laws through to calling for municipal shops to supply potatoes. The Dundee Trades Council (DTC) was also active in pressing for more controls, for example over sugar supplies.[95]

In April 1917 the DTC organised a public meeting with the LRC and the local shipbuilding and engineering unions calling on the government to take entire control of the 'production and distribution of the necessaries of life' and calling on the Council to petition for this. The Council had already agreed with the Board of Agriculture a scheme for the allocation and maximum prices of potatoes.[96]

A meeting of the Special Food Committee in May 1917 supported the idea of setting up a Food Control Committee, partly in response to pressure from central government concerned with labour unrest, partly in the light of the local manifestations of that discontent. One of its first discussions was about the desirability of establishing communal kitchens, one of the ideas being pushed by local labour organisations.[97] Local actions were linked to national activity: in June 1917 there were three women and three men delegates to a Conference on National Food Supply held in the city.[98]

Local Food Control Committees (FCCs) were one of the key initiatives of the Ministry of Food in the summer of 1917. Initially these were made up mainly of tradesmen and farmers, but the Ministry insisted that there be one woman and one labour representative.[99] The FCC in Dundee was established in August 1917. Under instruction from the Ministry of Food, its remit was to urge economising in food consumption, as well as applying regulations. The Council initially rejected the idea that trade unions and cooperatives be allowed to nominate members, but conceded this point the following month under pressure from central government.[100] The initial view of Lord Provost Don was 'Labour must be fully represented on the Committee, but he took up the ground that they all represented labour, and that no Councillor was entitled to say that he represented labour or capital any more than another'.[101] Labour's unsuccessful calls for more representatives on the FCC eventually led to their temporary withdrawal, and an inquiry into this by a Divisional Commissioner from Edinburgh. Labour wanted FCCs to have a majority of their members from external organisations, but the Council said it was legally bound to have a majority.[102] Initially there was one woman on the FCC, but with greater involvement in the complex of subcommittees that soon proliferated, with the Food Economy subcommittee having its own women's subcommittee convened by Miss Kynock, initially the only woman on the FCC.[103]

The activities of the FCC emphasise the fact that 'consumption' issues had become central to labour politics in a context where price increases and shortages were the biggest immediate threat to working-class standards of life. The composition and actions of the FCC were a source of strong dispute throughout its existence, until it was abolished in 1920.[104] The Trades Council and the LRC, in alliance with Scrymgeour and the small number of Labour Councillors, constantly pushed for a more interventionist stance, including municipal control of key products and communal kitchens.[105] The DDUJFW was prominent in supporting these arguments, with Sime, along with Crooks from the co-ops and James Gordon from the DTC, members of the Committee.[106]

Though the FCC was male-dominated, it did include specific representation of 'women's interests' as well as those of labour.[107] When a new committee was established in Dundee just as the war ended in

THE CITY AND THE FIRST WORLD WAR 263

November 1918, it consisted of sixteen people, ten from the Council, two to represent women's interests, three Labour representatives and one person from the co-ops. The Labour representatives were nominated by the LRC, the ILP and the DTC, while the two women came from 'the two textile societies and the National Union of Women Workers'.[108] Thus the women were clearly there to represent working women, not 'housewives'. Indeed, the terminology of 'housewives', while not entirely absent, was unusual in this period, a contrast with some of the experience of the Second World War.[109]

While political battles were being fought over the FCC, alongside this body, and encouraged by the WE: WNC, a Food Vigilance Committee (FVC) was established, which later mutated into a Consumers League.[110] The FVC was an unofficial, labour movement-based body that had a bigger role for women than in the local FCC. As elsewhere, the FVC appears to have given more space to women than the official and male-dominated FCC. The DDUJFW appointed two men and two women to the FVC in 1917, and two women and one man to the Consumers League in 1918. Three women were sent to a League meeting in September 1918.[111] The League, while strongly supported by the Union, was seen as being aimed particularly at women.[112] An advert for the League in April 2018 was characteristically headed '20,000 women wanted'.[113]

As elsewhere in Britain, across the war period there was increased attention to milk as a key commodity, rather than to bread, which historically had played a pivotal role in working-class diets and the politics of food. Whereas the issues surrounding bread had focused largely on price, the supply of milk brought more complex issues concerning purity and distribution as well as how much the consumer had to pay. In Trentmann's view, the milk crisis towards the end of the war 'cast a shadow over the entire liberal system of markets and trade that had ruled before the war'.[114] In doing so it encouraged a more collectivist political response as the route to effective regulation of this commodity.

In wartime Dundee we can see that the 'liquid politics' of milk did indeed come to play a central role. Issues over the supply and price of bread did continue, and bread was a fraught political issue because the bakery workers formed one of the strongest trade unions in the city, so those seeking to regulate the commodity had to negotiate multiple issues, including bakers' wages. Scrymgeour was chair of the bread sub-committee of the FCC and had to try and conciliate between the demand by bakers for higher wages and the calls to keep the price of bread in check. The issue became so heated over allegations that the Council was siding with employers in keeping these wages down, that it led to the temporary withdrawal of the labour members from the FCC in August 1918.[115]

But alongside these battles over bread, late in the war milk supply rose to unprecedented prominence. It was a national issue from 1917, when a Committee under Lord Astor was set up and, following this, a central Milk Control Board was created.[116] But much was left to local initiative. In Dundee, arguments about milk are evident from 1916. Scrymgeour raised the issue of milk supply by the Council to hospitals, children and, if possible, the general community.[117] In April 1917 the DDUJFW journal was talking of a 'Dundee milk scandal'.[118] In May 1917 a local milk supplier, Batchelors, was arguing that it could not supply at the prevailing controlled prices, and telling the Public Health Committee that the Council should take over its role.[119] Batchelors became part of a recurrent argument about the municipalisation of milk, repeating their argument that controlled prices made their company unviable, and that they should be allowed to sell off their dairy.[120] Many on the Left argued that municipalisation was indeed the answer, though this never looked likely to be achieved.[121]

Non-socialists were not convinced that this was the way forward, but it is notable that less partisan voices, such as the *People's Journal*, published a great deal on the topic, for example in January 1917 arguing that the city's dairying system needed to be reorganised, and that if this didn't happen, there was a case for municipal intervention.[122] This continued into the post-war period, with the *Journal* arguing in August and September 1919 that the trebling of the milk price since 1914 had put it out of reach of many children.[123]

A local Milk Control Committee was created, and in February 1918 it reported that 'the question of Dundee's milk supply promises again to develop features which will give it a prominent place in local municipal politics'.[124] Pressure on milk eventually led to a government committee of enquiry into Dundee's milk supply.[125] In June 1918 the *Advertiser* suggested that the average consumption per head of milk in Dundee was half a cup, and in particular argued that children were not getting enough.[126] The same month the paper argued that 'no one can pretend that the milk consumption, as revealed in the Food Committee figures, does not fall far short of what is desirable for the welfare of the consumers'.[127]

The question of milk was not in any intelligible sense solely a 'women's issue'. But it was argued that in Dundee the peculiarity of extensive married women's labour supply gave the milk issue special resonance: 'So long as the staple industry of the city depended upon the working

THE CITY AND THE FIRST WORLD WAR   265

mothers, and the cow was the foster mother of the child, it behoved the Town Council to do everything in their power to protect the milk supply.'[128]

Alongside the supply and price of food, the most contentious wartime 'consumer' issue in Dundee was rent. This of course was not unique: struggles over rent have long been recognised as one of the key issues in wartime discontent in several parts of Britain, especially on Clydeside.[129] But such struggles were also important in Dundee, where there was a pre-war precedent in the rent strike of 1912.[130] Before the war, Dundee had exceptionally overcrowded housing even by Scottish standards, but the cessation of housebuilding and the influx of workers underpinned a marked worsening of the situation in the war years. This was an issue around which trade unions and socialist activists were able to effectively mobilise in the city from 1915 onwards.[131]

The DDUJFW established a rents committee in 1915 partly to help with legal assistance for rent strikers. Benefits were also paid to workers who left work to help prevent evictions.[132] The strikes of 1915 encouraged a new 'politics of housing' in the city. For example, the February 1917 *Guide* noted that rent agitation had led to the creation of the Dundee Labour Housing Committee, formed at the beginning of 1915 and focused on giving housing advice and support. Housing issues figured prominently thereafter, and broader issues of housing provision were central to local (as well as national) politics around the end of the war. Post-war, the DDUJFW continued to focus attention on the issue. In 1920 it called for a one-day strike in support of 'rent protest day', against rent increases under the new Rent Act.

In relation to the rent strikes, Ann Petrie suggests that 'for a city that was so dominated by women there is little direct evidence to suggest that women led the battle in Dundee'.[133] This contrasted with Glasgow, where women leaders emerged. Nevertheless, as she notes, there was evidence of widespread support from women for the strike, and it was commonly framed as an issue of especial interest to women, partly because, of course, many men were away at the front, leaving women to cope with rent increases. For a typical framing in this way we can cite the 'Town Council notes' by ex-baillie John Reid: 'At the next meeting of the Housing and Town Planning committee, I am to recommend the co-option of a practical housewife to assist us in preparing future Housing schemes. Women have had too little to say in the planning of houses, and it is largely a women's question.'[134]

Alongside women's participation in the new, multidimensional consumer politics of wartime Dundee, some other political and civic activities also thrived. Activity related to the suffrage was largely suspended (though it revived later in the war), but the Dundee Women's Suffrage Society continued to meet, focusing its attention on war relief work.[135] Bodies specifically for relief were also created, notably the Dundee Women's War Relief Committee.[136] One of its successes was the organisation of a communal kitchen serving two thousand portions a week; those running it suggested that 'the demand arises not so much from the war conditions as from the normal conditions of work and domestic arrangements'.[137]

Anti-war politics were especially important in Dundee. Conscientious objection on a significant scale went on alongside very successful recruitment into the army, especially the Black Watch.[138] Directly, at least, these were largely male concerns, but this was not the case with drink, with prohibitionism especially prominent in the city.[139] Pre-war support for this movement was strong, particularly among women, and seems to have been strengthened by the war, with the Dundee Social Union calling for a complete ban on wartime alcohol sales.[140] Among women Liberals, concern about drinking was a persistent theme, with, for example, in December 1917 a meeting of the Women's Liberal Association stressing that 'all the more pressing social problems had drink as their leading factor'.[141]

Another body active in the city was the Union for Democratic Control, whose aims were primarily to do with achieving parliamentary control over hitherto secret diplomacy, but it was also a pro-peace body (and one founded by E. D. Morel, alongside Scrymgeour a victor in the 1922 election). While the UDC gained support from both men and women, Dundee women such as Agnes Husband played a prominent role.[142]

The financial situation of women whose husbands were away in the armed forces was a major welfare problem in the First World War.[143] This was another area where national concerns were matched by local initiatives, with, in August 1918, the setting up in Dundee of an Association on separation allowances. There were calls for action on these allowances from the local LRC, and a new association to campaign on these allowances was set up.[144]

Dundee women were widely involved in activities in support of or responding to the war. In the Liberal party there was a clear alliance with Unionists to encourage the war effort, including recruitment.[145] Women had played a big role in the Liberal party pre-war, with a separate association, and many were drawn into involvement in actions in support of the war. For example, they supported a March 1915 recruitment meeting organised by the 'ladies of the city' featuring Clementine Churchill and a range of other prominent women.[146]

POLITICS AND THE WAR

Fought in December, the month after the war ended, the 1918 general election, based on a franchise that had trebled in size in Dundee, shows no obvious evidence of radical change resulting from the war. As across the rest of Britain, the electoral outcome was framed by the impact of the 'Coupon' given to supporters of the Lloyd George Coalition. In Dundee this meant Winston Churchill, Liberal MP for the city since 1908, and Alexander Wilkie, the Labour member since 1906. Churchill and Wilkie achieved respectively 66 and 64 per cent of the votes cast against opposition from Scrymgeour and James Brown, an Independent Labour Party candidate. The turnout was very low at 47 per cent. Enthusiasm for Wilkie among the organised working class appears tepid – the local LRC had only endorsed him by twenty votes to nineteen.[147] Women outnumbered men among 'resident voters', with no evidence of any clear impact on the outcome of the (very recent) enfranchisement of women.[148] Consumer and food supply issues figured much less in the election campaigns than might have been expected given wartime developments. Instead, a focus on the outcome of the war and issues about reparations underpinned a Conservative victory – even if, as in Dundee, the party labels were non-Conservative: 'Dundee shared fully in the post-war hysteria which demanded that Germany pay for the war.'[149]

In local electoral politics in the aftermath of the war there was greater advance for the Left, and also some for women. In the November 1919 elections Labour won eight new seats on Dundee Town Council, but none of the victors were women. However, at the same time four women were elected to the Parish Council (of whom two were Labour: Agnes Husband and Mrs M. E. Gordon).[150]

The biggest women's organisation in interwar Dundee was the Dundee Women Citizens' Association (DWCA), founded in 1918 in expectation of the franchise extension. This was part of a wider movement in Scotland, but it certainly flourished in Dundee, with eight hundred members in its first year. Its early agenda unsurprisingly focused on securing women's voting registration, but beyond that housing was a key question. When the Association organised a meeting to press the candidates in the 1918 election on issues deemed crucial, housing was top of the list, with temperance fourth and equal pay fifth.[151]

By drawing women into a wider range of jobs, the war made Dundee even more of a 'women's town' in employment terms than it had been in peace. The entrenched women's role in the labour market allowed some women to build on that, especially through their role in the DDUJFW, and by expanding participation in locally important bodies like the Employment Exchange and the Trade Board. Beyond the labour market, the war, then the extension of the franchise, encouraged a wide range of women's civic activism. Some of this necessarily ended with the war, such as relief activity, but much of it, sometimes in mutated form, continued. The role of the DWCA was especially important in drawing women into a new kind of enfranchised citizenship.[152]

Some of the impetus to women's action was linked to the undoubted and under-recognised wartime surge of consumer-oriented politics. But we need to be careful about suggesting any simple relationship between women and this form of politics. The Dundee evidence bears out Karen Hunt's argument that 'The British politics of food offered women new formal and informal political spaces, created in response to the crisis of "total war".' But she cautions that women's participation was limited by the ambiguous understanding of who constituted a 'consumer' and thus who could speak for the 'ordinary housewife'.[153] That ambiguity was also evident in Dundee, where women's activism saw them acting as either workers or women, and often as both simultaneously.

The functioning of the FCC in Dundee also bears out the argument made by Hannam and Hunt that to a degree the rising cost of living at the beginning of the war made rising prices less of a 'women's issue': 'Food has shifted, not least in socialists' minds, from being a gender issue to one of class.'[154] But like involvement in trade unions, involvement in consumer activism could be a pathway into other forms of civic or political participation: 'the politics of food drew a wider range of women into local politicized structures. This could then be capitalized on when significant numbers of women were enfranchised in 1918.'[155]

CONCLUSIONS

While Dundee's jute industry was boosted by the war, this boost was far less dramatic, and long-lasting, than that felt by Calcutta. A poignant symbol of the new realities was the sale in May 1919 of the Angus jute works, with the whole of the machinery transferred to Calcutta.[156]

This shift in comparative strength was clearly recognised in Dundee, when just after the war's end the employers and unions briefly cooperated to press the Board of Trade into setting up an inquiry into the industry's prospects. This inquiry, aided by the temporary boom that came to the industry in the second half of 1919, fought off the employers' claim for protection and the unions' pressure for Calcutta wages to be raised to the level of Dundee's.[157] Doubts about the industry's future

THE CITY AND THE FIRST WORLD WAR 269

had been evident even before the war ended. The need for new industries to provide jobs for women and returning soldiers was a theme in the *Prohibitionist* in 1917.[158] In early 1918 there was a first meeting of the city council's development committee, also focused on bringing new industries to the city, and in May 1918 the Scotscraig site across the Tay in Tayport was purchased by the city for this purpose.[159]

How did the war impact upon the divisions in the city discussed in chapter 7? On income and wealth disparities it seems clear that, notwithstanding some improvement in real wages, the bulk of the benefits of the wartime boom accrued to the profits of the owners. These profits were sustained through the post-war boom of 1919–20, but then collapsed, never to recover. Their existence underpinned the major consolidation of the industry, which allowed many owners to exit the industry with large cash sums.

On the wage side, too, the gains of the war were temporary, not outlasting the collapse of the post-war boom. The tight labour market for labour in the city disappeared, not to return until the Second World War. The occasionally greater degree of cooperation between the jute employers and unions did not last long. They were able to agree a joint approach to the government into the future of the industry just at the end of the war, but once the boom disappeared battles over wages were bitter, as the employers sought to take away the support given by the Trade Board by pushing for its abolition.

But some gains by the Dundee workers were more permanent. The war laid the basis for welfare improvements, especially in housing, where wartime agitations fed into initiatives by the local authority which made the city something of a pioneer in the provision of public housing after the war.[160]

However, overall the legacy of the First World War in so weakening Juteopolis in comparison with the Indian industry was a dire one. Throughout the interwar period the industry, and hence the city, suffered huge problems of unemployment, at their worst in the world slump of the 1930s, when Calcutta made large inroads into the British market, on top of its dominance of (shrunken) global demand. The Second World War and the controls it led to stabilised the industry for a period in the 1940s and 1950s, but from the 1960s decline continued until all jute production ceased in the city in 1998.

Notes

1. *Dundee Year Book* (*DYB*) 1915, p. 21.
2. *DYB* 1916, p. 16.

3. J. P. Day 'The jute industry in Scotland', in David Jones et al., *Rural Scotland During the War* (Oxford, 1926), p. 275.
4. E. M. H. Lloyd, *Experiments in State Control* (Oxford, 1924), pp. 36, 66.
5. Board of Trade, *Jute Working Party* (London, 1948), table VII.
6. Controls in jute were easier to operate than in linen, given the limited range of outputs and the single source of supply of the raw material: Philip Ollerenshaw, 'Textile business in Europe during the First World War: The linen industry, 1914–18', *Business History*, 41 (1999), p. 71.
7. Day, 'The jute industry', pp. 277–9.
8. But the data show that exports never entirely ceased.
9. TNA, CAB 24/43/54, War Cabinet Secretary of State for War 'Cessation of shipments of jute', 27 February 1918.
10. *Dundee Advertiser*, 29 November 1917.
11. TNA, NATS1/1178, D. Young, 'Report on jute industry with reference to the 10 per cent reduction in use of raw material', 8 February 1918.
12. Day, 'The jute industry', p. 287.
13. Chris Whatley, *Onward from Osnaburgs. The Rise and Progress of a Scottish Textile Company: Don and Low of Forfar, 1792–1992* (Edinburgh, 1992), pp. 140, 157–8.
14. Jim Tomlinson, *Dundee and the Empire: Juteopolis 1850–1939* (Edinburgh, 2014), pp. 105–6.
15. Day, 'The jute industry', p. 279.
16. Ibid., p. 288.
17. Gordon Stewart, *Jute and Empire* (Manchester, 1998), pp. 54, 60.
18. Ibid., p. 77.
19. TNA, LAB 83/1176, Committee on Production, 'Jute Workers, Dundee', 20 January 1916.
20. DDUJFW committee meeting, 2 November 1915.
21. TNA, LAB 83/1176, Committee on Production, 'Jute Workers, Dundee', 20 January 1916.
22. William Walker, *Juteopolis: Dundee and its Textile Workers 1885–1923* (Edinburgh, 1979), p. 187.
23. The *Guide* was briefly the 'Dundee Textile Workers Guide' until it became the sole responsibility of the DDUJFW. It survived until 1923: copies are in DCA, GD/JF/12/1-4.
24. Walker, *Juteopolis*, p. 148.
25. DCA, GD/JF/1/9 DDUJFW, committee meetings, 24 December 1915, 9 June 1916; *Prohibitionist*, 25 December 1915.
26. DCA, GD/JF/12/1, *Guide*, 19 May 1916.
27. DCA, GD/JF/1/9 DDUJFW, committee meetings, 20, 21 May 1916; *Prohibitionist*, 22 January, 5 February 1916.
28. TNA, LAB 2/207/IC1370/1917, Sime to employers, 20 February 1917.
29. TNA, LAB2/207/IC1370/1917, T. Munro to I. Mitchell, 5 May 1917.
30. DCA, GD/JF/12/1, *Guide*, July and August 1917.

THE CITY AND THE FIRST WORLD WAR   271

31. GD/JF/1//9 DDUJFW, Committee, 29 August 1916.
32. GD/JF/1//9 DDUJFW, Committee, 7 August 1917, 10 April 1917; GD/ JF/12/1, *Guide*, October 1917.
33. In line with the conventions of the time, and as in 1908 when he was appointed President of the Board of Trade, Churchill had to resign his parliamentary seat on being given a new ministerial job.
34. *Dundee Courier*, 4 August 1917.
35. *Dundee Courier*, 13 July 1917; during the campaign Churchill expressed support for temperance ideas and emphasised that the election was not about Scrymgeour's prohibitionism: *Courier*, 28 July 1917; For Churchill's 1917 election address (which made no mention of Scrymgeour), CHAR 5/19/18-21, 26 July 1917.
36. *Dundee Courier*, 25, 28 July 1917; acceptance speech by Clementine Churchill, *Dundee Courier*, 4 August 1917.
37. *Prohibitionist*, 28 July 1917.
38. John Kemp, 'Drink and the labour movement in early twentieth-century Scotland with particular reference to Edwin Scrymgeour and the Scottish Prohibition Party' (unpublished PhD dissertation, Dundee University, 2000), pp. 171–3; *Prohibitionist*, 22 July; *Dundee Advertiser*, 24, 27, 28 April 1917.
39. Letter to *Dundee Courier*, July 1917.
40. TNA, NATS 1/1178, Henderson to Secretary, Ministry of National Service, 17 February 1918.
41. TNA, NATS 1/1178, Sime evidence to Conference on Jute and Flax, 13 December 1917, pp. 4, 5.
42. TNA, NATS 1/1178, Sime to F. McLeod, Ministry of National Service, 11 January 1918.
43. TNA, NATS 1/1178, R. Graves to F. Young, 25 January 1918.
44. TNA, NATS 1/1180, 'Jute Trade Restrictions: War Benefit Scheme', 20 March 1918. The scheme did not run smoothly: see, for example, TNA, NATS 1/1180, Sime to J. Cunningham, 1 April 1918.
45. Walker, *Juteopolis*, pp. 407–19.
46. *DYB* 1914, pp. 16–24; *DYB* 1915, pp. 17–27; *DYB* 1916, pp. 16–27.
47. Whatley, *Onward from Osnaburgs*, p. 155.
48. *People's Journal*, 27 September 1917.
49. TNA, LAB2/207/1C 155, 'Committee on Production. Jute workers. Dundee', 20 January 1916.
50. *Guide*, 18 November 1917, 5 August 1918.
51. *Guide* May 1917.
52. CHAR 11/16/187-192, 'List of trades from Miss Black, Miss Macarthur and Mr. Mallon'. Jute and linen was described as a 'very badly paid factory trade in which women rapidly displacing men. Many women earning 8s and 9s a week, and men in the trade as low in some cases as 11s 3d. Centralised and easily dealt with'; *Dundee Courier*, 6 February 1909.

53. Walker, *Juteopolis*, p. 420.
54. Dorothy Sells, *The British Trade Boards System* (London, 1923), pp. 4–5.
55. *Dundee Advertiser*, 20 August 1918 (these figures are probably exaggerated).
56. Cf Walker, *Juteopolis*, p. 419.
57. UDA, MS 84/3 (2), AJSM meetings, 25 November, 9 December 1918, 28 August 1919.
58. Sells, *Trade Boards System*; the wages set by the Board are detailed in UDA, MS 84/2, AJSM Annual Report 1939, Appendix H.
59. Dundee City Archives (DCA), GD/CC/4/9, Dundee Chamber of Commerce (DCC) minutes, 20 January 1916.
60. *Dundee Courier*, 14 June 1918; see also *Scotsman*, 14 June 1918; 'Report of the Departmental Committee appointed by the Board of Trade to consider the position of the Textile Trades after the War', Cd. 9070 BPP 1918, Vol. III.
61. Robert Boyce, *British Capitalism at the Crossroads, 1919–1932* (Cambridge, 1987), pp. 82–90.
62. *Dundee Courier*, 20 August 1918; UDA, MS 84/3 (2), 26 September 1918, for Sime's call for an Industrial Council.
63. *Dundee Courier*, 2 October 1918 and UDA, MS 84/3/1 (3), 11 October 1918. But the problem of hours of work dogged discussion between employers and unions, with employers wishing to revert to a fifty-five-hour week as more raw jute became available.
64. CHAR 5/20/13-15. In Churchill's letter to George Ritchie, President of the Liberal Association, 5 November 1918, he says that he hopes the Tories will support him, and Labour won't put anyone up against Wilkie, so the two will be easily returned.
65. Richard Rodgers, 'Employment, wages and poverty in the Scottish cities 1841–1914', in George Gordon (ed.), *Perspectives on the Scottish City* (Aberdeen, 1985), p. 29; *Guide*, July 1919.
66. *People's Journal*, 31 March, 8 September 1917.
67. *Dundee Advertiser*, 29 March 1917. There was considerable resistance to women working on the trams, and opposition was only overcome when the supply of discharged soldiers dried up: *People's Journal*, 3 February 1917.
68. *People's Journal*, 11 January 1919.
69. Neil Glen, '"Of Myth and Men": Dundee women's experience working and organising for change in Juteopolis through the Great War and after' (unpublished MA dissertation, University of Dundee, 1997).
70. *People's Journal*, 9 February 1918.
71. The secretary of the calenderers' union said that 1,600 to 2,000 of his 3,000 members had gone to fight in the war. The other main male monopoly was tenting, and here there seems to have been little change, the union

THE CITY AND THE FIRST WORLD WAR 273

saying women 'won't do tenting'; TNA, NATS 1/1178, Meeting of representatives of the jute industry, 15 December 1917, p. 6.

72. TNA, NATS 1/1178, Meeting of representatives of the jute industry, 15
December 1917, p. 4.

73. *Dundee Advertiser*, 30 March, 12 April 1917.

74. *Guide*, July 1917; the same sentiment can be found in the December
Guide.

75. TNA, MUN 5/98/350/1. Munitions Council Paper and Tables on estimated displacement of male and female labour on reduction of munitions
programme, 1918.

76. *People's Journal*, 24 December 1917; see also *Dundee Advertiser*, 30
December 1918.

77. *Guide*, July, August 1916.

78. *Guide*, November 1916, December 1917.

79. *People's Journal*, 30 June 1917.

80. DCA, GD/JF/1/1, DDUJFW general meeting, 28 June 1917, 25 September
1919.

81. For example, DCA, GD/JF/1/9, DDUJFW general meeting, 15 May, 12
June 1917.

82. DCA, GD/JF/1/16, DDUJFW general meeting, February 1915.

83. *Guide*, September 1917. Mary Brooksbank, Dundee's female poet and
member of the Communist Party (though later expelled), was not a trade
union activist: Siobhan Tolland, '"Jist ae wee woman" – Dundee, the
Communist Party and the feminisation of socialism in the life and works of
Mary Brooksbank' (unpublished PhD dissertation, University of Aberdeen,
2005).

84. DCA, DD/JF/1/2, DDUJFW general meeting, 15 August 1919 (the last two
of these had very few women members).

85. TNA, LAB2/327/ED27615/1918, Meeting of Dundee local advisory committee, 11 February 1918. When it became clear the unions were appointing women to these roles, the employers decided they should replace the
men previously nominated with women.

86. TNA, LAB 2/237, Meeting with DDUJFW, 20 June 1918. Four out of
fourteen union representatives on the Trade Board were women, with
three from Dundee (Mrs M. Nary, Miss J. Spence, Miss J. Steele) and one
from Aberdeen: *Guide*, December 1919.

87. *Guide*, December 1917; similar argument at DCA, GD/JF/1/2 DDUJFW,
committee meeting, 2 November 1915.

88. DCA, GD/JF/1/9, DDUJFW committee meetings, 22 June, 5 July 1915;
GD/JF/1/2, DDUJFW general meetings, 18 November 1917, 5 August
1918; GD/JF/1/10, DDUJFW general meeting, 6 August 1918; *Guide*,
May, November 1917, September 1918.

89. DCA, GD/JF/1/2, DDUJFW general meetings, 18 November 1917, 5
August 1918.

90. L. Margaret Barnett, *British Food Policy During the First World War* (London, 1985).

91. David Swift, 'Labour and the War Emergency: The Workers' National Committee during the First World War', *History Workshop Journal*, 81 (2016), pp. 84–105.

92. DCA, GD/JF/1/8, DDUJFW general meeting, 16 February 1915.

93. Dundee Central Library: Local History Collection (DCL: LHC), Minutes of Town Council, 8 November 1916, pp. 51–2.

94. DCL: LHC, Minutes of Town Council, 1 February 1917, pp. 317–18.

95. DCL: LHC, Minutes of Town Council, 1 February 1917, p. 313; 23 March 1917, pp. 454–6.

96. DCL: LHC, Minutes of Town Council, 5 April 1917, p. 538; Meeting of Special Food Committee, 24 April 1917, pp. 596–9; *Prohibitionist*, 31 March, 7 April 1917.

97. DCL: LHC, Meeting of Special Food Committee, 11 May 1917, pp. 657–8; 14 June 1917, pp. 781–3.

98. DCL: LHC, Minutes of Town Council, 12 June 1917.

99. Barnett, *British Food Policy*, pp. 115, 126–7.

100. DCL: LHC, Minutes of Town Council, 9 August 1917, pp. 657–8; 14 September 1917, p. 1138; *Dundee Courier*, 27 August 1917; *People's Journal*, 9 September 1917, says Jas Gordon, W. M. Crooks and John Sime added.

101. *Dundee Courier*, 10 August 1917.

102. *People's Journal*, 19 October, 16 November 1918; *Dundee Courier*, 13 November 1918; *Dundee Advertiser*, 28 October 1918.

103. DCL: LHC, First Meeting of FCC, 4 September 1917, pp. 1109–10; *Prohibitionist*, 11 August 1917: in the first six months of their existence the FCC and its subcommittees met over sixty times: DCL: LHC, Meeting of Town Council, 7 February 1918, appendix pp. 339–42.

104. DCL: LHC, Minutes of Town Council, 8 November 1920, p. 135.

105. *Dundee Advertiser*, 10, 13 August, 7 September 1917; *Dundee Courier*, 14 August 1917; *Dundee Evening Telegraph*, 6 September 1917; *Dundee Courier*, 3 September 1918. Scrymgeour was highly active on this issue, being a Council member with responsibilities for regulation of the grocery trade.

106. *Guide*, September 1917.

107. *Dundee Courier*, 30 September 1918.

108. DCL: LHC, Town Council meeting, 23 October 1918; *Dundee Courier*, 4 October 1918.

109. Karen Hunt, 'The politics of food and women's neighbourhood activism in First world War Britain', *International Labour and Working-Class History*, 77 (2010), pp. 19–20; 'Housewives' was used when Dundee Council set up an anti-profiteering committee in 1917: *People's Journal*, 27 September 1917.

THE CITY AND THE FIRST WORLD WAR
275

110. TNA, PRO 30/69/1833, Ramsay Macdonald Papers, WE: WNC, 'Food Vigilance Committee', June 1917. These committees were widespread in Britain: Hunt, 'Politics of food', pp. 14–15.

111. DCA, GD/JF/1/9, DDUJFW committee meeting, 2 October 1917; GD/JF/1/10, committee meeting, 17 September 1918.

112. *Guide*, March 1918.

113. *Guide*, April 1918.

114. Frank Trentmann, *Free Trade Nation* (Oxford, 2008), p. 200.

115. *Prohibitionist*, 29 June, 24 August 1918.

116. National issue of milk in 'Committee on Production and Distribution of Milk' Cd. 9095 1918, and papers in TNA, MAF60/472, 'Milk Control' 1917–1922. Trentmann, *Free Trade Nation*, pp. 202–3.

117. *Prohibitionist*, 7 October 1916.

118. *Guide*, April 1917.

119. *Prohibitionist*, 12 May 1917.

120. *Prohibitionist*, 23 March 1918.

121. In September 1918 the *Guide* argued that despite changes a year previously in the make-up of the FCC, this had had little impact. For example, discussion of municipalisation of the milk trade, *Dundee Courier*, 10 December 1918. Other issues relating to milk: prices, *Dundee Courier*, 3 August 1918, 17 September 1919; security of supply, *Dundee Courier*, 7 June 1918; costs of distribution, *Dundee Evening Telegraph*, 16 May 1919.

122. *People's Journal*, 13 January 1917; also 27 January, 14 April, 5 May 1917.

123. *People's Journal*, 30 August, 20 September, 6 December 1919.

124. *Dundee Advertiser*, 12 February 1918.

125. *Prohibitionist*, 27 April, 4 May 1918; *People's Journal*, 27 April.

126. *Dundee Advertiser*, 7, 8 June 1918.

127. *Dundee Advertiser*, 10 June 1918.

128. Councillor Fraser, reported in *People's Journal*, 5 May 1917.

129. Jo Melling, *Rent Strikes: People's Struggle for Housing in West Scotland 1890–1916* (Edinburgh, 1983).

130. Ann Petrie, *The 1915 Rent Strikes: An East Coast Perspective* (Dundee, 2008).

131. Petrie, *1915 Rent Strikes*, pp. 15–16, 30–8.

132. DCA, GD JF 1/1, general meeting, 28 October 1915; other union activities on rents in 1915 are discussed in GD/JF 1/9, committee meetings, 28 September, 26 October.

133. Petrie, *1915 Rent Strikes*, p. 37.

134. *Guide*, February 1920; Petrie, *1915 Rent Strikes*, p. 38.

135. *Dundee Courier*, 5 August 1916.

136. Leah Leneman, *A Guid Cause: The Women's Suffrage Movement in Scotland* (Aberdeen, 1991), pp. 210, 266; Mary Henderson, previously secretary of the Suffrage Society, became secretary of this new Committee.

137. *Dundee Advertiser*, 14 June 1918.
138. Kenneth Baxter and William Kenefick, 'Labour politics and the Dundee working class c. 1895–1936', in Jim Tomlinson and Christopher Whatley (eds), *Jute No More: Transforming Dundee* (Dundee, 2011), pp. 203–5; William Kenefick, 'War resisters and anti-conscription in Scotland: An ILP perspective', in Catriona Macdonald and Elaine McFarland (eds), *Scotland and the Great War* (Edinburgh, 1998), pp. 59–80; Julie Danskin, *A City at War: The 4th Black Watch Dundee's Own* (Dundee, 2013).
139. Kemp, 'Drink', pp. 144–222.
140. DCA, GD/OC/GL 1, DSU minutes, 22 December 1914.
141. *Dundee Advertiser*, 17 December 1917; see I. Donachie, 'World War One and the drink question', *Scottish Labour History Society Journal*, 17 (1982), pp. 19–26. Lloyd George had famously asserted that drink was more damaging to the war effort than submarines: *Hansard* (House of Commons), Vol. 81 col. 864, 29 April 1915.
142. *Dundee Advertiser*, 29 March 1917.
143. Though it was claimed, with no evidence, that these allowances had reduced married women's labour supply in the city: TNA, NATS 1/1178, 'Report on jute industry', 5 February 1918, p. 2.
144. *Guide*, August 1918.
145. DCA, GD/SM1/1, Liberal Association Organization committee meetings, 28 August, 24 November 1914.
146. *Dundee Advertiser*, 10 March 1915.
147. *Prohibitionist*, 3 August 1918; on Wilkie and the war, see *Dundee Courier*, 14, 16 March 1918; *People's Journal*, 15 March 1918.
148. Donald Southgate, 'Politics and representation in Dundee, 1832–1963', in J. M. Jackson (ed.), *The Third Statistical Account of Scotland: The City of Dundee* (Arbroath, 1979), pp. 302, 308: 'resident electors' in October 1918 numbered 34,000 women and 20,000 men, though men outnumbered women on the overall register: *Dundee Advertiser*, 15 October 1918.
149. Walker, *Juteopolis*, p. 450.
150. *Guide*, November 1919; Baxter and Kenefick, 'Labour politics', pp. 205–6.
151. Sarah Browne and Jim Tomlinson, 'A women's town? Dundee women on the public stage', in Tomlinson and Whatley, *Jute No More*, p. 112.
152. *Dundee Advertiser*, 29 April 1917.
153. Hunt, 'Politics of food', p. 9.
154. June Hannam and Karen Hunt, *Socialist Women: Britain, 1880s to 1920s* (London, 2002), p. 146.
155. Hunt, 'Politics of food', p. 21.
156. Day, 'The jute industry', p. 288.
157. *People's Journal*, 11 May 1918; Day, 'The jute industry', pp. 289–90.
158. *Prohibitionist*, 11 August 1917.
159. *Dundee Courier*, 18 January, 24 May 1918.
160. *Prohibitionist*, 7 April, 6, 13 November 1917.

Afterword

On 19 October 1998 the MV *Banglar Urmi* from the port of Chittagong in Bengal docked in Dundee harbour with a shipment of 310 tons of raw jute, the last shipment ever to come to the city. The following year, that jute was processed in the last remaining jute mill, the Taybank Works, and soon after the works closed.[1] The original Taybank Works was built in the early 1870s, right at the end of the great expansion in mill building as jute boomed; in 1949 a large extension was added, the most substantial addition to the city's twentieth-century textile buildings.[2] By the time of its closure, it was spinning jute for the carpet trade, the longest surviving sector of the industry.

The eighty years since 1918 had been one of unambiguous decline in Dundee jute, albeit with temporary reprieves, such as in the boom of 1920/21 and, much more sustainedly, in the years of war and post-war protection from 1939 until the 1960s. Employment in the industry went from around 40,000 at the end of the First World War to under 30,000 by the outbreak of the Second. It stabilised at around 20,000 in the early post-war years, but then fell from the mid-1960s, especially rapidly in the 1970s and 1980s. By the last decade of the twentieth century, the industry hovered on the verge of extinction.[3]

Competition from the Indian subcontinent must play a central part in any account of that protracted contraction. As we have seen, that competition was evident from the 1880s and was accelerating up to 1914. The economic conditions of the First World War stimulated the Calcutta industry further, while hampering Dundee. The war also shifted the political relationship between Britain and its largest colony, with the granting of fiscal autonomy to India, along with a much greater perceived need in London to make concessions to Indian nationalism, a nationalism partly spearheaded by the bosses of industries like jute. Even if the means had been readily available, Britain lacked the political will to impose restrictions on India's capacity to expand its jute industry in competition with Dundee.[4] This was clearly recognised in a lament by the editor of the *Courier* in 1937: 'nothing could do the Government more damage than a confirmation of the belief that out of a dread of offending Indian susceptibilities and of giving Indian politicians a handle for their propaganda it would permit a native industry to go to the wall'.[5] This issue had come sharply into focus in the late 1930s, when the weakening of the Indian jute cartel under the impact of the great depression lowered international prices and threw Dundee into profound crisis.[6]

Dundee did gain protection from imports from *outside* the empire following the commitment to imperial preference made at the Ottawa conference of 1932, but of course this had no impact on Indian competition.[7] Tariff bargaining with countries like Denmark and Argentina may also have given some aid to the industry by committing these countries to wrapping their exports to Britain in Dundee sacking.[8] But such measures could not prevent Dundee becoming a net importer of jute cloth, and in consequence experiencing some of the highest unemployment in Britain. The journalist James Cameron, working for D. C. Thomson in the city in the early 1930s, found it a place of 'singular desolation', where a city that 'had for generations dedicated itself to a kind of commercial single-mindedness that had come to fruition, in my day, in black and terrible industrial depression'.[9] In 1939 it was suggested that, 'At present the industry feels itself precariously balanced on the edge of a precipice and, if it falls over, the city of Dundee will be largely dependent on Unemployment relief.'[10]

But as so often, war came to the rescue. With that war came the treatment of jute as a strategic material, which led in 1939 to the establishment of Jute Control to regulate and effectively protect the industry. Initially, manufactured jute imports fell sharply to conserve shipping space, but they revived later in the war as Dundee production was cut back while, as in the past, demand for wartime uses expanded. The overall result was the concentration and decline of the Dundee industry, but now in conditions where there was no unemployment in the city given the overall level of economic activity (alongside the recruitment of workers into the armed forces). But it was clear to the post-war Labour government's enquiry into the industry what the consequences would be of a reversion to pre-war trade policy: 'without protection, however we see no possibility of a healthy home industry and contraction is inevitable'.[11]

Despite the broad commitment to move towards a more liberal trade policy for the British economy after the war, in practice the British government retained substantial trade controls, especially import quotas, in place for a considerable number of years after 1945.[12] One beneficiary was jute, where fears of a recurrence of mass unemployment provided a strong political argument against allowing free entry to imports. As a result, employment in the industry in the immediate post-war years was stable, with peak numbers employed in 1954. Contrary to what is often assumed, the protection of the industry went along with a marked improvement in productivity and innovation. Economists who studied technical change in the industry suggested that 'import controls and government purchasing had freed managers from the immediate struggle for existence, and they have been able to give attention to the introduction of new equipment which had been developed in other industries'.[13]

Only in the late 1950s and early 1960s did free traders in the British government manage to start to slowly erode these import restrictions (unsurprisingly urged on by the governments of India and Pakistan, independent since 1947). The general buoyancy of employment in Dundee, as post-war regional policies attracted new employers to the city, also helped undermine the case for the continued protection of jute. Regional investment grants attracted US companies like Timex and NCR, but also British companies like Ferranti, and together these incomers provided large amounts of mainly well-paid employment in the city until they, too, started to cut back their operations in the 1970s.

The culmination of the trend towards trade liberalisation came in 1969 when the Jute Control, hastily introduced in response to the war, was finally abolished. This was an important moment in the industry's history. Commenting on the significance of that year, the *Telegraph* later noted that, 'A nutcracker was being opened for the Tayside jute industry, and its jaws were polypropylene and growing competition from low cost jute imports ... By the end of that fateful year the lights began to go out in earnest in the jute industry.'[14]

The change was followed by two decades of shrinking employment and closures of mills, culminating in the shutdown of Taybank at the end of the century. While mill closures were the most dramatic evidence of decline, more important quantitatively was the preceding contraction: a striking case is the Camperdown Works, historically the largest of all jute employers in the city, with a peak workforce of over five thousand, but which by the time of its closure in 1981 employed only 340 workers.[15] Five hundred tons of equipment from the closed works were shipped to Calcutta.[16] The beginning of the 1980s was for jute, like so much of British industry, an especially bad time because of the loss of competitiveness due to the extraordinary rise in the exchange rate brought about by the Thatcher government's policies. Employment in the industry fell by 23 per cent in one year (September 1979 to September 1980).[17] By 1982 the *Courier* headline was 'Last ditch appeal to safeguard jute industry', as the employers sought to hang on to the remnants of protection against South Asian competition within the framework of the EEC.[18]

Dundee developed a desperate unemployment problem in the late 1970s and 1980s as both jute employment and jobs in the new manufacturing sectors sharply diminished. By 1979 the official rate (which underestimated the real figure by a substantial margin) had reached 9 per cent, peaking at 18 per cent in 1991. The belief that the city must decisively reinvent itself was the product of this alarming situation, and in 1982 Dundee was officially branded as the 'City of Discovery', a name which sought to link its heritage as a port (Scott's HMS *Discovery* became an important tourist attraction) with its hoped-for future as a centre of scientific and technological discovery in such areas as life sciences and video gaming. Linen and jute no longer figured in how the city sought to portray itself.

Over the long run, Calcutta's main impact on the Dundee industry was not its encroachment on Britain's home market, but its capture of export markets. Initially producing only the coarsest products, India gradually moved upmarket from basic sacking and bags into products such as linoleum backing. This process was well advanced before 1939.[19] Dundee had sought to escape from Calcutta competition by manufacturing more of the wider widths of cloth, used in lino and for other products where it was hoped India's lower wages and costs of production would be less of a competitive advantage. This trajectory was reversed during the Second World War, when the needs of the conflict increased demand for the cruder items, and production of more sophisticated products for consumer markets was curtailed. But after the war, helped by the creation of the British Jute Trade Research Association in 1946, new product areas were developed, aimed at serving market niches where Indian competition would be limited.[20] One of the most important was carpets. Dundee had long been involved in the production of woven carpets as one of its more sophisticated products. But the invention of tufted carpets opened new opportunities for jute to be used as the standard backing in key brands such as Axminster and Wilton. (Jute was also used in carpet underlays and underfelts.) However, the downside to the shift to mass-market fitted carpets was the decline in demand for linoleum, which before 1939 had been one of the expanding uses for jute.[21] By the early 1970s, about 80 per cent of total output was going to carpet-making.[22] However, carpet-making was not an easy route to prosperity.

AFTERWORD 281

By 1979 the Low and Bonar amalgamation was arguing that its carpet companies were 'not earning the profits their well-equipped plants should provide', blaming 'excess competition' and an influx of cheap American carpeting.[23]

The significance of Indian competition to the fate of Dundee jute diminished in the post-war years, and technological change, never absent, achieved much greater importance. Globally, bulk handling and containerisation reduced demand for many types of bagging and sacking. Alongside this trend was the rise of materials that substituted for jute. This meant, for example, the replacement of lighter and cheaper multi-wall paper sacks in many uses where jute had traditionally been employed. But most important in the last phase of Dundee jute's demise was the rise of artificial fibres, especially polypropylene. Developed from the late 1960s, this type of plastic provided a cheap, durable alternative to jute in many uses.[24] It also fundamentally undermined the geographical logic of jute, 'transforming Dundee's highly concentrated industry, based upon one product, into a part of a national textile industry'.[25] While there were major historically established locational advantages for jute firms in Dundee, once those firms moved into polypropylene they had no good reason to stay, and most shifted their activities to lower-cost locations. Eventually, of the old major Dundee jute firms, only Low and Bonar produced polypropylene in the city, while also developing plants in Belgium, Hungary and China.[26]

Ultimately, international competition and technological change did for the industry. The final, symbolic, end came when in 1999 the machinery from Taybank Works was loaded onto an Indian ship in Dundee harbour for transport to a mill near Kolkata (formerly Calcutta), marking the end of Juteopolis.[27]

Notes

1. Gordon Stewart, 'Endgame for jute: Dundee and Calcutta in the twentieth century', in Jim Tomlinson and Christopher Whatley (eds), *Jute No More: Transforming Dundee* (Dundee, 2011), p. 47; *Dundee Courier*, 1, 28 September 1998.
2. The only other significant post-war construction was the small Douglasfield Works, built in 1957.
3. Jim Tomlinson, Carlo Morelli and Valerie Wright, *The Decline of Jute: Managing Industrial Change* (London, 2011), p. 21.
4. Even if imperial considerations had not blocked protection against Indian goods, there was recognition that such a move was likely to have incited

282   THE TRIUMPH OF TEXTILES

retaliation against cotton exports to India, and these were far more economically significant than jute production.

5. *Dundee Courier*, 24 September 1937.

6. Bishna Gupta, 'Why did collusion fail? The Indian jute industry in the inter-war years', *Business History*, 47 (2005), pp. 532–52.

7. Board of Trade, *Working Party Reports. Jute* (London, 1948), p. 69; a 20 per cent tariff on manufactured goods, 10 per cent on yarn.

8. These deals were strongly pursued by the Conservative MP for Dundee after 1931, Florence Horsbrugh.

9. James Cameron, *Point of Departure: Experiment in Biography* (London, 1968), p. 28.

10. J. Eastham, 'Economic survey', in R. Mackie (ed.), *A Scientific Survey of Dundee and District* (Dundee, 1939), p. 101.

11. Board of Trade, *Jute*, p. 3.

12. George Brennan and Alan Milward, *Britain's Place in the World: Import Controls 1945–1960* (London, 1996).

13. Charles Carter and Bruce Williams, *Industry and Technical Progress* (London, 1954), p. 187.

14. *Dundee Evening Telegraph*, 20 August 1981.

15. Jim Tomlinson, Jim Phillips and Valerie Wright, 'De-industrialization: A case study of Dundee, 1951–2001, and its broad implications', *Business History*, 64 (2022), pp. 33–8.

16. *Dundee Evening Telegraph*, 12 December 1981.

17. *Dundee Courier*, 28 January 1981.

18. *Dundee Courier*, 6 November 1982. By this time Dundee was producing only 1 per cent of the world output of jute.

19. Board of Trade, *Jute*, p. 19.

20. Swapnesh Masrani, Peter McKiernan and Alan McKinlay, 'Strategic responses to low-cost competition: Technological lock-in in the Dundee jute industry', *Business History*, 62 (2020), pp. 965–7.

21. Tomlinson, Morelli and Wright, *The Decline of Jute*, pp. 97–8.

22. W. Stewart Howe, *The Dundee Textile Industry 1960–1977: Decline and Diversification* (Aberdeen, 1982), p. 160.

23. UDA, MS 24/1/8/5/1, 'Report '79 – A Report for Everyone in the Low and Bonar Group'.

24. Though not, of course, an ecologically sustainable one.

25. Christine Craig, Jill Rubery, Roger Tarling and Frank Wilkinson, 'Abolition and after: The Jute Wages Council', Department of Applied Economics, Cambridge University (Cambridge, 1980), p. 79.

26. Tomlinson, Morelli and Wright, *The Decline of Jute*, p. 113.

27. *Dundee Courier*, 28 June 1999. The Kolkata industry has also contracted in the face of competition (including from Bangladesh) and technological change, though recent attempts to restrict the use of plastics have helped stabilise the industry.

Index

Note: italic indicates figure; t indicates table; n indicates note

Act of Union (1707)
  arguments for, 5, 24, 26–7, 29
  effects of, 30, 33, 35
Admiralty *see* Royal Navy
agents, 37, 38, 100, 101, 108, 109,
    188–9, 198
agriculture, 28, 40, 41, 117, 135, 138
Albert Institute, 12, *14*, 86, 161–3, 235
Albert Square, 12, *14*, 16, 79
alcohol
  drunkenness, 1, 171–2, 178
  'pint' breaks, 49, 147
  temperance, 16, 164, 231, 266, 267
American Civil War, 5, 68–9, 73, 82,
    93, 179
Anderson, William, 76
apprentices, 97, 99, 151, 152, 158
architecture, 1, 11–13, 17, 162–3;
    see also Albert Institute; housing;
    mills
Armitstead, George (MP), 146, 163,
    228
Askwith, Sir George, 253, 254
Association of Jute Spinners and
    Manufacturers (AJSM), 249,
    253, 254, 255
'Auld Betty' (poet), 183

bagging
  jute products, 73, 77, 78, 82, 197
  linen products, 36, 38
  uses, 7, 50, 61, 63, 68, 281
Balfour & Meldrum, 76, 77, 99
Baltic Coffee Room, 79
Baltic flax imports, 25, 40, 63, 116

Baltic Works, 19
banks
  Bank of Scotland, 26
  British Linen Company, 33, 36,
    104–5
  credit availability, 47, 51, 100–1
Barnagore mill, Calcutta, 9, *10*, 188
Baxter and Sons, 37, 51
Baxter Brothers Ltd
  French mill, 102
  linen manufacture, 4, 7, 47, 65, 67–8,
    106
  managers, 9, 85–6, *98*, 114, *124*,
    159, 164
  origins, 95
  takeover of, 248
  see also Baxter family members;
    Dens Works
Baxter, Edward, 50, 69, 95, 101,
    109–10, 163
Baxter, John (Jnr), 95
Baxter, John, of Idvies, 39–40, 95
Baxter, John (Snr), 95
Baxter Park, 15, 143, 159, 161, 184,
    235
Baxter, Robert, 80–1
Baxter, Sir David
  Baxter Park, 15, 143, 159, 161, 184,
    235
  character, 86, *96*, 159
  within Baxter Brothers Ltd, 9, 95,
    100, 119, 149
Baxter, Sir George (MP), 206, 233, 234
Baxter, William, 37, 51, 69, 95, 101
beetling, 42, 106

Bell, Balfour & Meldrum, Messrs, 76
Bell, Thomas, 63, 101
Belmont Works, 63, 97, 101
Bengal
  direct imports from, 6, 109, 162, 277
  mechanised mills, 83, 189
  traditional jute industry, 73–4, 81,
    191–4
  see also Calcutta; India
Blairgowrie (Oakbank Mill), 80, 139
bleaching, 32, 33, 64, 67, 107
Board of Trustees for Fisheries,
    Manufacturers and
    Improvements, 5, 33, 104
Borneo Jute Company, 188
Bow Bridge Works, 71, 72, 123, 158–9,
    181, 258t; see also Grimond
    Brothers
Boyack, William, 76, 77, 142, 145
British Linen Company, 33, 36, 104–5
Brough, Robert, 62, 99
Broughty Ferry, 84–5, 103, 145, 224
Brown, G. (Baxter Brothers Ltd), 124
Brown, J. and W., 51–2, 61, 70–1
Brown, John see Brown, J. and W.
Brown, William, 9, 111, 114, 123, 138,
    139, 144, 174; see also Brown,
    J. and W.; East Mill
Buist, Alexander, 86, 103, 200, 216,
    234
Burns, Robert (statue), 12, 14, 16, 160,
    163

Caird, John K. (Hawkhill Works), 181,
    216, 217t, 237, 244n
Calcutta
  Barnagore mill, 9, 10, 188
  competition with, 18, 187, 196, 199,
    200, 206–7
  Dundee emigrants, 75, 190–1
  Dundee firms' branches, 82, 109
  First World War effects, 245, 248
  racist attitudes towards, 189–90, 206
  raw jute trade, 192–4, 195t
  working conditions, 202–5
  see also Bengal
Caldrum Works, 122, 221
calendering (finishing technique), 76,
    106, 107, 157, 218, 226, 259t
Camperdown Works, Lochee
  chimney, 8, 84
  closure, 279

site, 11, 69–70, 83, 108, 120, 122,
    247
  see also Cox Brothers
canvas
  meaning, 67
  producers, 7, 39, 63, 97, 149, 257t
  raw material supply, 78, 116, 125
  see also sailcloth
carding, 48, 52
Carmichael, James (engineer)
  family connections, 99
  statue, 12, 14, 163
  Ward Foundry, 63, 70
Carmichael, Peter
  character, 98, 102, 103, 136, 151,
    161, 184
  chimney design, 6–7
  expertise, 9, 97–8, 113, 113, 116,
    119, 157–8
  family connections, 99
  see also Baxter Brothers Ltd; Dens
    Works
carpets
  Dundee producers, 9–11, 12, 66
  hand weavers, 72, 120, 147
  jute, 9–11, 66–7, 77, 197–8, 280–1
  whale oil use, 81
Castleroy (stately home), 85
Catholics, 103, 175, 177–8
Chamber of Commerce see Dundee
    Chamber of Commerce (DCC)
Chartists, 65, 146, 150, 158, 214
children
  and crime, 178–9
  deaths, 18, 155–6, 172, 219, 223
  discipline of, 144, 145–6
  health of, 132, 145
  as labour, 40–1, 42, 141–2, 154, 202,
    203
chimneys, 6–7, 8, 50, 84, 174, 247
churches, 2, 28, 102–3, 111, 161,
    164–5, 177
Churchill, Winston, 1, 205–6, 230–3,
    251, 255, 267, 271n
clocks, 70, 84, 137
coal, 31, 64, 83, 96, 195, 204
coarse textiles, 7–8, 27, 33, 73, 105–6
Cock family see Cox Brothers
Cockburn, Lord, 2, 3, 172–3
codilla, 64–5, 71
collective action, 49, 118, 139, 149,
    227; see also trade unionism

INDEX

colonialism, 26–7, 34–5, 39, 60–1, 191, 277–8
Company of Scotland, 26
conscription (WW1), 249, 250, 261, 266
Conservatism, 200, 225, 228, 234, 236–7, 267; *see also* Unionism
Constable Works, 99
consumerism, 41, 45, 280
Consumer's League, 263
cotton, 38, 50, 82, 106, 110, 218
Cox Brothers
    Calcutta branch, 82, 189, 196
    carpets, 66, 106
    employees, 222, 259t
    family history, 51, 63, 94–5, 99–100, 104
    jute spinning, 72, 77, 217t
    wealth, 234, 247t, 248
    see also Camperdown Works, Lochee
Cox, Edward, 101, 190, 198, 234, 239n
Cox, George A., 84
Cox, James (Camperdown), 7, 99–100, 101, 102–3, 158, 161, 172
credit, reliance upon *see* banks
crime, 25, 144, 155–6, 171–2, 178–9
Crimean war, 68, 73, 78, 142, 216
Cunningham, James (Constable Works), 99

Dalgleish, William Ogilvy, 85–6, 152, 164–5, 234
Darien scheme, 26
Dens Works
    Lower Dens, 13, 50, 51, 125
    origins, 47, 95
    site, 4, 39, 83, 108, 122–3
    Upper Dens, 13–14, 69, 98, 120, 122
diaper, 50, 105
direct trade, 37–8, 63, 109–10
discipline, 122–3, 145–6
docks, 46, 65, 71, 121, 196, 214
domestic servants, 141, 151, 180, 197, 221, 256, 257t, 258
Don & Low, 19, 37, 105, 246, 253
Don, Robert & William *see* Don & Low
Douglas Foundry, 83, 190
Douglastown, 110, 111
Drummond, John (MP), 34, 74
drunkenness, 1, 171–2, 178

Dundee
    civic attainments, 11–13, 17, 19–20, 86, 161–3
    criticism of, 1–2
    industrial decline, 217, 277–81
    location, 95, *176*, 224
    secondary industries, 15–16, 79–80
Dundee and District Mill and Factory Operatives Union (DDMFOU), 226, 237–8, 249
Dundee and District Union of Jute and Flax Workers (DDUJFW)
    influence of, 249–51, *265*
    origins, 227
    women's role within, 260–1, 263, 267–8
Dundee Chamber of Commerce (DCC)
    formation, *14*, 79
    free trade vs protectionism, 200–1, 204, 205, 255
    and jute industry, *12*, 191–2, 196, 209n
    stance on slavery, 60–1
Dundee, Perth and London Shipping Co., 75
Dundee Social Union (DSC), 157, 218, 219, 220, 236, 266
Dundee Trades Council (DTC), 227–8, 229, 235, 244n, 261, 262
Dundee Women Citizens' Association (DWCA), 267
Dura Works, 63, 97

East India Company (EIC), 5, 73, 74–5, 78
East Mill, 47, 62, 114, 122, 159; *see also* Brown, J. and W.; Brown, William
economy, 25–7, 43, 51, 173, 179, 215, 216; *see also* free trade; protectionism
Edinburgs *see* Osnaburg cloth
education
    general, 19–20, 86, 161, 229, 237
    schools, 102–3, 158, 163, 177, 179, 257t
Edward, A. & D. & Co (Logie Works), 67, 69, 183
emigration, 38, 51, 63, 147, 215
employee numbers, 221–2, 277
employer–employee relations
    collaboration, 14–15, 157–8

employer–employee relations (*cont.*)
  industrial action, 118, 139, 179–82
  paternalism, 133, 143, 158–61,
    235–6
engineering
  importance of, 5, 15–16
  and trade unions, 152–3, 227
  unionism amongst, 18, 227
  women in WW1, 256, 257t
engineers, 49, 104, 106, 153; *see also*
    Carmichael, James; Carmichael,
    Peter
England
  as competitors, 50, 112
  exports to, 27, 28, 29, 32
  see also Act of Union (1707)
English East India Company *see* East
    India Company (EIC)
entrepreneurs, 9, 92–4, 101, 112–13,
    114
exports
  competition with Calcutta, 280, 281n
  export bounty, 34–5, 39, 43, 50, 61
  vs imports, 194–5
  see also direct trade

Factory Acts, 63, 201–2, 204, 235
Fairweather & Marr, Messrs, 38–9,
    47
Fairweather, Patrick, 37
Fairweather, Robert, 49
famines, 25–6, 29, 136, 187
Fife mills, 97, 111
fires, 62, 63, 99, 107–8, 172
First World War (WW1)
  female labour, 256–60
  food control, 261–5, 268
  jute trade effects, 245–8
  state intervention, 253–5
  unionism, 248–53
  War Benefit Scheme, 252
flax
  imports, 25, 50, 63, 64, 68
  vs jute, 4, 11, 66, 71, 77
  properties, 95, 107–8, 111
  spinning machinery, 48, 110, *113*,
    115
  supply, 40, 43, 78, 107–8
  see also linen; spinners (workers)
flax dressers *see* hecklers
food
  employment within, 135, 257t

prices, 203, 215, 223, 223t, 233,
    250, 253
riots, 26, 32, 44
WW1 controls, 261–5, 268
foremen, 9, 15, 123, 144–5, 160, 191
Forfar, 27, 32, 73, 95, 121, 150, 183;
    see also Don & Low
free trade
  and Liberalism, 199–200, 231–3, 236
  vs protectionism, 200–1

Gilfillan, Rev. George, 163, 164, 237
Gilroy Brothers
  employee disputes, 144, 179
  house building, 85, 175
  jute spinning, 76–7, 109, 217t
  Tay Works, 70, 70, 83, 85, 122, 123
Gilroy, George, 85, 109
Gilroy, James, 62, 65, 99, 100
Gilroy, Robert, 76–7
Glasgow Jute Company, 83, 84
Grimond, Alexander, 67, 86
Grimond Brothers
  Bow Bridge Works, 71, 72, 123, 258t
  'Brussels' carpets, 10, 67
  employer–employee relations, 104,
    139
  influence of, 104, 163, 200, 216
  Maxwelltown Works, 66, 104, 120
Grimond, James (Oakbank Mill), 76,
    80, 139
Grimond, Joseph, 67, 85, 109, 234

Halley Stevensons (Baltic Works), 19
Halley, William (Wallace Craigie
    Works), 62, 63, 86, 98–9, 100,
    101–2, 117
handloom factories, 42, 97, 99, 116–17,
    120, *150*; *see also* weaving sheds
handloom weavers
  and agricultural cycle, 40, 117, 138
  importance of, 72, 81
  industrial action, 117–18, 147–8, 150
  Irish, 82, 136–7
  wages, 43, 148–9, 154
  weaving sheds, 42
harbour, 6, 24, 52, 196; *see also* docks;
    shipping
health
  deaths, 18, 155–7, 229
  health and safety, 62, 62, 145
  illness, 172, 174, 219, 224–5, 237

INDEX

287

hecklers, 14, 48, 49, 115, 147, 151
hemp
  in carpeting, 66, 106
  imports, 64–5, 68, 71, 78
  origins of industry, 25, 50, 52
  varieties of, 67, 75
  see also flax; tow
hessian, 82, 248
house building, 175
housing
  and class divisions, 44–5, 46
  grand houses, 31, 84–6, *85*, 100, 183
  rents, 175, 223t, 265
  working class housing, 110, 172, 173–4, *180*, *182*, 222–3, 224

illness, 145, 172, 174; *see also* health
imperialism, 5, 73, 74, 190, 205, 207, 278, 281n
imports
  vs exports, 194–5
  flax/hemp, 25, 43, 50, 52, 63, 64–5, 68
  imperial preference, 246
  jute, 71–2, 82, 179, 195t, 246
  Jute Control, 278–9
  Jute Importers Mutual Protection Association (JIMPA), 191, 192–3
  see also exports; free trade; shipping
India, 5, 187, 277–8; *see also* Bengal; Calcutta
industrial action *see* strikes; trade unionism
industrial decline, 217, 277–81
infant mortality, 18, 155–7, 219
investments, 70, 82, 188–9, 217–18, 239n
Irish Home Rule, 18, 19, 200, 206, 234
Irish immigrants, 82, 118, 136–7, 142, 175, 177–8
Ivory, James, 9, 110

Johnston, Ellen, 15, 159
jute
  carpets, 9–11, 66–7, 77, 197–8, 280–1
  early uses, 73, 74
  hazards of, 62, *62*, 107–8
  imports, 46, 71–2, 72t, 82, 179, 195t
  industry decline, 277–81
  man-made substitutes, 281
  poem about, 15

  varieties of, 108
Jute Control, 277–9
Jute Importers Mutual Protection Association (JIMPA), 191, 192–3
Jute Industries Limited, 248
jute industry
  employee numbers, 199, 257t, 258t, 259t
  expansion, 4–5
  mill owners, 217t
jute palaces, 84–6, *85*, 183
'Juteopolis', 4, 5, 73, 162, 195, 215

Kendrew & Porthouse, 47, 110
Kinloch, George (MP), 12, *14*, 162
Kolkata *see* Calcutta

Labour Party, 18, 229–30, 232, 251, 260, 262, 267, 278
Labour Representation Committee (LRC), 260, 261, 262
lapping, 14–15, 106, 157–8
Leggatt, William, 114
Leighton, George, 76
leisure pursuits, 15, 41, 45, 143, 158–9, 160–1
Leng, John (MP), 203–4, 205, 222, 227–9, 237, 240n
Lennox, David, 217, 224–5, 237
Liberal Unionism, 200, 206, 230, 234, 266
Liberalism, 199–200, 205–6, 231–6, 266; *see also* Churchill, Winston; Leng, John (MP)
Lindsay, John (spinner), 139
linen
  bleaching, 32, 33, 64, 67, 107
  British Linen Company, 33, 36
  Calico Act 1721, 32
  coarse linen, 39, 47, 66, 81, 104, 105
  diaper, 50, 105
  export figures, 28, 35, 38, 43, 49–50, 52
  historic importance, 4–5
  Pomerania, 36, 104–5
  stampmasters, 31, 33, 101, 104, 118
  varieties of, 38
  see also Baxter Brothers Ltd; canvas; Osnaburg cloth
'Linenopolis', 65
linoleum, 18, 197, 199, 207, 280
lint (Osnaburgs), 37

288 THE TRIUMPH OF TEXTILES

Logie Works, 69
London
  London Jute Company, 83, 84
  shipping links, 74, 75–6
  stock market collapse, 51
Low and Bonar, 19, 248, 281
Low, James, 16, 49
Lower Dens Works, 13, 50, 51, 125;
  see also Dens Works

Macarthur, Mary, 2, 219, 227, 254
McManus Art Gallery and Museum see
  Albert Institute
machinery
  calendering, 106
  exported to India, 190, 267, 268,
    281
  heckling, 113, 115, 116, 119–20
  resistance to, 49, 65, 118, 147–8
  spinning, 16, 38–9, 48, 110
  see also power looms
Mackie, Charles, 48, 52, 104, 112, 122
Malcolm, George (Constable Works),
  99
Malcolm, Ogilvie & Co, 99, 109, 179,
  217t
managers, 9, 48, 111, 112, 114, 144,
  218; see also Baxter Brothers Ltd
map of Dundee (1889–90), 176
marriage
  married women employees, 13, 135,
    173, 218–19, 220
  mill-owning families, 79, 97, 99
Marshalls' Works, Leeds, 50, 97, 112
Maxwelltown Works, 66, 104, 120
Meldrum & Co., 49; see also Balfour &
  Meldrum
men
  abuse of women, 15, 144–5
  economic role, 219–20, 225, 226
  health of, 156–7, 224
  occupation bias, 15–16, 40, 115, 140,
    147, 152–3
  textile worker numbers, 135, 222,
    258t, 272n
  see also paternalism
merchant navy, 67, 68
middle classes
  homes, 44–5, 176, 178, 190–1, 221
  political power, 223–4, 242n
  social integration, 13, 46, 158, 163,
    235

migrant workers, 46–7, 52, 175, 177–8,
  259
milk, 157, 263–5
Miller, Ogilvy Gourlay, 70–1
mills
  architectural style, 6–7, 8, 70, 71,
    82–4, 122–3
  early mills, 39, 41–2, 47–8, 50, 51–2,
    110–11, 140
  expansion of, 61, 64, 69, 70
  resistance to, 50, 138–9
Moir, John, 38, 42, 51, 75, 109
Moncur, Alexander (Victoria Works),
  101, 143, 154
museums, 12, 16, 19–20, 86, 161

Napoleonic wars, 38, 43, 44, 46, 67,
  68, 148
Neish, James (Heathfield Works), 77,
  197
Neish, Thomas, 76, 98

Oakbank Mill, 80, 139
Ogilvie, David (Constable Works), 99
Osnaburg cloth, 33, 35–7, 39, 61, 68,
  105, 110, 118

Paisley (town), 2, 3, 99, 102, 148, 174
paternalism, 133, 143, 158–61, 235–6
Perth, 28, 30, 31, 75
philanthropists, 86, 228, 237
philanthropy (general), 155, 158, 202,
  235–6, 243n, 243
pigs, keeping of, 174, 261
plaiding, 27, 42
plantation system, 5, 34–6, 40, 60–1
poetry
  poems, 15, 28, 154–5, 224
  poets, 1, 16, 42, 45, 160, 183
  see also Burns, Robert
politics see Labour Party; Liberal
  Unionism; Liberalism; suffrage
  movement
polypropylene, 19, 279, 281
Pomerania linen, 36, 104–5
population growth, 52, 82, 133–6,
  134t, 215; see also migrant
  workers
poverty, 2–3, 18, 25–6, 153–5, 174,
  178, 234
power looms, 9, 69, 81, 118, 119–21,
  150–2

INDEX

price-fixing, 195–6, 206
profiteering, 253–4
prohibitionism, 251, 266, 269
protectionism, 18, 200–1, 205–6, 236, 255, 278–9
Protestantism, 102–3, 161, 177

quality control, 28–9, 67, 104–6, 192–3

racism
   towards Indians, 190
   towards Irish, 175, 177
   see also plantation system
radicalism, 44, 45, 133, 147–8, 162, 229
railways, 194, 247
religion, 45, 102–3, 164, 190, 193, 237–8; *see also* Catholics; Protestantism
rents, 175, 223, 223t, 250, 261, 265
riots, 26, 32, 44, 171, 177, 214
Rowan, Alexander, 76, 77
Roxburgh, William, 75
Royal Navy, 7, 27, 39, 67–8, 82, 120

sack sewers, 152–6, 254
sacking, 78, 101, 120, 149, 198; *see also* bagging
sailcloth, 38–9, 43, 67–8, 82, 148, 159
St Roque's Mill, 71
sanitation, 157, 161, 174, 222, 224
schools, 102–3, 158, 163, 177, 179, 257t
Scott, Sir George Gilbert, 12, *14*, 162
Scouringburn
   early mills, 19, 39, 52
   housing, 46, 174, *182*
Scrymgeour, Edwin, 164, 251, 261, 263, 264, 267
Scrymgeour, James, 1, 164
Scrymgeour, John, 26, 27, 30
seal oil, 79, 80, 81
Sharp, Frederick, 86
Sharp, John, 76, 81, 100, 109, 115, 147, 217t
sheeting, 37, 38, 61, 68, 118
shipping
   effects of WW1, 246
   shipping lines, 6, 63, 64, 75–6, 193–6, 210–11
   training ships, 179
Sime, John, 60, 62, 251, 252, 255, 259

slave trade *see* plantation system
Small, Rev. Robert, 29, 172
Small, William, 98
socialism, 225, 229, 230, 232, 237, 251, 265
spinners (workers)
   early mill work, 114–15, 137–46
   gender bias, 42, 110, 139, *140*, 226
   hand spinners, 28, 41
   reputation of, 3, 16, 151, 225
spinning frames, 48, 112, 139, 144
stampmasters, 31, 33, 101, 104, 118
state intervention, 157, 253–5
statues, 12, *14*, 15, 16, 143, 162, 163
steam engines, 38–9, 49, 52, 65, 69, 70, 145
steam ships, 194–6
Steell, Sir John, 96, 143
stock market collapse, 51
'Strelitz' Osnaburgs, 105
strikes
   1912 strike, 227, 238, 265
   1916 strike, 249–50
   amongst young people, 179–82, *231*, 250
   early instances, 49, 115
   'Great Strike in Dundee', 181–2
   management response to, 121, 145–6
   rent strike, 265
Sturrock, John, 153, 164, 177
suffrage movement, 19, 227, 238, 266, 267
Syme, James, 37
Symers, John, 82

tariffs, 26–7, 28, 31, 65–6, 200, 232–3, 253–4
Taws, James, 76, 77
tax, 31, 32, 200; *see also* tariffs
Tay Works, 70, *70*, 83, 85, 122, *123*; *see also* Gilroy Brothers
Taybank Works, 277, 279, 281
temperance, 16, 164, 231, 266, 267
textile worker numbers, 134, 221–2, 258t, 259t
Thomsons of Seafield Works, 67
Thrace Group, 19
tow, 37, 48, 52, 67, 80, 112, 116; *see also* flax; hemp
Trade Boards, 254–5, 260, 268, 269
trade unionism
   and bakers, 263–4

trade unionism (*cont.*)
early examples, 49, 148
and jute industry, 226, 227, 235, 236
and women, 219, 225–7, 260–1
in WW1, 248–53
see also strikes
Trades Councils *see* Dundee Trades
Council (DTC)

unemployment
causes, 179, 216, 269, 278, 280
political intervention, 232, 233,
243n, 280
Unionism, 229, 230, 233, 234
Unionists *see* Baxter, Sir George (MP);
Liberal Unionism; Unionism
unions *see* trade unionism
United States of America
American Civil War, 5, 68–9, 73, 82,
179
as competitors, 17, 92
as customers, 49–50, 61, 63, 64,
109–10
investments in, 93, 189
University of Dundee, 19–20, 184
Upper Dens Works, 13–14, 69, 98, 120,
122; *see also* Dens Works

V & A, Dundee, 19–20
Verdant Works (museum), 16, 19
voting rights
suffrage, 19, 227, 238, 266, 267
working class, 18, 223, 228, 230, 242n

wages
in Dundee, 18, 149, 220
Dundee vs Calcutta, 190, 196–7,
203–5
equal pay, 254, 261
male workers, 13, 16, 254
minimum wage, 254
money vs real wages, 138, 173,
215–16
wage reductions, 180–1, 183
Walker, Harry (Caldrum Works), 63,
86, 97, 122, 217t
Wallace Craigie Works, 62, 65, 86, 99
Walsh, William, 237–8, 240n
War Benefit Scheme, 252
War Emergency: Workers' National
Committee (WE:WNC), 261

Ward Foundry, 49, 70
Ward Mills, 19, 103
Warden, Alexander J., 4, 76, 81, 82, 99,
113, 121
wartime trade
American Civil War, 5, 68–9, 73, 82,
84, 179
Crimean war, 68, 73, 78, 142, 216
First World War, 245–8
Napoleonic wars, 38, 43, 148
water supply
for mills, 39, 64, 112, 123
for residents, 17, 172, 174
Watt Institution, 86, 111
Watt, James (East Mill), 62
wealth distribution, 184, 234–5
Weaver Trade, 28–9
weavers (workers)
female, 16, 119–20, 123, 150–1, 218,
220
household weavers, 116–17
industrial action, 151–2, 181
reputation, 102, 104
vs spinners, *221*, 225, 226
wages, 117, 151
see also handloom weavers; power
looms
weaving sheds, 13–14, 42, 117, 122,
123, *150*; *see also* handloom
factories
Webster, Thomas & Co., 42
welfare provisions, 224, 237, 254, 266,
269
West Ward Mill, 47
whale oil, 11, 73, 79–81, 174
whaling industry, 79–81, 210n
Wilkie, Alexander (MP), 18, 229–30,
250, 267
Williamson, Henry (DDMFOU), 226,
237–8, 249
women
behaviour of, 2–3, 16, 225
as committee members, 262–3, 266–8
in India, 204–5
and male abuse, 15, 144–5
married women employees, 13, 135,
173, 218–19, 220
occupation types (general), 221–2,
256–8, 257t
sack sewers, 152–6, 254
spinners, 41, 110, 139, *140*, 226

suffrage movement, 19, 227, 238, 266, 267
as supervisors, *140*, 152
and trade unionism, 219, 225–7, 260–1
wage disparity, 226, 254
weavers, 119–20, 151–2
working mothers, 157, 218–20, 254, 264–5
in WW1, 252, 256–60, 258t, 259t

Women's Trade Union League, 2, 219, 227
woollen industry, 27, 39

Yeaman, George, 30–1
young people
behaviour of, 178
as labour, 40, 42, 43, 137, 148
and strikes, 179–82, *231*, 250